**An Altitude
SuperGuide**

Classic Hikes
in the
Canadian Rockies

An Altitude SuperGuide

Classic Hikes
in the
Canadian Rockies

Graeme Pole

Altitude Publishing Canada Ltd.
Canadian Rockies/Vancouver

Publication Information

Altitude Publishing Canada Ltd.
The Canadian Rockies
1500 Railway Avenue
Canmore, Alberta T1W 1P6

Copyright 1994 © Graeme Pole

10 9 8 7 6 5

Revised reprint 1999

Extreme care has been taken to ensure that all information presented in this book is accurate and up-to-date, and neither the author nor the publisher can be held responsible for any errors.

Canadian Cataloguing in Publication Data
Pole, Graeme, 1956–
Classic hikes in the Canadian Rockies

(SuperGuide)
Includes index.
ISBN 1–55153–702-8 (binder)—
ISBN 1-55153-706-0 (pbk.)
1. Rocky Mountains, Canadian (B.C. and Alta.)—Guidebooks.* 2. Hiking—Rocky Mountains, Canadian (B.C. and Alta.)—Guidebooks.* I. Title. II. Series.
FC219.P64 1995   917.1104'4   C95–910842–4
F1090.P64 1995

Altitude GreenTree Program

Altitude Publishing will plant in Canada twice as many trees as were used in the manufacturing of this product.

Front cover scenic photograph: *Mt. Assiniboine*
Front cover inset photographs: *Moss Campion; Rocky Mountain Bighorn Sheep*
Frontispiece photograph: *Climbers on The Grand Sentinel, Sentinel Pass*
Back cover photograph: *Boom Lake*

Project Development

Concept/Art Direction	Stephen Hutchings
Design	Stephen Hutchings
Maps	Catherine Burgess
Electronic Page Layout	Stephen Hutchings
	Catherine Burgess
Technical Assistance	Mark Higenbottam
Colour separations	Friesen Printers
Halftones	Stephen Hutchings
Graphics	Stephen Hutchings
Financial Management	Laurie Smith

Made in Western Canada

Printed and bound in Canada by Friesen Printers, Altona, Manitoba.

A Note from the Publisher

The world described in Altitude SuperGuides is a unique and fascinating place. It is a world filled with surprise and discovery, beauty and enjoyment, questions and answers. It is a world of people, cities, landscape, animals and wilderness as seen through the eyes of those who live in, work with, and care for this world. The process of describing this world is also a means of defining ourselves.

It is also a world of relationship, where people derive their meaning from a deep and abiding contact with the land–as well as from each other. And it is this sense of relationship that guides all of us at Altitude to ensure that these places continue to survive and evolve in the decades ahead.

Altitude SuperGuides are books intended to be used, as much as read. Like the world they describe, *Altitude SuperGuides* are evolving, adapting and growing. Please write to us with your comments and observations, and we will do our best to incorporate your ideas into future editions of these books.

Stephen Hutchings
Publisher

Contents

Introduction

The Hikes

Banff National Park

Jasper National Park

Yoho National Park

Kootenay National Park

Waterton Lakes National Park

Reference

The Classic Hikes in the Canadian Rockies are organized according to this colour scheme:

Banff National Park	Kootenay National Park
Jasper National Park	Waterton Lakes National Park
Yoho National Park	Information

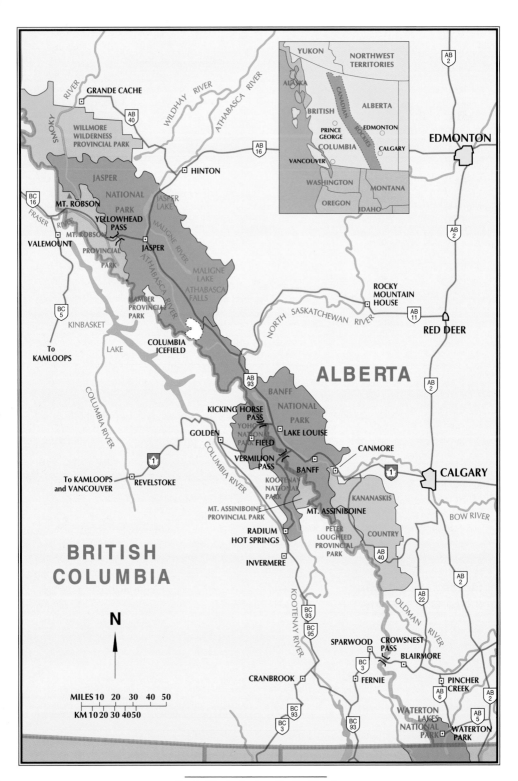

Foreword

The world has changed profoundly since the first steel tracks were laid through the Canadian Rockies just over one hundred years ago. Frontiers have retreated or been submerged under the flood tide of human enterprise. In the mountains, the time of exploration has passed, almost overnight, to a time of impending crisis for ecological diversity expressed in wild landscapes.

Trails too, have changed. Many had their genesis as the faint, ephemeral routes of wildlife. Their use was formalized by early guides and outfitters. Now, they have been institutionalized by guidebooks and management plans. For park administrators trails are part-attraction, part-infrastructure. For hikers, they facilitate travel. For wilderness, they signify intrusion.

But there is no reason for those of us who hike to behave like intruders. The easy part is learning the techniques; the hard part is knowing the reasons. Too often we hasten to destinations, ignorant of origins and oblivious to the places between. Drawn to the grand and spectacular, we pass unheeding the subtleties of relationships and processes, not caring that small mysteries are as intriguing as the large. We check our watches faithfully as if keeping this appointment like any other.

However, hiking can be a truly liberating experience, if measures of respect, humility and receptiveness are included in our gear and if filters of comfort, security and technology are left behind. Trails, those dotted lines on contour maps that provoke imagining, lead through real places. We are rained on, sunburned, windblown, mosquito-bitten and unnerved by bear scats. Senses dulled by disuse are re-activated. We grow aware of possibilities. As the landscape opens before us, we become open to it. We are participants, not mere observers. And, if we are lucky, exhilaration turns to memory.

Our civilization lives on gifts from the Earth. The time has come to reciprocate. Simply enjoying the magnificent areas that are the subject of this book is a self-indulgence, a luxury we can no longer afford. Threats to ecological diversity, wild land, and by extension, to the vital wildness in the human spirit, are real and must be resisted.

Even as this book goes to publication, the petroleum industry, eager to squeeze every last drop of profit from the land, is launching a frontal assault on the eastern slopes of the Rockies. To the west, logging trucks range farther and farther from their mills, the symbol of a desperate search for the last trees in over-committed forests. Roads proliferate. Mine development creeps higher into the mountains and closer to the parks. Helicopters provide quick fixes of alpine glory for passengers unwilling to spend the time and effort to earn genuine experience.

Within parks there are planners and managers who speak of underutilized capacity. With little thought for the needs of ecosystems, they too assume, that if some peculiarly human benefit is not being derived to the maximum from a natural landscape, opportunity is wasted. For such people, and the politicians who direct them, success for parks is gauged by numbers of visitors and revenue generated. The slide towards degradation is insidious and relentless.

There was time in the human past, when our bond to the Earth was more visceral, more sure, more crucial to our individual survival. Today, it seems the prospects for collective survival depend on repairing that bond where it has been broken. Hiking offers a hint of that past and stimulates dreams of the future: dreams of wildness restored and of humans sharing again the evolutionary journey with all life on the planet.

The useful thing about trails, is that although they may take us away, they also will bring us back. If we are responsive, if we concentrate and work at it, we may return with an enriched sense of belonging to the Earth. Action should follow. There will be different trails for different people, but if enough people find the trails back, there may be hope. This guide book points us in the right direction.

Mike Mclvor,
Banff, Alberta 1994

Acknowledgments

H ikes in Banff National Park were reviewed by Mike McIvor, a director of the Bow Valley Naturalists, and by Alex Taylor, trail crew. Hikes in Jasper National Park were reviewed by Ben Gadd, naturalist and author. Ben also reviewed the appendix material. Hikes in Yoho National Park were reviewed by Harry Abbott, park warden. The Lake O'Hara Alpine Circuit was reviewed by Allan Knowles, park warden. Hikes in Kootenay National Park were reviewed by: Joanne Cairns, park warden; Larry Halverson, chief park naturalist; Doreen McGillis, park naturalist; and Rosemary Langshaw - Power, independent naturalist. Joanne Cairns also reviewed hikes in Waterton Lakes National Park, as did Janice Smith, Assistant Chief Park Warden. All these reviewers also read the introductory material.

The text on bears was reviewed by Mike Gibeau, park warden. Text concerning first aid and safety was reviewed by Dr. Ron Oshry of Banff, and by Tim Auger, park warden and Public Safety Supervisor for Banff National Park. Text describing vegetation was reviewed by Andy MacKinnon, BC Forest Service, Victoria. Dr. Desmond Collins, Curator in Charge of Invertebrate Paleontology at the Royal Ontario Museum, reviewed the text describing the Burgess Shale. John Ricker provided a critical review of the text. His many insightful comments revealed a strong desire to maintain both the integrity of meaning and the integrity of the environment.

Notwithstanding the efforts of the above, any mistakes in the text are the responsibility of the author. Corrections and suggestions from users of *Classic Hikes* are welcomed. Please send them to the author in care of the publisher.

The author is grateful to the following people who provided assistance with research and fieldwork:

Harry Abbot, Dr. Peter Achuff, Wes Bradford, Joanne Cairns, Paul Cinnamon, Dr. Desmond Collins, William Cox, Glenn Crowe, Dr. Dave Cruden, Perry Davis, Beth Dunagan, Ben Gadd, Cia Gadd, Mike Gibeau, Dave Gilbride, Dorothy Gilbride, Larry Halverson, Mike Henderson, Tom Hurd, Perry Jacobson, Louise Jarry, Cindy Kelly, Dr. Brian Luckman, Doreen McGillis, Linda Morita, Hal Morrison, C. Simon Ommaney, Ian Pengelly, Gord Rutherford, Greg Slatter, Ian Spooner, Staff at the Banff Public Library, Staff at the Whyte Museum, Bob Thrale, William Warkentin, Candis Waugh, Jeff Waugh and Shelley Wright.

Last but not least, the author thanks Publisher Stephen Hutchings for his unflagging commitment to this book – a long-held dream finally realized.

Special Acknowledgement

Completion of *Classic Hikes* would not have been possible without the dedicated assistance and support of my wife, Marnie. During 1992, we hiked virtually every trail in this book together – a gruelling summer job that Marnie took on without complaint. Marnie's commitment to this project was equal to mine, as was the physical and creative energy she invested. Looking at the finished product, I am aware of countless examples of Marnie's input. Her insight, observations and photographic contributions enrich the work throughout. Although one person's name appears on the cover, *Classic Hikes* is very much the result of the considerable efforts of two people. Thank you, Marnie.

Preface

Authors of guide-books take a great risk, and have a tremendous obligation. Guidebooks to natural areas include landscapes that are unique or special. The risk lies in advertising these landscapes to a broader public, so that destinations subsequently become overrun and tarnished. Bears, wolves, wolverines and caribou require places where there are no people. Although it is an unintended effect, the unrestrained enthusiasm of a guidebook author can contribute to the many pressures confronting natural areas and species, and accelerate their declines.

Thus, *Classic Hikes* does not include descriptions of unbeaten paths leading to backcountry secrets. You will only find, as the title implies, 1070 km of trails that comprise the established hikes and backpacking trips for which the Canadian Rockies are renowned.

Some of the Classic Hikes have quotas that limit the number of overnight users allowed on the trail at any given time. Quotas and other management tools should insure the Classic Hikes do not become spoiled. However, the onus is on you, the hiker, to travel and camp responsibly, and thereby guarantee that the special qualities of these trails, and the species that dwell in the areas they traverse, are not lost.

The information provided in *Classic Hikes* reflects more than a decade of experience, observation and research, involving more than 11,000 km of travel in the backcountry of the Canadian Rockies. It is the author's sincere hope that many decades hence, these mountains will continue to be a haven for resident species, and offer visitors as vital a wilderness touchstone as they do today.

Assumption of Risk

As pursuits, hiking and backpacking, backcountry travel and backcountry camping have dangers not limited to insect bites, black bears, grizzly bears and other aggressive wildlife. There are also rough trails, slippery bridges, suspension bridges, and unbridged streams with their slippery logs and rocks. And if that were not enough there may be inclement weather, lightning, forest fires, falling trees, contaminated drinking water, avalanches, late-lying snow, rockfalls, mudslides and flash-floods.

The author has hiked every trail in this book at least once, and has endeavored to render trail descriptions with the greatest accuracy and with safety in mind. However, conditions in the backcountry are not static, and the inclusion or exclusion of any information does not mean that you will find conditions as described. In particular, bridges and trail signs may or may not be present as described in the text, and the locations of stream crossings, snow patches and ice-cored moraines may change from year to year.

Classic Hikes contains ample information to assist you in preparing for safe backcountry travel. However, *you* are responsible for your well-being in the backcountry of the Rockies. Neither the author nor the publisher can be held responsible for any difficulties, injuries, misfortune or loss of property that arises from using the information presented.

In *Classic Hikes*, "backpacking" means to hike and camp self-sufficiently in the backcountry. It does not imply that any of the services associated with low-budget travel (also called "backpacking" in Europe and Australasia) will be present.

How To Use This Book

Hike Descriptions

The boxed introductory information for each hike identifies it as a day-hike or an overnight trip, and summarizes the distance and route. Relevant topographic maps are indicated. Some of the shorter overnight hikes can be hiked in a day by fit hikers. Some of the longer day-hikes can be turned into overnight hikes by using campgrounds along the route. The introduction also indicates the best time of day for viewing the featured destination on day-hikes.

Distances are given between the trailhead and landmarks: passes, lakes, bridges, trail junctions and campgrounds. The elevations of these landmarks are also shown. By comparing elevations, you can estimate the elevation gain or loss for different sections of the hike. Many of the overnight trips incorporate sections of different trails. For instance, The Lakes and Larches Trail (#8) is routed along portions of the Healy Pass, Whistling Pass, Shadow Lake, Gibbon Pass and Twin Lakes trails. The important junctions are mentioned in the text.

If you read the entire text for a hike, you will be able to decide if it is appropriate for your ability and fitness and to consider the trail conditions and time of year. Consult a park information centre for current conditions, warnings and closure information. You can obtain a weather forecast, purchase topographic maps, and participate in the voluntary safety registration program. You will need a wilderness pass if camping.

Trails

In the descriptions, "trail" refers to designated and maintained trails. You will find maintenance standards vary between parks, and between heavily used and remote areas within

each park. "Path" and "track" refer to unmaintained routes where travel will likely be slower and more difficult. "Rooted" means a trail contains many tree roots that make walking difficult. All river, creek and stream crossings are bridged unless stated. On a few of the hikes the text will advise you to carry an ice axe if hiking early in the season. Do not attempt these hikes before mid-June if you do not have this equipment or if you are unfamiliar with its use.

Take note of trails that are shared with horses and mountain bikers. Some trails have horse/hiker barriers, designed to keep horses from sections of trail intended only for use by hikers.

Side Trips

This symbol placed on the coloured title bar indicates convenient outings that you can make from campgrounds along the route of overnight trips. The distance of side trips is not included in the overall distance of the outing.

Distances and Time

All measurements in the text are metric. Common abbreviations used are: cm (centimetres), m (metres), km (kilometres), ha (hectares), m^2 (square metres), and km^2 (square kilometres). For Metric/Imperial Conversions, see the Reference section.

For loop hikes or circuits, the distance given is the total for the outing. Otherwise, the distance indicated is one-way, from trailhead to destination. A minimum and a maximum number of days is suggested for overnight trips. The minimum means that no side trips are undertaken, and long days are spent backpacking. The maximum means that all the side trips are completed, and shorter days are spent backpacking. The distance for overnight trips does not include any side trip options.

The trail distances given in *Classic Hikes* are based on figures provided by the parks. These have been compared to those given in other

Abbreviations

Maps

FC▲.......Front Country (drive-in) campground
Ⓟ.........Parking Lot

Text

CG............CampGround
jct ....Junction

guidebooks, and then field-checked where discrepancies were noted. Most trailheads and junctions have signs. Those without signs are referred to as "unsigned." While out on the trail, you will often find that the distances given on trail signs are wrong. Don't worry. Unless the distance shown to your destination greatly increases on successive signs, at least you'll know you're going in the right direction! In recognizing that a completely accurate inventory of trail distances does not exist, and that creating one is a daunting task, Banff National Park has stopped putting distances on its newer signs.

Hiking times have not been given in the text because they are totally dependent on your experience, pace and ability, and the conditions of the day. As a general rule, if you are accustomed to backpacking in mountainous terrain you will average 2.5 km/hour, including all manner of stops during the day. The novice will average 1.5 km/hour, and those of intermediate ability will cover somewhere between these two figures. On day-hikes, strong hikers with light packs can cover 4 to 5 km/hour. However, most people average 2.5 to 3.5 km/hour.

Maps

Topographic maps are indispensable to backcountry travel and help you appreciate the scenery. Unfortunately, most trails in the Rockies are shown inaccurately or incompletely on the 1:50,000 map sheets of the National Topographic Survey. The exceptions are the large colour sheets that cover Yoho and Waterton Lakes parks. Because errors of trail location are the rule rather than the exception, the particular errors for each topographic map are not described in the text.

The maps accompanying the hikes have been created especially for this book. They indicate all trails as accurately as possible. The appropriate topographic map for each hike is listed at the bottom of the route information box.

When you see the name of a landscape feature in the text in quotation marks, it means the name is unofficial.

Access to the Rockies

Calgary is the closest major centre to most of the Classic Hikes, and is served by an international airport. Banff townsite is a 90 minute drive from Calgary. Daily bus service is available direct from Calgary airport to Banff and Lake Louise. Bus service also operates four times daily from Calgary from the Greyhound terminal (on Bow Trail downtown) to Banff, Lake Louise and Field; and daily to Canmore and Radium. There is no passenger train service west from Calgary.

Edmonton is a four-hour drive east of Jasper townsite. There is daily Greyhound bus service, and passenger train service twice a week. Daily bus service operates during peak season, northbound and southbound, between Banff, Lake Louise and Jasper, and will stop at Columbia Icefield on request.

Transportation

Public transportation is not readily available to and from most trailheads. If you will be spending an extended period of time backpacking without the convenience of a vehicle, the logistics of organizing food, and getting to and from trailheads can involve almost as much work as the hikes themselves. Hitchhiking cannot be advocated. However, the best success in securing rides is with local residents, who understand the problems of access. By talking to other people staying in campgrounds and hostels, or in town, your transportation needs can sometimes be met. If you hitchhike, make a cardboard sign that shows your destination.

Taxi service is available from Canmore, Banff, Lake Louise and Jasper, but will be prohibitively expensive for most. There is daily bus service between Banff and Jasper, and more frequent service along Highways 1, 16 and 93 south. You may be able to book a one-way seat on tour buses from Banff and Jasper. Shuttle service for hikers is available at Banff, Lake Louise, Jasper and Waterton. Check at park information centres for details.

For trails that begin and end at locations greatly distant from each other, you should make transportation arrangements for the end of your hike in advance. Otherwise, plan to arrive at trail's end early enough in the day to avoid being benighted in a parking lot. Most roads are not well travelled after dark.

Where to Stay in the Rockies

Commercial accommodation is available at: Canmore, Banff, Lake Louise, Field, Jasper, Hinton, Valemount, Golden, Radium and Invermere. Reservations are advised during peak season. The only low-budget accommodation is at frontcountry campgrounds scattered throughout the Rocky Mountain parks, and at a few hostels in Banff, Jasper and Yoho national parks. Campgrounds offer facilities for tents and motor homes only, and do not have dorms, cabins or kitchens.

Most of the Classic Hikes do not have accommodation or campgrounds within reasonable walking distance of the trailhead. The list below is for the convenience of those travelling without a car, and summarizes the trailheads that can be reached on foot. Supplies are available as indicated. For information on hostels, contact the Southern Alberta Hostelling Association: 403-762-4122, 403-283-5551.

Hike#	Accommodation
1, 2	Two Jack CG
10	Johnston Canyon CG (limited supplies at resort nearby)
11	Castle Mountain CG and Hostel (limited supplies at Castle Mountain Village nearby)
13–15, 18	Lake Louise CG and Hostel (supplies at Lake Louise village)
19, 20	Mosquito Creek CG and Hostel (limited supplies at hostel)
24, 25	Hilda Creek Hostel
26	Columbia Icefield CG and Wilcox Creek CG
27	Athabasca Falls hostel, Mt. Kerkeslin CG
28, 29	Mt. Edith Cavell Hostel
33	Robson River, Robson Meadows and Emperor Ridge CG (limited supplies at Robson jct)
37, 38	Takakkaw Falls CG, Whiskey Jack Hostel
41	Hoodoo Creek CG
42, 43	Marble Canyon CG
46, 48	Waterton townsite CG (supplies in townsite)

Geography, Geology and Vegetation

The Canadian Rockies extend from the US border to the Liard River in northern BC. In the text, the terms "Rockies" and "Canadian Rockies" refer to the Southern and Central Rockies Ecosystems, between Waterton Lakes National Park and Mt. Robson Provincial Park. References made to regulations and resource management objectives generally refer to those of Banff, Jasper, Yoho, Kootenay and Waterton Lakes national parks.

Points of geological interest are described in the text. Rock formations in the Rockies are named for locations where they are most prominent, or where they were first studied. To minimize cluttering of the text, ages of the formations are not often given. Refer to the geological column in the Reference section of this book for information on the age of rock formations and the dates of glacial events.

The common names of tree species are those given in *Native Trees of Canada*. The common names of wildflowers, shrubs and other vegetation are those given in *A Flora of Waterton Lakes National Park*.

Season Openers

These Classic Hikes are usually the first to become snow-free, and the last to become snowbound. In most years, you may attempt these outings as early as the third week of May, and as late as the fourth week of October. To prevent erosion and damage to surrounding vegetation, please make every effort to stay on the trail at these times of year. If your chosen trail is too wet, please select another outing.

#1. Aylmer Pass and Aylmer Lookout
#2. C-Level Cirque
#5. Elk Pass Loop
#10. Johnston Canyon
#21. Sarbach Lookout
#22. Glacier Lake
#32. Sulphur Skyline
#41. Mount Hunter

Modern Hiking

It has become clear in the late 20th century that humankind has tipped the natural balance on earth. Our interactions with nature are loaded with, and tainted by things that naturalist and philosopher Aldo Leopold would have deemed "wrong." Since the late 1700s, industrial societies have subjected the natural world to exploitation and turned it into fodder for machinery dedicated to the accumulation of wealth. In doing so, our outlook on nature has been transformed from one of fearful wonder and reverence to one of domination and control. For centuries we have been walking heavily on the land.

The consequences of our actions are now inescapable. Our lust for economic gain has created a poverty of clean air and water, fertile soil, and accessible yet untarnished places of spirit. It has displaced races of humans and wiped out natural ecosystems that required millennia to develop. Species, both celebrated and unknown, are disappearing at rates unparalleled since the onset of the last ice age.

As the air we breathe becomes more hazy, as the fires of industry force us further into smoggy, urban cocoons, as the waters of the earth dissolve our wastes and excesses into liquids which still the lakes and rivers, at last we must face a quandary of our own making.

Although it may be too late to heal the damage already done, too late to fully restore nature's balance on a large scale, there are still some places where the order of the natural world prevails. These places can both renew and inspire us. Despite considerable internal and external pressures, the parks of the Canadian Rockies are among these places. And yet, although the mountains themselves still stand indomitable, the ecosystems that they anchor are showing signs of the wear and tear that stem both from abuse and

"A thing is right when it tends to preserve the integrity, stability, and beauty of the biotic [natural] community. It is wrong when it tends otherwise."
—Aldo Leopold,
A Sand County Almanac

from being "loved to death" by the increasing number of park visitors.

If the 1990s are the decade when the agenda for the establishment of new protected areas will be completed in North America, and when the will must be exercised to guarantee that already-established protected areas remain inviolate, then we have an obligation to act in harmony with those objectives, both in our occupations and our recreation. In other words, we have a choice when we embark on a trail in the Canadian Rockies. We can consume the experience in the same manner that we have become accustomed to. Or we can make a conscious effort to experience the world differently. We can honour the ecological integrity that remains in the parks of the Canadian Rockies by leaving no trace of our passing through this incredible landscape.

No matter that in our imperfection we will always fall short of this mark. The caring for the land is what counts. For it is the seed whose nurturance is vital to a healing – the transformation of our relationship not just with these hiking trails, parks and their resident species, but with all the world.

Even though trails can be a quagmire, the modern hiker plows right through. Walking around mud spots on the trail severely damages the landscape.

Leaving No Trace

In caring for the land, we must also recognize the intangible spiritual value of hiking in the Canadian Rockies.

We should act in a manner that positively supports the experience and safety of others who are currently on the trail, and those who are yet to come.

The "how-to" of no-trace hiking and camping is easily listed. However, putting the knowledge into practice takes a focused and concerted effort. Please read the following before each hike. And, after you have completed your trip, review the list to see where you can make improvements on your next outing.

- Inform yourself thoroughly about where you are going. Plan ahead for the unexpected.
- Keep to maintained trails.
- Concentrate your impact in high-use areas.
- Spread your impact in pristine areas.
- Avoid places where human impact is beginning to show.
- Walk through snow and puddles to stay on the trail.
- Stay off trail sections that are closed for rehabilitation.
- Do not shortcut trail switchbacks.

- Pack out all your trash and garbage, and pick up any left by others. Make the effort to recycle what you can.
- Cigarette butts and spent matches are litter, too. Pack them out.
- Protect watercourses. Be responsible with human waste. Always use the facilities provided; if none are available, dispose of human waste properly.
- Use a campstove for cooking.
- Use fires responsibly and only where permitted; use only the wood provided, and only when necessary.
- Do not remove or disturb any natural objects.
- Respect wildlife. Do not feed them under any circumstances. Give them lots of space.
- Respect other's requirements for solitude and quiet. Hike in small groups.
- Share the facilities provided.
- Those hiking downhill have the right of way. Yield to them.
- Step to the downhill side of the trail to allow horse parties to pass. Do not speak or make any movement that might startle the horses.
- Mountain bikers should yield to hikers.
- Fish odours attract bears. It is advisable not to fish on overnight trips. For the safety of those who follow, pack out fish viscera.

This campsite sets a poor example for other visitors. Strive to leave no trace of your stay.

Hiking in the Rockies

One sentence sums up how to approach hiking in the Rockies: Be prepared and be self-reliant. Help is seldom close at hand. No matter how experienced, every hiker from time to time encounters difficult situations. In the Rockies, these could include: a bear encounter; a squirrel or jay eating your food; a lost backpack; a fall into a river; a fall on a patch of late-lying snow; a mid-summer blizzard; or an injury or illness. And there are the hazards you might create such as attempting an outing that is beyond your ability or venturing off-trail into hazardous terrain. If in doubt, be cautious.

The principal wildlife hazards are: bears, elk, moose, and wood ticks. Avoid elk and moose during the autumn rut and in spring when calves are born. The bite of the wood tick can cause complications. Wolves may take a curious look at you or your camp, but are harmless. Coyotes and cougars have been known to attack humans on extremely rare occasions, however these instances do not constitute grounds for general concern. (Be grateful if you see one!) Porcupines can damage unattended equipment around camp. Bighorn sheep, deer and mountain goats will almost always flee, except if the sheep or deer are accustomed to being fed, or, as in Waterton Lakes National Park, if the deer have acquired the taste of human urine around campsites. There are no poisonous spiders, venomous snakes or scorpions in the Rockies. However, bees, wasps and hornets are present.

In an emergency, preparedness will be your best ally. Your options should always include retreat, or pitching camp quickly in order to stay warm and dry. Carry reliable, lightweight equipment and make sure everyone is familiar with the operation of the stove. All members of the party should know the hiking route, potential escape routes, and the locations of campgrounds and park patrol cabins. Although there is no guarantee of finding other persons at these locations, they are the best choices when help is urgently required.

First Aid

All members of your party should carry a first aid kit and be familiar with the basics of first aid. Skills you should practise: treatment for shock, management of fractures and sprains using improvised splints, and hemorrhage control.

Leaving Word

Whether you are going on a short day-hike or on a multi-day backpacking trip, leave your itinerary with a responsible person. Do this in writing. Specify the number in your party, your route, where you intend to camp, and when you will be back. Describe your vehicle and where it will be parked. Tell your contact person when to report you overdue, and where to make the report.

If you do not have a responsible local contact person, you may use the voluntary registration system to insure someone will look for you if you are overdue. Contact a park information centre or warden office for details. Whichever safety plan you choose, always carry an extra night's rations with you. Searches are extremely costly and sometimes put rescuers at great risk. Parks Canada is considering charging overdue hikers for search and rescue costs.

Even on a day-hike close to the highway you should be equipped for changing weather and the possibility of having to stay out overnight. Warm clothing, rain gear, extra food, a space blanket and any essential daily medications should always be in your pack.

Park Regulations

National parks are protected by regulations that insure use is in harmony with the mandate of preservation. Although not exhaustive, the list below outlines the regulations pertinent to backcountry users. The onus is on you to be aware of the regulations. If you have doubts, inquire.

- Vehicles stopping in national parks must pay the appropriate fee at a park gate or at a park information centre.
- Firearms are not permitted, unless securely locked or dismantled.
- Hunting and trapping of wildlife is not permitted.

- Anglers must obtain a national park fishing permit, and be aware of regulations.
- It is illegal to: disturb, remove or deface any natural, cultural or historic object or artifact; approach, feed, entice or harass wildlife; or enter a closed area.
- Backcountry campers require a wilderness pass.
- Camp in designated campgrounds only.
- Mountain biking is permitted only on certain trails.
- There are restrictions on taking dogs into the backcountry in most parks.

The Wilderness Pass

In 1994, Parks Canada instituted the "wilderness pass" for overnight trips. You may purchase a wilderness pass for each outing, or a season pass for the year. If you will be camping seven nights or more, purchase the season pass. How much will it cost you? It now requires close to a hundred dollars in fees for one person to bring a vehicle into a national park and to go backcountry camping for a week. Refunds are not given for inclement weather.

Purchase your wilderness pass immediately prior to your hike, at a park information centre in the park where your hike is located. Groups of more than six persons are discouraged. Larger groups require the permission of the park superintendent. Even if you will not be camping, visit a park information centre before your hike to get information on weather, trail conditions, bear warnings and closed areas.

Camping within the core areas of Mt. Assiniboine and Mt. Robson provincial parks (*Classic Hikes* #7 and #33) is also subject to use fees. For The Berg Lake Trail, purchase your trail permit at the visitor centre at Mt. Robson Junction on Highway 16. No permit is required for Og Lake and Lake Magog campgrounds at Mt. Assiniboine. However, park rangers will collect a fee from you each night. Contact Mt. Robson Provincial Park (250-566-4325) and Mt. Assiniboine Provincial Park (250-422-3212) in advance to find out the current fees.

Quotas

At time of publication, the *Classic Hikes* with quotas were: The Brazeau Loop (#25), Fryatt Valley (#27), The Tonquin Valley (#28), The Skyline Trail (#31), and The Berg Lake Trail (#33). Some backcountry campgrounds have quotas: Aylmer Pass Junction (#1), Lake O'Hara (#36), those in the Yoho and Little Yoho Valleys (#38), Bertha Lake (#46), Crypt Lake (#47), Carthew/Alderson (#48), and The Tamarack Trail (#49). When these quotas are full, wilderness passes and trail permits will not be issued.

In the national parks (except in Waterton Lakes National Park), reservations are accepted for a portion of trail and campground quotas. Where quotas apply, a portion is set aside for issue on the day of use, so early risers can *usually* get onto their desired trail on the desired day. However, be flexible when scheduling a hike on a popular trail. For information on The Berg Lake Trail quota, contact Mt. Robson Provincial Park: 250-566-4325.

Although backcountry use has not increased significantly during the last decade (except on The Berg Lake Trail), cumulative impacts in heavily travelled areas have increased. More trails and campgrounds may have quotas in the future as managers attempt to control visitation and to protect park resources. Some trails may be closed permanently or seasonally to protect wildlife such as grizzly bears, wolves and caribou. The author has endeavoured to exclude trails that may be subject to outright closure. However, please abide by any new regulations that supercede information presented in *Classic Hikes*.

Protecting the Parks

The Rocky Mountain parks have been subdivided into Land Use Zones in order to protect the landscape and to regulate conflicting uses. Most of the area is zoned as "wilderness." You can help support the zoning by complying with the regulations. Insure your activities are permitted, and your desired experience is realistic, before you set out.

You can also help protect the parks by reporting apparent violations (fishing, poaching, vandalism, etc.) to a park information centre, park warden or ranger, or RCMP officer. Reports of required trail maintenance (i.e. downed trees), significant wildlife sightings, and discoveries of historical objects are also appreciated.

In the 1990's, park operational budgets are being slashed annually. The quality and frequency of trail maintenance and other services that affect trail users are in decline. Accurate reports of trail maintenance needs will assist the parks in getting the most out of their maintenance budgets.

Climate

The climate during the hiking season is summarized in the tables below. These records are from stations at Banff, Jasper, Field, Kootenay Crossing and Waterton Park townsite respectively. Values have been rounded to the nearest whole number.

As you can see, it rains or snows on average one day in three during the hiking season; slightly less frequently in Waterton. However, thunderstorms are more common in Waterton. The prevailing weather systems arrive from the southwest, and the overall trend is more precipitation on the western side of the continental divide (Yoho, northern Kootenay and Mt. Robson). In May and June, poor weather of an easterly system (known locally as an "upslope" condi-

tion) can plague Banff and Jasper. During these times, the weather will improve if you travel west to Yoho, Kootenay or Mt. Robson. On days where the weather pattern is mixed, marked changes often occur a short distance away. For example, if it is raining at Lake Louise, it might be partly cloudy with the odd shower north of Bow Summit, or in Yoho or Kootenay national parks. Of course, it could be worse!

You can usually hike in the Rockies from late May to early October at low elevations, and mid-June to mid-September higher up. At treeline, the average annual temperature is -4°C, and more than 75 percent of the annual precipitation falls as snow. In the high country you will frequently encounter snow, whether freshly fallen, or lingering from last winter. After a few outings you may agree with some locals, who sarcastically describe the climate of the Rockies as "nine months of winter, and three months of poor skiing!" There is a pattern to summer snowstorms. Significant snowfalls often occur: middle of July, first week of August, third week of August, and first week of September.

One of the most enjoyable times for backpacking in the Rockies is between mid-

Average Daytime Temperature

Average Daytime Temperature, rounded to nearest °C

	May		June		July		August		Sept		October	
	high	low	high	low	high	low	high	low	high	low	high	low
Banff	14	1	18	5	22	7	21	6	16	3	10	-1
Jasper	16	2	19	6	23	8	21	7	16	3	10	-1
Yoho	16	1	20	5	24	7	22	6	17	3	9	-2
Kootenay	16	-1	20	3	24	4	23	3	17	0	9	-4
Waterton	15	2	19	6	23	7	22	7	17	3	12	0

Average Monthly Precipitation

Average Monthly Precipitation, expressed in mm and in days with precipitation

	May		June		July		August		Sept		October	
	mm	days	mm	days	mm	days	mm	days	mm	days	mm	days
Banff	52	12	61	14	42	12	49	12	42	11	31	6
Jasper	33	10	55	13	50	13	49	13	38	11	29	10
Yoho	52	12	74	14	55	12	45	12	45	11	43	10
Kootenay	47	10	61	11	37	10	43	9	45	9	35	8
Waterton	70	9	116	10	44	7	61	8	64	8	51	8

September and late October. The fair weather that often persists during this time is characterized by cool, crisp nights; sunny days; colourful larch trees; and an absence of bugs.

Weather Lore

Mountain weather can change rapidly and is frequently harsh. A sunny start does not guarantee a day without rain or snow. The variety and extremes of weather in the Rockies can bewilder and beleaguer you. On a single day, you might experience rain, snow, hail, sleet, sun, cloud, fog and wind. (For tips on dressing appropriately, see the Reference section.)

Signs of Storm

- The rapid movement of high cirrus clouds (mare's tails) across an otherwise clear sky.
- A lunar halo, especially in late summer and autumn.
- Clouds developing on the windward sides of mountains.
- Small, puffy clouds developing on the leeward side of summits.
- Two layers of cloud developing during the day.
- A "buttermilk sky" developing after a period of good weather.
- The sun is rapidly covered by stratus clouds.
- A rapid clearing during a storm is often false.

Rained Out?

There is not much joy in backcountry travel when the weather is bleak. Banff, Waterton and Jasper offer diversions: park information centres, bookstores, libraries, cafés, museums, bike rentals and movie theatres. Lake Louise has a bookstore, deli and park information centre. There are hot springs at Banff and Radium, and public swimming at Jasper. The Banff Park Museum has an excellent reading room. The **Altitude SuperGuide** *Walks and Easy Hikes in the Canadian Rockies* describes an array of short walks and hikes, ideal for filling in a rainy afternoon, or making the best of a rainy week.

Signs of Improvement

- A "buttermilk sky" developing after a period of poor weather.
- If a valley bottom fog looks dark along its edges, it is sunny at higher elevations.
- Banner clouds pluming from summits, gradually dissipating during the day.
- If the day's weather has been improving gradually, take note of the sky about 5:00 p.m. If there is only one layer of cloud and it doesn't look threatening, then the clearing will continue overnight. The following day will be fine.
- A lingering, vividly coloured twilight (electric blues, pinks and yellows) foretells good weather next day.
- A gradual clearing indicates the arrival of a high pressure system.

During one August, we awoke to 15 cm of snow, a harsh wind and a temperature of -3°C. The previous day had been sunny and 25°C!

Banff National Park

E stablished in 1885, Banff is Canada's oldest national park.

Today it includes 6641 km² of the front ranges and eastern main ranges in the Rockies. Banff has approximately 1500 km of maintained hiking trails. Some are the most heavily used trails in the country. Others are remote outings completed by only a few hundred backpackers a year. The park features tremendous scenic diversity, including many of the trademark Rocky Mountain views.

The major centres are Banff townsite (129 km west of Calgary) and Lake Louise Village (187 km west of Calgary). Access is by car or passenger bus along Highway 1. A full range of services, supplies and accommodation is available at these centres, and at Canmore 22 km east of Banff. Basic groceries and fuel are available at Castle Mountain Village, Johnston Canyon and Saskatchewan River Crossing.

There are six hostels and the 10 frontcountry campgrounds have more than 2800 campsites. Park information centres are at Banff townsite and Lake Louise Village. The warden office is in the Banff industrial compound.

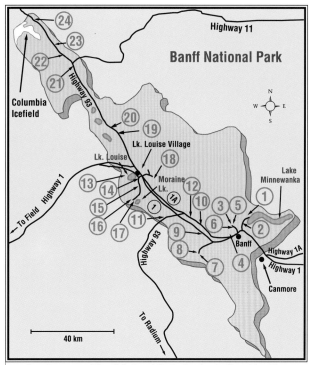

Overview map of Banff National Park showing trailhead locations

The view north across Aylmer Pass features the limestone peaks of Alberta's Ghost River Wilderness.

1. Aylmer Pass and Lookout

Route

Day-hike or overnight
Round trip: 30.4 km

Route	Elevation (m)	Distance (km)
Gate	1480	0
Stewart Canyon	1486	1.7
Aylmer Pass jct and CG	1488	7.8
Aylmer Lookout jct	1982	10.1
Aylmer Pass	2288	13.5

Topographic maps: 82 O/3, 82 O/6
Best lighting: mid-morning to late afternoon

Trailhead

Follow Banff Avenue 3 km east from Banff townsite to the Highway 1 interchange. Keep straight ahead (east) on the Lake Minnewanka Road for 5.9 km to the Lake Minnewanka parking area. Park on the north side of the road. Walk east from the parking lot to the gate. The trail begins as a road through the picnic area.

The Aylmer Pass trail takes you from shoreline to timberline in a landscape typical of Banff's front ranges. The trail features views of the largest body of water in Banff National Park, and forest burned in 1988 and 1990 as part of the park's prescribed burn program. Bighorn sheep are often seen.

On this hike you can visit the pass, visit the lookout, or include both destinations. Because it lies in a relatively dry part of the Rockies and traverses south-facing slopes, this trail is one of the first high-country outings to become snow-free. It is shared with mountain bikers as far as Aylmer Pass junction. The campground near this junction can be used as a base for an overnight trip.

Trailhead to Aylmer Pass Junction

The trail follows the lakeshore for 1.7 km to Stewart Canyon.

Here, the Cascade River flows along a fault in the limestone bedrock where two thrust sheets meet, creating a strike canyon. The canyon is named for George Stewart, first Superintendent of Banff Nation-

al Park. Cross the bridge and take the trail angling uphill to the north (left). Turn east (right) at the next junction.

The trail follows the north shore of Lake Minnewanka through a forest of lodgepole

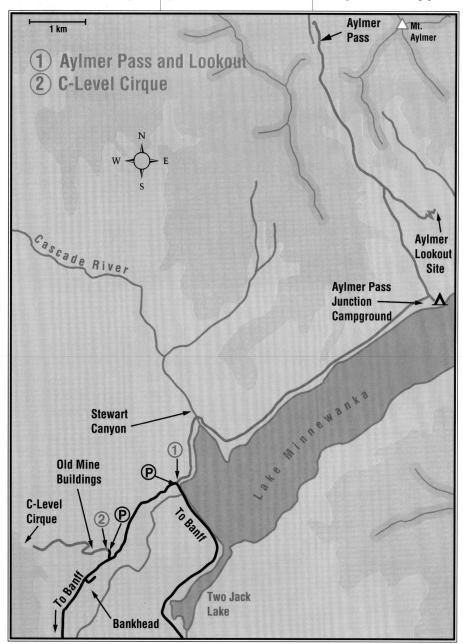

1 km

① Aylmer Pass and Lookout
② C-Level Cirque

N
W — E
S

Aylmer Pass

Mt. Aylmer

Aylmer Lookout Site

Cascade River

Aylmer Pass Junction Campground

Stewart Canyon

Old Mine Buildings

C-Level Cirque

To Banff

① P

② P

To Banff

Lake Minnewanka

To Banff

Bankhead

Two Jack Lake

pine, trembling aspen, Douglas fir and limber pine. This steep, south-facing slope is typical of the montane ecoregion in the front ranges. Colourful wildflowers grace these dry soils in late spring, including: blue clematis, blue columbine and scorpionweed.

After crossing a series of flash-flood stream courses,

the trail encounters the first evidence of the prescribed burns. The trail crosses the stream that drains Aylmer Pass, and 100 m later, reaches the Aylmer Pass junction. The campground is 200 m to the south (right). A campground reservation is required. Aylmer Pass and Lookout are to the north (left).

Aylmer Lookout Junction to Aylmer Pass

Until now, this outing has involved little elevation gain. In the remaining 5.7 km to Aylmer Pass, the trail climbs 800 m. The Aylmer Lookout junction is reached in 2.3 km.

The Lake of the Water Spirit

Lake Minnewanka is the largest of the 480 lakes and ponds in Banff National Park. Sir George Simpson, Governor of the Hudson's Bay Company, was probably the first white man to see the lake. He travelled its north

Mt. Inglismaldie and Lake Minnewanka

shore in 1841 on his way across Canada and around the world. The lake was well known to Natives long before Simpson's visit. It fills a massive breach in the eastern wall of the Rockies and offers an obvious travel route. Evidence of a 10,000 year old encampment has been found along the north shore near the mouth of the Cascade River.

Minnewanka means "lake of the water spirit." Natives believed the lake contained a creature, half-human and half-fish, that could move the waters at will. In the late 1800s and early 1900s, the lake was commonly called Devil's Lake in reference to this legend. Lake trout are the only native fish species. A 15 kg specimen was caught in

1987. At least eight other fish species have been introduced.

The lake we see today is a hydroelectric reservoir, the only one in a Canadian national park. The lake's outlet has been dammed three times, raising the water level a total of 25 m and lengthening the body of water eight km. The most recent dam was constructed in 1942 when the protection afforded national park waters was unfortunately superseded by the War Measures Act. The lake now has an area of just over 2217 ha, and is slightly more than 97 m deep.

Not only was the Lake Minnewanka valley bottom flooded by the 1942 dam, but the upper Ghost River at the east end of the lake was diverted from its

natural course to help fill the reservoir. A village called Minnewanka Landing was inundated. Today, exploration of the submerged ruins is a favourite outing for scuba divers. Adding to Lake Minnewanka's anomalous character: it is the only lake in Banff open to power boats.

Lake Minnewanka is part of the montane, an ecoregion under siege in the Rockies. The montane comprises only 2.95 percent of the area of Banff National Park. Highways, roads, townsites and the railway have severely impacted this ecoregion, disrupting wildlife habitat and severing travel corridors. The montane of Banff would be significantly larger today if Lake Minnewanka's area had not been doubled by the dam. The situation in the montane is even more grim in the Bow Valley just outside the park. Developments near Canmore are obliterating wildlife habitat.

A 1.7 km sidetrail leads southeast to the site of Aylmer Lookout. Constructed in 1946, this facility was one of seven fire lookouts in Banff National Park that saw use until 1978. The structures here were removed in 1985. The site provides an excellent overview of Lake Minnewanka, 654 m below. Bighorn sheep are often seen here – the lookout knoll reeks of their urine. Unfortunately a tower jack who worked here for 17 summers, put out salt blocks to attract sheep, and this has conditioned subsequent generations to return. The lookout is a haven for wood ticks in late spring and early summer. The 1990 prescribed burn consumed most of the trees nearby – a touch of irony that underscores the change in outlook toward forest fires, from one of prevention, to one of careful promotion.

Back on the trail to Aylmer Pass, the forest soon becomes distinctly upper subalpine in character. The trail crosses several avalanche slopes, where crimson-coloured paintbrush, white globeflower and western spring beauty thrive. Keep alert: this is grizzly country. The trail cuts through a shale ravine and drops to the creek just before the pass. Rock-hop to the west side. From here, the track is

Playing With Fire

Fire helps regulate the vitality of ecosystems, and periodic fires are normal in most forests. However, forest fires have been actively suppressed in the Rocky Mountain parks since the late 1800s. Fire suppression was so effective in the 1960s and 1970s, wildfires burned less than 6 km² of Banff National Park.

Park managers have inventoried the forests: mapping tree stands and determining the locations, dates, extent and intensity of past fires. They have also studied the frequency with which different forest types have burned. It is the frequency and intensity of fires that controls vegetation patterns and affects the vitality of the forest ecosystem. Research determined that within the Lake Minnewanka area, large, moderately intense fires should occur every 20 to 50 years. However, the most recent significant wildfires took place in 1884.

Park managers decided to "prescribe" a series of burns in the area, to reintroduce fire into

The 1988 fire at Lake Minnewanka

the ecosystem. Fire guards to contain the 1800-hectare Minnewanka burn area were prepared in the autumn of 1987. The forest was ignited April 17, 1988. This first burn affected 750 ha of forest. Park wardens studied the burn, and appraised its success in terms of duplicating a natural fire. The forest was re-ignited in September, 1990, and another 400 ha burned. In total, 36 percent of the forested area was burned with an intensity that killed all vegetation – a "crown fire." Another prescribed burn was set in 1994.

As you hike through the area, notice the patchwork of burned and unburned forest that resulted from the prescribed burns. You will see some trees that candled or "crowned." And you will see where fire crews excavated smouldering embers after the burns. The fire-resistant bark of many older Douglas fir trees enabled them to survive, while smaller trees nearby were consumed. The resulting mosaic of new and old growth will enhance the forest's vitality. Elk, which were absent before the burns, have rediscovered the area, attracted by the new growth of aspens.

Prescribed burns are being carried out elsewhere in the Rocky Mountain parks. Although most people agree that the burns will benefit the ecosystem over the long term, some argue that the program is manipulative. They would much rather see natural fires left to burn unimpeded if they do not threaten townsites or adjacent provincial forests.

Aylmer Lookout was one of seven fire lookouts constructed in Banff National Park in the 1940s. The lookout buildings are now removed. The site provides a view of Lake Minnewanka and the front ranges.

sometimes sketchy as it crosses the tundra of scree, sedges and snow patches, for the remaining 700 m to the pass.

Aylmer Pass is a favourite haunt of bighorn sheep, and marks the boundary between Banff National Park and the Ghost River Wilderness, a 153 km² provincial wilderness area. Self-reliant backpackers, competent at route finding, may explore farther north into this area. Random camping is allowed and permits are not required. Looking south, Mt. Inglismaldie (2964 m) forms the backdrop to Lake Minnewanka. Inglisdmaldie Castle is in Scotland, and was the home of the Earl of Kintore, who visited Banff in 1887. Mt. Aylmer (3163 m), the highest mountain in this part of Banff National Park, towers above the east side of the pass. The mountain was first climbed in 1889 by surveyor J.J. McArthur. He named the peak for his hometown in Quebec.

> "*After leaving timber line we entered a beautiful alpine valley which continued to the divide and which was bright with flowers. We startled many covets of ptarmigan and saw a number of marmots.*"
>
> —Surveyor J.J. McArthur describing a crossing of Aylmer Pass, *Report of the Department of the Interior,* 1891

"There are indications of coal along the cutbanks, and upon the slopes of Cascade Mountain. Anthracite (coal) of an excellent quality has been discovered."
—Surveyor J.J. McArthur,
Report of the Department of the Interior, 1890

C-Level Cirque and the limestone cliffs of Cascade Mountain

2. C-Level Cirque

Route

Day-hike, 4.0 km

Route	Elevation (m)	Distance (km)
Trailhead	1461	0
C-Level buildings	1646	1.0
C-Level Cirque	1920	4.0

Topographic map: 82 0/4
Best lighting: before noon

Trailhead

Follow Banff Avenue 3 km east from town to Highway 1. Keep straight ahead on the Lake Minnewanka Road for 3.7 km. Turn north (left) into the Upper Bankhead picnic area. The trailhead is on the west side of the parking area.

I n the short outing to C-Level Cirque, you climb from aspen parkland in the montane ecoregion, to avalanche swept slopes in the alpine. This ecological diversity coupled with interesting human history, makes the trail one of the most popular excursions near Banff townsite. Although the cirque itself is frequently snowbound well into summer, the trail is generally open early in the hiking season.

Trailhead to Mine Ruins

The trail climbs steadily for 1 km through a mixed montane forest to the remains of two mine buildings. This was the uppermost or "C-Level" mine. Fenced-off ventilation shafts are nearby. You can walk east from the buildings onto a coal tailings pile, which grants fine views: east to Lake Minnewanka, south into the Bow Valley, and north into the Cascade Valley. Look for the charred forest of a 1992 prescribed burn on the east side of the Cascade Valley.

Please see map on page 21

Bankhead Mine

"C-Level" refers to one of three mining galleries at Bankhead, a coal mine developed by the Canadian Pacific Railway, and operated from 1903-1922. Initially, the Bankhead mine was intended to supply coal only for the railway locomotives. However, the coal shortage of 1906-07 created a national demand for coal. The CPR quickly expanded its mining operations and built a townsite nearby.

Mine production peaked in 1911, when more than 250,000 tonnes were extracted. The population of Bankhead reached maximum the same year, with estimates varying from 900-2000 people. Most of the miners were immigrants from Europe and China. The mine featured a coal-burning power plant that also supplied electricity to Banff.

Bankhead's semi-anthracite coal was extracted in an unusual fashion. Instead of removing the coal through vertical shafts, miners excavated tunnels known as raises, slightly upwards into the mountainside. The coal was knocked down into railcars that coasted back down to the portals. Three galleries: A, B, and C levels, were in operation at different elevations above the valley floor. In all, more than 300 km of mining, transportation and ventilation tunnels were excavated in the flanks of Cascade Mountain.

Labour unrest and failing economics put an end to the Bankhead mine in 1922. Total production was 2.6 million tonnes of coal. Most of the buildings were soon demolished or moved, and Bankhead became a ghost town. New mining claims in national parks have not been allowed since the National Parks Act was proclaimed in 1930.

To C-Level Cirque

About 500 m beyond the mine buildings, the trail narrows and angles sharply west (left). The forest at trailside becomes subalpine in character. Between here and the entrance

Trembling Aspen

The trail begins in a stand of trembling aspen. This tree is common in the montane ecoregion of the front ranges, where it grows on glacial and alluvial rubble. Trembling aspen propagates principally by root suckering; hence the dense stands of uniform age. The trunks of aspens are often scarred up to several metres in height where elk or deer have stripped the protective outer bark to gain access to the sugary cambium layer.

Aspen groves

Small aspens may also be used as "rub trees" by elk and deer, to remove the velvet from their antlers before the autumn rut. Natives knew the aspen as "noisy leaf" – a most appropriate name when a breeze is blowing. The flat leafstems of the aspen readily catch the wind, causing the leaves to flutter. Natives reportedly used the silvery dust from aspen bark as both a sunscreen and a cure for headaches.

The tipple, where coal was sorted at the Bankhead mine, ca 1906.

to the cirque, the trail cuts through several coal seams—exposures of the Early Cretaceous Kootenay group of sedimentary formations.

In early season, you will be greeted by glacier lilies and calypso orchids along the last few hundred metres to C-Level Cirque. Although the elevation here is 300 m below the average for treeline in this area, the cirque is a treeless alpine environment. The northeast-facing slope, with its rocky soils and perennial snow patches is avalanche-prone in winter. It is too chilly here for a forest to grow. Many of the trees along the eastern edge of the cirque are in krummholz form, stunted by the cold, and damaged by avalanches.

An unmaintained path heads north along the eastern edge of the cirque, to a larch covered knoll. From the knoll you may enjoy a fine prospect south over the Bow Valley. The limestone boulders on the knoll exhibit *rillenkarren*—furrows eroded over centuries by naturally acidic rainwater and snowmelt, in a process called solution.

The Handiwork of Ice and Water

C-Level Cirque is not a classic, deeply eroded glacial cirque. Much of the cirque's shape has resulted from mechanical weathering, erosion by water, and avalanches. The hummock at the end of the maintained trail is moraine debris known as a kame. The lakelet is a kettle pond. Both indicate the area was once covered in glacial ice. The hummock is frequented by pikas, hoary marmots and golden-mantled ground squirrels. The reddish tinge in snowpatches is watermelon snow – coloured by an alga with a red eye-spot.

The cliffs that flank C-Level cirque display a sequence of sedimentary rock formations common in the front ranges. The lower cliffs are Palliser limestone (Late Devonian), the middle ledge is Banff shale (Early Mississippian), and the cliffs above are Rundle limestone (Middle Mississippian). This vertical world is home to mountain goats and bighorn sheep, and offers nesting sites for ravens.

The Cascade Amphitheatre trail climbs steeply from Forty Mile Creek to this glacier-carved hollow on the southwest flank of Cascade Mountain.

3. Cascade Amphitheatre

Route

Day-hike, 7.7 km

Route	Elevation (m)	Distance (km)
Trailhead	1701	0
Forty Mile Creek bridge	1555	3.1
Cascade Amphitheatre jct	1799	4.3
Cascade Amphitheatre	2195	7.7

Topographic map: 82 O/4
Best lighting: mid- to late-afternoon

Trailhead

Follow Gopher Street north out of Banff. Cross Highway 1 and follow the Mt. Norquay Road 6 km to the first parking lot on the north (right) at the ski area. The trailhead kiosk is at the north end of the parking lot.

Cascade Mountain forms the northern skyline in the view from Banff townsite. The Cascade Amphitheatre trail ascends into a steeply walled cirque on the southwest flank of the mountain, granting a unique perspective on this well-known landmark. The trail is generally snow-free by mid-May. However, snow patches linger in the amphitheatre until mid-June. The approach trail is used by mountain bikers and horses.

Trailhead to Forty Mile Creek

The first 4.3 km are shared with the Elk Pass trail, which begins as a Cat track through the Mt. Norquay ski area. Keep straight ahead at the Mystic Pass junction. Just past the Mystic chairlift, the trail begins a steady descent north through open lodgepole pine forest to a "T" junction on the banks of Forty Mile Creek. Turn east (right), and in 150 m cross Forty Mile Creek on a bridge.

To Cascade Amphitheatre

Across the bridge, the uphill toil begins: 640 m of gain in the remaining 4.6 km. The dogtooth spire of Mt. Louis (2682 m) in the Sawback Range is featured in views

west. At the Cascade Amphitheatre junction, turn east (right), and continue the steady ascent to the amphitheatre entrance.

During the climb from Forty Mile Creek, you pass from the montane ecoregion into the subalpine. The lodge-

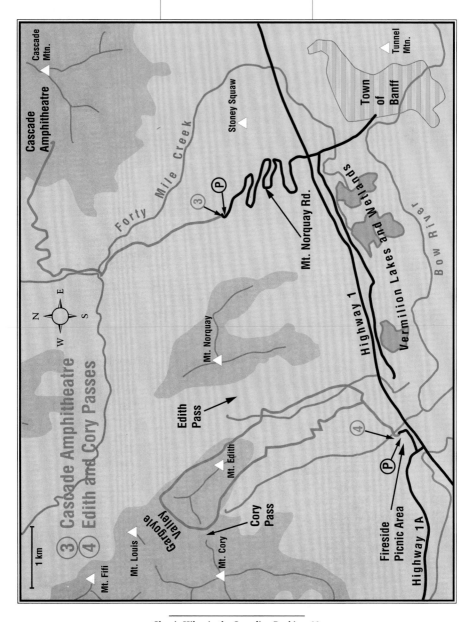

pole pines at trailside seeded after a large forest fire in 1894. The trail levels off at the entrance to the amphitheatre, where there is a marked transition from pine forest to a mix of Engelmann spruce and subalpine fir, typical of the upper subalpine ecoregion. The paths that branch south (right) join the approach to the regular mountaineering route on Cascade Mountain. Keep straight ahead.

Cascade Amphitheatre

Cirque valleys like Cascade Amphitheatre were created and enlarged by glacial erosion during the various ice ages of the last 2 million years. Glaciologists speculate there have been 20 to 30 glacial advances in this time. The trail undulates over a series of low recessional moraines as it enters the amphitheatre—evidence of the most recent maximum extent of glacial ice.

Although the glacial ice is now gone, a chill remains on the floor of the amphitheatre. Cold air flows downhill and collects in depressions, creating frost hollows where mature trees cannot develop. The many small mounds are frost hummocks, soil formations produced by a churning action in the damp soil during repeated freezing and thawing.

The trail is vague in places, but keeps to the southern edge of the meadows. It crosses rockslide debris from which several springs issue. About 1 km after entering the am-

phitheatre, you climb through a small stand of trees to where the trail ends on a knoll of rockslide debris. You may see white-tailed ptarmigan, pika, and hoary marmot in this area.

Cascade Mountain

The summit of Cascade Mountain (2998 m) is directly east of trail's end. The name, Cascade Mountain, is a rendition of the Stoney word Minnehappa: "the mountain where the water falls", and was given by James Hector in 1858.

Cascade is an overthrust mountain. Its tilted southwest-facing slope (the ridge south of the amphitheatre) ends on a northeast-facing cliff (seen from C-Level Cirque, Classic Hike # 2).

The rock layers of Cascade Mountain exhibit much folding. When deep within the earth's crust, the rock layers were made pliable by heat and then warped into folds by the forces of mountain building. U-shaped folds are known as synclines (SIN-clines). Arch-shaped folds are called anticlines. A prominent syncline is visible from the end of trail. You can see a tremendous assortment of folds in Cascade Mountain's eastern flanks, from the Lake Minnewanka Road.

The upper slopes of Cascade Mountain are Rundle limestone and dolomite comprised of sediments deposited during the middle Mississippian period. Although inhospitable looking, this terrain is excellent habitat for bighorn sheep, and large flocks may be seen.

Forty Mile Creek

The first explorers in the Rockies often named features for their distance from a known location. Forty Mile Creek is not forty miles long, so it was undoubtedly named because it is forty miles distant from a prominent feature. There is no record as to what this point of reference might be. However, the creek crossed the route of the Canadian Pacific Railway about forty miles distant from two points: the old railway siding of Padmore to the east, which was a major resupply point during the railway survey of 1881-1882; and the crest of Kicking Horse Pass to the west.

In the spring and summer of 1982, Banff endured an outbreak of "beaver fever", caused by contamination of drinking water with the parasite *Giardia lamblia*. (See the Reference section.) Beavers living in the town water reservoir on lower Forty Mile Creek were deemed the carriers. They were trapped and destroyed as a short-term solution to the problem. In July, 1983, the town of Banff completed the switch to three groundwater wells. This was good news for townsfolk, and for the beavers, for whom the meanders of Forty Mile Creek provide excellent habitat.

"*We stopped and looked back at our mountain, which towered up magnificently in the dusk, and Conrad spoke volumes when he said, "Ye Gods Mr. MacCarthy; just look at that; they never will believe we climbed it.*"

—A.H. MacCarthy,
*The First Ascent of Mt. Louis,
Canadian Alpine Journal,
1917*

The limestone spire of Mt. Louis is one of the most striking summits in the Rockies.

4. Edith and Cory Passes

Route

Day-hike, 13.6 km loop

Route	Elevation (m)	Distance (km)
Trailhead	1415	0
Cory Pass jct	1470	1.1
Edith Pass jct	1860	4.0
Entrance to Gargoyle Valley	2134	6.2
Cory Pass	2363	7.8
Cory Pass jct	1470	12.5
Trailhead	1415	13.6

Topographic map: 82 O/4

Best lighting: aim to be on Cory Pass before early afternoon

Trailhead

Follow Highway 1 west from the Mt. Norquay (Banff) interchange for 5.6 km to the Bow Valley Parkway exit (Highway 1A). Follow the Bow Valley Parkway 500 m and turn east into the Fireside picnic area. Follow this narrow road 600 m to its end.

The Edith and Cory passes loop is unquestionably the most spectacular and strenuous outing in the vicinity of Banff. Set amongst the rugged limestone peaks of the Sawback Range, the trail ventures from montane valley bottom to well above treeline, and displays tremendous ecological diversity. Bighorn sheep, white-tailed deer, mule deer and elk are often seen. In early summer, lingering snowpatches cover the steep side-slopes traversed by the trail. Early season hikers should carry an ice axe.

Please see map on page 29

Fireside Picnic Area to Edith Pass Junction

From the trailhead, cross the footbridge and turn south (right). Follow the broad trail 200 m to a junction and turn north (left). This part of the trail is in a forest typical of south-facing slopes in the montane ecoregion of the front ranges. Lodgepole pine is the most common tree. The understory contains the shrubs: buffaloberry, prickly wild rose and common juniper; along with Indian paintbrush, showy aster and groundsel. Stands of trembling aspen grow near stream courses and on grassy slopes. This deciduous tree propagates principally by root suckering. The sugary cambium layer within the bark of as-

pens is a food for elk and deer during winter. The animals strip the outer bark, uniformly scarring the tree trunks.

At km 1.1, the descent trail from Cory Pass merges from the north. Keep straight ahead, following signs for Edith Pass. The trail drops into the ravine that drains the pass, and abruptly enters a markedly different forest – one that hasn't burned since 1850. This cool, shaded ravine supports a damp forest of lodgepole pine, Douglas fir, and a few white spruce. The rocky soils are home to feathermosses and shade-tolerant wildflowers, including several species of orchids.

Douglas Fir

A few majestic Douglas fir trees grace the grassy slopes near the trailhead. The Douglas fir is the climax tree species of the montane forest in this part of the Rockies. The thick, corky bark of the mature tree allows it to withstand most ground fires and infestation by insects. The fires remove competing vegetation, creating open parkland dotted with stately firs. Douglas firs in such settings may be 600 years old. The last

Douglas fir tree

Douglas fir bark

forest fire on these slopes was in 1910.

Their are two varieties of Douglas fir: coastal and interior. Although the two interbreed, the interior or "blue Douglas fir" is most common in the Rockies. Large specimens are 30-40 m

tall and 1 m in diameter. In Pacific rainforests, the coastal variety attains heights of 80 m and diameters in excess of 4 m. The tree was named for David Douglas, a Scottish botanist who collected in the Rockies in 1826 and 1827. Intensive harvesting of Douglas firs in the commercial forests of British Columbia guarantees that old-growth stands of this tree will soon be non-existent outside protected areas.

Edith Pass High Route to Gargoyle Valley and Cory Pass

The trail ascends the ravine to an important junction at km 4.0. The low route over Edith Pass continues straight ahead. Turn northwest (left) to take the high route to Cory Pass. The trail levels out in a sub-alpine spruce/fir forest at another junction in 500 m. Turn north (right) for Cory Pass.

For the next 1.5 km, you ascend a rough trail across avalanche slopes beneath the slabby east face of Mt. Edith (2554 m). Edith Cox was a companion of the party of Prime Minister John A. Macdonald, when he visited Banff in 1886 following completion of the CPR. The mountain has three summits of which the most northerly is the highest. Mt. Norquay (NOR-kway) (2522 m) is east across the forested saddle of Edith Pass. John Norquay was Premier of Manitoba when he climbed this peak in 1888. The mountain to the north across Forty Mile Creek is Mt. Brewster (2859 m), named for Jim Brewster, trail guide, outfitter and Banff businessman. A huge limestone block sits on its southwest slope.

Each avalanche slope that you cross provides better views northwest to Mt. Louis (2682 m), the scenic focal point of this hike. The dog-tooth spire of vertically thrust Palliser limestone is one of the most striking peaks in the Canadian Rockies. First climbed in 1916, the south ridge is popular with rock climbers today. Keep straight ahead at unsigned trail junctions until the trail emerges on the southern edge of a large avalanche slope with an unobstructed view of Mt. Louis.

If snow covered, the next section can be treacherous. The trail contours across steep sideslopes to the col between Mts. Edith and Louis – the entrance to the Gargoyle Valley. This northeast-facing cirque is flanked by Mts. Louis, Edith and Cory (2802 m). The sidehill gouging continues in the cool of the shaded valley, as the trail angles upwards toward Cory Pass. Views back to Mt. Louis are superb.

Cory Pass and Descent

Cory Pass is a narrow, rocky and often windswept breach, that culminates the diversity of terrain on this hike. Set in the alpine ecoregion, the thin soils of the pass support only scattered mats of hardy wildflowers, like white mountain avens and moss campion. Views south include: the Bow Valley, Mt. Rundle, Sulphur Mountain, and the Sundance Range. West of this range is the Fatigue Thrust Fault, that separates the grey limestone peaks of the front ranges, from the eastern main ranges. The "gargoyles" flanking Cory Pass are shattered pinnacles of Eldon limestone. An opening or "window" has been eroded into one of them. Cory Pass and Mt. Cory commemorate William Cory, Deputy Minister of the Interior from 1905-1930.

The trail descends south from Cory Pass, traversing steep avalanche slopes to treeline on the south ridge of Mt. Edith. The open slopes feature a variety of wildflowers with yellow blooms: stonecrop, double bladder pod, golden fleabane, yellow beardtongue, and yellow mountain saxifrage. During the descent, Mt. Assiniboine (3618 m) looms to the south, and you can see the many meanders of the Bow River.

The trail is well defined as it re-enters the forest. However, it becomes vague for 25 m where it encounters a knoll on the ridge. Ignore the path that descends to the east. Make a short ascent to stay on the crest of the ridge, where the undulating trail resumes.

The trail leaves the ridge at its southern end, and begins a mercilessly steep descent to the southeast, dropping 350 m during the next 1.5 km. Please keep to the beaten path. The final descent is on a grassy, flower-filled slope, dotted with aspens. Elk, deer and bighorn sheep frequent this area. At the junction with the Edith Pass trail, turn west (right) to return to the trailhead.

"*Two gentlemen decided to ascend Cascade Mountain, one of the highest peaks in the neighbourhood. ... They started out with the intention of returning within twenty-four hours, but instead mysteriously disappeared for three days.... It appears that they had been lost in a region of burnt timber where they had wandered hungry and hopeless.... No one knows how far they went or where, but it is certain that upon reaching the hotel they retired to their rooms and remained there the greater part of the ensuing week.*"

—Walter Wilcox,
The Rockies of Canada, 1909

Elk Lake is reached by a short sidetrip from Elk Pass campground.

5. Elk Pass Loop

Route

2-3 days, 35.8 km loop

Route	Elevation (m)	Distance (km)
Trailhead	1701	0
Forty Mile Creek bridge	1555	3.1
Cascade Amphitheatre jct	1799	4.3
Elk Pass campground	2055	11.5
Elk Pass	2055	12.8
Cascade River bridge	1631	20.2
Stony Creek bridge	1631	20.4
Cascade trail jct	1640	21.0
Cascade Bridge CG	1545	29.2
Upper Bankhead parking lot	1461	35.8

Topographic maps: 82 O/4, 82 O/5, 82 O/6

Trailhead

Follow Gopher Street north out of Banff. Cross Highway 1 and follow the Mt. Norquay Road 6 km to the first parking lot on the north (right) at the ski area. The trailhead kiosk is at the north end of the parking lot.

Although close to Banff townsite, the Elk Pass Loop provides a taste of Banff's front-range hinterland of rugged limestone peaks; an area that is home to grizzly bear, wolf, coyote, elk, deer, mountain goat and bighorn sheep. The trail to Elk Pass, and the Cascade Fireroad are shared with mountain bikers. The entire loop is used by commercial horse parties.

Trailhead to Elk Pass

From the trailhead, follow the Cat track north through the facilities of the Mt. Norquay ski area. Keep straight ahead at the Mystic Pass junction. Just past the Mystic chairlift, the trail begins a steady descent through open lodgepole pine forest to a "T" junction on the banks of Forty Mile Creek. Turn east (right), and in 150 m cross Forty Mile Creek on a bridge.

The trail ascends for 1.2 km through lodgepole pine forest to the Cascade Amphitheatre junction. The surrounding pine forest resulted

from a large forest fire in 1894. The resin-sealed cone of the lodgepole cracks open at 45°C, scattering the seeds and producing a doghair forest of pines. At this elevation, most of the lodgepole pines would normally have been replaced after 60 years by the climax species of the subalpine forest: Engelmann spruce and subalpine fir. However, these steep, well-drained, sun-exposed slopes on Cascade Mountain offer a perfect niche for pines, and they have remained the dominant tree. A few small spruces can be seen beneath the canopy, where buffaloberry, bearberry and wolf willow also grow. Views west through the forest feature the dogtooth spire of Mt. Louis (2682 m) in the Sawback Range.

Keep straight ahead at the Cascade Amphitheatre junc-

tion. The wide and sometimes rocky horse trail continues north, crossing several flash-flood stream courses. As you climb toward Elk Pass, note the subtle transition to upper subalpine forest. From openings in the trees there are views south to Cascade Mountain, Mt. Norquay, Sulphur Mountain and the Sundance Range. The purple bloom of silky scorpionweed graces some of the shale banks at trailside. Open glades of willow mark the final approach to the pass. The slopes to the east are covered in silver spar trees from a 1914 forest fire.

Follow the Elk Pass campground trail 100 m northwest (left) from the main trail to the campground. This pleasant camping place is set in a grove of spruce trees. The water source is questionable – a small stream rich with organic material and frequented by deer and elk. Boil or filter the water before consumption.

While camped here we were visited by a mule deer doe and buck, who approached within 5 metres. While drifting off to sleep, I was awakened by the unmistakable snarl of a big cat close-by the tent – possibly a cougar. In the morning, we awoke to the yelping and commotion from a coyote den, 600 m from camp on the opposite side of the valley. We found the skin of a goat in the willow meadows near the campground junction. The goat may have been killed by a cougar or wolves.

Elk Lake, 2.2 km

An early morning visit to Elk Lake is the highlight of this outing. From the junction on the main trail just north of the campground, a wide and sometimes muddy trail climbs northwest into treeline forest. After crossing a spur of Mt. Brewster, the trail descends west to Elk Lake. Lyall's larch is common in the forest, and if you are hiking in early summer you will see white globeflowers and glacier lilies among the tufts of heather at trailside. On the north side of the trail, you may see moose and elk in a nearby slough.

Elk Lake is a classic cirque lake, harboured in a glacial depression beneath Mt. Brewster. The trail peters out at the lakeshore, which is buggy, boggy and fringed with alpine buttercup. The outlet on the north shore drains to the Cascade River. The cliffs of the cirque display the Palliser limestone, Banff shale, and Rundle limestone sequence, common to northeast-facing cliffs in the front ranges.

Cutthroat trout are present in the lake. Since there is no record of stocking of any species at Elk Lake, it is possible these fish represent a natural strain – a rarity among accessible lakes in the Canadian Rockies.

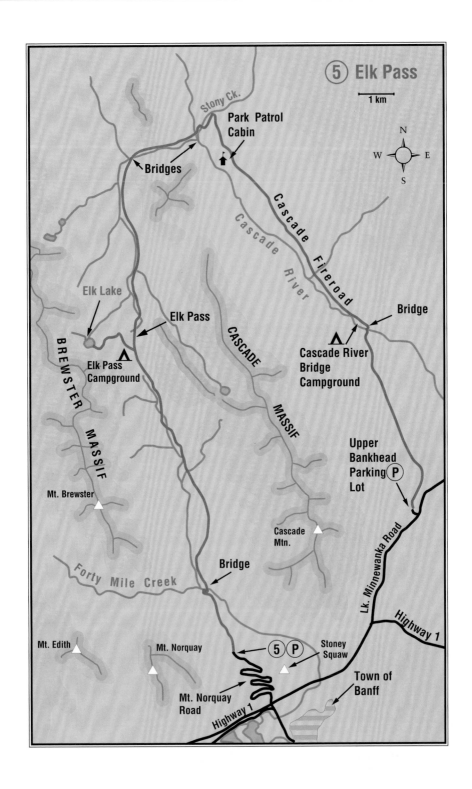

Coyote tracks

Elk Pass to the Cascade Fireroad

The willow meadow stretches for 1.5 km across Elk Pass. This is ideal habitat for prey species: snowshoe hare, mice, voles, least chipmunk and Columbian ground squirrel. Hence, the predator species: wolf, coyote, lynx and cougar frequent this area. You may see tracks and scats at trailside. From the north edge of the pass, the trail descends parallel to the stream course. During wet weather, there are some awful mud holes here, churned up by horse traffic. However, fine views west to Mt. Brewster compensate for the difficult travel.

Roughly 5 km north of Elk Pass, the trail crosses the stream to its north bank on a bridge, and turns east toward the Cascade Valley. The bridge is built from railway ties, soaked in creosote. In the 1960s and 1970s, many backcountry structures were built from this weatherproof wood. Unfortunately, creosote is toxic and readily leaches into streams. When you also consider these timbers were flown here by helicopter, this bridge is not "environmentally friendly".

The final 2.2 km to the Cascade River is through a montane valley typical of the front ranges. Bright and attractive wildflowers are common: yellow and orange false dandelions, goatsbeard, yellow columbine, prairie groundsel, Indian paintbrush, yellow and blue beardtongues, and yellow hedysarum. Common dandelion is also abundant. This flower is not native to the Rockies. The seeds are often transported to the backcountry in the feed and dung of horses.

The steep, grassy slopes to the north of the trail are ideal habitat for mountain goats and bighorn sheep. The shaded avalanche slopes to the south offer good food sources for bears. Toward the mouth of the creek, the trail passes through several groves of trembling aspen. Visibility is limited and the creek is noisy. Make lots of noise in this area to alert bears to your presence.

The trail cuts through a limestone bluff and emerges onto the west bank of the Cascade River at its junction with Stony Creek. Cross the river on two footbridges, located 50 m to the south (right). Turn north (left) 20 m beyond, and follow this trail for 30 m. Angle northeast (right) onto a well-beaten trail that parallels the north bank of Stony Creek. Cross this creek on a series of split-log bridges. There is a maze of horse trails, paths and fireroads on the south bank of the creek. Disregard them. Follow Stony Creek upstream for 600 m to the concrete bridge on the Cascade fireroad.

A Road in the Backcountry?

The headwaters of the Cascade River are in the wilderness heartland of Banff Na-

Strike Mountains

The topographic maps clearly show that Elk Lake occupies one of more than a dozen east-facing cirques along the 21 km length of Mt. Brewster. With its numerous summits, Mt. Brewster is a fine example of a massif – a miniature mountain range. The front range landscape of Banff and Jasper national parks is dominated by a series of parallel massifs, oriented along the northwest/southeast strike of the Rockies. Cascade Mountain is another example. Parallel to these massifs, major streams and rivers erode their courses. Secondary streams enter the major streams at right angles, producing a pattern known as trellis drainage. A few older streams have managed to bisect the massifs, eroding downwards as the mountains were thrust upwards.

Mt. Brewster was named for Jim Brewster, who rose from humble beginnings in Banff to gain control of a transportation empire in the early 1900s. The summits immediately above Elk Lake are 2805 m. Elsewhere north and south, the summits are slightly higher. The southernmost peak of the Brewster massif, to which the name Mt. Brewster is formally applied, is visible from places in Banff townsite.

tional Park; an area important to many large mammals, especially wolves and grizzly bears. It may seem unthinkable today that a road was built here. However, the existence of the Cascade Fireroad underscores the history of changing attitudes toward resource management in the Rocky Mountain parks.

The most extensive wildfires in Banff National Park this century occurred in 1936. Three major burns consumed about 70 km² of park forests. Almost 90 percent of this total resulted from a single fire at Flints Park in the upper Cascade Valley. Park managers of the day were obsessed with protecting timber, and quickly mobilized crews to extinguish the fire. The aggressive response to the Flints Park burn was also prompted by the fact that the fire was caused by campers.

As part of the firefighting efforts, a Cat bulldozed a road north to Flints Park. In the years following the fire, the road was upgraded and lengthened northwards over Wigmore and Snow Creek

Summits to the Red Deer River, and then east to the park boundary – a total distance of 70 km.

By the 1950s, fireroads had been constructed in most major backcountry valleys to facilitate firefighting. Patrol cabins sprang up along the roads, and park maintenance and warden vehicles were brought into the heart of prime wildlife habitat, causing untold disruption. At times, there was even political intent to pave the fireroads and open them to public traffic. Fortunately for ecosystem integrity, this did not happen. In recent decades, the use of helicopters for smoke patrols and initial attack on fires has rendered fireroads obsolete.

The 1988 national park management plans called for the closure of all fireroads to motorized traffic. Some fireroads have had "tank traps" installed at the trailheads. Others have had key bridges removed, or like the Cascade, have had bridges downscaled to pedestrian width.

Unfortunately, old ways

die hard. When the new Stony Creek park patrol cabin was built on the Cascade fireroad in 1992, the logs were hauled to the building site. The heavy equipment bypassed the narrow bridge by driving through the Cascade River.

Stony Creek to Upper Bankhead Parking Lot

The Elk Pass Loop concludes with an enjoyable walk south along the undulating Cascade Fireroad. The Stony Creek patrol cabin is on a sideroad, approximately 1.3 km south of Stony Creek. The Cascade River Bridge campground is located on the west side of the fireroad, just before it crosses the Cascade River. Beyond the bridge, the trail climbs into lower subalpine forest that features a number of sloughs created by beavers. With views of the Bow Valley ahead, the outing concludes with a rapid descent to the Upper Bankhead parking lot on the Lake Minnewanka Road.

You should remain alert for grizzly bears while hiking the Cascade fireroad. The valley offers extensive areas of good habitat, and grizzlies are more commonly observed here than anywhere else in Banff National Park.

Space for Grizzlies and Wolves

In May 1993, Banff National Park temporarily closed the Cascade River Valley above Stony Creek to recreational use. The closure was to protect resident populations of grizzly bears and wolves. Previously, park areas had only been closed because of avalanche hazard, or following bear/human, or bear/elk incidents. The Cascade closure was one of the first proactive closures intended to provide space for wide-ranging carnivores. Although the closure temporarily removed some of the wildest country in Banff from the backpacker's domain, it was necessary to help reduce the pressures confronting bears and wolves. At the time of publication, it was likely that the closure will be enacted each year.

The waters of Baker Lake make a tranquil mirror for Ptarmigan Peak shortly after sunrise.

6. Sawback Trail

Route

Mystic/Pulsatilla/Boulder Passes
4-7 days, 73.5 km

Route	Elevation (m)	Distance (km)
Trailhead	1701	0
Forty Mile/Mystic jct	1707	0.7
Forty Mile Creek bridge	1631	4.0
Cockscomb Mtn CG	1723	8.2
Mystic Pass jct	1838	15.9
Mystic Valley CG	1921	18.6
Mystic Lake jct	1951	19.1
Mystic Pass	2285	22.7
Johnston Creek jct	1692	29.3
"Larry's Camp" CG	1685	29.5
Luellen Lake jct	1890	37.8
Johnston Creek CG	1875	38.0
Badger Pass jct	2027	43.7
Badger Pass jct CG	2043	44.2
Pulsatilla Pass	2365	47.6
Baker Creek jct	1814	54.0
Wildflower Creek CG	1814	54.0
Baker Lake CG	2210	60.0
Boulder Pass	2345	64.9
Hidden Lake CG	2195	66.4
Fish Creek parking area	1698	73.5

Topographic maps: 82 O/4, 82 O/5, 82 N/8

Trailhead

Follow Gopher Street north from Banff. Cross Highway 1 on the overpass and follow the Mt. Norquay Road 6 km to the first parking lot. The trailhead kiosk is at the north end of the parking lot.

The Sawback Trail connects a series of spectacular alpine passes as it winds over the crest of the Sawback Range from Banff to Lake Louise. This long outing includes sections of the following trails: Forty Mile Creek, Mystic Pass, Johnston Creek, Wildflower Creek, Baker Creek and Boulder Pass. The many campgrounds allow for short days on the trail and time for exploration. Be forewarned: the Sawback Trail traverses prime grizzly habitat, and its entire length is shared with horse traffic. Avoid this outing during spells of poor weather, when much of the trail is quagmire.

Trailhead to Mystic Valley Campground

The trail begins as a Cat track through the Mt. Norquay ski area. Just past the Spirit chairlift, branch left, following signs for Mystic Pass. The trail then contours around the north flank of Mt. Norquay, and descends to a bridge over Forty Mile Creek at km 4.0.

For the next 12 km, the trail climbs gradually through open coniferous forest along the east bank of Forty Mile Creek. In places the trail has been crowned and hardened with gravel to withstand the impact of constant horse travel. Views are limited, except where the trail crosses avalanche paths or abuts the creek. The dogtooth spires of Mt. Louis (2682 m) and Mt. Fifi (2621 m) dominate the west side of the valley.

The Edith Pass junction is 6.0 km from the trailhead. Keep straight ahead. If you use the Cockscomb Mountain campground at km 8.2, treat all drinking water from Forty Mile Creek.

The unmarked trails that branch west prior to the Mystic Pass junction lead to a horse outfitter's camp. Keep straight ahead until the junction. The trail is very poor in this area. Turn west (left) and descend to a bridge over Forty Mile Creek. The trail skirts the north side of the Mystic patrol cabin. Keep straight ahead (west) at the junction just beyond. After traversing a forested sideslope for 2 km, the trail descends avalanche paths to a bridge across Mystic Creek to reach the Mystic Valley campground. The campground is situated on a bench between the creeks draining Mystic Pass and Mystic Lake. Upstream, both creeks are forded by horses. Treat all drinking water.

Mystic Valley to Mystic Pass

The Sawback Trail heads west toward Mystic Lake for 500 m to a junction. Turn north (right). The trail climbs moderately with one bridged stream crossing and one rock-hop to reach treeline at the southern entrance to Mystic Pass.

Mystic Lake, 1.1 km

Mystic Lake is nestled in a glacial cirque under the eastern ramparts of Mt. Ishbel. The trail to the lake departs west from the campground, crosses the lake's outlet stream and ascends to a junction in 500 m. Keep straight ahead. The muddy and rocky trail improves dramatically after the horse/hiker barrier, about 300 m beyond the junction.

Mystic Lake has an area of 8 ha and is 15 m deep. It is fringed by an ancient forest of spruce and fir that last burned in

Mystic Lake is bordered by an ancient forest.

1645. The wildflowers: arnica, fleabane and leather-leaved saxifrage grow on the damp shoreline, along with the sedge, cotton grass. Cutthroat trout and bull trout are the fish species in the lake.

The first white visitor to Mystic Lake was Jim Brewster, who was led here by William Twin of the Stoney tribe in 1891. Mt Ishbel was named for the daughter of Ramsay MacDonald, a former British prime minister. Although it is possible to make a rough circuit of this enchanting body of water, most visitors are content to gaze at the lake and Mt. Ishbel from near trail's end on the east shore.

Mystic Pass is a narrow cleft between two parallel ridges of the Sawback Range. The axis of the pass lies direct-ly on the Sawback Thrust Fault which separates the drab, grey Devonian Palliser limestone on the east side of the pass, from the more varied and old-er Cambrian rocks to the west. These include the purple Arc-tomys (ARK-toe-miss) shales

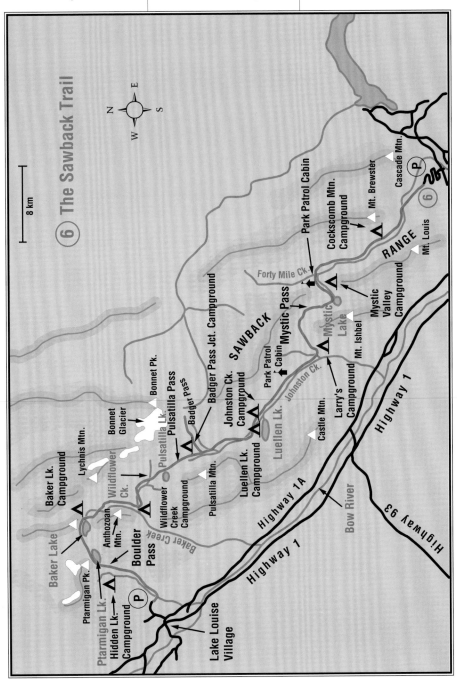

6 The Sawback Trail

8 km

N E W S

Park Patrol Cabin

Cockscomb Mtn.

Campground

Mt. Brewster

Cascade Mtn.

P

6

Forty Mile Ck.

SAWBACK

RANGE

Mt. Louis

Mystic Valley Campground

Mystic Lake

Mystic Pass

Badger Pass Jct. Campground

Bonnet Pk.

Pulsatilla Pass

Badger Pass

Johnston Ck. Campground

Park Patrol Cabin

Mt. Ishbel

Larry's Campground

Bonnet Glacier

Lychnis Mtn.

Wildflower Ck.

Pulsatilla Lk.

Pulsatilla Mtn.

Luellen Lk.

Luellen Lk. Campground

Johnston Ck.

Castle Mtn.

Highway 1A

Highway 1

Bow River

Highway 93

Baker Lk. Campground

Anthozoan Mtn.

Wildflower Creek Campground

Baker Creek

Boulder Pass

Baker Lake

Ptarmigan Pk.

Ptarmigan Lk.

Hidden Lk. Campground

P

Lake Louise Village

at trailside. Bighorn sheep and mountain goats frequent the kilometre-long tundra of the pass. Game trails criss-cross the surrounding slopes.

The Sawback Range

The Sawback Range was named by James Hector in 1858, for the serrated appearance of its ridges. The limestone slabs, capped by weak shales, were thrust vertically during mountain building. This created steep southwest-facing slopes that are now oriented directly perpendicular to the prevailing weather systems. The shales atop the slabs are readily eroded through mechanical weathering, solution, and abrasion, creating the sawtooth ridges and hourglass-shaped gullies below. The gullies collect runoff from vast areas near the ridgetops, and funnel the water through resistant limestone slots onto the lower slopes. Flash-floods are therefore common at the base of the Sawback Range.

Mystic Pass to Johnston Creek

Leaving Mystic Pass, the trail swings west and plunges toward Johnston Creek. Sedimentary formations in the mountain to the north display extensive folding and small solution caves. As it levels out, the trail alternates between rockslides and willow plains. Some sections are routed along a flash-flood stream course. Look for cairns that

Mystic Pass crosses the backbone of the Sawback Range. Bighorn sheep and mountain goats are often seen here.

mark the way where the trail becomes faint.

The stream that drains Mystic Pass emerges from the base of a rockslide about 2.5 km below the pass. Cross another flash-flood stream course and rock-hop the creek to its north bank. A multitude of colourful montane wildflowers blooms in July on the steep, dry slopes north of the trail. There are views south along Johnston Creek to Copper Mountain (2795 m). Johnston Creek was named for a prospector who frequented the area near Silver City in the Bow Valley in 1882.

Johnston Creek to Luellen Lake

At the Johnston Creek junction, turn south (left) if you would like to stay at Larry's Camp campground. You can also make an emergency exit from this point to the Bow Valley Parkway, 7.9 km south.

The Sawback Trail continues northwest (right) from the junction – as a mucky, rooted

horse trail along Johnston Creek. It is difficult walking – the 8.5 km to the Luellen lake junction seems half that far again. Horsetails grow at trailside. Their genus, *Equisetum*, is the most primitive and ancient group of vascular plants on earth. There are nine species of horsetail in the Rockies. They prefer damp habitats and are a favourite early summer food of black and grizzly bears.

A wooden fence and gate marks the horse pasture at the Johnston Creek patrol cabin. Please close the gate behind you.

The upper Johnston Creek valley is oriented along the Castle Mountain Thrust Fault. Bedrock in the lower slopes on the west side of the valley is purple and brown Miette (mee-YETT) gritstone and shale. Miette rocks underlie much of the eastern main ranges. Miette sediments accumulated to a maximum thickness of 9 km.

There are two campgrounds near Luellen Lake

junction, both reached by turning west (left). Johnston Creek campground is 200 m downhill from the junction, on the near bank of the creek; an excellent choice for those wishing more solitude and fewer bugs than at nearby Luellen Lake campground.

Luellen Lake to Badger Pass Junction

The Sawback Trail continues northwest from the Luellen Lake junction, along the east bank of Johnston Creek. This section of trail is narrower and much less travelled. The trail crosses to the west bank 500 m north of

the junction. The forest becomes more open and views improve toward the head of the valley. The trail descends to the creek and crosses it again. There is a massive teepee frame on the east bank amidst the willows. This structure is filled with the innovative "furniture" of an outfitter's camp, packed away some decades ago, and evidently not used since.

For the next 3 km, the trail is routed through willow and shrub thickets near the creek. Some of the willow stands are more than two metres tall. Visibility is poor. Make lots of noise while travelling here to alert bears to your presence. This could be a miserable sec-

tion during or shortly after rain. Keep to the hiker trail at the horse/hiker barrier, or you may be forced to ford and reford numerous braids of the creek.

Rock-hop Badger Creek to

Fishing

To Stock or not to stock? Luellen Lake is one of the most popular backcountry fishing destinations in Banff National Park, and was named for the daughter of a fish hatchery superintendent. Cutthroat trout are present. Luellen and many other lakes were formerly stocked with non-native species to promote angling. Some introduced species flourished to the detriment of native species. As a result, few backcountry lakes in the Rockies are in a "natural" state.

Sport fishing is the only extractive activity still permitted in the Rocky Mountain national parks. Park managers are contemplating various measures to re-establish natural regimes in backcountry lakes. This may include increasing catch limits for introduced species, until they are "fished out," and then closing the lakes to angling; or managing the lakes as "catch and release" fisheries only. Although many anglers support this kind of management, some continue to advocate stocking. The revised National Park Policy of 1993 no longer permits stocking to promote angling. Native species may be stocked only to assist recovery or to re-establish populations.

Luellen Lake, 750 m

The route to Luellen Lake crosses Johnston Creek and climbs a rough track for 750 m to the campground on the north shore of this beautiful lake. Luellen Lake is an attractive ribbon of water, 1750 m long, with an area of 47 ha. The peculiar blocky summit to the west is Stuart Knob (2850 m), named for Benjamin Stuart, the son of Charles Walcott. Walcott is best known for his discovery of the Burgess Shale in 1909. The 500 m high quartzite cliffs of Helena Ridge form the backdrop for Luellen Lake. Walcott climbed the ridge in 1910, and named it for his second wife.

You may hear the call of the Common loon at Luellen Lake: "who-EEE-ooo." Many backcountry lakes in the Rockies are home to a pair of loons in summer. Loons eat fish and aquatic insects. They nest near water and are unable to take off from land. Loons in the Rockies migrate to the west coast during winter.

the Badger Pass trail junction. The Sawback Trail continues north, reaching the Badger Pass junction campground in 500 m.

Badger Pass Junction to Baker Creek

For 2 km beyond Badger Pass junction campground, the Sawback Trail works its way through shrub thickets in the valley bottom. Boulder-hop Johnston Creek to its west bank. Wet meadows here feature an astounding array of wildflowers, including: elephant head, fleabane, bracted lousewort, yellow hedysarum, and yellow paintbrush.

Pulsatilla Mountain (3035 m) dominates the west side of the valley. The east face of the mountain is a 6 km long cliff, riddled by cirques. One of

these cirques is still home to a sizeable glacier, which formed part of mountain's first ascent route in 1930. From bottom to top, the cliffs display the Cathedral limestone, Stephen shale, Eldon limestone sequence of formations. This "castle building" arrangement is known as the "Middle Cambrian Sandwich," and is common in the eastern main ranges.

The shrub thickets give way to larch forest as the trail nears Pulsatilla Pass. There is a picturesque waterfall in the creek, where upturned edges of rock capture the flow and create a Z-shaped cascade. Rock-hop the creek to its east bank, take the northwest (left) trail fork, and climb toward the pass.

It's steeper and farther than it looks to Pulsatilla Pass. Impressive wildflower displays make the climb enjoyable.

No Badgers Here

Badger Pass is named for the American badger, a nocturnal member of the weasel family. The alpine terrain of Badger Pass is not good badger habitat. The animal prefers low elevation grasslands and shrub meadows where it seeks the small rodents that comprise most of its diet. However, southeast of the pass in the Cascade River valley, badgers are sighted more frequently than in any other watershed in Banff National Park.

"Pulsatilla" is an old genus name for the western anemone (*Anemone occidentalis*). This showy member of the buttercup family grows here in profusion. "Anemone" means "wind flower." Along with other typical upper subalpine wildflowers, these meadows contain two species normally found at lower elevations: white camas and cow parsnip. Contorted lousewort is also common.

The view north from Pulsatilla Pass reveals one of the most exquisite alpine landscapes in Banff National Park. The centrepiece is Pulsatilla Lake, framed perfectly between the wild crags bordering upper Wildflower Creek. In the distance, with its perennial snowpatch, is Fossil Mountain (2946 m). While you stop to take in the view, keep an eye on your packs. The pass is inhabited by bold hoary marmots, high-country highwaymen who will quickly depart

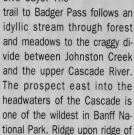

Badger Pass, 5.0 km

Fortunate is the backpacker who can visit the exquisite alpine realms of Badger and Pulsatilla passes on successive days. The trail to Badger Pass follows an idyllic stream through forest and meadows to the craggy divide between Johnston Creek and the upper Cascade River. The prospect east into the headwaters of the Cascade is one of the wildest in Banff National Park. Ridge upon ridge of sawtooth mountains rear up like waves in an ocean of rock and sky. Badger Pass can be snowbound until mid-July. The horn mountains northwest of Badger Pass feature extensive grassy slopes that are excellent habitat for bighorn sheep and mountain goats.

with any loose object they find.

Descend steeply north from the pass on a good trail that stays high to avoid wet meadows. About 500 m from the pass, the trail forks. The lefthand path descends to the shore of Pulsatilla Lake. The righthand path traverses the sideslope above the lake. The two routes converge a kilometre to the north.

Pulsatilla Lake is a sink lake. It has no visible outlet, indicating subterranean drainage in the limestone bedrock, known as karst. The lake is impounded behind an upturned edge of glacier-worn rock – a *riegel*. The front ranges of Banff feature many sink lakes dammed in a similar fashion. However, few are as large as Pulsatilla Lake.

The descent into Wildflower Creek is very steep. The trail passes an unnamed pond, dammed by rockslide debris. It was near this pond that Mary Vaux Walcott, third wife of Charles Walcott and a gifted botanist and artist, collected 82 species of flora during a visit in July 1921. In his diary, Charles Walcott recorded that Mary found "50 species in bloom within 200 feet of our tent." Mary called the valley "Wild Flower Canyon", the origin of today's name.

The forest in the confined valley bottom is ancient Engelmann spruce and lodgepole pine. Some of the spruce trees are 45 m tall. The trail is vague where you rock-hop a tributary stream coming in from the east. About 5.5 km from Pulsatilla Pass, ford Wildflower Creek (straightforward) to its west bank. The steep descent continues to the Wildflower Creek campground and Baker Creek junction, skirting ancient mounds of moraine en route.

Baker Creek to Baker Lake

You can exit along the Baker Creek trail to Highway 1A (14.9 km) from this point. However, the route is vague, wet, exasperating and not maintained. Turn north (right) to continue the Sawback Trail. You may have to ford Wildflower Creek (straightforward) if the artful, felled-tree bridge has collapsed.

Climbing north from the confluence of Wildflower and Baker creeks, you cross several avalanche slopes that offer views southwest to the Wenkchemna Peaks. Vegetation here is incredibly lush. The trail drops into a clearing where the route can be lost – a

Finding Faults

Although the ragged peaks of the front ranges seem chaotic, there is pattern and symmetry in this landscape. Mountain passes and valleys are oriented along weaknesses in the underlying bedrock. These weaknesses can be a fold, where the rock formations have been stretched or compressed; or a fault, where they have been shorn.

Pulsatilla Pass, Wildflower Creek, and upper Johnston Creek lie on the Castle Mountain Thrust Fault. Like most faults in the front ranges, this fault is oriented along the strike of the mountains, northwest to southeast. This creates a symmetrical

landscape. Each strike valley is walled by parallel mountain ranges, that are composed of the leading edges of thrust sheets. The effect is repeated many times farther east in the front ranges.

On the crest of Pulsatilla Pass, you can see the contact surfaces of the Castle Mountain Thrust Fault. The trail follows the dividing line between Gog quartzite (early Cambrian) to the west, and Survey Peak shale (late Cambrian) to the east. This Gog quartzite is the leading edge of the thrust fault, brought up from near the sedimentary basement of the Rockies to rest atop the younger shales. This rocky seam also separates two of the geological provinces of the Rockies: the front ranges to the east, from the older eastern main ranges to the west.

taste of things to come. At the north edge of this meadow is an outfitter's camp. From here the trail descends to an extensive wet meadow along Baker Creek. Keep to the east side of this boggy area, and do the best you can to keep your feet dry.

North of the wet meadow, the trail crosses the alluvial rubble of a flash-flood stream course – the handiwork of Lychnis Creek. The bridge here has been knocked out by a surge of water and débris. *Lychnis* is the genus name for species of campion – showy wildflowers of the upper subalpine and alpine. If you lose the trail here, don't look for it in the forest. It keeps to the open willow plain.

On the west side of the valley two waterfalls on Anthozoan Mountain (2695 m) emerge from underground. They drain a series of lakes concealed on the bench above. Anthozoans are reeflike deposits of coral found in the dolomite bedrock of this and other mountains nearby.

The steep ascent to the meadows south of Baker Lake demonstrates the full range of ills resulting from horse travel: braiding, muck holes, damaged drainage control, churned up rocks and trampled tree roots. Thankfully, this section of trail lasts but a kilometre. Delightful upper subalpine meadows greet you at the top of this climb, and will silence your curses.

Rock-hop Baker Creek to its west side just above a picturesque shale canyon. You reach an important junction

The conclusion of the Sawback Trail follows Corral Creek. Mt. Temple and the Wenkchemna Peaks form the distant skyline.

800 m beyond. Turn northwest (left) for the final kilometre to Baker Lake campground. The lake is contained by a series of upturned rock benches that mark the edge of the Castle Mountain Thrust Fault. The outlet stream has eroded an interesting channel

Little Baker Lake, 1.2 km

Little Baker Lake is one of three lakes tucked under the east flank of Brachiopod Mountain. Rock-hop the outlet of Baker Lake and follow beaten paths through larch forest to the southeast. Look back at Fossil Mountain to see the incredible Z-shaped overturned fold in the upper part of the south face.

The maze of paths here defies sensible description. Pass a small unnamed pond (not shown on the topographic map) along its east shore. Using a topographic map to keep your orientation, continue to Little Baker Lake. There are views to Tilted Lake en route. Brachiopod Lake is farther south. However, this seasonal pond frequently dries up by late summer.

through these formations. Look for the American dipper here, the only aquatic songbird in North America.

Baker Lake is another popular backcountry fishing destination, and is home to rainbow trout and cutthroat trout. Besides a multitude of campers, you will undoubtedly share this campground with mosquitoes, porcupines and snowshoe hares.

Baker Lake to Fish Creek

The Sawback Trail concludes by heading west along the north shores of Baker and Ptarmigan lakes to Boulder Pass, where views are exceptional. The mountains of the Slate Range are close at hand, and Mt. Temple (3543 m) looms to the southwest. Halfway Hut and Hidden Lake campground are 1.5 km beyond the pass. The hut was built as a stop-over for pack-

ers supplying Skoki Lodge, and is located halfway between the Lake Louise train station and Skoki. (See Classic Hike # 18.)

Beyond the hut, the trail re-enters subalpine forest, and after 3 km emerges onto a ski run at the Lake Louise ski area. It is 3.5 km of steady downhill on a gravel road to trail's end at the Fish Creek parking lot, with occasional views of Mt. Victoria en route. If you need a telephone to arrange transportation, follow a Cat track north from the Fish Creek parking lot, for 1 km to Whiskeyjack Lodge at the Lake Louise ski area. Otherwise, walk 3.5 km down the road to reach Lake Louise Village.

"Our next trip was up Forty Mile Creek. To avoid the canyon, we entered by the pass to the east of Mt. Edith. It is about 5 miles across on a good trail ... to the valley which runs in a northwest direction parallel to the Sawback Range. About 7 miles from the crossing, a good sized creek comes in from the west, and along this a trail leads across the Sawback Range to Johnston Creek.... We made a trip to the lake [Mystic Lake] and caught two dozen trout."

Surveyor, J.J. McArthur,
Report of the Department of the Interior, 1891

Hoary Marmots: Indolent Rodents

The hoary marmot is a large rodent that resembles the woodchuck, to which it is related. Its preferred habitat is upper subalpine boulderfields and meadows. The marmot eats grasses, leaves, flowers and berries, within safe range of its den. Grizzly bears, lynx, hawks and eagles are its principal predators. Grizzlies will expend considerable time and energy, excavating in quest of this apparently delicious rodent.

The shrill whistle of the marmot warns its fellows that a threat is near, and gives rise to its folk name: "whistle-pig." "Hoary" refers to its grayish-tipped coat. The marmot disdains the hardships of winter, autumn and spring, hibernating nine months of the year. Marmots have little fear of humans, and a fondness for exploring packs, boots and lunches without invitation. Please do not feed them.

"*The majestic mountain, which is a noble pyramid of rock towering above snow fields, was clearly reflected in the water surface. Such a picture so suddenly revealed aroused the utmost enthusiasm of all our party, and unconsciously everyone paused in admiration.*"

—Walter Wilcox
describing Mt. Assiniboine in 1899,
The Rockies of Canada

Mt. Assiniboine is one of the most celebrated mountains in the Rockies.

7. Mt. Assiniboine

Route		
Citadel Pass-Wonder Pass, 3-6 days, 62.2 km		
Route	Elevation (m)	Distance (km)
Sunshine parking lot	1675	0
Sunshine Village	2195	6.5
Rock Isle Lake jct.	2300	7.6
Quartz Ridge	2385	11.5
Howard Douglas Lake & CG	2286	12.3
Citadel Pass	2360	15.9
Porcupine CG jct.	1829	20.4
Simpson River jct	1996	22.5
Og Lake and CG	2060	28.0
Lake Magog CG	2165	35.5
Wonder Pass	2395	39.8
Marvel Lk. connector trail jct	1795	47.4
Marvel Lake	1782	47.9
Marvel Lake CG	1753	49.0
Bryant Creek trail jct	1750	49.6
Big Springs (Br 3/9) CG	1740	52.9
Bryant Creek Trail Centre	1737	55.8
Mt. Shark trailhead	1768	62.2
Topographic maps: 82 O/4, 82 J/13, 82 J/14		

Trailhead

Follow Highway 1, 8.3 km west from Banff to the Sunshine Village exit. Follow the Sunshine road 9 km to its end at the ski area parking lot. Follow the Sunshine Village access road from the locked gate east of the gondola terminal.

Mt. Assiniboine (3618 m) is the sixth highest mountain in the Rockies. Straddling the continental divide, "The Matterhorn of the Rockies" is the highest mountain in both Banff National Park and Mt. Assiniboine Provincial Park (386 km²). Ever since the mountain was noted and named by surveyor G.M. Dawson in 1884, it has been an irresistible backcountry icon, attracting travellers from around the world. The mountain was named for a Native tribe of the Sioux

Confederation. Known elsewhere as the Nakoda or Dakota peoples, they are known locally as the Stoney. Assiniboine (ah-SIN-ni-boyne) means: "those who cook by placing hot rocks in water."

A half dozen backpacking routes lead to Lake Magog at the base of Mt. Assiniboine.

This outing describes a traverse of Mt. Assiniboine Provincial Park via Citadel and Wonder passes. This traverse, combined with the day-hiking options described, will provide you with the most complete experience of Mt. Assiniboine's spectacular scenery. Do not expect solitude at Mt.

Assiniboine. You will be sharing the area with hikers, helicopters and horse traffic. The Lake Magog campground is frequently crowded, and the Naiset cabins are overcrowded during poor weather.

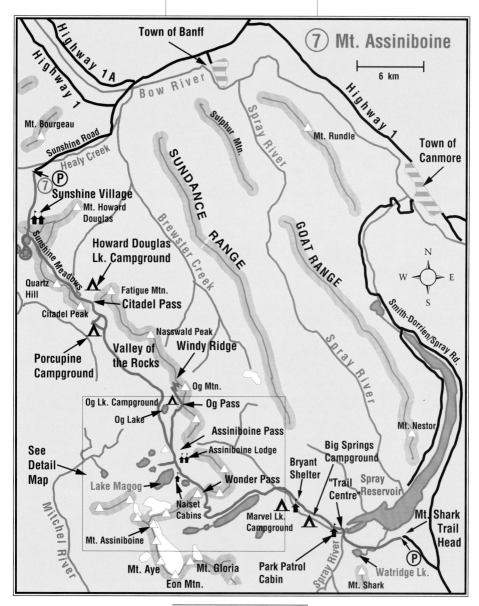

Trailhead to Sunshine Meadows

You pay some dues on the first 6.5 km of this outing. The trail climbs a gravel access road with the trappings of the Sunshine ski area at hand. The ski area originated with a cabin built by the Canadian Pacific Railway in 1928. Between 1929 and 1932, several ski parties from Banff visited the area, and were delighted with the winter snow conditions they found. Jim Brewster, then owner of Brewster Transportation, was one of these skiers. In 1934, he leased the cabin for the winter, buying it outright in 1936. Brewster hired mountain guides to teach skiing, and the area's popularity grew rapidly.

Sunshine Village is at road's end. Follow the red, crushed stone path toward the Customer Service building, and turn east (left). Fifteen metres past the avalanche station turn east (left) again onto a gravel trail and ascend through open larch forest to the Sunshine Meadows – a spectacular hiking environment. Open vistas fill all directions, and the towering horn of Mt. Assiniboine beckons from the south.

Sunshine Meadows occupy a 14 km arc along the continental divide, at an average elevation of 2225 m. Linked together with other meadows around Simpson Pass, around Healy Pass and above Lost Horse Creek, they form one of the largest alpine meadow systems in the world. The vegetation here is a heath tundra, and features: mountain heather, woolly everlasting, fleabane, valerian, arctic willow, western anemone and sedges. In addition, 340 other species have been identified. This represents more than one third of the plant species of Banff and Jasper national parks. Some of the species are rare, and many are at either the extreme northern or southern limits of their ranges.

The average temperature on the meadows is -4°C, and more than 7 m of snow falls annually. Snowbanks linger well into July. Vegetation is specially adapted, storing nutrients from summer's sun-

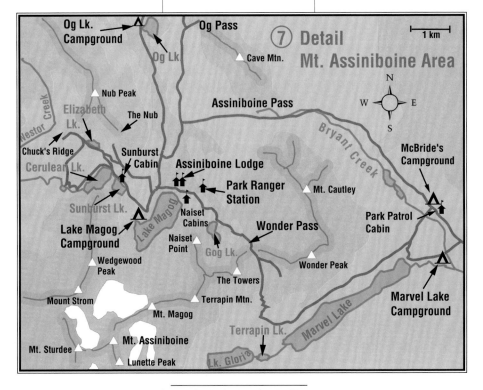

shine to release in a burst that promotes rapid growth the following year. Still, with a growing season so short, it may take many decades before some plants mature enough to carry blooms – 20 years is typical for moss campion. The thin soils are saturated with snowmelt for much of the summer, and travel off-trail causes immediate and sometimes permanent damage to the ground cover. Please keep to maintained trails.

After 1.1. km, the trail crests the continental divide and crosses the boundary from Banff National Park, Alberta, into Mt. Assiniboine Provincial Park, BC. The trail forks. The wider, righthand trail leads to Rock Isle Lake. If you do not want to make this side-trip, continue on the lefthand trail.

Sunshine Meadows to Citadel Pass

For 2.5 km beyond the Rock Isle junction, the Assiniboine trail rambles through Sunshine Meadows, re-entering Banff National Park. The meadows are dotted with limestone erratics – boulders deposited by retreating glaciers. After descending into a hollow northeast of Quartz Hill, the trail climbs over Quartz Ridge, with unimpeded views south to Mt. Assiniboine. Here, the trail improvements end, and a heavily braided, often slippery trail drops to the first campground on the east shore of Howard Douglas Lake (incorrectly called "Sundown Lake" on the topographic map). Howard Douglas was the second superintendent of Banff National Park. Mountaineers may readily ascend Quartz Hill (2580 m) from either the campground or the trail's high point on Quartz Ridge. Eastern brook trout inhabit Howard Douglas Lake.

Beyond Howard Douglas Lake lies a classic alpland dotted with lakelets. It was in this vicinity in August 1933, that three hikers watched two wolves attack and kill a grizzly bear. After crossing Citadel Pass, you re-enter Mt. Assiniboine Provincial Park. A sign optimistically informs you

Rock Isle-Grizzly-Larix Lakes, 5.0 Loop

This 5 km loop visits three picturesque lakes in the northern part of Mt. Assiniboine Provincial Park. Follow the trail around the north and west shores of Rock Isle Lake, keeping left at the first junction. The trail descends from the lake through a delightful, flower-filled larch forest.

Keep straight ahead at the next junction, and pass along the east shore of Grizzly Lake. The trail then curves south to a viewpoint overlooking the upper Simpson Valley. After circling around Larix Lake, with impressive views west to The Monarch (2904 m), the trail climbs back up to the loop junction below Rock Isle Lake.

The three lakes have different characteristics. Rock Isle Lake is dammed by an upturned lip of Outram limestone and its outlet is underground. Another bedrock exposure creates the "isle". Grizzly Lake is shallow and filling with vegetation. Larix Lake is deep with underwater ledges visible. *Larix* is the genus name of the Lyall's larch. You must carry your backpacks on this loop hike, since there is no safe place to cache them.

that Lake Magog is 17 km and 5.5 hours distant. In reality, you should add 3 km and 3 hours to these numbers, respectively.

Citadel Pass to Og Lake

A kilometre south of the pass, the trail drops below treeline into larch forest, passes beside a small tarn (the last good water source for 13 km), and then begins a steep switchbacking descent through avalanche paths. This is excellent bear habitat. Though it is within Mt. Assiniboine Provincial Park, the Simpson River Valley below is open to black bear hunting from April 1 to June 30, and from September 10 to November 30 inclusive, annually. Wear a vest or jacket of "hunter's orange" during these times. Grizzly bears were formerly common on Sunshine Meadows. One bear researcher has stated that overhunting in the Simpson Valley has rendered the bears scarce in recent decades.

After traversing south onto a sideslope, you reach the Porcupine campground junction. If you make the very steep descent to this campground, you don't have to climb back up to continue next day. Follow a faint track south from the campground for 2.1 km, to rejoin the main trail at the Simpson River junction.

From the Porcupine campground junction, the high trail continues its southward traverse of the sideslope. More than 25 wildflower species bloom here in early July. At the south end of this traverse, the trail contours around a rockslide that heralds the entrance to the Valley of the Rocks.

The Valley of the Rocks is not a valley, but a depression in the débris of an enormous landslide that originated from the mountains to the east. This landslide is estimated to contain more than a billion cubic metres of material, making it by far the largest known rockslide in the Rockies, and one of the twenty largest in the world. The winding trail through the Valley of the Rocks seems double its 6 km length, and is virtually devoid of water. At the Simpson River junction turn southeast (left). The small rockslide depression lake nearby is the only source of water before Og Lake. You should treat this water before drinking it.

You will know the travail through the Valley of the Rocks is over when Mt. Assiniboine again becomes visible, directly ahead. The trail descends to Og Lake and campground. Og Lake is a sink lake.

Preservation and Development in the National Parks

As with most commercial enterprises in the national parks, over the years the various owners of Sunshine Village have pressured for expansion of their facilities and lease area. With its high profile and sensitive vegetation, development at Sunshine has long been a thorny issue. Environmentalists question the appropriateness of private, commercial enterprise on national park land, due to the negative effects caused by incessant incremental expansion. Skiers and Banff business people note the area has excellent snow, and many advocate that Sunshine should be allowed to expand to cater to a larger market. In 1993, the Canadian Parks and Wilderness Society filed suit to stop the most recent proposed development.

When Sunshine Village was granted permission to open as a hiking resort for the summer season in 1984, trails were hardened with gravel in an attempt to mitigate anticipated impacts. Between 1984 and 1990, more than 30,000 people visited the meadows each summer. In 1991, the owner of the ski area abandoned summer operation, rendering redundant the trail hardening which had cost Banff and Mt. Assiniboine parks 1.4 million dollars. Perhaps only a thousand backpackers now use the trails each summer. With greatly reduced hiking traffic, the gravel and pressure-treated wood trail structures now appear as permanent and unnecessary impacts in the landscape. It is precisely this kind of manipulation of national park land by private commercial interests, subsidized by taxpayers, that has fuelled the ire of environmental groups.

Mt. Assiniboine is reflected in the still waters of Lake Magog.

Windy Ridge, 8.7 km

Follow the Assiniboine Pass trail northeast from the campground. At all junctions follow signs for Og Pass-Windy Ridge. The trail climbs toward Og Pass, and levels out in meadows at a final junction at km 6.5. Og Pass is 300 m east. The Windy Ridge trail veers north (left) from the junction, and climbs 2.2 km to the barren ridge crest north of Og Mountain, at an elevation of 2635 m. The ridge provides a splendid panorama. Especially picturesque is an unnamed lake, immediately northeast in the upper reaches of Brewster Creek.

Its waters drain underground. Many of the lakes near Mt. Assiniboine empty in a similar fashion. Although the karst system fed by the lakes is unstudied, a century ago Walter Wilcox speculated that the disappearing water is the source of the Simpson River, 6 km to the northwest .

Og Lake to Lake Magog

From Og Lake, it is 6.8 km to the campground at Lake Magog. Half of this distance is across a flat subalpine meadow, the probable location of an ancient lake. At the trail junctions, follow signs directing you to the campground, which is set on a terrace of glacial moraine on the northwest shore of Lake Magog. The campground offers a commanding view of Mt. Assiniboine, whose graceful summit towers 1400 m above. Like many high mountains, Assini-

Sunburst Circuit-Chuck's Ridge, 9.1 km loop

Follow the trail north past Sunburst Lake to Cerulean (seh-ROO-lee-an) Lake. "Cerulean" means "resembling the blue colour of the sky". At the junction on the far side of Cerulean Lake, turn west (left) and follow the north shore. There are fine views of Sunburst Peak (2820 m) across the lake. At the west end of the lake, the trail descends to the north. After 200 m, angle east (right) at a junction, and climb 1.4 km to Elizabeth Lake. The aquamarine lake was named for Lizzie Rummel, who operated Sunburst cabin as a tourist lodge from 1951 to 1970. The cabin has since been moved from its original location. Remarkably, a bald eagle frequented Elizabeth Lake in 1992.

At the outlet of Elizabeth Lake the 800 m sidetrail to Chuck's Ridge veers north. Chuck's Ridge (2347 m) pro-

Cerulean Lake

vides an excellent overview of this area, and of the meadows and lakes at the head of Nestor Creek. The glacier-draped form of The Marshall (3190 m) dominates the view southwest from the ridge, and Wedgewood Lake is visible. The ridge was a favourite haunt of Chuck Millar, a packer for Mt. Assiniboine Lodge.

Return to Elizabeth Lake and follow the trail along the west shore to a junction in 400 m. If you would like to ascend to The Nub, turn east (left). Otherwise, continue straight ahead and descend to Cerulean Lake. Return via Sunburst Lake to the campground.

boine creates its own local weather. Clouds frequently adorn the summit, and precipitation is common nearby.

Mt. Assiniboine was the object of intense interest, competition, and several mountaineering attempts in the 1890s. The mountain's remote location and difficult approach added to the challenge.

In 1901, Edward Whymper, of Matterhorn fame, visited the Rockies. It was widely hoped he would make Assiniboine's first ascent. However, Whymper was past his mountaineering prime. The first ascent of the "Canadian Matterhorn" was made in September 1901, by Sir James Outram (OOT-rum) and guides. They ascended the southwest face of the mountain, and descended the northeast arête, toward Lake Magog. This arête is the "regular" ascent route today. Although the climb is not difficult by contemporary standards, unpredictable weather, poor rock, and the presence of snow or ice make any attempt on Mt. Assiniboine a serious undertaking.

After the energy you've invested in reaching Mt. Assiniboine, you will probably want to spend several days in the area. The best day-hiking options are described in this section. All outings begin at Lake Magog campground.

Mt. Assiniboine's popularity assures you will have lots of company during your visit. Many visitors stay at the

The Nub, 6.7 km loop

Follow the trail north past Sunburst Lake to Cerulean Lake. At the junction on the far shore of Cerulean Lake, turn northeast (right) for Elizabeth Lake. After a short climb, you reach The Nub junction. Turn east (right) and climb steadily to Nub Ridge (2390 m).

If you would like to ascend higher onto Nub Peak, watch for a faint track that angles sharply to the north where the trail levels out. By following this rough path to the prominent high point, you obtain superb views of the soaring, tooth-like form of Mt. Assiniboine. Six lakes are visible: Gog, Magog, Sunburst, Cerulean, Elizabeth and Wedgewood. For those inclined, a beaten track leads north for 2 km along a shattered

The view from the Nub features the glaciated horn of Mt. Assinboine and six of the area's many lakes.

limestone ridge, and grants access to the summit slopes of Nub Peak (2748 m). The view from this modest mountain is without equal in the vicinity.

From Nub Ridge you can return to the campground via your route of ascent (more direct), or make a loop by following the trail south from the end of the ridge to the Assiniboine Pass trail. At this junction, turn southwest (right) to reach the campground in 1.5 km.

Naiset Cabins or Mt. Assiniboine Lodge. The five original Naiset Cabins were built in 1925 by A.O. Wheeler, founder of the Alpine Club of Canada. The cabins provided accommodation for clients on "Wheeler's Walking Tours" of the Rockies. Wheeler's enterprise soon went bankrupt, and the cabins were leased to various interests until 1944, when the ACC assumed ownership. In 1971, ownership of the decrepit cabins passed to BC Parks, and they refurbished them for use by hikers (capacity 31). Bunk space is first-come, first-served in summer. Rangers collect a nightly fee. Naiset is a word from the Sioux language, meaning "sunset."

Mt. Assiniboine Lodge was built by the CPR in the summer of 1928, at the behest of Italian sportsman Marquis delgi Albizzi and Norwegian skier Erling Strom. The two had skied to Assiniboine the previous spring and were delighted with the skiing terrain. Strom subsequently operated the lodge for more than four decades. The lodge is now owned by the BC government, and is operated privately under lease. The park ranger station is located southeast of the lodge and cabins.

Lake Magog to Marvel Lake

Because it is difficult to arrange transportation at the Mt. Shark trailhead at trail's end, many backpackers exit from Mt. Assiniboine via Sunshine. If you choose to backtrack, be sure to include Wonder Pass as a half-day-hike from Lake Magog.

The trail to Wonder Pass skirts the shore of Lake Magog to Naiset Cabins. Half a kilometre south of the cabins, the trail crosses the outlet of Gog Lake. Great blue herons nested at this lake in 1983 – the highest nesting elevation yet recorded for this species. The names Gog, Og and Magog refer to legendary giants of Biblical times. The cliffs south and west of Gog Lake are quartzite and siltstone of the Gog Formation. Gog quartzite is a metamorphic quartz-rich sandstone, and one of the hardest and most common rocks in the central Rockies.

Continuing south from Gog Lake, the trail climbs through wildflower meadows and larch forest to a viewpoint overlooking a small waterfall and canyon. This canyon is cut in Miette (mee-YETT) shale. The trail here was rehabilitated and rerouted in 1992. Please avoid using trail sections that have been closed. You reach treeline about 500

Helicopters: An Evil Necessity?

As you have probably noticed, many people who visit Mt. Assiniboine fly to the area by helicopter (64 percent in summer). BC Parks' policy allows helicopters to land near the ranger station three days a week. The Mt. Assiniboine area is also a highlight of "flightseeing" trips which originate at Canmore. Although the helicopters used for this purpose do not land, they are frequently overhead. On a single day in 1993, there were 40 round-trip flights from Canmore to Naiset Cabins, and 30 additional flightseeing flights over the area.

Helicopters create an exceptional aesthetic disturbance in the backcountry. Some backpackers take advantage of helicopter access. Many others begrudgingly tolerate noisy helicopter presence as an evil necessity. Imagine what your overall experience of the Rockies would be like if all the parks permitted helicopter access everywhere. If you do not like the presence or amount of helicopter traffic at Mt. Assiniboine, write the park manager and express your concerns. Apparently, BC Parks receives few negative comments regarding helicopter use.

The negative effects of helicopter traffic go beyond aesthetics. Most helicopters that visit Mt. Assiniboine have flown over areas of Banff National Park zoned as wilderness. Recreational helicopter landings are prohibited in these areas, however national parks cannot control the airspace above. Helicopter traffic subjects wildlife to stress. Particularly vulnerable are mountain goats, bighorn sheep, elk and caribou, especially when with young. Thus, BC Parks' helicopter access policy thwarts the wildlife protection objectives of adjacent national parks. (See Issues and Contacts in the Reference section).

m before Wonder Pass. From the crest of the pass, located on the Banff National Park boundary, there are inspiring views south to the overthrust limestone peaks of the Blue Range. On a clear day, the view north will include the mountains that flank Sunshine Meadows. Look for mountain goats on the cliffs of The Towers (2846 m), west of the pass.

South of Wonder Pass, a faint track branches southeast (left) to a viewpoint overlooking Marvel Lake. This is an excellent extension for day-hikers, however it inconveniently adds extra distance for those carrying heavy packs. The main trail descends gradually. At treeline it cuts southwest across a gully. From this sideslope you have a spectacular vista of Marvel Lake, 550 m below. Marvel Lake is the sixth largest in Banff National Park, and is 67 m deep.

The next 1.8 km involves a steady descent. Initially the trail heads west, providing spectacular views of the extensive glacier beneath Mts. Gloria (2908 m), Eon (3310 m) and Aye (3243 m). Two more lakes are now visible through the trees in the valley above Marvel Lake – Lakes Gloria and Terrapin. The remarkable colours of these lakes result from the concentration of glacial rock flour suspended in their waters. These lakes act as settling ponds, preventing much of the rock flour from entering Marvel Lake. Hence the water of Marvel Lake is much more clear. A waterfall marks the outflow of Terrapin Lake.

Keep straight ahead at the Marvel Pass junction. Although this trail is well travelled, the Marvel Lake valley is a wild corner of Banff National Park. As you begin the 5 km long sideslope traverse above the north shore of Marvel Lake, watch for grizzly bears. Although not lushly vegetated, these south-facing avalanche slopes offer early season foods for grizzlies. They are also decorated with a variety of attractive wildflowers.

Marvel Lake to Mt. Shark Trailhead

The trail re-enters forest at the east end of Marvel Lake. Keep straight ahead at the first, unsigned junction. At the second junction, turn south (right) to reach the outlet of Marvel Lake in 500 m. Head east from Marvel Lake to the Br 7/13 campground in 1 km. (The older trail signs measured the 7 km distance to this campground from the Bryant Creek trailhead. Newer trail signs indicate the 13 km distance from the Mt. Shark trailhead.)

From this campground, it is 600 m to the Bryant Creek trail. Turn southeast (right), and follow this rolling backcountry artery through lodgepole pine forest to the mouth of the Bryant Creek valley. The trail is fireroad width and is shared with horses. The tread surface has been covered with wood chips in an attempt to mitigate damage from horses. Henry Bryant was an explorer who made the first attempt to climb Mt. Assiniboine in 1899.

The junctions at the Banff National Park boundary are often referred to as "Trail Centre". Take the south (right) trail branch for the Mt. Shark trailhead, and descend toward Bryant Creek. Cross the creek on the footbridge and continue south for 500 m. This is part of the historic Palliser Pass trail, travelled by the Palliser Expedition in 1858. The southern Spray Lakes Reservoir is to the north. The Spray Lakes area was removed from Banff National Park in 1930 for a hydroelectric reservoir, completed in 1951.

Turn east (left) at the next junction, and cross the Spray River at a small canyon. The remaining 5.8 km to the Mt. Shark trailhead is along old logging roads. Watridge Lake and the nearby Karst Spring (one of the largest by volume in North America) are interesting short sidetrips from this trail.

The Mt. Shark trailhead is a very long day (26.7 km) from Lake Magog campground. Many backpackers use one of the campgrounds along Bryant Creek to break the journey into two days. If you do not have transportation prearranged, plan to arrive at the Mt. Shark trailhead early in the day. The trailhead is 4.6 km along a gravel road from the Smith Dorrien/Spray Road. The junction of these two roads is 37 km south of Canmore. Traffic is light in the evening.

The still waters of Shadow Lake reflect the image of Mt. Ball.

8. Lakes and Larches

Route

Healy Pass-Egypt Lake-Whistling Pass-Gibbon Pass, 40.4 km, 3-6 days

Route	Elevation (m)	Distance (km)
Healy Pass trailhead	1692	0
Healy Creek CG	1973	5.5
Healy Pass	2330	9.2
Pharaoh Creek jct	1992	12.2
Egypt Lake CG	1997	12.4
Whistling Pass	2292	15.7
Haiduk Lake	2067	17.9
Ball Pass jct and CG	1921	21.2
Shadow Lake	1851	25.5
Gibbon Pass jct	1814	26.4
Shadow Lake CG	1814	26.5
Gibbon Pass	2300	29.5
Lower Twin Lake	2058	32.2
Upper Twin Lake CG	2088	33.2
Arnica/Twin Lake Summit	2287	34.6
Arnica Lake	2149	35.4
Vista Lake	1570	39.0
Kootenay Parkway	1707	40.4

Topographic maps: 82 O/4, 82 N/1

Trailhead

Follow Highway 1, 8.3 km west from Banff to the Sunshine Village exit. Follow the Sunshine road 9 km to the ski area parking lot. The trailhead kiosk is west of the gondola terminal.

With its ease of access, attractive options for day-hiking, and a landscape dominated by lakes and larches, the Lakes and Larches trail is one of the most popular in Banff National Park. The trail traverses a series of passes along the eastern flank of the continental divide, a spectacular terrain of cliff, meadow and tarn; scenery that is the hallmark of the Canadian Rockies.

Trailhead to Healy Pass

The trail begins as a bulldozed track along Healy Creek. Keep right at the junction in 400 m. The trail narrows and drops to a bridge over

Sunshine Creek, and then gradually ascends Healy Creek valley. Healy Creek is northeast of a break on the continental divide. Moisture-laden air that would normally be blocked from reaching the eastern slope of the Rockies, spills over. Nearby, annual snowfalls are more than 7 m at higher elevations. This damp environment sustains a forest of Engelmann spruce, subalpine fir and feathermosses, and gives rise to the profusion of wildflowers you will see at Healy Pass. Listen for the long, sweet, bubbling song of the winter wren, a common resident in this dark forest.

At km 3.1, you cross Healy Creek to its north bank. The trail passes through several broad avalanche slopes en

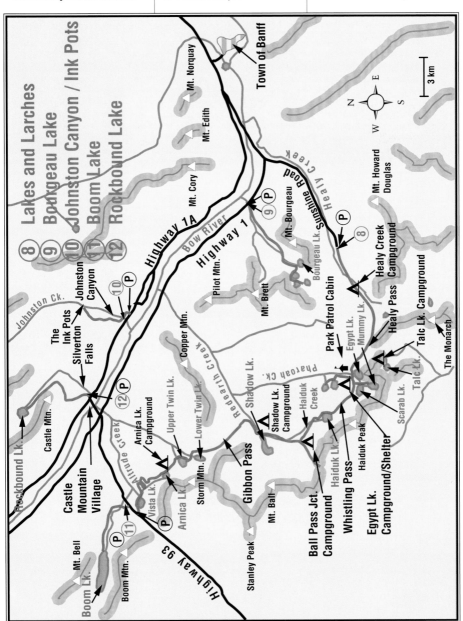

route to Healy Creek campground at km 5.5. Keep right at the junction 200 m west of the campground. The trail to the left leads to Simpson Pass, named for Sir George Simpson, a governor of the Hudson's Bay Company. Simpson and his entourage crossed the pass on their way across Canada and around the world. In 1904, Simpson's initials and the date 1841 were found carved in a fallen tree on the pass.

By the late 1970s the trail to Healy Pass was in poor condition due to excessive use, especially horse traffic. The trail was closed to horses and reconstructed to improve drainage and to harden the tread surface. Hikers now find it easier stay on the rebuilt trail, thus protecting the fragile upper subalpine environment from further impact.

The first Lyall's larch trees are about 1 km beyond the

Larch forest and wildflower meadows highlight the hike to Healy Pass. The view west includes Egypt, Scarab, Mummy and Talc lakes.

Simpson Pass junction. Larches are deciduous conifers; their needles turn gold and are shed annually. Lyall's larch often forms pure stands at treeline. The colourful display of larch trees adds to the delights of late season hiking.

Healy Pass to Egypt Lake Campground

After you cross a tributary stream, the trail emerges from forest into the meadows at the head of Healy Creek. Just be-

Glacier Lily (Dogtooth Violet)

In early summer, you may be treated to an astounding display of glacier lilies at Healy Pass. The glacier lily's nodding yellow bloom is the first to appear in the upper subalpine ecoregion, growing through receding snowbanks. Its bloom is testimony to nature's remarkable means for ensuring that plants survive in harsh climates. Here, the growing season is less than two months, and the average annual temperature is -4°C. The bulb of the glacier lily stores nutrients synthesized from last year's sunshine, and it releases them in a

burst, promoting rapid growth in late spring. Grizzly bears relish the protein-rich bulb, and will often excavate entire meadows in quest for this food.

Healy's Many Fortunes

John Gerome Healy was a classic character of the Wild West. He could list half a dozen professions and enterprises behind his name when he arrived in the Rockies in 1884. He prospected in Healy Creek and near Copper Mountain. Like most of his kind, Healy soon moved on. However, unlike many of his contemporaries, Healy's fortunes changed. He established a successful trading company in Dawson City, lived long and died a wealthy man.

yond is a junction with another trail to Simpson Pass. Keep right. The meadows of Healy Pass, Simpson Pass, Lost Horse Creek, Harvey Pass, Citadel Pass and Sunshine are part of an extensive alpland, covering approximately 40 km^2. Magnificent displays of upper subalpine wildflowers carpet the rolling slopes from mid- to late-July.

Healy Pass provides a wonderful prospect over the southern Rockies. The Healy Pass Lakes, sustained by snowmelt and springs, occupy the basin between Healy and Simpson passes. The quartzite bluff of the Monarch Ramparts extends southwest from Healy Pass, providing a backdrop to the scene. Mt. Assiniboine (3618 m), highest in the southern Rockies, soars skyward 30 km to the south. From Mt. Assiniboine to Crowfoot Mountain in the north, the view encompasses a 110 km length of the continental divide.

To the west, the cluster of

Egypt, Scarab and Mummy Lakes, 3.5 km

From the trail sign in front of the Egypt Lake shelter, head south through the campground on the Whistling Pass trail for 300 m to the Egypt Lake junction. Turn south (left) and follow a rough, undulating trail, 150 m to the north shore of Egypt Lake. The lake is 32 metres deep and has an area of 16 ha. Cutthroat trout and eastern brook trout are present. A waterfall that drains Scarab Lake cascades over the colourful quartzite cliffs west of Egypt Lake.

The Egyptian motif for the names in this area originated with the Interprovincial Boundary Survey in 1922. It all started with a flight of fancy – a supposed resemblance of the outline of nearby Scarab Lake to that of a beetle, viewed from above. The scarab beetle was an Egyptian symbol of resurrection. With their minds in Egyptian mode, the surveyors applied the names Egypt, Mummy and Pharaoh nearby.

Backtrack to the Whistling Pass trail, and turn west (left). The next 1.4 km of trail is poor and involves an extremely steep ascent of the headwall above Egypt Lake. The trail descends slightly from the top of the headwall through a stand of larches to reach the Scarab Lake junction in 200 m. Turn south (left), and descend to the outlet of Scarab Lake in 600 m. Of the three lakes visited on this day-hike, Scarab Lake has the most remarkable colour. The lake is glacially fed, and rock flour in the water reflects the blue and green spectra of light.

Rock-hop the outlet of Scarab Lake, and continue south on a rough track. After an initial climb, the trail drops into a meadowed basin . Follow cairns through rockslide débris, angling upwards toward a break in the cliff that grants access to

Egypt Lake

rocky slopes above the east shore of Mummy Lake. This large lake occupies an extremely barren setting, but is exceptionally beautiful in its primal simplicity. Travel is difficult along the boulderfields on the lakeshore.

exquisite lakes in the vicinity of Egypt Lake catches the eye. The arrangement of the three largest – Mummy, Scarab and Egypt – are known as paternoster lakes, or a cirque staircase. Glacial ice that flowed from the south created the three basins, each at a progressively lower elevation. Today, only a remnant glacier remains at the western end of Scarab Lake.

Leaving Healy Pass, the trail descends rapidly through wet subalpine meadows and glades of larch forest to reach the Pharaoh Creek trail in 3 km, just south of the Egypt Lake patrol cabin. Turn south (left). Cross Pharaoh Creek on a bridge in 150 m and ascend the west bank to the Egypt Lake campground and shelter.

A reservation and park use permit are required for overnight use of the shelter. Given the area's popularity, this building is often crowded, especially during poor weather. In 1993, Parks Canada was considering turning it over to private interests. Plan on spending several days at Egypt

The National Talc Company

Talc is magnesium silicate, one of the softest minerals. It is used in talcum powder, explosives and insulators. The Talc Lake claim was staked by outfitter and guide Bill Peyto (PEE-toe) in 1917. Peyto was a talented amateur geologist, who constantly kept an eye out for minerals during his extensive mountain travels. Peyto was thwarted in his attempt to develop the claim by the government's erroneous contention that it lay within Banff National Park. (Kootenay National Park did not exist at that time.) The National Talc Company took over the claim, and mined talc during the 1920s. The claim passed to

The National Talc Company mine bulidings in August, 1944

Western Talc Holdings, and finally to Wartime Metals. They mined it in 1943. The talc was shipped by horse and cart to Massive, a railway siding in the Bow Valley. One marvels today at the energy of this enterprise, in what was then a remote corner of the Rockies.

Lake, to take advantage of the many day-hiking options.

Egypt Lake to Ball Pass Junction

From Egypt Lake campground, the Lakes and Larches trail tackles the headwall above Egypt Lake en route to Whistling Pass. The 1.4 km climb is excessively steep. Water frequently runs down bedrock exposed in the trail, and the tread is covered in loose rubble. Persevere, for matters soon improve and scenic rewards lie just ahead.

From the top of the headwall, the trail descends slightly to contour around a rockslide

Talc Lake (Natalko Lake) 4.2 km

From Egypt Lake campground, backtrack to the Pharaoh Creek bridge. Cross the bridge and turn south (right). Follow the east bank of Pharaoh Creek on a rough and often ill-defined trail, for 2.3 km to a poorly marked junction. Turn west, cross the wet meadow, and pick up the trail that ascends the opposite bank. The trail between here and Talc Lake

is an old cart track, constructed by the National Talc Company. Boulders cleared from the track are lined up along the trail edges. In this vicinity, the trail enters Kootenay National Park, BC.

Talc Lake occupies an austere setting, walled by precipitous cliffs. A hundred-metre-high waterfall cascades to the west shore. The presence of a small

drift glacier harks back to colder climes and the glacial origin of the cirque containing the lake. The portals of the talc mine are visible in the cliffs to the south. You can inspect the old foundations and waste rock from the mine by hopping the outlet of Talc Lake and walking south. Camping is allowed here, with a park use permit.

Whistling Pass was named for the whistle of hoary marmots, which are often seen nearby. Mt. Ball and Haiduk Lake are the focal points in the view north.

at the base of the southern Pharaoh Peak. Keep straight ahead (west) at the Scarab Lake junction. The trail swings northwest and works its way through rock benches and sparse forest, climbing to the rocky saddle of Whistling Pass. The pass is named for the whistle of the hoary marmot. You may see these rodents in the quartzite boulderfields nearby.

The views from Whistling Pass are exceptional. To the north stands glacier-capped Mt. Ball (3311 m), highest mountain on the 80 km length of the continental divide between Mt. Assiniboine and Moraine Lake. Haiduk (HAY-duck) Lake lies on the floor of the U-shaped valley north of the pass. The lake was named by the Interprovincial Boundary Survey. Haiduk has various meanings: a group of Balkan rebels; a band of Hungarian mercenaries; a district in Hungary; or a village in Romania! The people who

gave the name failed to record whether any connection exists with the Canadian Rockies. The pass is a good place to see or hear rosy finches. These alpine birds are opportunistic feeders: they often congregate on snow patches to eat insects, snow worms, seeds and spiders, which are easy to see on the white background.

The descent to Haiduk Lake is steep, on a trail beaten in-

to screes and boulderfields. If hiking in early summer, you will undoubtedly encounter snow on this north-facing slope. Several easy rock-hops of the adjacent stream lead to a boggy area on the south shore of Haiduk Lake. Follow the east shore on a rough trail to another inlet at the north end. Spectacular views north to Mt. Ball and south to the waterfalls draining the cirque below Haiduk Peak (2920 m), compete for your attention.

The trail parallels an extensive wet meadow for 300 m before crossing Haiduk Creek to its west bank on a log bridge. For the next 2 km, you descend gradually through subalpine forest before swinging west, and plunging down forested moraines to the Ball Pass junction and campground.

Hoary marmot tracks

Pharaoh and Black Rock Lakes 2.4 km

The mountain wall north of Egypt Lake is riddled with five northeast-facing cirques. Pharaoh Lake occupies the largest, and is backed by the quartzite cliffs of the Pharaoh Peaks. Walk north from Egypt Lake campground on the west side of Pharaoh Creek, 500 m to a junction. Turn west (left) and ascend a steep, rough trail for 800 m to

the lakeshore.

To continue to Black Rock Lake, rock-hop the outlet of Pharaoh Lake and follow a track northwest for 1.1 km. The last 100 m is alongside a delightful stream. There is a massive rockslide at the west end of the lake. "Black Rock" describes the lichen-covered cliff to the south.

Ball Pass Junction to Gibbon Pass Junction

It is 4.2 km from the Ball Pass junction to the outlet of Shadow Lake. The first 2 km feature open views as the trail skirts wet meadows along the west fork of Haiduk Creek. Cross the principal meltwater stream from Ball Glacier on a bridge, slightly west of where the horse trail fords the stream.

After you cross Haiduk Creek on a log bridge to its east bank, the trail becomes wet, muddy and rocky, slowing your pace. This trying section ends just before the outlet of Shadow Lake, where the trail has been gravelled for the clients of nearby Shadow Lake Lodge. The outlet of the lake is bridged by a tremendously

The climb from Redearth Creek brings you to Gibbon Pass, a larch-dotted meadow frequented by mountain goats. The quartzite cliffs of Storm Mountain rise to the north.

overbuilt, pressure-treated wood structure; every piece of which was transported here by helicopter at great expense.

The bridge however cannot detract from one of the most inspiring scenes in the Rockies: Shadow Lake at the foot of the awesome, glacier-draped northeast face of Mt. Ball. The lake is 25 m deep,

has an area of 57 ha, and is home to cutthroat trout and eastern brook trout. Haiduk Creek has created a sizeable alluvial fan at the inlet on the south shore, almost dividing the lake in two. As its name suggests, the lake spends the latter part of each day in the shadow of Mt. Ball. Best lighting is early morning. If you

Ball Pass, 2.7 km

This short sidetrip takes you southwest from Ball Pass junction to the crest of the continental divide. It offers detailed views of the incredible south face of Mt. Ball, and a panorama over the valley of Redearth Creek.

The first 1.5 km climbs gently to the upper reaches of the west fork of Haiduk Creek. Rock-hop the stream and commence the steep ascent to Ball Pass. The route ahead looks unlikely, since the trail aims straight toward the boulderfield and cliff beneath the pass. However, a well-conceived series of switch-

backs breaks through the headwall, and delivers you easily to the craggy north entrance of the pass. The red, iron-rich soil underfoot is a possible origin of the name "Redearth."

Mt. Ball dominates the view. Its cascading south glacier defies the peril inherent in a sunny southern exposure, and clings magnificently to the mountainside. The southwest ridge of Mt. Ball acts as a snowfence, trapping snow in the south cirque, sustaining this glacier and another on the bench below.

James Hector brought the name "Ball" to the Rockies to

commemorate John Ball, a British public servant who rallied government support for the Palliser Expedition. Ball later became an accomplished mountaineer and first president of The Alpine Club in England. It is likely that Hector intended the name for the peak now known as Storm Mountain.

Walk 500 m south across the pass to obtain a view over the upper Hawk Creek valley into Kootenay National Park. Hawk Creek's source is a stream that discharges from the ground, southwest of the pass.

Upper Twin Lake is one of three attractive lakes tucked under the northeast flank of Storm Mtn.

Canadian Pacific Railway (CPR) in 1928, as part of a system of backcountry shelters for its clientele. Brewster Transport purchased the building in 1938, and sold it to Bud Brewster in 1950. In 1991, the lodge was redeveloped, adding six new outlying cabins. In 1993, additional development was proposed which would increase the capacity (including staff) to 40, making this one of the largest backcountry facilities in the Rockies. The development was approved despite the fact that the environmental assessment identified 20 negative impacts.

The Shadow Lake camp-

will be camping at the nearby campground, return to the outlet for sunrise. East of the outlet, you will see an unusual view of Pilot Mountain (2935 m), a well known landmark in the Bow Valley.

The original Shadow Lake Rest House was built by the

ground is 1.2 km east of the lake, 125 m east of Shadow Lake Lodge and the Gibbon Pass junction. For those who would like to exit the Lakes and Larches trail at this point, follow the Redearth Creek trail 13.1 km northeast to Highway 1. There is a backcountry campground en route, approximately halfway, at Lost Horse Creek.

Gibbon Pass Junction to Arnica Lake

The steady climb to Gibbon Pass earns you the delights of another beautiful upper subalpine landscape. Numerous game trails crisscross the expansive, larch-dotted alp of the pass. You may be fortunate to see mountain goats here. On the slope east of the pass, treeline is approximately 2400 m, well above the local norm of 2200 m. Why? The slope is southwest-facing and is in the lee of Storm Mountain. Perhaps the soils are warmer and drier than normal. On the pass itself,

Succession

The heat of the Vermilion Pass Burn cracked open the resin-sealed cones of lodgepole pines, resulting in a mass seeding and the subsequent growth of a doghair pine forest. Lodgepole pines are not shade tolerant, and usually thin themselves out, allowing for a transition to a forest dominated by Engelmann spruce and subalpine fir. This process of transformation is called succession,

and is usually complete within 130 years. However, the north-facing slope and windiness of this location create harsh growing conditions. New growth of lodgepole pines in the upper part of this burn is taking place slowly, and the succession to a spruce-fir forest here will likely be delayed. A quarter century after the burn, the average height of the young pines was only two metres.

young Lyall's larch trees are colonizing the tundra, transforming it to upper subalpine forest. Gibbon Pass was named in 1929 for John Gibbon, public relations manager with the CPR and founder of the Trail Riders of the Canadian Rockies.

From Gibbon Pass, the trail makes a gradual, sideslope descent north along the eastern side of the valley. After about 2.5 km, it switchbacks rapidly down to the outlet of lower Twin Lake. This is the first of another series of lakes that occupy northeast-facing cirques – this time beneath the stupendous cliffs of Storm Mountain (3161 m). The cirques are separated by arêtes – narrow rock ridges that descend from the summit area. All of these arêtes, and many of the gullies between, have been climbed by mountaineers. The east arête, rising between the Twin Lakes, is considered one of the most enjoyable alpine rock-climbing routes in the Rockies.

The trail is boggy in the vicinity of Lower Twin Lake. Cotton grass grows in abundance. Cross the outlet on a bridge to an important trail junction. Ahead, the "up and down" nature of this hike continues, with two more stiff climbs and descents in the remaining 8 km to the Kootenay Parkway. For those who want to exit at this point, hike downhill on the trail northeast (right) from this junction, for 8.0 km to Castle Junction on Highway 1.

Upper Twin Lake and campground is 800 m north of the junction. The campground is a popular overnight destination for backpackers travelling south from the Kootenay Parkway. Rock-hop the outlet and ascend steeply to the forested saddle on the northeast buttress of Storm Mountain: the Arnica/Twin Lake Summit. A steep descent brings you to Arnica Lake. Arnica is the genus name of common subalpine wildflowers that feature showy yellow blooms. There are fifteen species in the southern Rockies. The flowers of each arnica plant bloom only in alternate years.

Arnica Lake to the Kootenay Parkway

Leaving Arnica Lake, the trail descends onto the north flank of Storm Mountain. After passing the east shore of a rockslide-depression lake, the trail emerges onto the southern edge of the Vermilion Pass Burn. This lightning-caused forest fire consumed 2630 ha of subalpine forest in July 1968. The open area of the burn offers fine views east to Mt. Ishbel, Castle Mountain and Protection Mountain.

The lowest elevation on this hike is reached just 1.4 km from trail's end, at Vista Lake. This deep valley is an unusual landscape feature. It was not eroded over eons by the tiny creek we see today, but by a meltwater surge from a detached block of glacial ice at the end of the Wisconsin Glaciation. This meltwater also eroded the canyon west of

"On 16th September, I started up Healy's Creek … To the west of the Divide there is a beautiful piece of alpine park country, about one mile wide and several miles in length, dotted with emerald lakes and open groves of mountain larch..."
Surveyor J.J. McArthur, *Report Department of the Interior,* 1891

the lake. The stagnant ice block created a series of kettle lakes of which Vista is the lowest. The higher, Altrude Lakes are on the continental divide, farther west. "Altrude" is an odd but appropriate name, created when a surveying crew combined the Latin words for "high" (altus) and "beautiful" (pulchritude).

From the outlet of Vista Lake, a well-graded trail climbs to the Kootenay Parkway, bisecting a remarkable hoodoo-like formation en route. The final advance of the Wisconsin Glaciation in the Bow Valley ended near here. Irregular mounds of moraine dot the forest. This hoodoo may have been eroded from such a moraine.

Trail's end is at the Vista Lake/Twin Lakes trailhead on the Kootenay Parkway, 39 km by road from the starting point. There is a pay phone 2 km east at Storm Mountain Lodge.

Bourgeau Lake occupies a deep cirque eroded into the limestone cliffs of Mt. Bourgeau.

9. Bourgeau Lake

Route

Day-hike, 7.4 or 9.8 km

Route	Elevation (m)	Distance (km)
Trailhead	1403	0
Bourgeau Lake	2150	7.4
Harvey Pass	2440	9.8

Topographic map: 82 O/4
Best lighting: anytime

Trailhead

West side of Highway 1, 11.6 km west of the Mt. Norquay (Banff) interchange; 43.9 km east of Lake Louise. There is a highway sign for eastbound travellers only. This is a dangerous turnoff for westbound travellers. Use extreme caution.

Nestled in a massive glacial cirque beneath Mt. Bourgeau, Bourgeau Lake is a gem of a destination, and one of the most popular in the vicinity of Banff. The elevation gain is distributed along the length of this well-graded trail, making for relatively easy access to the upper subalpine environs at Bourgeau (boor-ZJOWE) Lake. Because it ascends a shaded valley, you should not hike this trail until mid-summer when the way will be clear of lingering snow. This trail is of recent origin compared to most in the Rockies. It was built in the late 1950s. The trail passes through excellent grizzly habitat. Use caution.

Low Larkspur

Highway 1 to Bourgeau Lake

The first 2.5 km of trail winds through forest on the slopes above Wolverine Creek. There are subtle changes in the vegetation at almost every turn. Most noticeable is the "doghair" forest of lodgepole pines and Douglas firs, evidence of a 1904 forest fire. The trail passes between two stately Douglas firs, one of which shows bark blackened by the fire. Beyond this point, Engelmann spruce is the most common tree. You may see spruce grouse here.

About 1 km from the trailhead there is a wonderful squirrel midden. Red squirrels nest on the ground in middens – accumulations of seed shells discarded from Engelmann spruce cones.

The first avalanche slope features fine views northeast to the Bow Valley and the Sawback Range. The meandering course of the Bow River reveals oxbow lakes, including Muleshoe Lake. The charred forest created by prescribed burns in 1991 and 1993 covers much of the eastern slope of the valley. Hole-in-the-Wall, a solution cave eroded by glacial meltwater, sits high and dry on the southwest face of Mt. Cory.

North of Wolverine Creek, terraced limestone cliffs dip eastwards toward the Bow

Please see map on page 59

Valley. Look for mountain goats here.

The cliffs are an outlying ridge of Mt. Brett (2984 m). Their dip reveals the eastern arm of an anticline. Dr. R.G. Brett was a businessman and politician, prominent in the affairs of Banff and the province of Alberta from 1886 to 1925. Roughly a kilometre beyond the first avalanche slope, the trail crosses a tributary stream, and then curves gradually south. This stream, and the south fork of Wolverine Creek, crossed at km 5.5, are choked with trees avalanched from the surrounding mountainsides. The first creek is bridged. However, any bridge across the second creek would be destroyed by avalanches. Gabion (GAY-bee-on) bags have been installed as stepping stones.

Gabion bags are wire-mesh baskets filled with rock from the stream bed. By nature of their tremendous weight and low profile, gabions can resist moving snow. They also dissipate the force of water by allowing some of the flow to pass between the rocks. Gabions are often successfully used for bridge footings and shoring in

Who Maintains the Trails?

Most hiking trails in the Rocky Mountain parks are maintained by trail crews employed by each park. The principal jobs are to keep the trails clear of fallen trees, avalanche debris and rocks; and to insure that tread surfaces remain well-drained. The trail crews also construct bridges, boardwalks and campground facilities, and they install and maintain signs. Most tools and materials are packed to the worksites each day. However, a helicopter is sometimes used to reach remote worksites, or for projects involving extremely heavy materials. Rewarding physical work in spectacular mountain scenery creates heavy interest annually in the few available trail crew positions. Unfortunately, trail maintenance is on the decline in most parks. In the summer of 1993, Banff National Park employed only six people to maintain more than 1500 km of trails.

In US national parks, the Wilderness Act precludes the use of motorized equipment for backcountry maintenance, thus minimizing disturbances to wildlife and visitors. Budgetary restraint in the Canadian Rocky Mountain parks could result in a revival of traditional non-motorized techniques for trail maintenance here.

sites prone to erosion.

A waterfall tumbles from the hanging valley west of Wolverine Creek. After crossing the creek, you climb steadily on switchbacks to the subalpine wet meadow adjacent to Bourgeau Lake. Here, the trail becomes muddy and indistinct. Do your best to keep to the beaten path. Cold air collects in the hollow of this meadow, and the damp soils are subject to frequent frosts. Mature trees cannot grow. However, on the slightly higher ground surrounding the meadow, a stunted forest of subalpine fir and a few Lyall's larch ekes out a chilly existence in the shade of Mt. Bourgeau.

Bourgeau Lake has been dammed by a rockslide. The lake drains beneath the débris. The massive cliffs ringing the lake are Livingstone limestone. This rock is made of fossilized remains of crinoids – marine animals related to the starfish of today.

Bourgeau Lake to Harvey Pass

When the slopes beyond Bourgeau Lake are free of snow, you may extend this outing by following any of several paths along the northwest shore to the west end of the lake. Look for low larkspur here. This uncommon member of the buttercup family has blue flowers. The leaves contain alkaloids that are poisonous to most wildlife.

Ascend a rough track on the north side of the inlet stream, and follow cairns. A stiff climb along the stream course brings you to a picturesque lakelet, set amongst beautiful alpland. Keep straight ahead. Another, shorter climb leads to a large basin that features yet another lakelet, not shown on the topographic map. You may be fortunate to see bighorn sheep here.

A 1981 estimate gave a population of 120-130 sheep for the vicinity of Mt. Bourgeau. Sixty-five mountain goats also live in this area, and the meadows are frequented by grizzly bears.

A faint track swings south and climbs a compacted scree slope to the climax of this exceptionally scenic hike: Harvey Lake nestled in the hollow of Harvey Pass. The pass was named for Ralph Harvey, who accompanied Jim Brewster here in the 1920s. Mt. Assiniboine (3618 m) soars skyward in the view south. From the southern brink of the pass, you have a wonderful vista over the larch-filled forest of Healy Creek, to Sunshine Meadows and the lake-dotted terrain of Simpson Pass.

A Modest Man, An Imposing Mountain

James Hector named Bourgeau Lake and mountain for Eugene Bourgeau, botanist with the Palliser Expedition of 1857 to 1860. Bourgeau was a likeable man and a first-rate botanist. He collected 60,000 specimens in 460 species during the expedition. The mountain was named in 1858, and the lake was named in 1912. The 2930 m mountain was first climbed in 1890 by J.J. McArthur and Tom Wilson. Although the mountain appears formidable, a "walk-up" route exists along the west slopes from Harvey Pass.

"Looking up the valley... we had before us a truncated mountain, evidently composed of massive horizontal strata, and which I named Mount Bourgeau."
—Journal of James Hector, August 17, 1858; The Palliser Expedition

"*At many points the towering cliffs reach up on both sides of the noisy stream and almost exclude the rays of the sun at noon. The creek bed is one long boulder strewn gorge where rapids and waterfalls alternate. The end of the trail is reached and there you will find a silvery cascade of water in a setting which brings visions of Hiawatha to the imagination.*"

—from Banff *Crag and Canyon*, March 17, 1917; written after completion of the Bow Valley Parkway as far as Johnston Canyon.

The deep, narrow cleft of Johnston Canyon is typical of limestone canyons in the Canadian Rockies.

10. Johnston Canyon

Route

Day-hike, 5.9 km

Route	Elevation (m)	Distance (km)
Trailhead	1430	0
"Lower Falls"	1463	1.1
"Upper Falls"	1483	2.7
Ink Pots jct	1524	3.2
Ink Pots	1631	5.9

Topographic maps: 82 0/4, 82 0/5
Best lighting: late morning to mid-afternoon in Johnston Canyon; anytime at The Ink Pots

Trailhead

Northeast corner of the Johnston Canyon parking lot. East side of the Bow Valley Parkway (Highway 1A), 23.6 km west of Banff; 6.5 km east of Castle Junction.

The Johnston Canyon trail is one of the four most heavily used trails in the Rockies. The most interesting features are next to the trail, making this hike an excellent choice for poor weather days. The trail will be less crowded early and late in the season. Wildlife you may see includes: mule deer, red squirrel, porcupine, gray jay, American dipper and common raven. Johnston Canyon is one of two known Alberta nesting sites for the black swift. The creek and canyon were named for a prospector from Silver City who frequented this area in 1882.

Bow Valley Parkway to Lower Falls

From the parking lot, cross Johnston Creek and turn north (right). The trailhead is at an elevation normally described as montane. However, canyons chill the air within them, creating environments more typical of higher elevations. The vegetation on shaded, north-facing slopes in lower Johnston Canyon is distinctly subalpine in character, and features lichen-draped Engelmann spruce and subalpine fir. On the south-facing slopes, lodgepole pines and a few Douglas firs prevail.

Johnston Canyon has a maximum depth of 30 metres, and features seven waterfalls, from 2 to 30 metres in height. Each waterfall marks the place where a layer of dolomite bedrock has been uncovered by the flowing water. Dolomite is more resistant than limestone, and naturally becomes the brink of a waterfall in this canyon. At the base

of each waterfall, the incessant pounding of the water creates a plunge pool. The plunge pool eventually undercuts the brink, causing it to collapse. As a result, the waterfall "migrates" slightly upstream, where the process is repeated.

The trail in the lower canyon has been designed to accommodate the tremendous number of visitors. In places, a concrete slab catwalk is suspended from the canyon wall on steel girders. Although it might seem intrusive, you gain an appreciation of the effects of flowing water that would not be possible from the canyon rim.

The Lower Falls are at km 1.1. The plunge pool is clearly visible. On the opposite side of the creek you can walk through a natural tunnel to a balcony drenched by the spray of the falls. The shattered cliffs nearby have been coated with a man-made compound to prevent rockfall.

Please see map on page 59

Lower Falls to Upper Falls

Many people turn back at the Lower Falls, hence the trail beyond is less crowded. The character of the canyon also changes. The bedrock here is principally soft shales. The canyon is often wider and V-shaped, in contrast to the narrow, deep slot of the lower canyon. The creek makes a prominent bend beneath a viewpoint. Looking downstream, you can see the strike, or orientation of the Johnston Creek Thrust Fault.

At km 2.7, you can descend a catwalk to the base of the 30-metre-high Upper Falls. On the opposite wall of the canyon is a travertine drape. Travertine is crumbly limestone, precipitated from lime-rich water. In one method of forming travertine, algae remove carbon dioxide from the water during photosynthesis, and deposit a film of calcium carbonate as a waste product. The calcium carbonate even-

The Hillsdale Slide

Johnston Creek has not always followed its present course. At the end of the Wisconsin Glaciation, Johnston Creek flowed east of here, along the base of Mt. Ishbel. It emptied into the Bow River farther south. However, the slopes of Mt. Ishbel had been undercut by ice during the glaciation, and then collapsed about 8000 years ago. The resulting landslide is known as the Hillsdale Slide. This landslide blocked Johnston Creek, and forced it to seek another course to the Bow River. The creek followed the line of least resistance, and is eroding the canyon along a fracture system known as the Johnston Creek Thrust Fault.

tually builds up into banded limestone. This is the largest of the six travertine drapes in Johnston Canyon, and may be the largest in the Rockies. Twenty-five species of algae have been identified here.

Upper Falls to the Ink Pots

Back on the main trail, you climb to the crest of the Upper Falls and a viewpoint at the canyon's edge. Please keep within the guard rails. Five people have died from falls into the canyon at this point. The trail reverts to a natural surface just beyond. Twenty metres past the "end of interpretive trail" sign, a short spur trail leads left to an abandoned canyon. Johnston Creek formerly flowed here as a waterfall. Downward erosion along the current stream course captured and redirected Johnston Creek, leaving this channel dry.

The trail angles away from the canyon, and the sound of rushing water quickly fades. The forest becomes drier. At km 3.2, the trail joins the horse route from Moose Meadows. Turn north (right) for the Ink Pots. The trail climbs and becomes narrower, before descending to the willow plain on Johnston Creek at the Ink Pots. The high, shale banks of the upper canyon are visible in places en route. They are capped by a 20 m thick overburden of glacial till.

East of the Ink Pots, Mt. Ishbel (2908 m) is prominent. Its slabby sedimentary layers and serrated ridges epitomize

The Ink Pots

The Ink Pots are karst features that mark the outlets of seven cold mineral springs. Fed by rainwater and snowmelt that has percolated into the surrounding bedrock, the spring water emerges at a constant temperature of 4.8°C. The combined volume of flow is 1800 litres per minute. The bases of the Ink Pots are covered in fine sediments that have the consistency of quicksand. Two of the springs run murky due to sediments disturbed by the rising water – hence the name, The Ink Pots.

the sawtooth mountain form, so common in the front ranges. The hills and dales of the Hillsdale Slide are clearly visible to the south. To the north, grassy terraces on Castle Mountain provide excellent range for bighorn sheep and mountain goats.

Rockbound Lake is ringed on two sides by impressive cliffs of Eldon limestone. James Hector named the lake and nearby Castle Mountain in 1858. It would be hard to improve these descriptive names.

11. Rockbound Lake

Route

Day-hike, 8.4 km

Route	Elevation (m)	Distance (km)
Trailhead	1395	0
Silverton Falls jct	1395	0.3
Tower Lake	2128	7.7
Rockbound Lake	2210	8.4

Topographic map: 82 O/5
Best lighting: mid-morning to mid-afternoon

Trailhead

East side of the Bow Valley Parkway (Highway 1A), 29.5 km west of Banff, 200 m east of Castle Junction.

Nestled beneath the colossal ramparts of Castle Mountain, Rockbound Lake is part of an elemental landscape of water, rock and sky; inspiring in its simplicity. Beautiful wildflower displays, larches, and intriguing geology and human history add interest to this outing.

Bow Valley Parkway to Tower Lake

The first 5 km of trail is fireroad width, and climbs steadily through the lodgepole pine forest that cloaks the Bow Valley. This forest grew in the aftermath of an 1892 forest fire. At approximately km 2.4, the trail angles sharply east (right) at an unmarked junction. Straight ahead is an unmaintained path to the now removed Castle Mountain fire lookout. Storm

Mountain (3161 m) is prominent in the view west.

The forested mounds on the floor of the Bow Valley are piles of moraine. These mark the greatest extent of the massive Bow Valley Glacier during the last advance of the Wisconsin Glaciation.

As the trail climbs over the ridge south of Castle Mountain, the forest becomes more subalpine in character. After it swings north behind the ridge, the trail narrows, the grade eases, and the tread surface becomes poor. In early season, it requires great effort to remain on the trail. As a consolation to the mud underfoot, the moist glades at trailside feature one of the best displays of white globeflowers you will see in the Rockies.

Please see map on page 59

The trail undulates over a series of forested recessional moraines, then becomes indistinct as it crosses a wet meadow to Tower Lake. This shallow lake mirrors the southernmost summit of Castle Mountain (2752 m) – "the tower." This summit was first climbed in 1926. Rockslides near the lake are home to hoary marmots. The surrounding forest contains Lyall's larch. The needles of this tree turn golden yellow in autumn, adding to the attraction of late season hiking.

Tower Lake to Rockbound Lake

After you rock-hop the outlet of Tower Lake, the trail switchbacks steeply up the headwall to Rockbound Lake, passing through a stand of ancient Engelmann spruce trees. Drummond's anemone and alpine spring beauty are common wildflowers here. The trail braids and becomes indistinct as it approaches Rockbound Lake.

Rockbound Lake is a perfect glacial tarn. Cliffs of Eldon limestone, up to 220 m high, provide a spectacular backdrop. Cutthroat trout, rainbow trout and eastern brook trout in the lake attract osprey. You may see these raptors circling the lake, and with fortune witness them diving for fish. The osprey is specially adapted for grabbing fish from the water. It has an opposable outer talon, that works much the same as a human thumb.

Rockbound Lake marks the southernmost point of the Castle Mountain Syncline, a

Castle and Controversy

Castle Mountain is one of the best-known landmarks in the Rockies, and one of the most appropriately named. James Hector first described it in 1858, and called it a textbook example of a "castellated mountain". Castle's lower cliff is Cathedral dolomite and limestone, the middle terrace is Stephen shale, and the upper cliff is Eldon limestone. This particular sequence of alternating resistant and recessive rocks is known as the "Middle Cambrian Sandwich," and helps to create the castellated appearance of many mountains in the eastern main ranges.

In 1946, politicians decided

Castle Mountain would be renamed in honour of Dwight D. Eisenhower, World War II commander of allied forces in Europe, and later US president. The change of name was not popular with Canadians, and after much lobbying, the name Castle Mountain was reinstated in 1979. As a compromise, the tower is now called Eisenhower Peak. It is not the highest point on Castle's 6.5 km long ridge. The true summit (2804 m) is the one farthest north, and is not visible from Tower or Rockbound lakes.

Silverton Falls

> "*Above the edge of the cliff, however, the going was easy, so that the highest part of the Castle (nine thousand feet) was not hard to reach, and the wonderful view of the valley of the Bow River, four thousand feet below, was quite worth seeing. The tower standing in front of the Castle to the southeast looked as unscalable as it was reported to be.*"
>
> —A.P. Coleman
> describing the first ascent of
> Castle Mountain in 1884,
> *The Canadian Rockies,*
> *New and Old Trails*

U-shaped fold in the bedrock that extends 260 km north to Mt. Kerkeslin in Jasper National Park. The Cathedral limestone slab underlying the lake is tipped upwards toward the south, damming the waters. You can walk east along this natural pavement to the high water outlet of the lake. Most of Rockbound Lake's outflow now drains underground through karst fissures eroded into the bedrock.

Silverton Falls

On your return, a sidetrip to Silverton Falls is recommended. (The falls are shaded in the morning.) Turn southeast (left) at the junction 300 m be-fore you reach the trailhead, and follow the sidetrail to the bridge across Silverton Creek. Do not cross the creek. Face downstream at the bridge and take the unmarked trail that ascends the slope to the north (right). This leads to an unfenced viewpoint overlooking the upper cataracts of the falls. Use caution.

"Silverton" refers to the railway and mining boom town of Silver City, that flourished nearby from 1882 to 1884. In its heyday, Silver City boasted a population of 2000 people and was larger than Calgary. A round-trip visit to Silverton Falls adds 1.3 km to the Rockbound Lake outing.

A Shattered Landscape

The valley above Rockbound Lake was called "Horseshoe Valley" by A.P. Coleman. This valley is renowned for its "clint and grike" landscape – extensive limestone pavement that has been shattered by millennia of frost action. The "clints" are limestone blocks and the "grikes" are the fissures that separate them. The words come from the dialect of Yorkshire, England, where this type of landscape is common.

A late summer snowfall blankets the mountains above Boom Lake. The trail to the lake passes through dense subalpine forest where moose, American marten and ruffed grouse may be seen. Common loons nest at the lake.

12. Boom Lake

Route

Day-hike, 5.1 km

Route	Elevation (m)	Distance (km)
Trailhead, Boom Creek picnic area	1723	0
Taylor Lake jct	1814	2.3
Boom Lake	1894	5.1

Topographic maps: 82N/1, 82 N/8
Best lighting: morning

Trailhead

Boom Creek picnic area, north side of the Kootenay Parkway (Highway 93), 7.0 km west of Castle Junction, 97.7 km east of the junction with Highway 95.

The hike to Boom Lake is one of the easiest Classic Hikes – an undemanding stroll through a remarkable ancient subalpine forest. The destination is a superb backcountry lake in a wilderness setting, the match of any in the Rockies. The shores of the lake are a wonderful place to wile away the hours.

Kootenay Parkway to Boom Lake

After crossing Boom Creek on a bridge, the broad trail (formerly a tote road to a mine) commences its gradual climb. Keep straight ahead at the Taylor Lake junction at km 2.3. The trail continues its rolling ascent for another 2 km, and then descends gradually, becoming narrow, rocky and rooted for the last 200 m. It emerges on the north shore of Boom Lake about 600 m west of the outlet. Rockslide debris makes travel farther along the lakeshore difficult .

Boom Lake is 2.7 km long, 30 m deep, and 366 m wide. With an area of roughly 100 ha, it is the tenth largest lake in Banff National Park. It is remarkably clear given its proximity to glacial ice. Measurements have documented a reduction of silt in the water during the 20th century – an indication that the glaciers that feed the lake are dwindling.

Boom Lake is home to cutthroat trout. The log booms are natural formations created from avalanched trees swept into the lake. The trees then drifted toward the outlet and became lodged, perhaps as Walter Wilcox theorized, on submerged moraines. The first boom is several hundred metres east of where the trail reaches shoreline. The cold, damp, north-facing avalanche slopes on the south side of the lake support stands of Lyall's larch, a tree usually found 300 m higher.

The prominent snow and ice clad mountains northwest of the lake are Chimney Peak (3000m) and Mt. Bident (3084 m) and Quadra Mountain (3173 m). People familiar with these latter two mountains as viewed from the Moraine Lake Road or Consolation Lakes may have difficulty recognizing them here. The basin beneath is heaped with moraines, indicating the extent of glacial ice less than two centuries ago.

The rockslide boulders and the dark cliffs that back the lake contain Gog quartzite. This rock was created from quartz-rich sediments deposited in prehistoric seas during the early Cambrian period. Gog quartzite frequently contains iron. Indeed, many of the quartzite boulders at water's edge are "rusted" brown with iron oxide. These rockslides are home to colonies of pikas, tiny members of the rabbit family whose call is a shrill "EEEEP". You may hear or seen the common loon on Boom Lake.

American marten track

Please see map on page 59

> "*One of its most curious features is a crescent-shaped dam of logs and tree roots about one mile from the lower end. This extends from shore to shore, and probably marks the shallow water made by some old glacier moraine. I thought at first of naming the lake from this instance, but was unable to make anything euphonious out of "log dammed lake."*
>
> —Walter Wilcox, on the first recorded visit to Boom Lake in 1899, *The Rockies of Canada*

The Subalpine Forest

The trail to Boom Lake is located just a few kilometres east of the continental divide, in an area of high precipitation. Engelmann spruce and subalpine fir comprise the damp, mature subalpine forest here. The spire-like form of the subalpine fir, with its downsloping branches, helps shed the heavy snow load. Labrador tea, dwarf birch, feathermosses, and fungi are prominent in the undergrowth.

This forest, with its deadfall and tree lichens, represents the climax vegetation for this area. It provides ideal habitat for mice and voles, which are standard fare for the American marten, the most widespread carnivore in the Rockies. Moose use this forest for cover, and ruffed grouse and pileated woodpeckers may be seen. Varied thrush, hermit thrush and golden-crowned kinglet are common songbirds. The bark of some Engelmann spruce trees is reddish purple, where the brown outer scales have been removed by three-toed woodpeckers in quest of grubs and insects.

The damp and decay is in contrast to the dry lodgepole pine forest you saw at the trailhead. The pines were seeded naturally after the 1968 Vermilion Pass Burn. Spruce and fir will probably replace the pines within 130 years.

This process of transformation in the forest is called succession. Each forest type favours certain species of vegetation and wildlife. Nature uses fire to promote succession and revitalize stagnant forests. The mosaic, of new and old, of burned and unburned, creates the diversity of habitat required to maintain all species in the forest ecosystem.

The Boom Lake trail travels between the extremes of forest succession habitats in the Rockies. The forest at the trailhead is less than thirty years old. Near Boom Lake you will see Engelmann spruce trees that measure 1 m in diameter at the base, and are 40 m tall, indicating ages of about 350-450 years.

Cloud shadows dapple the surface of Lake Louise and the Bow Valley in this view from Big Beehive. Lake Louise is typical of glacially fed lakes in the Rockies. Rock flour in the water reflects blue and green spectra of light. The Château sits on a glacial moraine that partially dams the lake's outlet.

13. The Beehives and Plain of Six Glaciers

Route

Day-hike, 20.0 km

Route	Elevation (m)	Distance (km)
Lake Agnes trailhead	1732	0
Mirror Lake	2027	2.4
Little Beehive jct	2104	3.1
Lake Agnes connector jct	2170	3.6
Little Beehive	2253	4.2
Lake Agnes	2118	5.2
Big Beehive jct	2260	6.5
Big Beehive	2270	6.8
Highline jct	2010	8.3
Plain of Six Glaciers trail jct	1950	10.1
Plain of Six Glaciers Teahouse	2135	11.5
Victoria Glacier viewpoint	2150	13.1
Château Lake Louise	1732	20.0

Topographic map: 82 N/8

Best lighting: most features on this hike are lit best in the morning

Trailhead

From Lake Louise Village, follow Lake Louise Drive 5.5 km to the parking lots at the lake. Paved walkways lead to the lakeshore. Walk along the lakeshore to the trail junction on the far side of the Château. The trail branches uphill to the north (right).

I f you have time for only one hike in the vicinity of Lake Louise, The Beehives should be your choice. As you climb to the modest summits of Little Beehive and Big Beehive, you will see all that is scenically special in the area, and you will frequently be reminded of its rich human history. However, this is not a hike for those seeking solitude. Two of the Rockies' most popular trails, Lake Agnes and Plain of Six Glaciers, are part of this outing. The trail on the north side of Big Beehive is often snowbound until July.

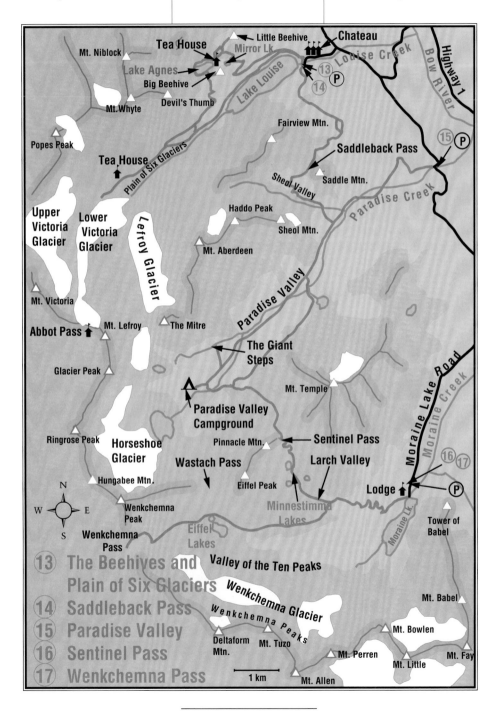

Lake Louise to Little Beehive

The broad Lake Agnes trail climbs steadily through sub-alpine forest for 1.6 km to a switchback overlooking Lake Louise and the delta at its inlet. You may see plumes of glacial sediment dispersing into the lake. Across the lake rise the quartzite cliffs of Fairview Mountain (2744 m). The trail narrows, turns sharply north and crosses a section of the wooden pipeline that once provided drinking water from Lake Agnes to the Château. At the horse/hiker barrier, turn west (left) to reach Mirror Lake. The quartzite buttress of Big Beehive forms the backdrop for this picturesque pond, which has no visible surface outlet. Mirror Lake and nearby Lake Agnes were referred to by the Canadian Pacific Railway (CPR) as "the lakes in the clouds," in promotional material in the late 1800s. Mirror Lake was known to Stoney Natives as the "goat's looking glass."

The trail continues north from Mirror Lake, and switchbacks up into larch trees on an avalanche slope on Mt. St. Piran. The mountain is named for the English birthplace of Willoughby Astley, first manager of Chalet Lake Louise. Astley supervised the cutting of many trails in the area, including this one.

At the junction at km 3.1, turn sharply northeast (right) onto the Little Beehive trail, which ascends higher onto the avalanche slope. Western anemone, Sitka valerian, arni-ca, common fireweed, common yarrow, white rhododen-dron, fleabane, dwarf dog-wood, cinquefoil and pink mountain heather are common here. There are fine views southwest to Big Beehive, Fairview Mountain, Haddo Peak (3070 m) and glacier-clad Mt. Aberdeen (3151 m). The icy summit of Mt. Temple (3543 m) rises above them all.

After 500 m you reach another junction. Turn northeast (right), and follow this trail 700 m across an avalanche slope onto the larch-covered knoll of Little Beehive. Lake Louise and the Château are visible from the cliff edge at the far side of the avalanche slope. Partway across, you pass a large quartzite boulder, around which grows red-stemmed saxifrage. The name saxifrage is derived from Latin words that mean "rock break-er." Seven species of saxifrage grow in the Rockies.

Little Beehive commands a superlative view of the Bow Valley, from Hector Lake in the north to Pilot Mountain (2935 m) in the south. Little Beehive was an obvious choice for the fire lookout that operated here from 1941 until 1978. The lookout building was removed in 1985. Parks Canada has installed an informative display concerning forest fires. Unfortunately, Cyclone Mountain and Fossil Mountain are misplaced on the accompanying diorama. From the lookout site, you can see the extensive habitat fragmentation that has been caused by developments in this part of the Bow Valley.

Little Beehive to Lake Agnes

On your descent from Little Beehive, keep straight ahead at the first junction. As you approach the Lake Agnes Tea House, the trail passes along-side a Gog siltstone bluff. The

Who was Agnes?

Officially, Lake Agnes is named for Lady Susan Agnes Macdonald, wife of Prime Minister John A. Macdonald. Lady Agnes had been informed by the CPR that when she visited the lake in 1890, she would be the first woman to do so. Unfortunately, chalet manager Willoughby Astley, unaware of this arrangement, had guided another woman to the lake a few days earlier. By coincidence, the other woman's name was Agnes Knox. A member of the first lady's party defused the situation, pointing out that by giving the name "Agnes" to the lake, everyone would be kept happy.

Walter Wilcox, an early visitor to Lake Agnes, called it "a wild tarn imprisoned by cheerless cliffs." The lake occupies one step in a glacial cirque staircase that descends from the slopes of Mt. Niblock toward Lake Louise.

Red Squirrel tracks

Devil's Thumb (2458 m), and Mts. Whyte (2983 m) and Niblock (2976 m) form a massive cirque around the lake. Sir William Whyte was second vice-president of the CPR, and John Niblock was a railway superintendent in the 1890s. The lake was their favourite fishing hole in the Rockies. Fishing is no longer allowed.

The Lake Agnes Tea House was one of a series constructed by the CPR to entice its hotel clients into the mountains. The first structure here was built in 1901. The present tea house was privately reconstructed in 1981. It is open daily from mid-June to early October, serving lunch, refreshments and baked goods. You can learn more about the history of the tea houses at an interpretive display on the south side of the lake's outlet.

bluff is tilted upwards to the northeast. Within this overall plane, some layers of sediments are at widely varying angles, known as cross-bedding. These layers are the record of shifting deltas where sediments were deposited in the early Cambrian period. Beyond the bluff, the trail climbs a staircase to the tea-house on the lakeshore.

Lake Agnes

Walter Wilcox, an early visitor to Lake Agnes, called it "a wild tarn imprisoned by cheerless cliffs." True to Wilcox's description, the lake is a glacial tarn, occupying a 20.5 m deep hollow. The wilderness character of the lake is now lost amongst the throngs of visitors, but the scene is impressive nonetheless. From south to north: Big Beehive (2270 m),

The upper subalpine forest at Lake Agnes provides the seeds, berries, fungi and insects eaten by Clark's nutcrackers, gray jays, golden-mantled ground squirrels, Columbian ground squirrels, least chipmunks and red squirrels. Please do not feed these birds and animals. Your "kindness" will ultimately kill them. Reliant on handouts, the non-hibernating species may not cache enough food to tide them through the winter. Those that do hibernate may go to sleep with bodies run-down by junk food diets, never to reawaken.

Lake Agnes to Big Beehive

From the tea house, head west through boulderfields along the north shore of the lake. Hoary marmots and pika are common here. Damp areas support dense growths of false hellebore and red-stemmed saxifrage. At the west end of the lake, the trail swings south beneath the shattered cliffs of the Devil's Thumb. Use caution crossing any lingering snow. The scrunching underfoot is caused by coarse, hard sand eroded from the quartzite

The trail beyond the Plain of Six Glaciers Tea House follows the crest of a lateral moraine. Massive, glacier-draped limestone cliffs tower above. The rubble-covered surface of Victoria Glacier stretches below. Rockfalls and avalanches echo through the valley.

bedrock.

The trail switchbacks steeply upwards to the saddle between Big Beehive and Devil's Thumb. Take care not to dislodge rocks onto people below. Scan the cliffs of Mts. Niblock and St. Piran (2650 m) opposite, for mountain goats. From the crest of the climb,

rough paths lead northeast (left) for 300 m to a shelter on the Big Beehive. Here, you obtain a stunning overview of Lake Louise, more than 500 m below.

Lake Louise is 2 km long, has an area of 85 ha, and a maximum depth of 70 m. It is the 11th largest lake in Banff

Plain of Six Glaciers

The Plain of Six Glaciers is the forefield of Lower Victoria Glacier, from where six glaciers are visible: Lower and Upper Victoria, Lefroy, Upper Lefroy, Aberdeen and Popes. (A seventh glacier, which does not flow into this valley is visible on the north peak of Mt. Victoria.) The complex of moraines surrounding the plain records stages of glacial advance and retreat. Lower Victoria Glacier has

receded 1.2 km since the maximum of the Little Ice Age in the early 1800s. You can see the former extent of the ice in the trimline. All forest between the trimline and the present glacier position was destroyed during the Little Ice Age advance.

The surface of Lower Victoria Glacier is covered in moraine and rockfall debris. For many years, the glacier toe contained a large ice cave. Undermined by

glacial retreat, this cave collapsed in 1992. After the dry winter of 1992-1993, the glacier receded a staggering amount and the profile of the terminus changed dramatically. With this trend in glacial recession, the present terminus may soon become separated from the main mass of the glacier – a feature known as a dead-ice moraine.

National Park. The lake occupies a hanging valley, and is dammed by a moraine that was pushed up alongside the Bow Valley Glacier during the Wisconsin Glaciation.

Big Beehive to the Plain of Six Glaciers

Return to the main trail, and turn south (left). The trail switchbacks steadily down to join the highline route that connects Lake Agnes and the Plain of Six Glaciers. Turn southwest (right), and follow this trail 1.8 km to the Plain of Six Glaciers trail. (At the first junction in 700 m, you can exit from this hike by turning left. By this route it is 4.4 km to the Château. Otherwise keep straight ahead.)

After passing through a tunnel of overgrown water birch, the trail joins the Plain of Six Glaciers trail. Keep straight ahead (southwest). The view to the south features The Mitre (2889 m), named for its resemblance to a bishop's hat. At the series of switchbacks just before the tea house, look upslope for mountain goats.

Common butterwort, one of seven species of carnivorous plants in the Rockies, grows in the seeps nearby. At the base of the purple flower is a rosette of pale green leaves . The leaves are coated in a sticky enzyme that traps and digests insects. Their exoskeletons cannot be digested, and remain as black specks on the leaves.

The Plain of Six Glaciers Tea House was constructed by Swiss Guides employed by the CPR in 1924. The building is just out of harm's way, beside a large avalanche path. Originally, the tea house served as a staging area for mountaineers. Overnight accommodation is no longer offered. Lunch, refreshments and baked goods can be purchased in season, which generally runs from mid-June to late September.

Tea House to Victoria Glacier Viewpoint

The tea house is the ultimate destination for many hikers. For those with stamina remaining, this hike can be extended southwest for 1.6 km to the exposed crest of a lateral moraine overlooking the Lower Victoria Glacier. Here, you are face to face with an ice age landscape. Massive limestone and quartzite cliffs glisten with glacial ice. Rockfalls and avalanches echo about.

In the view southwest, Abbot Pass (2925 m) separates Mt. Lefroy (3423 m) and Mt. Victoria (3464 m). At the crest of the pass is Abbot Pass Hut, built by the Swiss Guides in 1921-22. Although most of this building is made from stone obtained on-site, more than two tonnes of supplies were packed by horse across the glacier, and then winched and carried by the guides to the pass. Named for Phillip Stanley Abbot, who died on Mt. Lefroy in 1896, the hut was the highest inhabitable building

in Canada until the Neil Colgan Hut was constructed above Moraine Lake in 1982.

Travel beyond Plain of Six Glaciers viewpoint is for experienced and properly equipped mountaineers only.

It is 6.9 km from this viewpoint to the Château via the Plain of Six Glaciers trail. Keep straight ahead at all trail junctions. If the short section of trail along the edge of a bluff is not to your liking, you can bypass it on moraines to the south. If you reach the lake in early evening, you may witness the comings and goings of beavers. They often venture onto the trail to nibble willows, oblivious to human traffic.

"For some time we sat and smoked and gazed at the gem of beauty beneath the glacier [Lake Louise]. My Stoney guide told me that higher up were two smaller lakes, one of which his people called the "goat's looking glass," as the goats came down to it to use it as a mirror while they combed their beards."

—Tom Wilson,
on the discovery of Lake
Louise in 1882,
Trail Blazer of the Rockies

The ice-capped summit of Mt. Temple looms over boulderfields and larch forest on Saddleback Pass.

14. Saddleback Pass

Route

Day-hike, 3.7 km or 14.7 km loop

Route	Elevation (m)	Distance (km)
Saddleback Pass trailhead	1738	0
Saddleback Pass	2330	3.7
Saddleback jct Paradise Valley	1845	7.5
Moraine Lake trai jct	1814	10.3
Saddleback Pass trailhead	1738	14.7

Topographic map: 82 N/8
Best lighting: morning or late afternoon

Trailhead

From Lake Louise Village, follow Lake Louise Drive 5.5 km to the parking lots at the lake. Paved walkways lead to the lakeshore. The Saddleback Pass trailhead is located southeast of the World Heritage Site monument, on the south side of Louise Creek.

S addleback Pass is set amongst pleasant glades in a treeline larch forest. For the adventurous, a beaten path leads to the summit of Fairview Mountain. You can have your appetite whetted for many another outing among the vast array of peaks revealed in the summit view. By continuing over the crest of Saddleback Pass, you can extend this hike into a loop outing through Sheol and Paradise valleys.

Cleared in 1893, the trail to Saddleback Pass was one of the earliest recreational hiking trails in the Rockies. For a century, its ascent has served many as an introduction to the alpine wonders of the Lake Louise area, and as a test of fitness. Few trails in the Rockies are so intent of purpose. With an average grade of 16 percent, this trail makes a beeline for the "saddle" connecting Fairview and Saddle mountains, and leaves many hikers breathless long before the pass is attained.

Lake Louise to Saddleback Pass

The first hundred metres set the tone for this outing. On the Saddleback trail you toil upward across the shaded northeast slope of Fairview Mountain. More than 4 m of snow falls in this vicinity annually. The damp climax forest of Engelmann spruce and subalpine fir has not burned since 1630. Feathermosses are prominent in the undergrowth.

Keep straight ahead at the Fairview Lookout and Moraine Lake trail junctions. The trail crosses a broad swath in the forest, created by avalanches from the quartzite cliffs of Fairview Mountain. From the switchback at the south edge of this avalanche path, there is a fine view north to Chateau Lake Louise and distant Mt. Hector (3394 m), rising above the expansive glacially carved trough of the Bow Valley.

At about km 2, the trail forks. Both trails lead to Saddleback Pass, converging again in 400 m. The lefthand trail is less steep and offers views across the Bow Valley to the Slate Range. You can see

Please see map on page 80

the slopes of Whitehorn Mountain, criss-crossed by the ski runs of the Lake Louise ski area. After it swings south to approach the pass, the trail crosses more avalanche terrain and switchbacks through the first stands of Lyall's larch. The winding route into the pass is planned to circumvent snow patches that linger in early summer. Please do not short-cut the switchbacks.

The icy crest of Mt. Temple (3543 m) looms majestically over a foreground of larch trees on Saddleback Pass. The glacier on Mt. Temple is Macdonald Glacier, named after Canada's first prime minister– and the chief proponent of the Canadian Pacific Railway (CPR). The dark, rocky peak to the west of the pass is Sheol Mountain (2779 m). The name refers to the Hebrew abode of the dead, and was inspired by the gloomy appearance of the valley at its base.

The CPR built a tea house on Saddleback Pass in 1922. It had an unreliable water supply and operated for only one summer. You may find weathered boards in various locations on the pass – the remains of the building's siding. Sections of the water line from Sheol Valley still run across the flanks of Fairview Mountain.

Fairview Mountain

From the cairn on the pass, a track leads northwest toward

Pikas – EEEEP!

So goes the call of the pika (PEE-kah or PIE-kah), one of two members of the rabbit family in the Rockies. The quartzite boulderfields below Saddleback Pass are perfect terrain for this tiny (less than 20 cm long) mammal. The pika has a gray coat and a minuscule tail. It has been affectionately described as "a tennis ball with ears." Pikas live in colonies. You will probably hear a pika long before you see it. The shrill call warns its fellows of your presence.

Pikas eat grasses, lichens, leaves and wildflowers. Since the animal does not hibernate, it must stash food to tide it through the winter. It spends the summer gathering vegetation and drying it on flat rocks, before hiding the hay in its bouldery home. The winter diet is augmented by partially digested pellets of its own dung. Eagles, hawks, owls and members of the weasel family are the pika's principal predators.

Fairview Mountain (2744 m). First climbed by surveyor J.J. McArthur in 1887, Fairview is today probably the most frequently ascended mountain in the Rockies. If Fairview is snow-free and the weather is good, any reasonably fit and well-prepared hiker can accomplish the ascent. It is an excellent introductory peak for novice mountaineers. As the mountain's name implies, the summit panorama is one of the finest near Lake Louise. Be sure to descend from Fairview by retracing your route of ascent. Accidents, sometimes fatal, are common on this "easy" mountain when hikers attempt to "take a shortcut" down the northeast face to Lake Louise.

Loop Hike Option

To extend this outing into a loop hike, continue over Saddleback Pass and descend the switchbacks into Sheol Valley. As you lose elevation, the relatively minor summit of Sheol Mountain gains in stature, blocking the afternoon sun. One can see why Samuel Allen chose the name Sheol. The trail crosses the creek and descends to meet the Paradise Valley trail. Turn east (left) and follow this pleasant trail 3.1 km to the Moraine Lake trail junction, making two crossings of Paradise Creek en route. Turn north (left) at the junction, from where it is 4.3 km through subalpine forest to the starting point at the Saddleback Pass trailhead.

> "*Lake Louise was in the door-yard, and Fairview the house-top from which we descended to seek the fields beyond the bounding sky-line.*"
> —James Monroe Thorington; *The Glittering Mountains of Canada*, 1925

From Yale to Paradise

Sheol, Fairview, Saddle, Paradise and many other names in the Lake Louise area were given by members of the Yale Lake Louise Club. These five school mates spent a blissful and somewhat perilous summer on the heights around Lake Louise in 1894. Although lacking significant mountaineering experience, their adventures included the first ascents of Mts. Temple and Aberdeen, discoveries of Paradise Valley and Moraine Lake, and the first crossings of Sentinel, Wastach, Wenkchemna and Mitre passes. Two members, Walter Wilcox and Samuel Allen, each published maps of the area. Many of the names Allen applied were of Native origin. Wilcox also wrote *The Rockies of Canada*, a best selling book that went through numerous printings and editions, establishing him as the authority of the day on the Canadian Rockies.

Hungabee Mountain dominates the head of Paradise Valley. The mountain's native name means "Chieftain."

15. Paradise Valley

Route

Day-hike or overnight, 19.7 km loop

Route	Elevation (m)	Distance (km)
Paradise Creek trailhead	1729	0
Moraine Lake trail jct	1799	1.1
Paradise Valley jct	1814	1.3
Saddleback Pass jct	1845	4.2
Lake Annette jct	1887	5.1
Lake Annette	1970	5.7
Sentinel Pass jct	2119	8.8
Paradise Creek bridge	2012	9.4
Paradise Valley CG	2020	9.7
Giant Steps	2012	10.7
Paradise Creek trailhead	1729	19.7

Topographic map: 82 N/8

Best lighting: morning

Trailhead

From Lake Louise Village, follow Lake Louise Drive 3 km to the Moraine Lake Road. Turn south (left). Follow this road 2.3 km to the Paradise Creek trailhead.

With its alluring combination of forest, lakes, glaciers, meadows, waterfalls and imposing mountains, Paradise Valley provides one of the most complete hiking experiences in the Canadian Rockies. From the backcountry campground at the head of the valley, you can leisurely explore The Giant Steps, Sentinel Pass, Wastach Pass and Horseshoe Glacier. This outing is an excellent choice for novice backpackers, and is

American dipper

Moraine Lake Road to Lake Annette

The trail commences with an ascent over forested moraines. These moraines were pushed up where the ancestral Paradise Valley and Bow Valley glaciers merged during the Wisconsin Glaciation. The open subalpine forest features a variety of wildflowers. Yellow columbine, false hellebore, fleabane, arnica and dwarf dogwood are common. The undergrowth is dominated by club mosses, spike mosses, feathermosses, grouseberry and false huckleberry.

Keep straight ahead at the bike/ski trail junction. The trail follows the crest of an ancient creek bank through a doghair pine forest to the Moraine Lake trail. Here, turn north (right).

Please see map on page 80

Follow this trail 240 m to the Paradise Valley junction, ascending a rolling sequence of ancient creek terraces. Turn west (left) at the junction – the sign was missing in 1993. The Paradise Valley trail climbs a short distance over more moraines, and then begins a gradual descent to the first crossing of Paradise Creek.

Boggy areas along the south bank of Paradise Creek feature elephant head, cotton grass, fleabane, cinquefoil and yellow paintbrush. The trail recrosses the creek and in 1 km reaches the Saddleback Pass junction. Keep straight ahead to the Lake Annette junction. Here, turn south (left), and again cross Paradise Creek. Just past the bridge are a number of ancient tree stumps – too many to have been used in building bridges. The stumps suggest there may have been a cabin in this vicinity in the early 1900's.

The trail climbs moderately to the outlet of Lake Annette. Look directly above and through the trees to see the Black Towers on the east ridge of Mt. Temple. The slope west of the trail is covered in white mountain heather, and white globeflowers grow along the outlet stream. Watch for the American dipper (water ouzel) here. The dipper is the only aquatic songbird in North America, and a marvel of adaptation. It is a year-round

Mt. Temple-A Mountain Crucible

The north face of Mt. Temple (3543 m) dominates the view from the first bridge over Paradise Creek. Mt. Temple is the highest peak in the Lake Louise area, third highest in Banff National Park, and eleventh highest in the Rockies. The summit is more than 1700 vertical metres above the valley floor. Mt. Temple is also one of the largest mountains in the range, occupying 15 km².

Mt. Temple has long been a testing place for mountaineers. It was first climbed in 1894 by members of the Yale Lake Louise Club, led by school mates Walter Wilcox and Samuel Allen. They followed a route from Sentinel Pass on the opposite side of the mountain. The imposing north flank was first climbed in 1966, and now features eight challenging mountaineering routes. The mountain was named for Sir Richard Temple, patron of a British scientific expedition to the Rockies in 1884.

best between mid-July and mid-September.

resident of the mountains, protected from winter's chill by thick, soot-coloured, down that is impregnated with oil. The dipper feeds on insects and fish fry in turbulent streams. It has flaps which cover its nostrils during dives, allowing it to remain submerged for more than a minute.

Bordered by boulderfields, moraine and larch forest, Lake Annette sits at the base of Mt. Temple's stupendous north face. A krummholz forest of subalpine fir stands on the north shore of the lake. The upper part of each tree is a lifeless spike, killed by the chilling blast of avalanches from Mt. Temple. The gnarled mat of the lower trees has survived, insulated within the snowpack. Lake Annette was named by Walter Wilcox for a woman he presumed to be the wife of Willoughby Astley, the first manager of the Chalet Lake Louise. Annette was actually Astley's mother.

Lake Annette is fed by melting ice and snow from Mt. Temple.

Lake Annette to Upper Paradise Valley

From Lake Annette the trail climbs steeply southwest onto a bench covered in rockslide débris. This is a good place to see pikas, and perhaps a wolverine. This section of trail is usually snowbound and muddy until mid-July. The apex of the trail features a grand prospect ahead to the tremendous cirque of Horseshoe Glacier and the peaks that ring the head of Paradise Valley. Highest is Hungabee Mountain (hun-GAH-bee) (3493 m). This Native name was bestowed by explorer Samuel Allen in 1894, and appropriately means "Chieftain." You can see the Slate Range to the northeast, and the glacier serac wall on the north face of Mt. Temple to the southeast.

Near the end of the 3 km traverse beneath Mt. Temple,

Porcupine

Protected by a coat of 30,000 barbed quills, the porcupine is often seen ambling comically along trails and through the undergrowth in upper subalpine forests. The quills cannot be shot at a would-be attacker, and are not poisonous. However, they detach easily, barbed end first, and work their way painfully into flesh.

The porcupine's natural diet consists mostly of the sugary cambium layer beneath the bark of coniferous trees. As with

many animals, artificial additives have been added to the porcupine diet: salt-stained boots and backpacks, plywood glue, and antifreeze and brake fluid on parked vehicles.

The porcupine is nocturnal, and will often keep campers awake by chewing on outhouses or by serenading with an eerie, child-like cry.

Lynx, bobcat, cougar, wolverine and bears are predators of porcupines. They kill a porcupine by reaching beneath it and tearing open the abdomen. This is dangerous; a muzzle full of quills can mean death by starvation.

The Giant Steps

everyone who has camped here has a good porcupine story. Porcupines eat leaves and the tender cambium layer within tree bark. Like many other animals, they also have a fondness for anything salty. Boots and pack straps are prime porcupine cuisine, especially at night . Keep your boots inside your tent!

From the campground, a maze of paths leads northeast, merging into a single trail to the Giant Steps, 1 km distant.

Day-hikers should take the righthand fork at the creek junction before the campground. This provides a more direct approach to The Giant Steps, which are reached by turning north (left) in 200 m at the subsequent junction.

The Giant Steps are a series of overlapping quartzite slabs in the north fork of Paradise Creek. Scratches on the slabs are striations, caused by rocks imbedded in the underside of Horseshoe Glacier when it most recently advanced across this area. By looking at the striations, you can tell the glacier's direction of flow. Depressions in the slabs have filled with thin soil, in which miniature gardens of lichens, mosses and wildflowers have taken hold. Please avoid stepping on them.

> *"We saw a new group of mountains in the distance, while a most beautiful valley lay far below us. Throughout a broad expanse of meadows and open country, many streams were to be seen winding through this valley, clearly traceable to their various sources in glaciers, springs and melting snowdrifts."*
>
> —Walter Wilcox,
> the discovery of
> Paradise Valley in 1894,
> *The Rockies of Canada*

The trail emerges at the uppermost cascades. To reach the more picturesque lower falls, backtrack to the approach trail, and follow faint paths downstream. Use caution on the slippery rock slabs, and be on the lookout for ice on cold days.

Loop Hike Exit

To complete this loop hike, keep left at junctions on your return from The Giant Steps to reach the Paradise Valley trail in 800 m. Turn northeast (left), and descend the valley to the Lake Annette junction, crossing the creek twice on bridges. From the Lake Annette junction, retrace the first 5.1 km of this hike to the trailhead.

the quartzite towers that flank Pinnacle Mountain (3067 m) come into view. Highest of the pinnacles is the Grand Sentinel. At the base of Mt. Lefroy across Paradise Valley, "Mitre Glacier" terminates in a classic moraine-dammed lake. The cliffs of Mt. Ringrose (3281 m), Glacier Peak (3283 m) and Mt. Lefroy (3423 m) are alive with snow avalanches on warm afternoons. At the Sentinel Pass junction, turn northwest (right) and descend over a rock glacier to Paradise Creek. En route, Neptuak Mountain (3237 m) is framed through Wastach Pass to the southwest. A wooden sign points toward the pass, however there is no maintained trail in that direction.

Cross Paradise Creek on a bridge. The trail forks. The lefthand fork leads to the campground in 300 m. Almost

Sentinel Pass is the highest point reached by maintained trail in the Rockies. The Wenkchemna Peaks ring the horizon in this view south. The Minnestimma Lakes dot the meadows beneath the pass. Their name means "sleeping waters."

16. Sentinel Pass

Route

Day-hike or overnight, 11.6 to 19.4 km

Route	Elevation (m)	Distance (km)
Trailhead, Moraine Lake	1888	0
Larch Valley/ Sentinel Pass jct	2241	2.4
Sentinel Pass	2611	5.8
Paradise Valley jct	2119	8.1
Lake Annette	1966	11.2
Paradise Creek trailhead	1729	16.9

Topographic map: 82 N/8
Best lighting: any time

Trailhead

From Lake Louise Village, follow Lake Louise Drive 3 km to the Moraine Lake Road. Turn south (left). Follow this road 12 km to its end at Moraine Lake. The trailhead is on the lakeshore, south of the lodge.

Few destinations better exemplify the primal nature of the Rockies than the barren cleft of Sentinel Pass.

Sandwiched between the shattered ramparts of Pinnacle Mountain and Mt. Temple, the pass is the highest point reached by maintained trail in the Rockies, and provides you with a toehold in the domain of mountaineers. The steep slopes on either side of the pass will be treacherous when snow covered. If you are hiking this trail before mid-July, you should carry an ice axe and be proficient in its use.

This excursion lends itself to four variations:
1. Ascend to the crest of the pass and return the same way to Moraine Lake, 11.6 km round-trip.
2. Cross Sentinel Pass to Paradise Valley. Exit from Paradise Valley via Lake Annette to the Moraine Lake Road, 16.9 km total.
3. Cross Sentinel Pass to Paradise Valley. Visit

Columbian ground squirrel

the Giant Steps and exit along the valley bottom trail to the Moraine Lake Road, 19.4 km total.

4. Same as #3, but stay overnight at the Paradise Valley campground.

You can commence this outing with a short sidetrip along the interpretive trail to the top of the Moraine Lake Rockpile (see Classic Hike # 17).

Moraine Lake to Sentinel Pass

From the trailhead kiosk in front of the lodge, follow the trail southwest for 35 m to a junction. The Sentinel Pass/Wenkchemna Pass trail branches north (right), and

Please see map on page 80

immediately begins its steep climb. In the next 2.5 km, the trail gains 352 m to the entrance to Larch Valley. Moraine Lake is visible through the trees. The climb concludes with a series of 10 switchbacks that lead to a trail junction and a well-placed bench. The trail to Larch Valley and Sentinel Pass branches north (right).

Larch Valley occupies a broad glacial cirque centred on a bedrock fault south of Sentinel Pass. The trail winds its way into the lower valley and crosses a footbridge to a meadow. As early morning visitors will discover, the meadow is a frost hollow where cold air collects. Trees along the northern edge of the meadow display branches stunted by the cold. The meadow contains frost hummocks, formations caused by a churning action during repeated freezing and thawing of the damp soil. Columbian ground squirrels are common in this area. Directly southwest is Deltaform Mountain (3424 m), highest of the Wenkchemna Peaks. Walter Wilcox named the mountain for its resemblance to the Greek letter "delta."

The trail swings north and climbs to treeline, passing some ancient larches, and glades filled with western anemone. The three lakes in

Lyall's Larch: Gold in the Hills

Larch Valley is named for the tree, Lyall's (LIE-ulls) larch. Of the three larch species in Canada, Lyall's is the least extensive in range. In the Rockies, the species is found no farther north than Clearwater Pass, 28 km north of Lake Louise. It grows only in the upper subalpine forest, frequently forming pure stands at treeline. The mature tree is 5-10 metres tall and has a ragged top. Bright green needles grow from black knobby twigs that are covered in dark woolly down. The wood burns easily, but because the tree usu-

ally grows in rocky terrain, larch forests are seldom consumed by forest fires. Some trees in Larch

Valley may be more than 400 years old.

Lyall's larch is a deciduous conifer – it sheds its needles in early autumn. Then the tree goes dormant with the buds for next year's growth already formed. Before shedding, larch needles turn golden yellow, transforming the treeline forests of the southern Rockies into a wonderful sight. Visitors flock to Larch Valley in autumn – more than 8300 came in September 1992. The tree was named for David Lyall, a Scottish surgeon and naturalist with the British Boundary Commission.

the tundra below Sentinel Pass were called Minnestimma Lakes by Samuel Allen, a companion of Wilcox. The name means "sleeping waters." From the outlet of the middle lake, the trail heads east and begins the stiff climb along the lower flank of Mt. Temple to the switchbacks that lead into Sentinel Pass.

Sentinel Pass to Paradise Valley

Sentinel Pass is a vast ruin of nature indeed. The chief agent of erosion at work here is mechanical weathering. Water expands 9 percent when frozen. Repeated freezing and thawing of water in cracks, wedges the fissures open. Eventually, boulders, cliffs and mountainsides succumb to this incessant process.

The view south from the pass features the Wenkchemna Peaks, from Mt. Fay (3234 m) in the east, to Deltaform Mountain in the west. Mt. Fay was named for Professor Charles Fay, mountaineer and founder of the Appalachian Mountain Club and the American Alpine Club. Fay made 25 visits to the Rockies between 1894 and 1930, the year of his death. The large pinnacle to the north of the pass is the 120 m high Grand Sentinel, a favourite objective of rock climbers.

Sentinel Pass was first reached in 1894 by Samuel Allen, who ascended from a camp in Paradise Valley. A few days later, Allen, Wilcox and L.F. Frissell returned to the pass and climbed Mt. Temple,

the first time a mountain exceeding 3353 m (11,000 ft) had been climbed in Canada. Today it is the "regular route" on the mountain. On a fair summer day, as many as a hundred mountaineers may make the trip to Mt. Temple's summit by this route.

North from the pass, the trail is poorly defined as it switchbacks steeply down through scree and boulders on the west side of the valley. Take care not to dislodge rocks onto people below. After the initial descent, the trail angles across the valley floor (follow cairns) to the east side. The grade lessens and the way becomes obvious. The pinnacles on the north slope of Pinnacle Mountain are silhouetted against the sky, offering intriguing possibilities to photographers.

Paradise Valley Options

At the trail junction 2.3 km north of Sentinel Pass, you can chose between two options for concluding this hike. If you would like to visit The Giant Steps or camp in the backcountry campground in Paradise Valley, keep straight ahead at this junction. The trail descends across a rock glacier to Paradise Creek, from where a sidetrail leads to The Giant Steps. It is 10.9 km from the junction to the Moraine Lake Road via The Giant Steps.

A shorter exit is to turn northeast (right) at this junction and follow the highline route beneath the north face of Mt. Temple to Lake An-

nette, and then to the Moraine Lake Road. Distance for this option is 8.8 km. Either way you should have transportation prearranged. The Paradise Creek parking lot is 9.7 km by road from Moraine Lake, and 5.3 km from Lake Louise Village.

"Opposite was a pinnacled mountain stained red and grey, rent into thousands of narrow gullies or beetling turrets by the wear of ages. It was a vast ruin of nature, a barren mass of tottering walls and cliffs, raising two lofty summits upwards."

—Walter Wilcox describing Pinnacle Mountain and the environs of Sentinel Pass in 1893, *The Rockies of Canada*

The Wenkchemna Pass trail traverses the length of the Valley of the Ten Peaks to the lofty pass on the continental divide, the second highest point reached by maintained trail in the Rockies.

17. Wenkchemna Pass

Route

Day-hike, 9.7 km

Route	Elevation (m)	Distance (km)
Trailhead, Moraine Lake	1888	0
Larch Valley/ Sentinel Pass jct	2241	2.7
Eiffel Lakes	2287	6.0
Wenkchemna Pass	2600	9.7

Topographic map: 82 N/8
Best lighting: morning

Trailhead

From Lake Louise Village, follow Lake Louise Drive 3 km to the Moraine Lake Road. Turn south (left). Follow this road 12 km to its end at Moraine Lake. The trailhead is on the lakeshore, south of the lodge.

The Wenkchemna Pass trail travels the length of the Valley of the Ten Peaks to a barren, rocky saddle on the crest of the continental divide. The hike is dominated by the imposing northern aspect of the Wenkchemna Peaks. Forests of Lyall's larch, intriguing geology and human history add to the appeal of this hike. Wenkchemna Pass is the second highest point reached by maintained trail in the Rockies, and most years is snowbound until early July.

Moraine Lake to Eiffel Lakes

From the trailhead kiosk on the shore of Moraine Lake, follow the trail southwest for 35 m to a junction. The Sentinel Pass/Wenkchemna Pass trail branches north (right), and immediately begins its climb. In the next 2.5 km, the trail gains 352 m to the entrance to

Larch Valley. Moraine Lake is visible through the trees. The climb concludes with a series of 10 switchbacks, leading to a trail junction and a well-placed bench. The trail to Larch Valley and Sentinel Pass branches north (right). Keep straight ahead (west) for Wenkchemna Pass.

For the next 2 km, the trail travels at treeline across the southern flank of Eiffel Peak (3084 m), offering views ahead to Wenkchemna Pass and back to the western end of Moraine Lake. In 1893, Walter Wilcox and Samuel Allen were the first to see the upper part of this valley. Wilcox was so taken aback by the austere appearance of the Wenkchemna Peaks and the chaos of rubble at their bases, he coined the name Desolation Valley.

Most of the rubble in the

Please see map on page 80

Valley of the Ten Peaks is surface moraine that covers the 4 km² Wenkchemna Glacier. This peculiar body of ice is sustained primarily by snow and ice avalanches from couloirs on the north faces of the Wenkchemna Peaks. The more easterly part of the glacier is now stagnant and detached from the active glacial ice. Insulated by the moraine on its surface, this huge mass of ice will take centuries to melt if the glacier does not advance again and re-incorporate it.

The rubble-covered glacier features conical talus (TAY-luss) piles, mounds of rock created by avalanches. These piles have been carried from the base of the cliffs by the moving ice. The glacier's surface is dotted with kettle ponds, formed by slumping and melting of ice-cored

moraines. A sinuous terminal moraine winds along the glacier's northern margin. Wilcox was right: it is a scene of desolation, but not without beauty.

Samuel Allen named ten of the mountains in this valley with the Stoney words for the numbers, 1 to 10 – "Wenkchemna" means "ten." Allen's application of nomenclature was somewhat arbitrary, since there are eighteen mountains in the valley. Only three of the Wenkchemna Peaks still bear Allen's names. Tonsa or "Peak 4" (3054 m) is directly south across the valley from this point. Wenkchemna Pass is flanked by Wenkchemna Peak (3173 m) on the north, and by Neptuak Mountain, "Peak 9" (3237 m) on the southeast.

After you cross an avalanche slope, the picturesque Eiffel Lakes come into view. These lakes, fringed with larch trees, occupy depressions in rockslide debris.

The Rockpile: When is a Moraine Not a Moraine?

Y ou can begin this hike with a short side-trip along the interpretive trail to the top of the Moraine Lake Rockpile. Samuel Allen called the lake Heejee Lake in 1893. Walter Wilcox paid the first visit to its shores in 1899, and called it Moraine Lake because he thought it was dammed by a glacial moraine. The rockpile is now thought to be rockslide debris, although

Moraine Lake and the Wenkchemna Peaks

some geologists think it may be rockslide débris that was transported on the surface of a glacier

– which would make it both rockslide and moraine.

Most of the boulders in the rockpile are Gog quartzite, one of the oldest and hardest rock types in the Rockies. You can see fossilized worm burrowings and an example of ripple rock. This rock records the action of wavelets on a prehistoric shoreline, 560 million years ago.

The Eiffel Lakes are shallow ponds that occupy depressions in rockslide debris. The forbidding north faces of the Wenkchemna Peaks are the backdrop.

"Immense piles of débris rested against the mountain opposite, at the base of which was a desolate valley half filled with glacier and confused moraines. No tree or green vegetation of any kind appeared in all this barren scene."

—Walter Wilcox, describing the first view of the Valley of the Ten Peaks in 1893, *The Rockies of Canada*

They were a favourite destination of Wilcox, who would pack his 11x14-inch plate camera here late in the summer, when he thought the scenery was at its best. Wilcox called them the "Wenkchemna Lakes." The name "Eiffel" refers to a tower of rock on the mountain to the north. This tower supposedly resembles the Eiffel Tower in Paris. The lakes do not support fish.

The massive rockslide that contains the Eiffel Lakes originated on the north face of Neptuak Mountain, and carried across the valley floor. The prominent peak to the northwest is Hungabee (hun-GAH-bee) Mountain (3493 m). Hungabee means "Chieftain." The mountain is the second highest in the area after Mt. Temple, and commands the head of nearby Paradise Valley.

Eiffel Lakes to Wenkchemna Pass

West of the Eiffel Lakes, the trail is rough as it crosses boulderfields. The going becomes easier as the trail winds through an upper subalpine meadow bisected by several streams – the last water sources before the pass.

From the meadows, the trail angles southwest and then switchbacks upwards through more boulderfields. The quartzite boulders underfoot rest on the surface of a rock glacier – an accumulation of rock and ice that allows the entire mass to creep slowly downhill. There are several small kettle lakes northwest of the trail. The ground-dwelling white-tailed ptarmigan are often seen as you approach Wenkchemna Pass. Their plumage changes colour from white in winter to a mottled brown, grey and black in summer. The tail is always white.

On the final section of trail you toil across a scree slope before descending slightly onto Wenkchemna Pass.

The trackless west slope of the pass plunges to the upper reaches of Tokumm Creek in Yoho National Park. The rock formation in the meadows there is called Eagle Eyrie. Golden eagles do frequent this area, and when seen from ground level, the rock formation resembles an eagle. The summit of Neptuak Mountain, southeast of the pass, is the only point in Canada where the boundaries of three national parks meet: Yoho, Banff and Kootenay. Looking northeast, the massive bulk of Mt. Temple (3543 m) dominates all other mountains in the area.

Boulder Pass is the gateway to the lakes and valleys of Skoki country. The waters of Ptarmigan Lake lap against the eastern edge of the pass.

18. Skoki

Route

Ptarmigan-Baker-Red Deer-Skoki Valleys
3-5 days, 40.3 km loop

Route	Elevation (m)	Distance (km)
Fish Creek parking lot	1698	0
Temple Research Station	2012	3.7
End of gravel road	2018	3.9
Halfway Hut	2195	7.1
Hidden Lake jct and CG	2195	7.2
Boulder Pass	2345	8.7
Deception Pass jct	2348	10.5
Baker Lake CG	2210	13.2
Baker/Red Deer Divide	2180	15.0
Red Deer Lakes CG	2088	19.0
"Jones' Pass"	2210	22.4
Skoki Valley jct	2195	23.0
Skoki Lodge	2164	23.4
Merlin Meadows CG	2119	24.6
Skoki Valley jct	2195	26.2
Deception Pass	2485	29.2
Boulder Pass	2345	31.6
Fish Creek parking lot	1698	40.3

Trailhead

From the Lake Louise interchange on Highway 1, follow signs for the Lake Louise ski area, northeast along Whitehorn Road for 1.5 km. Turn south (right) onto the Fish Creek road. Follow this gravel road 1.0 km until it becomes restricted access. Park in the parking lot on the south (right).

Topographic maps: 82 N/8, 82 N/9, 82 O/5, 82 O/12

The area known as Skoki encompasses a series of compact valleys in the Slate Range northeast of Lake Louise. Much of the Skoki (SKOWE-key) area is at or above treeline, and sixteen lakes, each with its own unique character, will be found nearby. Grizzly bear, moose, wolverine, mule deer, elk, coyote, bighorn sheep and mountain goats frequent these valleys. In recent years, wolves have also been seen.

This outing is a counterclockwise loop hike. You can add a variety of day-hikes from the four backcountry campgrounds. Mountaineers can make straightforward ascents of more than a dozen nearby summits. Completing the charm of the Skoki area is its vibrant human history.

Fish Creek to Boulder Pass

The outing commences with a stiff climb along the Temple access road. Views are limited, except from the top of "Ford Hill," where Mt. Victoria (3464 m) and other summits near Lake Louise are visible to the west. Keep straight ahead at junctions until the road ends 200 m beyond the Temple Avalanche Research Station at the Lake Louise ski area. Angle steeply uphill across the ski run to the Skoki trail.

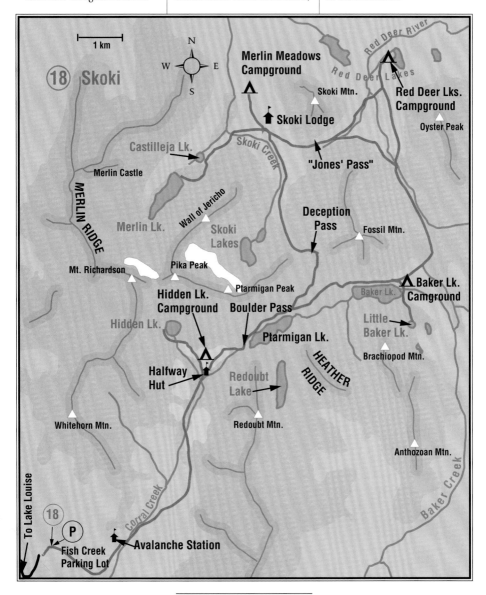

The trail follows Corral Creek through upper sub-alpine forest. Some work on the Skoki trail was done by Ukranian prisoners during World War I. Common wildlife species here are: red squirrel, porcupine, gray jay, Clark's nutcracker, American marten and mule deer.

At km 6.8, the forest thins. Cross Corral Creek to its west bank. Use caution if the bridge is frosty. Directly ahead are the three highest summits of the Slate Range, from west to east: Mt. Richardson (3086 m), Pika Peak (3052 m) and Ptarmigan Peak (3059 m). Mt. Richardson was named by James Hector, for John Richardson, surgeon and naturalist with the Franklin Arctic expeditions of 1819 and 1825. The Slate Range is home to approximately 40 mountain goats.

Halfway Hut (also called Ptarmigan Hut) is on the opposite bank of the north fork of Corral Creek. The cabin was constructed in 1931 as a stopover for ski guests of Skoki Lodge, and for guides and packers making supply trips. The

Mt. Temple is the highest mountain in the Lake Louise area, and is visible from meadows along Corral Creek en route to Boulder Pass.

building is halfway between the Lake Louise railway station and Skoki Lodge.

Many sober and reputable travellers have reported unusual sights and sounds near Halfway Hut. The ghosts of four skiers killed in avalanches are said to haunt the building. They schuss down from Ptarmigan Peak to convene a nightly poker game in winter. Today, the hut is a day-use shelter only. It is located on the site of a prehistoric Native encampment. There are fine views of Mt. Temple (3543 m) and some of the Wenkchemna Peaks from the meadows nearby. Porcupines, Columbian ground squirrels and wolverines are frequently seen here.

The Hidden Lake junction

Hidden Lake, 1.3 km

The sidetrip to Hidden Lake is recommended if you are staying at the nearby campground, or day-hiking to Boulder Pass. The trail departs from the campground and follows the north fork of Corral Creek. Wildflowers fill the glades in the treeline larch forest. Rock-hop the stream just below the lake's outlet, and follow the wet track to the lakeshore.

Hidden Lake is a typical glacial tarn, 32.3 m deep. Cutthroat trout inhabit the waters. Mountain goats and bighorn sheep are often seen on the cliffs north of the lake. Redoubt Mountain (2902 m) looms across the valley to the southeast.

is 100 m north of Halfway Hut. The adjacent backcountry campground is less than four hours travel from the trailhead for most parties, making it possible to start this hike late in the day in early summer, with the assurance of reaching a campground before dark.

Horse traffic makes the initial 500 m of trail between Halfway Hut and Boulder Pass very muddy. The final kilometre winds through massive quartzite boulders of rockslide débris from Redoubt Mountain. The mountain was named because of its "redoubtable," fortress-like appearance. If you look back during the climb, you may see the large boulder that perfectly matches the shape of dis-

tant Mt. Temple.

Boulder Pass is the gateway to the spectacular upper subalpine environment of Skoki. The centrepiece in the view is Ptarmigan Lake, which laps against the eastern side of the pass. On rare calm days, the lake mirrors Fossil Mountain (2946 m) and the distant summits of Mt. Douglas (3235 m) and Mt. St. Bride (3312 m), the two highest mountains in the Sawback Range. True to the name of the lake and nearby peak, the white-tailed ptarmigan, a ground-dwelling grouse, is often seen on the pass.

Boulder Pass to Baker Lake

The Skoki trail is rocky and wet in places as it contours along the north shore of Ptarmigan Lake. Krummholz tree islands of spruce and fir dot the tundra. Cotton grass grows along the lakeshore. You should be prepared for poor weather in this vicinity. When the clouds are down on the hills, Ptarmigan Lake can be one of the bleakest places in the Rockies. Summer snowfalls are common and winds are often strong and bitterly cold. The Deception Pass junction is 1.9 km from Boulder Pass. Keep straight ahead for Baker Lake.

The trail contours through

A Textbook Landscape

The vicinity of Ptarmigan Lake marks the transition from the eastern main ranges to the front ranges. The eastern main ranges were created 120 million years ago. The mountains contain resistant limestone, dolomite and quartzite cliffs alternating with layers of recessive shale. The strata are horizontal or angle slightly upwards to the northeast.

If you look at Ptarmigan Peak, you can see it rests on a massive sandwich of alternating resistant and recessive sedimentary layers. This rock sandwich is the Pipestone Pass

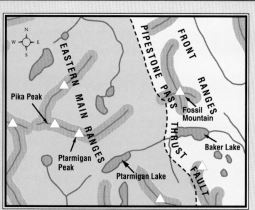

Thrust Sheet, an assemblage of rocks that slid 60 km during mountain building, upwards and over younger rocks. The steep drop between Ptarmigan and Baker Lakes indicates the leading edge of the thrust sheet.

In contrast, the younger rocks of mountains farther east

were thrust skyward 85 million years ago when the front ranges were created. The sedimentary formations of front range mountains, like Fossil Mountain, are tilted steeply upwards to the northeast, creating sawtooth and overthrust mountain forms.

In few places in the Rockies is it as easy to grasp the complex concept of thrust sheets, and the differences between the eastern main ranges and front ranges. Here you can look at the profile of Ptarmigan Peak and compare it with mountains to the east.

several shale gullies southwest of Fossil Mountain, and then descends through stunted subalpine forest to Baker Lake. Follow the north shore of the lake through willows to the Baker Lake campground near the outlet. The lake is popular for fishing cutthroat trout and eastern brook trout. During July and August, the campground is one of the buggiest spots in the Rockies. Porcupines and snowshoe hares frequent the tenting area.

Baker Lake to Red Deer Lakes

At the junction 50 m east of Baker Lake campground, keep north (left). From the junction, the trail contours through open subalpine forest dotted with larches, and then descends to the

Moose tracks

treeless tundra of the valley floor. The exceptional wildflowers here include elephant head and dense clumps of vibrantly coloured Indian paintbrush.

Cyclone Mountain (3041 m) and its eastern outlier Pipestone Mountain (2970 m) are prominent directly north. Cyclone was named in 1910 by a mountaineering party who studied routes on the mountain while a thunderstorm gathered over its summit. The sedimentary formations of Pipestone Mountain feature an anticline.

About 2 km from the campground, you cross the unremarkable height of land that separates Baker Creek from the Red Deer River. Perhaps because it is almost un-

recognizable as a mountain pass, this well-travelled feature is yet to be officially named. Broad mountain passes are frequently boggy like this one. Without a steep gradient to direct the flow of streams and springs, water collects into pools and marshes. The sedges and willows that grow in these areas make them excellent habitat for moose.

A trail branches northwest (left) to the Skoki Valley, 2.8 km from Baker Lake campground. Those who do not want to include the Red Deer Lakes in this outing should follow this trail. It climbs over the shoulder of Fossil Mountain into "Jones' Pass." Using this route, the distance between Baker Lake and Merlin Meadows campgrounds is

Little Baker Lake, 1.2 km

Little Baker Lake is one of three lakes tucked under the east flank of Brachiopod Mountain. Rock-hop the outlet of Baker Lake and follow beaten paths through larch forest to the southeast. Look back at Fossil Mountain to see the incredible Z-shaped overturned fold in the upper part of the south face.

The maze of paths here defies sensible description. Pass a small unnamed pond (not shown on the topographic map) along its east shore. Using a topographic map

Baker Lake is the first night's stop for many hikers on the Skoki loop. The lake is situated at the transition between the eastern main ranges and the front ranges.

to keep your orientation, continue to Little Baker Lake. There are views to Tilted Lake en route. Brachiopod Lake is farther

south. However, this seasonal pond frequently dries up by late summer.

shortened to 8.5 km, and the total distance for the loop hike is reduced to 34.3 km.

To continue to Red Deer Lakes, keep straight ahead at this junction, and the one following. The trail enters a 250-year-old spruce-fir forest, and soon deteriorates into horse-churned muck. You must make several awkward, stream hops during the next 700 m, after which the sidetrail to Red Deer Lakes campground

branches east (right).

The nearby Red Deer Lakes are popular fishing holes, and were formerly stocked to promote angling. Research has indicated that the rainbow trout, eastern brook trout and cutthroat trout present are no longer reproducing. Continued fishing will ultimately deplete the lakes. There is a maze of muddy trails on the surrounding willow plain. Mt. Hector (3394 m), the highest

peak in this part of Banff National Park, dominates the view west. The middle Red Deer Lake was called "Hatchet Lake" by participants of the 1915 Alpine Club of Canada camp, because of the shape of its shoreline. The Red Deer River was known to the Cree as "Elk River," because of the numerous elk (wapiti) in the upper watershed. Europeans know the elk as "red deer," and the first white visitors ap-

Skoki Lodge and Ken Jones

Skoki Lodge

Ken Jones

The unofficial name for the pass between Skoki and Fossil mountains was suggested by the late Jon Whyte. In 1936, Skoki Lodge was enlarged and a new ridgepole was sought for the roof. Outfitter and woods-man Ken Jones scoured the Skoki area for a tree of suitable length, finding one at Douglas Lake, more than 13 km to the east. Using a horse team, it took Jones a week to skid the tree to Skoki Lodge via 'Jones' Pass." Ken Jones is testimony to the youth-giving properties of a mountain life. He was still helping out with maintenance and chores at the lodge in 1993, at the age of 80.

Merlin Lake, 2.9 km

Mt. Richardson rises from the shores of Merlin Lake. Like many lakes set in limestone bedrock, Merlin Lake drains underground.

In a landscape overflowing with lakes, Merlin Lake is without question the most scenic. However, the trail to the lake will not be to everyone's liking. It's an up-and-down affair, routed across boulderfields and up a steep limestone headwall. The destination more than compensates for the demands of the approach. Lawrence Grassi, renowned for his trail construction in the Lake O'Hara area in Yoho, worked on part of this trail.

The trailhead is at creekside, directly opposite the front door of Skoki Lodge. The purplish rock in the creek bed is Miette shale. The trail winds through pleasant upper subalpine forest for 300 m to a junction. Turn west (right). You then climb onto a sideslope of quartzite boulders, which have appropriately tumbled from the Wall of Jericho. The blooms of red-stemmed saxifrage, mountain sorrel, yellow columbine and arnica brighten up the rocky slopes. Views north include Mt. Willingdon (3373 m), Cataract Peak (3333 m), Cyclone Mountain and unnamed summits on the west side of the Drummond Icefield.

The trail crosses a low ridge west of the boulderfield. The author once encountered a wolverine here. The Merlin Valley is ideal habitat for this largest terrestrial member of the weasel family.

Descend from the ridge on a rocky trail, and follow cairns where necessary. Unfortunately a number of paths have been marked, only serving to confuse the route. During the descent your eyes will no doubt be fixed on remarkably coloured Castilleja (cass-TIH-lee-uh) Lake. *Castilleja* is the genus name of the wildflower, Indian paintbrush.

The trail draws alongside the south shore of Castilleja Lake. Then you commence an excruciatingly steep climb south on scree slopes. At the top of this climb, follow cairns west to the Merlin Lake headwall. Ascend a scree gully through the headwall and then descend west over limestone pavement to the lakeshore. Take care not to knock rocks onto your companions while you are in the gully.

The glaciated north face of Mt. Richardson creates an exceptional backdrop for Merlin Lake. The lake takes its name from nearby Merlin Castle, an assembly of quartzite pinnacles that J.F. Porter likened to an Arthurian castle.

Merlin was a prophet and magician of Arthurian legend. Porter may have had another intention in mind when he gave the name, for Merlin Lake demonstrates some of nature's magic. If you walk along the lake's northeast shore, you may be puzzled at the absence of an outlet stream. Yet you probably noticed Castilleja Lake received an inlet stream from above. As with many lakes set in limestone bedrock in the Rockies, Merlin Lake is a karst feature, and it drains underground.

When Porter's party visited the lake, they noticed evidence of an abandoned surface outlet, along with driftwood that marked an ancient high-water level. This indicates Merlin Lake's subterranean outlet is, in geological terms, of recent origin. Since the driftwood has not yet completely decomposed, the change to underground drainage probably occurred within the last 200 years. With care, you can search the upper headwall northeast of the lake for a natural "window" that allows a glimpse within the Cathedral limestone bedrock to the underground stream. It's a remarkable sight, for the stream is an underground waterfall. Merlin indeed!

plied this name to the river and lakes.

Red Deer Lakes to Merlin Meadows Campground

From Red Deer Lakes campground, backtrack south 700 m to the first junction. Turn west (right), hop the creek, and follow the trail heading west into "Jones' Pass." The trail from the Baker/Red Deer Divide merges with this trail at an avalanche slope just before the crest of the pass. This area is often fragrant with the resin of spruce trees downed in avalanches of the previous winter. Straight ahead (southwest) is the Wall of Jericho (2910 m), and Ptarmigan Peak. West from the pass, sections of trail have been gravel-capped. The trail swings northwest and descends to the Skoki Valley junction. Turn north (right). Skoki Lodge is in 400 m.

The first detailed exploration of the Skoki area was by the J.F. Porter mountaineering party in 1911. Porter bestowed many names still in use today. The name "Skokie" was given to the wet meadow at the present site of Merlin Meadows campground. Skokie is a native word Porter brought from his Illinois home. It means "marsh."

In 1930, ski enthusiasts Cliff White and Cyril Paris of Banff sought a place to build the first ski lodge in the Rockies. Because of abundant snowfall and variety of skiing slopes, they chose the Skoki Valley. Originally intended to be a ski club cabin only, the lodge opened in the winter of 1931. But soon it became a commercial enterprise. It now operates seasonally in summer and winter. To reach Merlin Meadows campground, continue north through the lodge grounds for another 1.2 km.

Merlin Meadows to Fish Creek

The homeward trail departs south from Merlin Meadows campground. Keep straight ahead at the junction 400 m south of Skoki Lodge. The trail climbs 300 m in the next 3 km, to Deception Pass. The pass was named by skier Cyril Paris for a reason that will soon be obvious: it's farther to the crest than it looks.

Deception Pass provides a tremendous panorama of the Slate Range, Ptarmigan Lake, the Bow Range near Lake Louise, and more distant points north and south. White-tailed ptarmigan are frequently seen here. Skiers in winter find ascent and descent of this pass can be perilous.

Descend south on slopes of compacted shale to the Boulder Pass trail, and turn west (right). The remainder of the trail is on familiar ground, retracing the first 10.6 km of this outing along the shore of Ptarmigan Lake and over Boulder Pass, to the Fish Creek parking lot. There is a pay phone at Whiskeyjack Lodge in the Lake Louise ski area, 1 km north from the parking lot along the Cat track.

"*We moved our camp to the lower of the two small lakes west of Fossil Mt., one of the most beautiful sky-blue nameless foundlings. We called it Lake Myosotis, not only on account of its colour, but also because of its forget-me-not qualities. It is in fact a miniature Lake Louise. Ptarmigan Peak, Pika Peak and a thin jagged mountain we called the Wall of Jericho, embrace it on three sides. A fine hanging foot from the Ptarmigan and Pike [Pika] glaciers almost reaches the shores of the lake above and sends down a daily avalanche of icebergs. Both of these lakes are held back by high perpendicular dams over which water flows in attractive falls.*"

—Mountaineer J.F. Porter describing Lower Skoki Lake, *Canadian Alpine Journal*, 1912. (*Myosotis* is the genus of the alpine forget-me-not.)

Upper Fish Lake is one of several destinations accessible from Mosquito Creek.

19. Mosquito Creek

Route

Day-hike or overnight
Molar Pass 10.3 km
Molar Meadows & North Molar Pass 11.5 km
Fish Lakes 14.8 km

Route	Elevation (m)	Distance (km)
Mosquito Creek trailhead	1828	0
Mosquito Creek CG	2012	5.4
Molar Pass jct.	2195	6.9
Molar Pass Option:		
Molar Pass	2365	10.3
North Molar Pass/Fish Lakes Option		
"Mosquito Lake"	2302	8.8
North Molar Pass	2593	11.5
Upper Fish Lake CG	2220	14.8

Topographic map: 82 N/9

Trailhead

Mosquito Creek on the Icefields Parkway (Highway 93), 25.6 km north of Lake Louise. The parking lot is on the west side of the Parkway, south of the bridge. The Mosquito Creek trailhead is on the opposite side of the Parkway, north of the bridge. Cross the road with caution.

With its high starting elevation, the Mosquito Creek trail grants quick access to one of the loftiest and most sublime alpine environments described in *Classic Hikes*. You have several options. You can day-hike from the highway to either Molar Pass or North Molar Pass; you can make an overnight trip to Fish Lakes; or you can use the Mosquito Creek backcountry campground as a base for leisurely exploration of all three destinations. This is a wonderful way to immerse yourself for a few days in the high alpine environment of Banff National Park. The Mosquito Creek trail is used by commercial horse parties. Avoid this trail during wet weather, when muck and mire prevails. The valley, meadows and passes are frequented by grizzly bears. Travel accordingly.

Icefields Parkway to Molar Pass Junction

The trail climbs steeply up the bank of Mosquito Creek and then angles across the right-of-way cleared in the 1930s for the Wonder Road, precursor of the Icefields Parkway. The next 1.9 km is through open coniferous forest with a vari-ety of subalpine wildflowers in the undergrowth. The forest in this valley last burned in 1830, in a large fire that also con-sumed much of the upper Bow Valley. The rooted and rocky trail drops to creekside and then travels across willow plain. Rock-hop as necessary.

The trail crosses the north

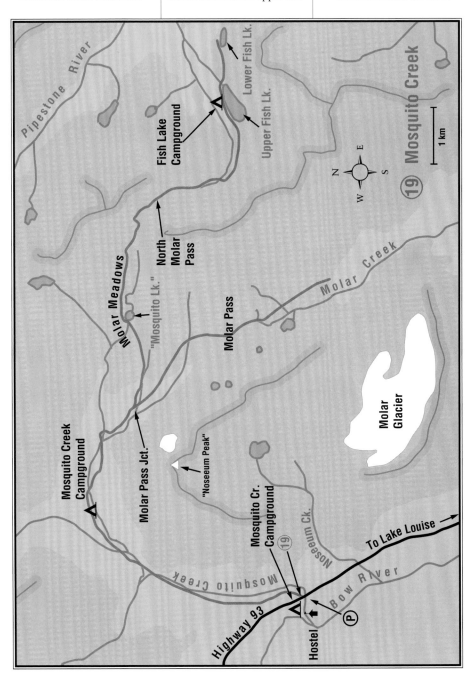

Molar Pass

fork of Mosquito Creek on a two-log bridge, and continues through forest to the Mosquito Creek campground at km 5.4. The campground is set amongst Eldon limestone boulders of an ancient rockslide. Given the horse traffic in this area, you should treat all drinking water here.

The trail beyond the campground is notorious for its muck holes and braiding, especially during early summer and after rains. The trail crosses the creek on a bridge and follows the bank for roughly 1 km. It then recrosses the creek. The Molar Pass junction is 500 m farther.

Molar Pass

For 1.5 km beyond the Molar Pass junction, you hike on a wet and sometimes sketchy trail through glades of open upper subalpine forest. The exceptional wildflower displays here more than compensate for the poor trail. Look for mountain marsh marigold in the tributary streams. The cliffs to the west are part of the group of summits at the head of Noseeum Creek. The northeast cliffs of the highest peak, "Noseeum Peak" (2988 m), feature a niche glacier. Ahead are views to the craggy entrance to Molar Pass.

Upper subalpine areas, especially those with limestone

A Cold and Rocky Home

At approximately km 3, the trail crosses an alluvial fan that marks the entrance of a tributary stream from the north. Vegetation on this fan is scant. Not only does the rocky soil make tree growth difficult here, but both the tributary stream and Mosquito Creek channel cold air into the valley bottom, shortening the growing season.

Mountain fireweed (river beauty), yellow mountain saxifrage (see photo), red-stemmed saxifrage, yellow paintbrush, ele-

phant head and butterwort are wildflowers that thrive in this cold, damp environment. Butterwort is the most common of the seven carnivorous plants in the Rockies. The pale green leaves at the base of the pretty purple flower, trap and digest insects.

This habitat is also good for sedges. Sedges resemble grasses, but have triangular, solid stems. One of the most common sedges in the Rockies is cotton grass. Its brilliant white tufts contain minuscule flowers. The tufts grace the banks of subalpine streams and marshes in late July and August.

North Molar Pass and Fish Lakes

From the junction 1.5 km beyond Mosquito Creek campground, keep straight ahead and begin a steep climb through treeline. Above is the alpine tundra of Molar Meadows, an exquisite backcountry landscape. The flower-filled meadows occupy 5 km², and

Descending from North Molar Pass to Upper Fish Lake

are a favourite haunt of grizzly bears. An unnamed quartzite spire rises above the southern edge of the meadows, and the castellated towers of Dolomite Peak are prominent in the view west. "Mosquito Lake" (unnamed on the topographic map), its shores fringed with cotton grass, completes this idyllic scene. The lake is an ideal place to rest before the hard work ahead – the climb to North Molar Pass, 280 m of elevation gain in the next 2.7 km.

Rock-hop the lake's outlet and climb away from the north shore. The trail crosses a beautiful alpland, the match of any in the Rockies. On the final approach to North Molar Pass, you may be intrigued by the two rock types visible. Weathered and lichen-covered blocks of Gog quartzite are to the south of the trail. Pink and buff fragments of Cathedral limestone are to the north. The seam between these two rock formations leads directly to the pass.

The ascent culminates in a steep track scraped out of the rubble. The narrow, barren crest of North Molar Pass (2593 m) is the third highest point reached by maintained trail in the Rocky Mountain parks. The pass is named for its proximity to Molar Mountain (3022 m), the summit of which is framed perfectly in the view southeast just before you cross the pass. Those day-hiking from the Icefields Parkway should return at this point. If you are day-hiking from the Mosquito Creek campground, assess your stamina for the 373 m descent to Upper Fish Lake, which you will have to climb on your return.

A perennial snow and ice patch clings to the southeast side of North Molar Pass. Give this treacherous feature a wide berth by crossing high on the slope to the north, then descending steeply to pick up the trail. After an initially abrupt drop, you cross the stream that drains the pass. The trail then begins a rambling, braided descent through sedge and heath meadows toward Upper Fish

Lake. Where the trail again angles to the edge of the stream, rock-hop to the east side. The location of this crossing is sometimes marked by a cairn. It is otherwise easy to miss. Cross the stream again in 1 km on a log bridge upstream from a small canyon.

From the rise just beyond this crossing, you get your first full view of Upper Fish Lake, 100 m below. Cataract Peak (3333 m) is beyond the lake on the east side of the Pipestone Valley. It is one of the highest mountains in the front ranges. Surprisingly, this fine summit was not climbed until 1930.

The Upper Fish Lake campground is set in a grove of spruce, fir and Lyall's larch, 100 m north of the upper lake. The larch trees here are near the northern limit for the species. With fishing no longer allowed at the Fish Lakes, this heavily used campground may see less traffic, and the surrounding vegetation may also recover from the abuses of undisciplined firewood gathering.

If you would like to add more distance to your outing, rock-hop the outlet of Upper Fish Lake and continue to Lower Fish Lake in 1 km.

bedrock, often contain seeps – outlets for rain and snowmelt that has drained underground. As it percolates downwards, the water is intercepted by resistant rock layers. These channel the water laterally to the surface. Woe be to the trail builder who constructs a trail through seep areas like the ones in upper Mosquito Creek! – and to the park manager who permits horse traffic in the mire that results. It is impossible to keep water and mud from underfoot. Please keep to the trail to spare the surrounding vegetation.

The grade steepens as the trail climbs onto drier ground above the creek. Rock-hop a stream that cascades down tilted slabs of quartzite bedrock. Mountain sorrel, leather-leaved saxifrage, alpine forget-me-not, and dense blooms of yellow columbine grow here. The trail switchbacks easily through the cliff at the northern entrance to Molar Pass. From the top of this climb there is an exceptional view north over upper Mosquito Creek, and onto the extensive, rolling alpland of Molar Meadows to the northeast.

Molar Pass is a heath and avens tundra, two kilometres long, that separates the headwaters of Mosquito and Molar creeks. The view south improves as you travel through the pass. Eventually, you can see the summit of Mt. Hector (3394 m), the peaks of the Slate Range, Molar Mountain (3022 m) and its outlying tower (2901 m). James Hector named Molar Mountain in 1858. Viewed from the vicinity of Lake Louise, the mountain and its tower resemble pointed teeth.

The trail traverses the hillside on the east side of the pass. On a visit in 1993, we watched a grizzly bear here from a kilometre away. The bedrock of the pass is Cathedral limestone. Above it to the west is a ledge of Stephen shale. Above this are massive cliffs of Eldon limestone. This is the "Middle Cambrian sandwich" of sedimentary formations that builds many imposing mountain walls in the central Rockies.

The axis of Molar Pass lies along a bedrock fault. On the west side of the pass are huge sheets of fissured Cathedral limestone pavement known as a "clint and grike" landscape. This indicates underground drainage called karst. The "clints" are limestone blocks and the "grikes" are the fissures that separate them. The words come from the dialect of Yorkshire, England, where this kind of landscape is common. There are four picturesque lakelets on the benches west of the pass. They drain underground.

When you start to descend into the upper reaches of Molar Creek it is time to turn around. Your ramblings in Molar Pass will add a few kilometres to the length of this hike.

The Fish Lakes: Poor Fishing

When the Fish Lakes were stocked with cutthroat trout, they offered good prospects to fishermen. Stocking of lakes in Banff to support angling was discontinued in 1988, and angler success here soon decreased rapidly. The Fish Lakes and two other unnamed lakes nearby were closed to angling in 1992 to allow fish stocks to recover through natural regeneration. In these cold, unproductive waters, recovery may take many years. If the Fish Lakes are reopened to angling, it may be as a "catch and release" fishery only. The revised National Parks Policy of 1993 permits stocking of lakes with native species only to assist in recovery or re-establishment of native populations, not to support angling.

"Unworldy beauty was all around us; Hector, the Dolomites, the icy Wahputiks [Waputik Mountains] rising blackly from the ice field behind them ... There rose, too, Mt. Gordon, Bow Mountain and unnumbered others, each demanding to hold the centre of this titanic stage."

—B.W. Mitchell,
Trail Life in the Rockies, 1924

Most of the Dolomite Pass hike is above treeline. The wildflowers in the Helen Creek valley are superb.

20. Dolomite Pass

Route

Day-hike or overnight, 8.9 km

Route	Elevation (m)	Distance (km)
Trailhead	1944	0
Helen Lake	2363	6.0
South shoulder of Cirque Pk	2500	6.9
Lake Katherine	2370	8.1
Dolomite Pass	2393	8.9

Topographic map: 82 N/9
Best lighting: anytime

Trailhead

East side of the Icefields Parkway (Highway 93), 34.5 km north of Lake Louise, opposite the Crowfoot Glacier viewpoint.

For more than 5 km of its length, the Dolomite Pass trail traverses an exceptional alpine environment.

The wildflower displays in the meadows before Helen Lake are superb. Dolomite (DOE-loh-mite) Pass and the valleys it connects are a principal travel route and prime summer habitat for grizzly bears. Two of the rarest mammals in the Rockies, the mountain caribou and the wolf, are also sometimes seen. The trail is used by commercial horse parties.

Icefields Parkway to Helen Lake

The first 3 km of trail ascends steadily as it contours around the south end of the outlying ridge of Cirque Peak. From treeline there are expansive views into the Bow Valley. Mt. Hec-

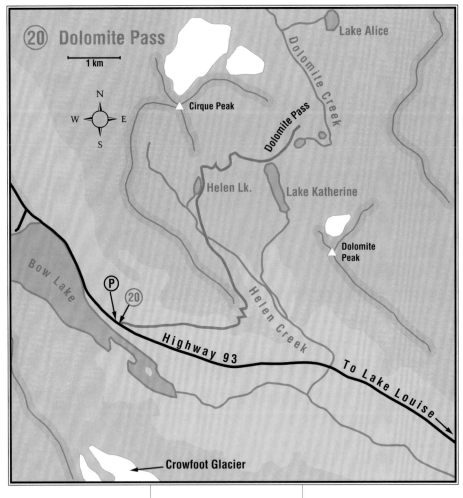

㉕ **Dolomite Pass**

1 km

N W E S

Lake Alice

Cirque Peak

Dolomite Creek

Dolomite Pass

Helen Lk.

Lake Katherine

Dolomite Peak

Bow Lake

P ㉕

Helen Creek

Highway 93

To Lake Louise

Crowfoot Glacier

tor (3394 m) is the prominent glacier-clad peak, 14 km south. Directly west, above the outlet of Bow Lake, is Crowfoot Glacier. Early travellers in the Bow Valley called it "Trident Glacier," because it terminated in three separate lobes of ice, two of which draped the headwall toward Bow Lake. The present name likens the glacier's form to the foot of the American crow, which has three splayed toes. The extent of glacial recession makes the origin of the name

less obvious today, as two of the "toes" have virtually disappeared. One of them fell off in the 1920s, in an avalanche reportedly (but not likely) heard as far away as Lake Louise.

After a series of switchbacks, you make a hairpin turn north into the valley of Helen Creek. Cirque Peak (2993 m) is straight ahead, and the castellated summits of Dolomite Peak tower over Helen Creek to the east. The highest point of Dolomite

Peak, 2782 m, is the fourth tower from north. It was first climbed in 1930. Many of the other towers were first ascended on days-off by workers employed in the construction of the original Icefields Parkway, between 1931 and 1939.

The meadows nearby are a veritable sea of colour from middle to late July, and contain all the common upper subalpine wildflowers: western anemone, bracted lousewort, Indian paintbrush, fleabane, glacier lily, Sitka valerian, mountain heather, yellow columbine, and arnica. After the first frosts of August, the pungent stench of valerian fills the air – one of the harbingers of autumn in the Rockies.

The trail crosses the base of a quartzite rockslide – a good place to look for hoary marmots – and then descends into a ravine. Rock-hop the stream and continue north on a braided trail across the alpine tundra toward Helen Lake. Braids develop when hikers and horses avoid muddy sections of trail. As few as 20 pairs of feet travelling across untracked tundra may create a permanent trail. There were five prominent braids leading toward Helen Lake in 1992. After the wet summer of 1993, a sixth braid had developed in places. Please keep to the most beat-

The south slopes of Cirque Peak feature an anticline; an arch-shaped fold of Arctomys shale.

en path, thereby preventing the development of additional braids, and allowing the marginal braids to recover.

For many, Helen Lake is the ultimate destination on this hike. The knoll just south of the lake provides pleasing views south to the Bow Valley. The lake-dotted alpland in the foreground is reminiscent of highland Britain. Indeed, one member of the first party to cross Dolomite Pass suggested the name "Doone" for features in this area. Doone is Gaelic for "down." Confusingly, "The Downs" are uplands of central Britain. The quartzite cliffs at the head of the valley are nesting grounds for golden eagles.

Helen Lake to Dolomite Pass

The trail to Dolomite Pass continues north from Helen Lake to the base of Cirque Peak. The steep climb over the shoulder of Cirque Peak is the high point on this hike. Views of Dolomite Peak and the environs of Dolomite Pass are superb. On clear days, Mt.

Assiniboine (3618 m) is visible, 110 km to the south. We have seen caribou tracks here.

Many hikers are confused as to why they must now descend to approach Dolomite Pass. The explanation is simple. Unlike most trails that follow streams directly to their sources on mountain passes, this trail traverses into Dolomite Pass from another drainage, and crosses this high ridge en route.

The steep descent east from the ridge crosses an outcrop of purple Arctomys (ARK-toe-miss) shale. In the southeast face of Cirque Peak you can see a prominent anticline, an arch-shaped fold, in a layer of this formation. From the meadows at the north end of Lake Katherine, Mt. Temple (3543 m) is visible to the south, as is the glaciated horn of Mt. Daly (3152 m). You may be surprised to see hoary marmots in these open meadows, away from their customary sanctuary of boulderfields. It seems these particular animals are content to burrow deeply into the meadows,

The Crowfoot Dyke

Beneath the trail at km 1 is the Crowfoot Dyke, the most accessible exposure of igneous rock in the central Rockies. You can see it on the Icefields Parkway – a dull green outcrop of diabase, 1.1 km south of the trailhead. A dyke is an intrusion of molten rock that flowed underground along cracks in pre-existing rock, and then consolidated. The Crowfoot Dyke was created between 570 and 730 million years ago. It extends 2.8 km east from the outlet of Bow Lake to the banks of Helen Creek.

rather than using boulders for partial cover.

Rock-hop the lake's inlet and climb the hillside to the east into Dolomite Pass. The trail becomes vague. The travelled route is on the rise north of the small lake that drains east into Dolomite Creek. Random camping is allowed eastwards from this point, but is not recommended. There are no trees in which to cache your food. The only reasonable option for food storage is atop the large boulders nearby.

Dolomite Pass was first crossed in 1898 by a party from the Appalachian Mountain Club. The mountaineers named a number of nearby features for family members. Alice was the wife of party leader, Reverend H.P. Nicholls. Helen and Katherine were two of his daughters. Other names were descriptive:

The alpine tundra of Dolomite Pass

Observation Peak (3174 m) for the view from its summit; Cirque Peak for the cirque glacier on its north flank; and Dolomite Peak for its resemblance to The Dolomites, a group of mountains in The Alps, renowned for their sheer north-facing cliffs. If you continue 1 km northeast from Dolomite Pass, you will be re-

warded with views to the south of another lake, and the glacier on the northeast side of Dolomite Peak.

Dolomite Peak

One way dolomite rock can be formed is when water seeps into limestone sediments before they have lithified. Calcium in the limestone is replaced with magnesium. The magnesium-enriched rock is tougher than the original limestone, and often more colourful too. Dolomite Peak does not contain massive dolomite cliffs like the Dolomites of The Alps. It displays mostly limestones and shales. From the shore of Lake Katherine to the summit of the peak, the formations are: Arctomys shale, Waterfowl limestone, Sullivan shale, and finally, cliffs of Lyell limestone.

These formations are middle to late Cambrian in age. The recessive shales have eroded into ledges; the more resistant limestones have endured as cliffs. Together they create the "layer cake" or castellated form of Dolomite Peak.

"*At last one of the party put the question flatly to me: 'Have you any idea where we are?' I replied: 'I know perfectly well where we are; we are between the valley of the Pipestone and the Bow. What I do not know is where we are going to come out.'*"

—Ralph Edwards, guide on the first crossing of Dolomite Pass in 1898; *The Trail to the Charmed Land*

Mt. Murchison dominates the view east from Sarbach Lookout. Stoney and Kutenai natives believed it was the highest mountain in the Rockies. Mt. Murchison doesn't place among the 50 highest Rockies' summits. However, the impression that it is the highest is understandable: the summit rises 1920 m above the North Saskatchewan River.

21. Sarbach Lookout

Route

Day-hike, 5.3 km

Route	Elevation (m)	Distance (km)
Trailhead	1520	0
Mistaya Canyon	1479	0.5
Sarbach jct	1488	0.7
Mistaya River overlook	1517	1.7
Sarbach Lookout	2043	5.3

Topographic map: 82 N/15
Best lighting: anytime

Trailhead

West side of the Icefields Parkway (Highway 93), 72.1 km north of Lake Louise, 5.1 km south of the junction with Highway 11, 157.1 km south of Jasper.

Banff's fire lookout system was completed between 1941 and 1950, and contained seven lookouts. Each was staffed by a "tower jack." Connected to warden stations in the valleys below by telephone, the tower jacks were often able to provide early warning of forest fires.

Aerial smoke patrols during times of high fire hazard rendered the lookouts obsolete in the 1970s. Although the lookout towers in Banff were all abandoned by 1978, and removed by 1985, the trails to most lookout sites are still maintained. And they provide easy access to lofty viewpoints. The Sarbach (SARback) Lookout site is unique in that it grants

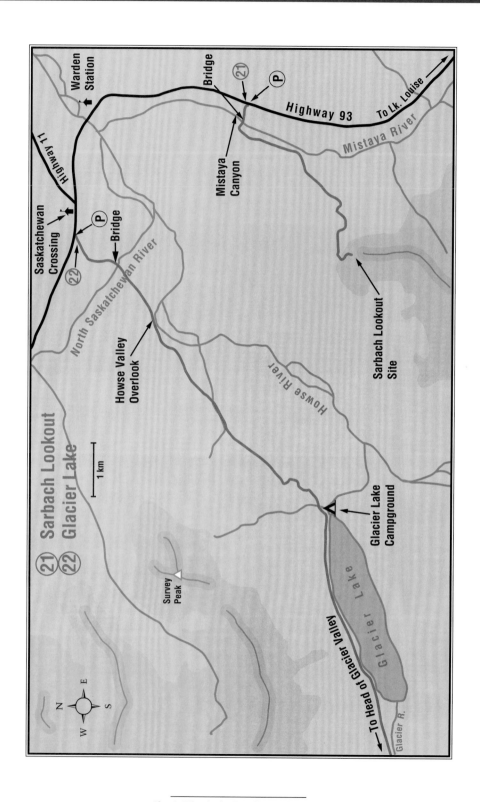

21 **Sarbach Lookout**
22 **Glacier Lake**

Warden Station

Highway 11

Saskatchewan Crossing

P

22

Bridge

North Saskatchewan River

Howse Valley Overlook

1 km

Survey Peak

To Head of Glacier Valley

Glacier R.

Glacier Lake

Glacier Lake Campground

Howse River

Sarbach Lookout Site

Bridge

21

P

Highway 93

To Lk. Louise

Mistaya River

Mistaya Canyon

N E S W

an overview of three of Banff's largest valleys.

Icefields Parkway to Mistaya River

The initial 450 m of trail is road width, and descends to Mistaya Canyon. Cross the bridge over the canyon and in 15 m, turn right (north). The trail ascends a bank of glacial till. Till overlies the bedrock here to a depth of more than 30 m.

Because most till in the Rockies came from limestone bedrock, it contains a high percentage of calcium carbonate (lime). Water percolating through the till creates a natural cement that binds the rock particles together. Thus, these gravel banks are deceptively tough. In places, rainwater and snowmelt are eroding hoodoos into them.

At the junction in 200 m, turn southwest (left) onto the Sarbach Lookout trail. The forest on this river terrace is an ancient one of Engelmann spruce and lodgepole pine, that last burned in 1640. The lodgepole pines here are as old and tall as you will see anywhere in the Rockies. One spruce tree at trailside shows charred heartwood exposed by a lightning strike. At first glance, the tree appears dead. However, a few upper branches are still growing. In the absence of recent fire, new habitat in this forest is created by blowdowns that remove weakened trees. The downed trees are piled like jackstraws, and provide abundant fuel for the

Sarbach Lookout was built in July 1943. The cabin and the tower supports were constructed from trees felled on site. The lookout housing was carried to the site in sections by packhorse.

inevitable day when the forest will burn.

At km 1.7, the trail regains the bank of the Mistaya River, from where there is a fine view south to the tremendous mountain wall along the western slope of the Mistaya Valley. The glacier-draped cliffs of The White Pyramid, Epaulette Mountain, the Kaufmann Peaks and Mt. Sarbach create an archetypal Rockies image.

Mistaya River to Sarbach Lookout

The trail veers west from the river, and for a kilometre crosses boggy terrain toward the north ridge of Mt. Sarbach. You may see moose in this area. The "snow course markers" on trees, indicate locations where snow core samples were taken by the Water Survey of Canada until the early 1980s. By melting the snow, its water equivalent was determined. Data obtained from snow at these sites was combined with other data from the Rockies, allowing the annual run-off to be predicted.

To this point, the trail from the Mistaya River has climbed gradually. Now the hard work begins, 370 m of gain spread over 2.5 km. There are limited views en route to the lookout site. However, the blooms of arnica, few-flowered anemone and the exquisite calypso orchid brighten up the trailside. You will know the relentless climb is nearing its end when the trail swings onto the north

Mistaya Canyon

Mistaya (miss-TAY-yah) Canyon is cut into Cambrian-age Eldon limestone. The canyon features a natural arch, and potholes eroded by rocks trapped in depressions. The river has exploited the weakness presented by a joint set – an arrangement of parallel cracks in the bedrock. This creates the dogleg course of the canyon, visible looking north. In places, the canyon is scarcely 2 m wide. Rather than attempting to cross the Mistaya River in places where it was wider, Stoney Natives would cross here on felled trees during their hunting trips into the mountains. Mistaya is a Stoney word for "grizzly bear."

Whitebark Pine

Whitebark pine is an indicator tree for the upper subalpine ecoregion, and is usually found in exposed locations. The tree bark is silvery and smooth on young trees, and grey and scaly on older trees. Needles are in bunches of five. The stand of whitebark pine on Mt. Sarbach exhibits the diverse forms possible for this species. The tree is a gnarled and twisted krummholz, where fully exposed to the elements. Where protected in the forest it has a robust form and attains a height of 10 to 12 m. "Spike tops" indicate where the tops of trees have suffered die-off from the chill of winter winds. The whitebark pine is one of the longest-lived tree species in the Rockies. Ages in excess of 1000 years have been recorded.

end of the ridge, and white-bark pine becomes the most common tree in the surrounding forest.

The last 200 m of trail is bordered with rocks – the handiwork of a tower jack. Snow patches linger here until early July. A Sacramento rain gauge, stumps of trees, the cabin foundation, and the trail borders are now all that remains of the Sarbach fire lookout, which was built in 1943. Even without the advantage of a tower, the site commands a grand perspective of the three valleys that merge below: the Mistaya to the south, the Howse to the west, and the North Saskatchewan to the north and east.

The mountains of the Amery Group are immediately north, and Mt. Wilson (3260 m) looms to the northeast, above the right-angle bend in the North Saskatchewan River. The mountain was named for Tom Wilson: trail guide, outfitter, and the first white visitor to the shores of Lake Louise. Wilson's heyday was the late 1800s. In the early 1900s, he became a fixture at the Banff Springs Hotel and at Château Lake Louise, regaling guests with stories of the trail, both tall and true.

Directly east from the lookout site is the stupendous form of Mt. Murchison (3333 m). James Hector named the mountain in 1858, for R.I. Murchison, the man who recommended Hector to the Palliser Expedition. Mt. Murchison is a massif, a miniature mountain range that contains 10 summits. Hector reported

that Natives considered Murchison to be the highest mountain in the Rockies. The impression is understandable since the northerly summit towers 1920 m above the North Saskatchewan River. However, Mt. Murchison does not even rank among the 50 highest Rockies' summits. Although the first ascent of Mt. Murchison was claimed in 1902, the highest summit (second from the north) was evidently not ascended until 1985.

Mt. Murchison is a wonderful example of a castellated mountain. Resistant limestone and dolomite cliffs alternate with recessive ledges of shale. If you trace the sedimentary formations of the lowest tier of cliffs, you will see a place where they become fractured vertically, and offset in a normal fault. The formations on one side of the fault have moved downwards relative to the other.

Cirque basins have been eroded into Mt. Murchison's flanks, and waterfalls cascade from them. The mountain's many summits are glacially sculpted horns. Farther south in the Mistaya Valley, Mt. Chephren (KEFF-ren) (3266 m) and the White Pyramid (3275 m) also exhibit horn mountain shapes.

The summit of Mt. Sarbach (3155 m) is hidden from view, 5 km south of the lookout site. The mountain was first climbed in 1897 by J.N. Collie, G.P. Baker and Peter Sarbach. Sarbach, the first Swiss Guide to work in Canada, spent only one summer in the Rockies.

However, he led a number of important first ascents, including Mt. Lefroy and Mt. Victoria at Lake Louise. You may be fortunate to see mountain goats on the slopes above the lookout site. Bears frequent the avalanche slopes to the south in autumn.

"Bear Creek [Mistaya River] safely crossed, we pushed on up the main valley of the Saskatchewan to the westward. On the 25th we climbed a peak 10,700 feet high, which was named after our guide, Sarbach. The first thousand feet was through primeval forest; then up a steep gully in a limestone escarpment, and over steep screes to the foot of the final peak."

—During the first ascent of Mt. Sarbach in 1897. Hugh Stutfield and J.N. Collie, *Climbs and Explorations in the Canadian Rockies*

Glacier Lake at dawn

22. Glacier Lake

Route

Day-hike or overnight, 9.1 km

Route	Elevation (m)	Distance (km)
Trailhead	1439	0
North Saskatchewan R bridge	1418	1.1
Howse River overlook	1433	2.3
Glacier Lake CG	1435	9.1
Head of Glacier River valley	1493	18.6

Topographic maps: 82 N/15, 82 N/14
Best lighting: morning

Trailhead

Trailhead: West side of the Icefields Parkway (Highway 93), 1.2 km north of the junction with Highway 11, 78.4 km north of Lake Louise, 150.8 km south of Jasper.

Renowned fur-trader and mapmaker David Thompson was the first European to record an impression of Glacier Lake. Visiting in 1807, he wrote: "all the Mountains in sight from the end of the Lake are seemingly of Ice." Nearly every visitor since has been equally impressed. The colossal icefall of the Southeast Lyell Glacier, which tumbles from Division Mountain west of the lake, is one of the most spectacular sights in the Rockies.

The Glacier Lake trail is one of the first Classic Hikes to become snow-free. Although the trailhead and destination are at nearly equal elevations, there is enough up and down en route to make the outing an ideal early season "shake down" trip. Random camping is permitted in the valley west of the lake. The area is prime habitat for black bears.

Black bear tracks

Icefields Parkway to Glacier Lake

The trailhead is in a dense lodgepole pine forest, the product of a July 1940 forest fire – the Survey Peak Burn. This was the last extensive wildfire in Banff National Park. It consumed 40 km², and forced closure of the recently opened Icefields Parkway. Buffaloberry and bearberry, whose fruits are favourite foods of bears, are common in the undergrowth near the trailhead. Ruffed grouse will often be seen.

The trail descends a series of ancient river terraces to an I-beam bridge over the North Saskatchewan River at km 1.1. Here, the river's course has been captured by a bedrock fault, creating a small canyon.

The North Saskatchewan River is 1216 km long. More than 80 percent of the water it carries to Hudson's Bay (via Lake Winnipeg and the Nelson River), is of glacial origin. The 49 km section within Banff National Park was proclaimed a Canadian Heritage River in 1989. Canadian Heritage Rivers are those that have played an important role in the human and natural history of Canada. The province of Alberta refuses to participate in the Canadian Heritage Rivers Program, so the designation stops at the park boundary.

The trail climbs away from the river and continues through burned forest to the Howse River overlook at km 2.3. Directly ahead (south-

Please see map on page 116

west) in the view from the overlook is Mt. Outram (OOT-rum) (3240 m), named for reverend and mountaineer James Outram, who made first ascents of many high peaks in the Rockies in 1901 and 1902. Tucked in behind Mt. Outram is Mt. Forbes (3612 m), seventh highest mountain in the Rockies, and the highest mountain entirely within Banff National Park. James Outram teamed up with the party of Scottish mountaineer J.N. Collie to make the first ascent of Mt. Forbes in 1902. Edward Forbes was James Hector's professor of natural history at the University of Edinburgh.

The trail swings west from the viewpoint and descends to riverside. To the southeast, the many summits of Mt.

The Howse Valley: A Once and Future Highway ?

The heavily braided appearance indicates that most of the flow of the Howse River is glacial. The meltwater comes from numerous glaciers, as well as three icefields: Freshfield (70 km²), Mons (16 km²) and Lyell (35 km²). Howse Pass, 16 km south, was part of the first fur trade route across the Rockies, and saw use between 1800 and 1810, when it was closed by hostile Peigan Natives. The Howse Valley is a haven for many species of large mammals: elk, mule deer, moose, black bear, grizzly bear, wolf, mountain goat, and coyote.

The city of Red Deer has repeatedly advocated construction of a highway across Howse Pass. Such a highway would decrease transportation times and costs between some places in Alberta and BC, but would destroy one of the last wilderness enclaves in the Rockies. The 1988 Banff National Park Management Plan precludes the construction of new roads. However, in 1993 the boundaries of two provincial ridings in Aberta were redrawn, with the sole objective of placing the Howse Valley in the same riding as the city of Rocky Mountain House. This will help consolidate renewed political arguments for a Howse Pass highway. At time of publication, pressure for this most inappropriate development had been renewed.

Murchison (3333 m) tower above the mouth of the Mistaya Valley. The trail veers away from the river, and you spend the next 5 km climbing and descending a forested spur of Survey Peak, to reach the shore of Glacier Lake and the campground near its outlet.

Glacier Lake is 3750 m long, 750 m wide, and has an area of 263 ha. It is the fourth largest lake in Banff National Park. Its waters are dammed by a moraine created where the ancestral Southeast Lyell and Freshfield glaciers merged. Glacier Lake was named in 1858 by James Hector. The osprey or "fish hawk" may be seen circling over the lake in quest of lake trout, rocky mountain whitefish and the increasingly rare bull trout.

The Glacier River Valley

The rough trail along the north shore of Glacier Lake originated earlier this century as a mountaineering approach to Mt. Forbes and the Lyell Icefield. In 1992 it was cleared for the first time in decades.

The Southeast Lyell Icefall

Less than a century ago, the head of the Glacier River valley was covered in glacial ice. Mountaineers J.N. Collie and Hugh Stutfield described the icefall in 1902: "Incomparably the finest we have seen in the Rockies, it is a larger scale than anything of the kind in Switzerland. It is of immense width, with a band of cliffs, surmounted at their northern end by blue ice-pinnacles, dividing the upper from the lower glacier for the greater part of the distance. The meltings of the higher snows fall over these cliffs in a series of waterfalls, and the roar of the ice avalanches was constant and deafening."

Beyond the inlet, the trail meanders across alluvial flats, following the north shore of the Glacier River and passing the site of the 1940 Alpine Club of Canada Camp. Though the trail is sketchy in places and has slumped into the river at others creating some awkward corners, the route to the head of the valley is fairly obvious.

About 9.5 km from the campground, look for a faint track that climbs steeply northwest (right) onto a series of knife-edged moraines. From this hard-won vantage there are astounding views of the icefall of the Southeast Lyell Glacier and its marginal lake, along with the tremendous glaciated fang of Mt. Forbes.

"The lake, which is 3 or 4 miles long, is beautifully set amongst the high peaks, and at the further end a snow-mountain sends down a glacier nearly to its level. The lake was nearly calm, and reflected the beautiful picture of mountain and sky from a tremulously moving surface ... There was something wonderfully impressive in the isolation and awful solitude of such a grand scene under the spell of evening calm."

—W.D. Wilcox,
Sources of the Saskatchewan,
The Geographical Journal,
April 1899

Glaciers: The Beginning and End of Lakes

If you look at the topographic map, you will see Glacier Lake occupies the eastern end of a 13 km long plain. At the conclusion of the Wisconsin Glaciation, the lake may have filled the entire valley. Over time, rubble and sediment carried by the Glacier River have filled much of the lake. As with many glacial lakes in the Rockies, if glacial recession continues, inevitably the day will come when the filling will be complete, and Glacier Lake will cease to exist.

Sunset Lookout commands an unobstructed view of the North Saskatchewan Valley. The U-shape of the valley and the many braids of the river testify to the past and present effects of glaciers in the Rockies.

23. Sunset Pass and Lookout

Route

Route	Elevation (m)	Distance (km)
Day-hike or overnight, 12.0 km		
Trailhead	1438	0
Sunset Lookout jct	1860	2.9
Sunset Lookout	2043	4.5
Sunset Lookout jct	1860	6.1
Norman Lake CG	1973	7.4
Sunset Pass, park boundary	2165	11.4
Pinto Lake viewpoint	2134	12.0

Topographic map: 83 C/2
Best lighting: anytime

Trailhead

East side of the Icefields Parkway (Highway 93), 93.6 km north of Lake Louise, 16.4 km north of the junction with Highway 11, 32.9 km south of the Icefield Information Centre, 135.6 km south of Jasper. The turnoff was not marked in 1992.

The trail to Sunset Pass is a backcountry artery into the remote northeast corner of Banff National Park, and is used principally by backpackers and horse parties bound for Pinto Lake in the adjacent White Goat Wilderness Area. Exceptional views of the surrounding terrain highlight this lengthy day-trip. In particular, the sidetrail to Sunset Lookout offers a breathtaking prospect over the North Saskatchewan Valley.

Icefields Parkway to Sunset Lookout Junction

The trail initially climbs steeply on a south-west-facing slope that is cloaked in a dry forest of lodgepole pine. Buffaloberry is common in the undergrowth. The glossy leaves of this shrub are pale and fuzzy on the underside, with rust-coloured spots. The yellow flowers yield red and amber berries in late July. By August, 95 percent of the typical black bear's diet is buffaloberries. Grizzly bears may consume 200,000 of these berries in a single day. If the berry crop is on, you are cau-

tioned to look for recent bear sign, and to make lots of noise on this trail. The author has surprised a grizzly here at very close range. The bear made a no-contact charge, passing within two metres.

At km 1.0, sidetrails lead south to the edge of the shale

canyon cut by Norman Creek. The steep slope on which you have been travelling is a product of glacial overdeepening of the North Saskatchewan Valley. Tributary valleys, such as Norman Creek, were not as deeply eroded by glacial ice during the Wisconsin Glacia-

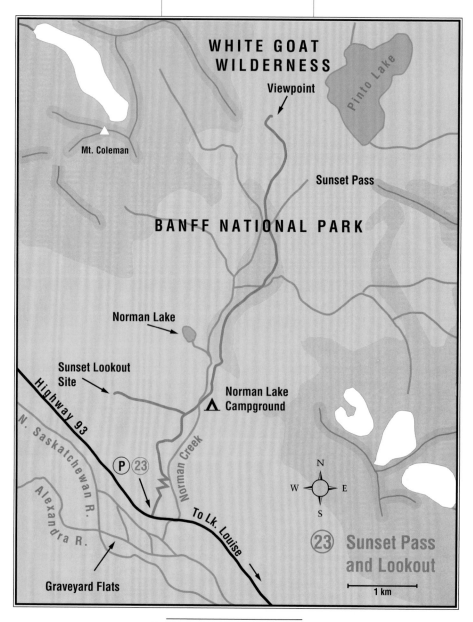

WHITE GOAT WILDERNESS

Pinto Lake

Viewpoint

Mt. Coleman

Sunset Pass

BANFF NATIONAL PARK

Norman Lake

Sunset Lookout Site

Highway 93

N. Saskatchewan R.

Alexandra R.

Norman Lake Campground

P 23

Norman Creek

To Lk. Louise

N
W E
S

23 Sunset Pass and Lookout

Graveyard Flats

1 km

tion, and were left hanging above the main valley floor. With the energy created by its steep gradient, Norman Creek has carved this impressive canyon. The creek may have been named for John Norman Collie, one of the leading alpinists of the late Victorian era. Collie made six mountaineering trips to the Rockies between 1897 and 1910.

From the canyon, the trail works its way north before switchbacking upwards to the Sunset Lookout junction. A few stately Douglas fir trees grow amongst the pines on this slope. This may be the northern limit for the Douglas fir in Banff National Park. The grade moderates just before the junction. Turn north (left) for Sunset Lookout.

Sunset Lookout

On the sidetrail to Sunset Lookout you make a rambling ascent along a bluff for 1.6 km to an opening in the subalpine forest. Then you descend steeply for 60 m through a stand of whitebark pines to the edge of a 500 m cliff overlooking the North Saskatchewan Valley. The former site of Sunset Lookout is no place for acrophobics. It is more suited to mountain goats, which are often seen nearby. The foundations and lightning conductor cables of the lookout ruins pose a genuine tripping hazard. Be careful.

Sunset Lookout was built in 1943 and operated until 1978, when smoke patrols by helicopter rendered it and the other towers in the fire lookout system obsolete. The site was extremely well chosen. Mt. Saskatchewan (3342 m), guardian of the southeastern edge of Columbia Icefield, dominates the view to the west, where the upper reaches of the Alexandra River are visible. The valleys of the North Saskatchewan, Mistaya and Bow align to the south, allowing an unrestricted view to Crowfoot Mountain, 60 km distant. Some glaciologists speculate that before mountain building, the North Saskatchewan River flowed directly south along this alignment, toward Lake Louise. The northern vista includes Nigel Pass and the environs of Columbia Icefield.

Sunset Lookout Junction to Sunset Pass

After backtracking to the lookout junction, turn northeast (left). The trail undulates through flower-filled glades to the edge of a vast subalpine willow meadow, and an unsigned junction. Keep right and descend to a bridge over Norman Creek. The campground is in the stand of trees just beyond.

Mt. Coleman (3135 m) dominates the north side of the valley. A.P. Coleman was a geology professor from Toronto. He made seven exploratory

The Graveyard

From Sunset Lookout you can compare the North Saskatchewan and Alexandra Rivers, which merge directly below at an area known to early explorers as Graveyard Flats. The North Saskatchewan is a glacially charged stream, with multiple braids and extensive gravel flats. Although it too has glacial origins, the Alexandra shows a more meandering course, with abandoned channels, ox-bow lakes and sloughs. The Graveyard Flats were a natural camping place for Natives, who dressed the kills of their hunts there. Explorer Mary Schäffer named the flats after she found animal skeletons in 1907.

"Saskatchewan" is Cree for "swift current." The North Saskatchewan River is 1216 km long. The portion within Banff National Park was designated a Canadian Heritage River in 1989. Princess Alexandra was the wife of King Edward VII.

journeys into the hinterland of the Rockies between 1884 and 1908, named many features and contributed greatly to the growing knowledge of the landscape. His book of 1911, *The Canadian Rockies, New and Old Trails*, is a landmark of Rockies'

Pinto Lake

history. The north side of the mountain features a spectacular glacier and two large lakes that drain underground.

The trail to Sunset Pass follows the east side of wet meadows and willow plain for several kilometres, and then angles northeast into forest. En route, there is a frustrating stream crossing: too deep to rock-hop, too narrow to bother fording, and a bit too wide to jump! The trail reaches the height of land and the national park boundary to the north of Sunset Pass proper. It then descends slightly onto a limestone bench above the headwaters of the Cline River.

you are day-hiking, do not descend to Pinto Lake. It's much farther than it looks (5 km), and will result in a 34 km day by the time you return to the Icefields Parkway!

Mr. Amery's Mountain

The prominent mountain to the southwest of Sunset Lookout, its flanks riddled with glacial cirques, is Mt. Amery (AY-muh-ree) (3329 m). The mountain was named in 1927 for British statesman, publisher and mountaineer, L.S. Amery. Two years later, Amery came to Canada with the express purpose of making the first ascent of "his" mountain. In wretched weather, Swiss Guide Ernest Feuz (FOITS) Jr. led Amery and a partner to the summit by a difficult route, or so they thought. A 1985 ascent found no evidence of the cairn they claimed to have built, and no suitable rocks with which to build one. In the poor visibility of his ascent, it is possible Mr. Amery did not quite reach the true summit.

Pinto Lake Viewpoint

After you travel 600 m along the bench northeast of Sunset Pass, walk east from the trail to the edge the cliff. This provides a wonderful prospect over Pinto Lake and the Cline River valley. The lake was named for one of A.P. Coleman's most troublesome packhorses on the 1893 expedition. Pinto went missing on the journey home. None were sad to see him go. Still, to quote Coleman: "... we immortalized him by giving his name to an exquisite lake near the head of Cataract River." If

"*Not far from its head Cataract River forks, one branch coming from a splendid valley to the south, where it begins in an exquisite lake about a mile long and broad, fed by an enormous spring forty feet wide. Pinto Lake, as we named it, is 5,850 feet above the sea, and on three sides of it mountain walls rise to seven or eight thousand feet, making a wonderful amphitheatre ... if it were not so far from a railway this romantic pool among the woods should be as attractive to mountain-lovers as Lake Louise.*"

—A.P. Coleman, 1893, *The Canadian Rockies: New and Old Trails*

Saskatchewan Glacier is the centrepiece in the view from Parker Ridge. It is the largest of the eight outlet valley glaciers that flow from Columbia Icefield.

24. Parker Ridge

Route

Day-hike, 2.4 km

Route	Elevation (m)	Distance (km)
Trailhead	1997	0
Parker Ridge crest	2271	1.9
Saskatchewan Gl viewpoint	2256	2.4

Topographic map: 82 C/3
Best lighting: morning

Trailhead

South side of Icefields Parkway (Highway 93), 117.5 km north of Lake Louise; 9 km south of the Icefield Information Centre; 111.6 km south of Jasper.

Although it is by far the shortest Classic Hike, the trail to Parker Ridge confirms the adage that "good things often come in small packages." With a minimal investment of time and energy, you can explore an alpine ridgetop, with views of the largest icefield and one of the largest alpine valley glaciers in the Rockies. Parker Ridge is often cold and windy. Carry warm clothing, including gloves and a hat.

Icefields Parkway to the Ridge Crest

The Parker Ridge trailhead is located in a treeline forest. Here, vegetation growth is hindered by: high elevation, cold glacial air, near constant winds, poor soils, avalanches and a northeast aspect. From the parking lot, the trail crosses a subalpine meadow – a frost hollow, typical of areas adjacent to glaciers. Cold air from Hilda Glacier collects here, creating a local growing season so short, mature trees cannot develop.

The horn mountain shapes of Mt. Athabasca (3491 m) and its outlier, Hilda Peak (3060 m), are prominent to the west. The summits of these mountains protruded above the kilometre thick ice sheets of the Great Glaciation. Since the retreat of the ice sheets, alpine glaciation has continued to whittle away at the upper mountainsides, creating the horns.

Across the meadow, the climb begins. The trail enters a small but ancient forest. At one point you squeeze between two massive Engelmann spruce, that are probably at least 400 years old. However, most of the vegetation here is in stunted, krummholz form.

Krummholz is a German word that means "crooked wood." The gnarled, dense, evergreen mats with silvery bark are subalpine fir trees. Taller, Engelmann spruce grow from within the mats. Although they appear to be shrubs, these are mature trees, possibly hundreds of years old.

The treeless areas on the northeast slope of Parker Ridge are either avalanche swept rock, or tundra comprised of sedges, white mountain avens, mountain heather, snow willow, arctic willow, woolly everlasting and purple saxifrage. Saxifrage is derived from Latin words that mean "rock breaker." Purple saxifrage is one of the pioneering alpine plants whose roots help break apart rock and create primitive soil. Vegetation here is low in stature to reduce wind exposure, and to enable the plants to absorb heat from the dark soils. Thick, waxy

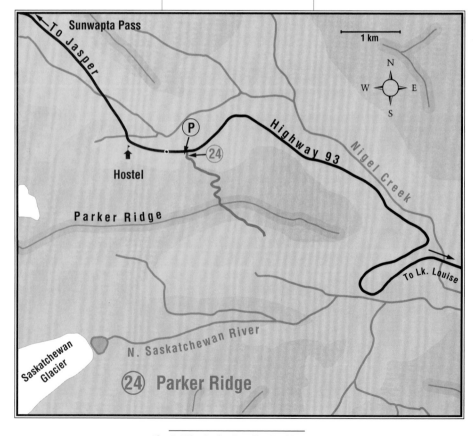

leaves help retain moisture. More than 6 m of snow falls annually at Parker Ridge. this snow takes a long time to melt because of the shaded northeast aspect and cold temperatures – resulting from the elevation and proximity to Columbia Icefield. A few of the drifts are perennial features. Needless to say, the slopes of Parker Ridge are popular with skiers in winter and spring. However, don't be surprised if you see some die-hards carving turns on a Parker Ridge snowpatch in mid-summer – to the possible detriment of underlying vegetation.

The Ridge Crest

The trail gains the open ridge at an elevation of 2271m. From here, follow the beaten path southeast (left) for 500 m to a vantage overlooking Saskatchewan Glacier. With a

Keeping On Track

On your way to the ridgetop you will see dozens of signs that indicate where shortcut trails have been closed. By the late 1970s, heavy traffic and uneducated hiking practices had combined to transform the slopes of Parker Ridge into a maze of trails. Vegetation was trampled, and erosion was widespread. The trail was rehabilitated in a costly project. Seeds from plants on Parker Ridge were grown in greenhouses, and the resulting seedlings were transplanted back to the ridge to revegetate redundant trails. Please help protect this fragile landscape and the considerable investment, by keeping to the gravel path.

length of 9 km, this outlet valley glacier of the 325 km^2 Columbia Icefield is one of the longest in the Rockies. It descends 750 m in elevation from the icefield rim to terminate in a marginal lake, the principal headwaters of the North Saskatchewan River.

Compared to Athabasca Glacier, the surface of Saskatchewan Glacier is relatively unspectacular. It has no icefalls and few large crevasses. Of interest is a medial moraine, a strip of lengthwise rubble on the glacier's surface. This type of moraine forms where two tributary glaciers merge. Saskatchewan is a Cree word that means "swift current". Mt. Saskatchewan (3342 m) is the high peak protruding above rounded summits, 8 km south of Parker Ridge.

Immediately south (left) of the head of the Saskatchewan Glacier is Castleguard Mountain (3070 m). South of this mountain is the entrance to Castleguard Cave, one of the largest cave systems in Canada, and the third deepest in Canada and the US. More than 18 km of passages have been explored. Some of these follow ancient drainages beneath Columbia Icefield, and terminate in dead-ends that are choked

Rock Lichens: Old Timers

In some areas, the thin soils of Parker Ridge support little but rock lichen colonies. Rock lichens are an example of a symbiotic relationship. They contain a fungus and an alga. The fungus protects the alga, and the alga produces food for both. One byproduct of this relationship is humic acid, which accelerates the chemical breakdown of rock and the creation of soil. Rock lichens grow outwards at an incredibly slow, though consistent rate. It is thought some rock lichen colonies in the Rockies may have begun life at the end of the Wisconsin Glaciation, 11,000 years ago! Two of the

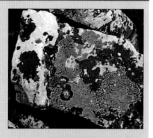

more common rock lichens are: the brilliant orange *Xanthoria elegans* found on a variety of rock types; and the green and black map lichen (*Rhizocarpon geographicum*), found principally on quartzite boulders. Rock lichens are eaten by caribou, bighorn sheep and mountain goats.

Golden Eagle

with glacial ice. If the day is clear, the view beyond Castleguard Mountain will include the lofty summit of Mt. Bryce (3487 m), 19 km distant.

If you look uphill along the crest of Parker Ridge, you will notice how the outlying ridge is rounded in appearance, becoming much more rugged toward Mt. Athabasca. The rounded parts of the ridge were completely covered by moving ice during the Great Glaciation, while the jagged areas were probably not. If you choose to explore along the ridge to the cairn at the high point (2350 m), please stay on the beaten path. The ridge crest features krummholz forms of whitebark pine, a common tree in windy locations, and coral-like fossils called *Syringopora*. Please do not remove the fossils.

Mountain goat, white-tailed ptarmigan, gray jay, Clark's nutcracker, pika and common raven are among frequently observed wildlife on Parker Ridge. Grizzly bear, wolverine and golden eagle may also be seen by fortunate visitors. The ridge was probably named for Herschel Parker, a mountaineer who made several first ascents of mountains near Lake Louise at the turn of the century.

> "At daybreak, without difficulty, we took the horses northward over a meadowed shoulder east of Mt. Athabaska, about 7500 feet in elevation, whence we looked back and over the tremendous expanse of green ice to Castleguard."
>
> —James Monroe Thorington, on the first recorded crossing of Parker Ridge in 1923, *The Glittering Mountains of Canada*

The Glacier Trail

Mountaineering parties in the early 1900s, intent on ascending peaks at the southern edge of Columbia Icefield, followed the Alexandra River to a base camp in Castleguard Meadows. If they wished to continue farther north, they were obliged to return along the Alexandra River to the North Saskatchewan River, and then cross Sunwapta Pass – a journey of approximately three days. This backtracking frustrated outfitter Jimmy Simpson and his clients. The supplies used descending the Alexandra could be better put to use exploring new ground. On the 1923 expedition of mountaineer James Monroe Thorington, Simpson decided to take a one-day shortcut from Castleguard Meadows to Sun-

wapta Pass – he led the pack-train down the Saskatchewan Glacier and over Parker Ridge.

Apparently the horses took to the ice with little fuss. The ploy was repeated on the Smithsonian Institution Columbia Icefield expedition of 1924, when Byron Harmon took this photograph. Thereafter, the crossing of Saskatchewan Glacier with horses became standard fare. In the late 1920s, outfitter Jack Brewster incorporated a visit to Castleguard Meadows via Saskatchewan Glacier into his pack trips from Jasper to Lake Louise – an outing known appropriately as "The Glacier Trail."

E stablished in 1907 as Canada's sixth national park, Jasper is the largest of the Rocky Mountain parks, and includes 10,878 km² of the front ranges and eastern main ranges. The park has almost 1000 km of maintained trails. The Classic Hikes in Jasper feature long backcountry outings as well as day-hikes to spectacular alpine landscapes.

Jasper townsite provides a full range of supplies, accommodation, and services. The townsite is 362 km west of Edmonton on Highway 16, and 237 km north of Lake Louise via the Icefields Parkway. Access is by car, passenger bus or train. Basic supplies are available at Columbia Icefield, Sunwapta Falls and Pocahontas. The park has 10 frontcountry campgrounds, with more than 1700 campsites. There are five hostels. Park information centres are in Jasper townsite and at Columbia Icefield. The warden office is on the Maligne Lake Road, 7 km from the town of Jasper. Emergency assistance is available at the Sunwapta warden station on the Icefields Parkway at Poboktan Creek, and at Pocahontas.

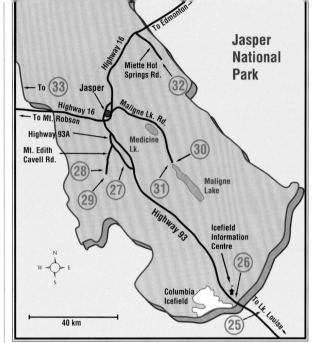

Overview map of Jasper National Park showing trail head locations

Mt. Robson Provincial Park

The Jasper Classic Hikes include The Berg Lake Trail in Mt. Robson Provincial Park. Mt. Robson was established in 1913 as the second provincial park in BC. Basic supplies are available at Robson Junction.

The park has five frontcountry campgrounds. Robson Meadows, Robson River, and the privately operated Emperor Ridge are all near Robson Junction.

The Brazeau Loop traverses three alpine passes and visits one of the Rockies' largest backcountry lakes.

25. Brazeau Loop

Route

Nigel-Jonas-Poboktan Passes
5-7 days, 78.6 km loop

Route	Elevation (m)	Distance (km)
Nigel Creek trailhead	1864	0
Nigel Pass	2225	7.2
Boulder Creek CG	2030	10.7
Four Point CG	1910	13.9
Jonas Pass jct.	1910	14.0
Jonas Pass	2320	23.8
Jonas Shoulder	2470	29.6
Jonas Cutoff CG	2140	32.8
Poboktan Creek jct	2115	33.0
Poboktan Pass	2304	36.0
John John CG	2020	40.3
John John Creek bridge	1830	44.5
Brazeau R. bridge and jct	1805	48.3
Brazeau R. Bridge CG	1805	48.7
Brazeau Valley jct. & bridge	1720	51.2
Brazeau CG	1720	51.3
Brazeau R. bridge east bank	1790	54.5
Wolverine South CG	1860	59.8
Brazeau R bridge west bank	1875	62.1
Four Point CG	1910	64.8
Boulder Creek CG	2030	67.9
Nigel Pass	2225	71.4
Nigel Creek trailhead	1864	78.6

Topographic maps: 83 C/3, 83 C/6, 83 C/7

Trailhead

Nigel Creek, east side of the Icefields Parkway (Highway 93), 113.8 km north of Lake Louise, 115.4 km south of Jasper, 12.7 km south of Columbia Icefield Information Centre. Southbound travellers should use caution making the awkward turn into the trailhead parking area. Walk north from the parking area on the old road. The trail veers east (right), and crosses Nigel Creek on a bridge, 50 m north of the gate.

The Brazeau Loop traverses three exquisite upper subalpine passes, the shattered crest of a mountain ridge, and the delightful, broad Brazeau (brah-ZOE) Valley. En route you visit one of the largest backcountry lakes in the Rockies. The area is home to grizzly bear, elk, moose, wolf, coyote, wolverine, cougar, deer, and mountain caribou. There is much spectacular scenery to savor on this hike. Take your time, and enjoy. Backpacking in the Rockies simply does not get any better.

Icefields Parkway to Nigel Pass

Fifty metres north of the parking lot, the trail crosses to the east bank of Nigel Creek. For the next 7 km it follows the creek to its sources in the extreme northeastern corner of Banff National Park. For the first 1.5 km, the trail alternates between ancient upper sub-alpine forest and avalanche

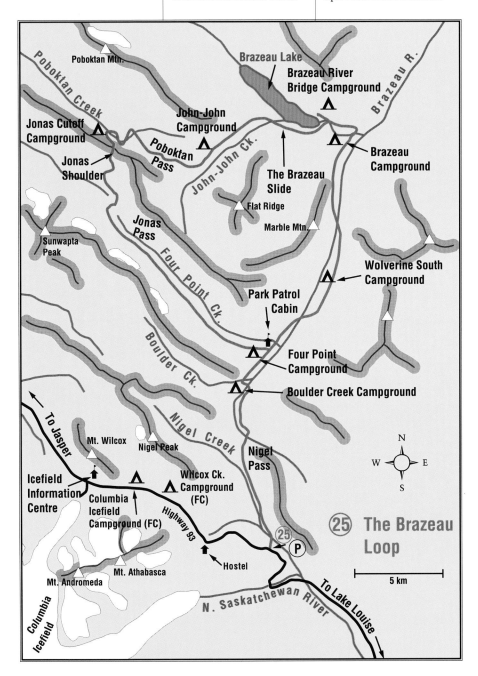

Poboktan Mtn.

Poboktan Creek

Brazeau Lake

Brazeau River Bridge Campground

Brazeau R.

Jonas Cutoff Campground

John-John Campground

Poboktan Pass

John-John Ck.

Brazeau Campground

Jonas Shoulder

The Brazeau Slide

Flat Ridge

Jonas Pass

Marble Mtn.

Sunwapta Peak

Four Point Ck.

Wolverine South Campground

Park Patrol Cabin

Boulder Ck.

Four Point Campground

Boulder Creek Campground

To Jasper

Nigel Creek

Mt. Wilcox

Nigel Peak

Nigel Pass

Icefield Information Centre

Columbia Icefield Campground (FC)

Wilcox Ck. Campground (FC)

Highway 93

N
W — E
S

Mt. Athabasca

Hostel

25 P

25 The Brazeau Loop

Mt. Andromeda

5 km

Columbia Icefield

N. Saskatchewan River

To Lake Louise

slopes, which support exceptional wildflower displays in late July. The trail climbs onto the bank above the junction of Hilda and Nigel creeks. Many trees nearby feature carvings, the handiwork of travellers along the Icefields Parkway in the 1940s. In the days before the Parkway was paved, the 237 km journey from Lake Louise to Jasper was a two-day adventure. This grove of trees was near the halfway point, and was evidently a popular resting and camping place.

The horn shapes of Mt. Athabasca (3491 m) and its outlier, Hilda Peak (3060 m), form the backdrop to the west. To the northwest is the southern summit of Nigel Peak. It displays the U-shaped fold of the Castle Mountain Syncline, a bedrock feature that extends 260 km through Banff and Jasper national parks.

The trail swings north into the upper valley of Nigel Creek. Although close to the Icefields Parkway, this area is frequented by grizzly bears. Make lots of noise while you cross the avalanche slopes. The last kilometre of the climb is on a steep eroded trail that leads to a craggy limestone bluff overlooking the Brazeau River. This point is 1 km to the east of, and slightly higher than Nigel Pass. Here, you are astride the boundary between Banff and Jasper national parks, and between two geological provinces of the Rockies: the eastern main ranges to the west, and the front ranges to the east.

Parker Ridge, Mt. Saskatchewan (3342 m) and the rounded peaks adjacent to Saskatchewan Glacier are prominent in the view south from Nigel Pass. To the southeast, you can see Cataract Pass and the source of the Brazeau River. The glaciated summit of Nigel Peak (3211 m) rises above massive limestone cliffs and dominates the view west.

Nigel Pass to Upper Brazeau Valley

Leaving Nigel Pass, make a straightforward ford of the Brazeau River. We were entertained here as a ptarmigan hen, fleeing our presence, coerced her chicks into crossing the river. Ptarmigan are ground-dwelling birds. However, as this hen and her brood demonstrated, they are capable of short bursts of flight when they feel threatened.

The trail climbs away from the river and for the next kilometre winds through rockslide debris dotted with hardy alpine flowers: moss campion, sawwort, cinquefoil, white mountain avens and alpine milkvetch. Just before it commences a steep descent, the trail crests a small bluff that offers a panorama of the upper Brazeau Valley. This is a graphic overthrust landscape: the steeply tilted southwest-facing slopes of the front range peaks lead upwards to terminate on northeast-facing cliffs. The peaks are separated by parallel valleys, creating a symmetry that has led more than one visitor to comment: "all the mountains look the same." The colourful quartzite ridge to the north divides the drainages of Boulder and Four Point creeks. Particularly pleasing to the eye are the meanders, verdant wet meadows and waterfalls along the Brazeau River. The wet meadows are lush with the showy white tufts of cotton grass in late summer.

Good Stew, Nigel!

Nigel Vavasour was cook on the 1898 expedition that made the first ascent of Mt. Athabasca and discovered Columbia Icefield. The expedition included mountaineers John Norman Collie, Herman Woolley and Hugh Stutfield, and was guided by Bill Peyto (PEE-toe). On the way north from Lake Louise, the party lost many supplies when its testy pack horses plunged into the North Saskatchewan River. The larder was almost empty before serious climbing could begin. While Collie and Woolley claimed glory on the heights of Mt. Athabasca, Stutfield and Peyto undertook a more mundane pursuit. They hunted bighorn sheep near Nigel Pass in an area they called "Wild Sheep Hills." The hunt was successful, and the sheep stew that became the party's staple for the next two weeks must have been a success too, for the cook's name was applied to a number of features in the area.

Upper Brazeau Valley

The meandering course of the Brazeau River ends at a small canyon. The trail follows the east bank of the river to this point, then crosses to Boulder Creek campground. Beyond the campground, the trail undulates in forest alongside the canyon. There are many rocks and roots underfoot. You cross Boulder Creek in 600 m, on an artistically constructed log bridge.

Upper Brazeau Valley Forest

The forest in the upper Brazeau Valley is a curiosity. Although the elevation (2000 m) classifies the area as subalpine, the forest is a homogenous stand of lodgepole pine, typically a tree found at lower elevations in the montane ecoregion. These lodgepoles indicate the area was burned by an intense fire, for the resin-sealed cone of the lodgepole requires a heat of 45°C to crack open and release its seeds.

At this elevation, the first generation of lodgepole pines to follow a fire is normally replaced by a forest of Engelmann spruce and subalpine fir trees within 60-130 years, in a process called succession. In this forest, spruce and fir are almost absent. As the first growth of pines reached maturity and died off, they were replaced not by spruce and fir, but by another generation of widely spaced pines. Thus, lodgepole pines have become the climax species in this forest.

Why are spruce and fir absent here? The dry soils and open, sunny slopes are a per-

Backcountry Construction, Au Naturel

The use of natural materials for bridges prevails in Jasper's backcountry. In other parks, pressure-treated wood structures have been the norm for many years. By the time pressure-treated wood is purchased and flown to the work site (along with the trail crew), these structures involve a tremendous expense. Although supposedly "maintenance free" for 30-50 years, pressure-treated wood structures succumb to the vagaries of flash floods and undercut stream banks just as easily as bridges built from materials found on-site. The manufactured look of pressure-treated timbers is often an eyesore in remote settings, detracting from the experience of wilderness. Hopefully, the philosophy and woodworking skills associated with using natural materials will be revived in all the parks in future.

The Woodland (Mountain) Caribou

The caribou has a brown coat with lighter patches on the neck, rump, belly and lower legs. The neck is fringed on its underside. Both males and females sport antlers that feature a forward-reaching "shovel." In summer, it is usually the females that carry antlers, and their "rack" is smaller than that of mature males. When they run, caribou carry their heads high and tilted back, and they lift their legs in a distinctive prance. If you are close enough you will hear the clacking made by tendons in the animal's legs. The caribou's large hooves help support it in deep snow, leaving a track that is more rounded than that of other deer family members.

Jasper's caribou migrate between the high alpine of places like Jonas Pass in summer to lower forests in winter. Their staple foods are ground, tree and rock lichens. Caribou "crater" through the snow to obtain these in winter. Because of their seasonal migration, these animals have earned the unofficial designation, mountain caribou. In the nothern part of Jasper, the caribous' migration takes them out of the park onto provicincial lands, where they are not protected.

Between 1960 and 1990, Alberta's caribou population decreased from 9000 to 3000. Population estimates for Banff and Jasper parks suggest 350 to 400 animals, grouped into six herds. The herd that frequents Jonas Pass is thought to number 40 to 65 animals. Clearcut logging on provincial land has fragmented caribou habitat, and destroyed much of the old-growth forest that provides winter habitat and food for those caribou that migrate out of the parks. Logging roads have also opened up habitat to hunting and poaching. Further destruction of caribou habitat may initiate an "extinction vortex" – a situation in which the caribou's natural breeding rate cannot keep pace with deaths resulting from natural and unnatural causes.

In light of the grim situation facing Alberta's caribou, the provincial government has accomplished virtually nothing in the way of regulation or policy to help protect the species. In 1992, the Committee on the Status of Endangered Wildlife in Canada listed western woodland caribou populations as "vulnerable" for the first time. This means they are "particularly at risk because of low or declining numbers." In reality, with their small herd-size, Alberta's scattered caribou populations are in a much more precarious situation – they are endangered.

A multiyear study of Jasper's caribou was due for publication as this book went to press. It is expected to confirm the pressures facing the species. In 1992, the Jasper Environmental Association proposed establishment of Woodland Caribou Conservation areas within Jasper. Seasonal or permanent closures of some areas may be required to help protect the species.

Please abide by any new regulations. Only a concerted effort by governments, industry, hunters and hikers will insure the caribou's local survival. See Issues and Contacts in the Reference section at the back of this book.

fect ecological niche for the lodgepole pine, whereas spruce and fir prefer damper areas. "Old-growth" forests of lodgepoles are not common. It is especially surprising to find one at this elevation. Buffaloberry is prevalent in the undergrowth. This makes the forest excellent feeding habitat for grizzly bears in late July and August.

Four Point Campground

Most hikers travel as far as Four Point campground on the first day. Officially, "Four Point" refers to the fact that four trails converge here. However, the name was probably intended to described the number of points on the antler rack of a particular deer, caribou, moose or elk. Although in a pleasant setting, the campground shows the wear and tear of heavy use. Please do your part to minimize impacts at the campgrounds on this loop.

Four Point Campground to Jonas Cutoff Campground

The second day involves an energetic 18.9 km to Jonas Cutoff campground. All but the concluding 3.2 km are uphill. Since camping is not allowed until you reach Jonas Cutoff, you must complete the entire distance in one day. Start early to allow plenty of time to enjoy the alpine glory of Jonas Pass.

The Jonas Pass junction is 100 m northeast of Four Point campground. Turn northwest (left). The trail climbs into the hanging valley of Four Point Creek over a series of recessional moraines. Each moraine marks a position of temporary halt during the northward retreat of the glacier that once filled the valley. In the forest and on the river flats nearby, there are several drumlins – teardrop shaped mounds of glacial débris. The blunt end of each drumlin faced into the ice flow, and the tapered end faced away.

After a steady climb of 4 km, the trail levels out in open forest. The valley bottom is a frost hollow, devoid of trees, but bedecked with wildflowers. The shrub thickets and tundra are important habitats for the rarest member of the deer family in the Rockies, the woodland or mountain caribou.

As it approaches Jonas Pass, the trail is routed between Four Point Creek and a rocky bench to the west. The cliffs on the west side of the valley are riddled with glacial cirques. Meltwater from these glaciers is the source of the numerous silty tributary streams you must rock-hop. Some of the streams feature picturesque cascades, made colourful by dense blooms of

A.P.Coleman, A Professor of Mountaineering

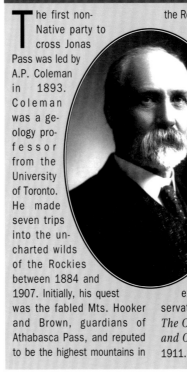

The first non-Native party to cross Jonas Pass was led by A.P. Coleman in 1893. Coleman was a geology professor from the University of Toronto. He made seven trips into the uncharted wilds of the Rockies between 1884 and 1907. Initially, his quest was the fabled Mts. Hooker and Brown, guardians of Athabasca Pass, and reputed to be the highest mountains in the Rockies.

During his journey of 1893, Coleman received advice on his route from a Stoney elder, Chief Jonas. Coleman named many features using Stoney, Cree and Iroquois words. Jonas Pass was named for his adviser. Coleman's considerable exploits and detailed observations were recorded in *The Canadian Rockies, New and Old Trails*, published in 1911.

Jonas Pass epitomizes the alpine country of Jasper's front ranges. Mountaineer A.P. Coleman named the pass in 1893 for a Stoney elder who gave advice about travel routes.

mountain fireweed and ragwort along their banks. Look for the mauve bloom of the alpine harebell on drier slopes.

The crest of Jonas Pass is typical of upper subalpine passes in the Rockies. Four lakelets and numerous seasonal ponds mark the imprecise height of land. Trees cannot grow in the pass itself because it is a frost hollow. The soil is frozen for much of the year, preventing the supply of water required for tree growth. However, just upslope on either side of the pass, a few islands of krummholz mark the uppermost limit of the forest. Alpine gentians can be found growing among the boulders in the pass. In 1992, a group of hikers watched spellbound as a cougar stalked a caribou herd nearby.

From Jonas Pass, the trail angles away from the upper reaches of Jonas Creek toward Jonas Shoulder. Several small tributary streams filter from the base of rockslides and cross the trail. These are the last water sources for 5 km.

The initial climb toward Jonas Shoulder is very steep. However, the grade moderates as the trail contours north. Three rock glaciers are visible to the west. They extend from the base of the cliffs across the valley onto the meadows near Jonas Creek. A rock glacier is an assemblage of rockslide débris that contains just enough ice to allow the entire mass to creep downhill. There are 119 rock glaciers in Jasper National Park. Many are stagnant or in decline. These rock glaciers are evidently advancing.

During this climb, there is a wonderful prospect south to Jonas Pass. The ridge east of the pass culminates nearby in a striking quartzite tower. Sunwapta Peak (3315 m), its north face cloaked in glacial ice, looms to the west. The mountain was first climbed in 1906 by guide and outfitter Jimmy Simpson. An unwilling mountaineer but a legendary hunter, Simpson was no doubt lured summitward while in pursuit of mountain goats or bighorn sheep.

The climb ends even more steeply than it began, on the crest of Jonas Shoulder – the ridge that separates the Jonas and Poboktan (poh-BOCK-tun) valleys. This is the 10th highest point reached by maintained trail in the Rockies. At the high point, you are greeted with a view north to Poboktan Mountain (3323 m).

The trail on the Poboktan side of Jonas Shoulder is snow-covered in early sum-

The alpine meadows of Poboktan Pass are frequented by caribou, bighorn sheep and grizzly bear.

mer, when an ice axe may prove useful. The trail angles sharply south (right), then switchbacks steeply down on scree. After crossing an intervening ridge, the trail rambles over boggy meadowland, paralleling the stream and descending rapidly north toward Poboktan Creek. Please keep to the beaten path to avoid creating braids in the trail. You will get your boots wet here. Shortly after you enter forest, look for a signed trail that branches west (left) to Jonas Cutoff campground. The campground is 200 m before the Poboktan Creek bridge and trail junction.

The Brazeau Lake Slide: The Walls Came Tumbling Down

When park warden Charlie Matheson rode down John-John Creek on a routine patrol in July 1933, he was the first person to see the aftermath of the tremendous Brazeau Lake Slide. He found the trail obliterated by a morass of mud and rocks. The debris was "still quivering." Needless to say, the backcountry telephone line was destroyed. Matheson reported that the water of Brazeau Lake had an odd taste for about a month, no doubt due to sediments from the slide.

The Brazeau Lake Slide is the largest landslide in the Rockies that is known to have occurred in the 20th century. The

slide was caused by separation of one or more of the underlying rock layers on the slope above. A build-up of pressure caused by water or ice within crack systems may have forced the layers apart. The rock that failed is Cambrian-age Pika limestone and dolomite. The bedding plane of the slide slope dips at 27° to the northeast (the direction of the lake), and is typical of

slopes that produce this kind of landslide.

Because the dead trees in the slide debris lie parallel to the direction of flow, the slide was probably not an instantaneous catastrophe such as the famous Frank Slide. (The wind blast from an instantaneous slide flattens trees at right angles to the flow.) The conical mounds in the runout of the slide are called mollards. Vibration of the ground during the slide caused sifting and sorting of rock and sediments, building the mollards. As unlikely as it seems, the effect has been duplicated in laboratory experiments.

Jonas Cutoff Campground to Brazeau Lake

The splendors of this loop hike continue into the third day. At the Poboktan Creek junction, turn southeast (right) and commence the climb to Poboktan Pass. Poboktan is Stoney for "owl." A.P. Coleman gave the name in 1892, when his party saw owls in the valley below.

The trail crosses and re-crosses the creek on bridges, and then angles steeply away from the east bank to climb through treeline. During the ascent you will see weathered posts, 5 m long, lying near the trail. These were formerly part of a backcountry telephone system, erected by park wardens in the 1920s. The advent of portable radios rendered the system obsolete, and the wires were removed.

Poboktan Pass is the third upper subalpine setting visited on this hike – a heath and avens tundra, dotted with krummholz, carpeted with wildflowers, and frequented by caribou and grizzly bear. The pass divides waters flowing north to the Arctic Ocean via the Athabasca, Slave, and Mackenzie rivers, from waters flowing east to the Hudson's Bay via the Brazeau, Saskatchewan, and Nelson rivers. Duncan McGillivray, a fur-trader with the North West Company, was probably the first non-Native to cross Poboktan Pass, in 1800. Flat Ridge (2820 m), directly southeast of the pass, features sev-

Brazeau Lake is one of the largest backcountry lakes in the Rockies. It is fed principally by meltwater from the Brazeau Icefield. Mt. Brazeau, the highest peak in the front ranges, is visible in the centre of the photograph.

eral rock glaciers on its north slopes.

The trail from Poboktan Pass descends at first gradually, then abruptly, into the forest along John-John Creek. John-John Harrington was father of Mona Matheson, Jasper's first female trail guide. She married Charlie Matheson, a park warden who was stationed in the Brazeau District during the 1930s.

For those who have wiled away the hours on Poboktan Pass, or who would otherwise like a short day on the trail, John-John campground makes a pleasant, creek-side stopping place.

From the campground, the trail follows the north bank of John-John Creek toward Brazeau Lake, then descends steeply through a forest of lodgepole pine to cross John-John Creek. On the east side of the bridge, the trail enters the debris of the Brazeau Lake

Slide.

The trail continues southeast beyond the slide, climbing into lodgepole pine forest that frustratingly offers only partial views of nearby

Joseph Brazeau

The features bearing the name "Brazeau" commemorate Joseph Brazeau, a trader, clerk and postmaster with the Hudson's Bay Company. Brazeau worked at fur-trade outposts along the eastern edge of the Rockies from 1852 to 1864. With his knowledge of Native languages, Brazeau was of great assistance to the Palliser Expedition. James Hector named the river for him in 1860. The lake and mountain were named by A.P. Coleman in 1892 and 1902 respectively. The mountain had appeared on earlier maps as "Mt. McGillivray."

Brazeau Lake. A steep descent east through a spruce-fir forest leads to the Brazeau River bridge, southeast of the lake's outlet. Be thankful for this bridge. The raging river would otherwise not be negotiable, except perhaps to daring souls on horseback. Across the river, turn northwest (left) to reach Brazeau River Bridge campground and the trail to the lakeshore. Turn southeast (right) to continue the loop.

From the campground, a rough track leads along the northeast shore of Brazeau Lake. With a length of 5 km, a maximum width of 900 m, and an area of 360 ha, the lake is one of the ten largest in the backcountry of the Rockies. It is fed by meltwater from the 25 km² Brazeau Icefield to the north. Mt. Brazeau (3470 m), highest mountain in the front ranges, towers over this domain of ice.

Brazeau Lake to Four Point Campground

From Brazeau River bridge, follow the north fork of the Brazeau River southeast for 2.9 km to a junction. Turn south (right) and cross the river on a high bridge to the Brazeau campground. The following 3.2 km of trail undulates over ancient rockslides forested with lodgepole pines, and makes for tedious travel.

After traversing high above the cleft of a canyon, the trail descends to the main branch of the Brazeau River and crosses to its east bank. Head downstream for 20 m to pick up the trail. The hiking immediately improves, with expansive vistas of the broad Brazeau Valley and surrounding peaks. Marble Mountain (2960 m) is to the north. By technical definition, "marble" is limestone or dolomite that has been recrystalized through heat or pressure. True marble is rare in the Rockies. However, in common usage marble refers to any limey sedimentary rock that can be polished. The effects of erosion by glacial ice and flowing water have created an abundance of this kind of "marble" in the Rockies.

The Brazeau River, like the Bow, Red Deer, Clearwater, North Saskatchewan and Athabasca rivers, cuts across the northwest/southeast grain, or strike of the Rockies. These rivers are thought to be as old as the mountains themselves. Their downwards erosion kept pace with uplift during mountain building. Hence the rivers maintained their unlikely courses.

Wolverine South campground is a wonderful stopping place for those who would like to extend their time in the Brazeau Valley. Views to the southwest include Mt. Athabasca (3491 m) on the fringe of Columbia Icefield, 20 km distant. The trail recrosses the Brazeau River on a bridge. Alternating between shrub meadows and pine forest, you may complete the loop back to Four Point campground. From here, it's an easy day's hike over familiar ground to the Icefields Parkway via Nigel Pass.

"Crossing the barren pass next morning, we followed a creek flowing northwest toward a wide river valley which we had looked at longingly from a mountaintop some days before. We named the pass and creek Poboktan, from the big owls that blinked at us from the spruce trees ..."

—A.P. Coleman (1892),
The Canadian Rockies: New and Old Trails, 1911

The Wilcox Pass hike features views of Athabasca Glacier and seven of the 25 highest mountains in the Canadian Rockies.

26. Wilcox Pass

Route

Day-hike, 12.0 km

Route	Elevation (m)	Distance (km)
Wilcox Creek CG	2035	0
Wilcox Pass	2360	4.5
Tangle Falls	1830	12.0

Topographic maps: 83 C/3, 83 C/6
Best lighting: morning

Trailhead

Wilcox Creek campground, on the east side of the Icefields Parkway (Highway 93) 124 km north of Lake Louise, 103.5 km south of Jasper, 2.8 km south of Columbia Icefield Information Centre.

When Walter Wilcox travelled north from Lake Louise in 1896, the toe of Athabasca Glacier blocked the upper Sunwapta Valley. The terrific rocky jumble of the Mt. Kitchener Slide lay just beyond, making travel directly north into the Sunwapta Valley impossible for horses. Wilcox's party skirted these obstacles by climbing over a pass to the northeast, to regain the Sunwapta Valley farther north. The Wilcox Pass-Tangle Creek trail retraces this historic route and offers panoramic views of the peaks and glaciers in the vicinity of Columbia Icefield.

Icefields Parkway to Wilcox Pass

From the trailhead at the entrance to Wilcox Creek campground, the trail climbs steeply into an ancient forest of Engelmann spruce. Given their proximity to Columbia Icefield and the resulting harsh local climate, some of these trees are remarkably old – 300 to 350 years is common. The oldest known Engelmann spruce in Jasper National Park(690 years) is just 3 km west of here. The high stumps you see are of trees cut for bridge timbers during construction of the original Icefields Parkway in the late 1930s.

The trail reaches treeline in 1 km at the edge of a cliff overlooking the Icefields Parkway. In the view south, from left to right the features are: Mt. Athabasca (3491 m), Mt. Andromeda (3450 m), Athabasca Glacier, Snow Dome (3451 m), Dome Glacier, and Mt. Kitchener (3480 m). Mt. Athabasca was first climbed in 1898 by the party that discovered Columbia Icefield. Today, it is one of the most frequently ascended alpine peaks in the Rockies. Look for climbers on the icy faces of this mountain and on Mt. Andromeda.

The trail veers north from the edge of the cliff and begins a rambling ascent through stands of ragged krummholz to Wilcox Pass. To the east is

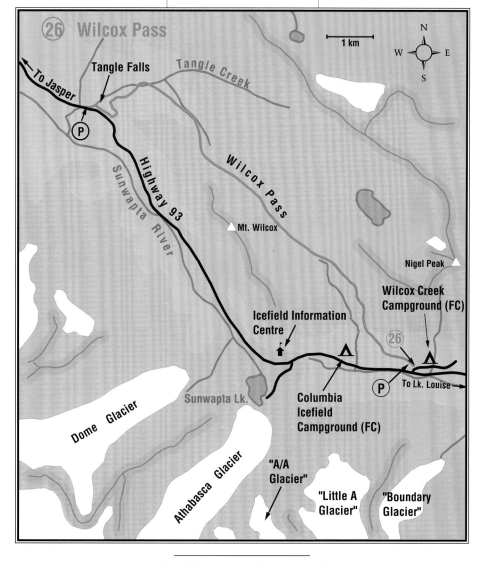

Nigel Peak (3211 m), named for Nigel Vavasour, cook on the expedition that discovered Columbia Icefield.

Wilcox Pass is alpine tundra at its best—a broad, U-shaped valley, 3 km in length. Wildflowers and wildlife abound. Flocks of bighorn sheep frequently congregate on lingering snow patches in the pass, seeking escape from heat and bugs. Other wildlife you may see include grizzly bear, moose, wolverine and golden eagle. Many of the ponds and bogs in the height of the pass are decorated with the showy, white tufts of cotton grass in early August. Cotton grass is a sedge with minuscule flowers concealed in its tufts.

Wilcox Pass to Tangle Falls

The trail becomes indistinct in the wet meadows as you cross the pass. Work your way up-slope toward Mount Wilcox, following occasional cairns, to gain the rocky bench about 20 m above the level of the pass. Please spread out to avoid repetitive trampling of vegetation. Continue north on this bench, usually without benefit of defined trail. The thistle-like purple bloom of sawwort colours the screes here.

At the north end of the bench, a faint track descends northeast toward upper Tangle Creek. This track soon becomes a well-beaten trail. The glaciated summits of Mt. Woolley (3405 m) (left), Diadem Peak (3371 m) and Mushroom Peak (3210 m) are grouped together in the northwest. Hermann Woolley was in the first ascent party on Mt. Athabasca and also made the first ascent of Mount Wilcox. Diadem refers to the snowy crest of the mountain. Mushroom Peak was named for an unusually shaped cornice of snow, noticed on the summit by renowned mountaineer N.E. Odell, who made the first ascent alone in 1947.

The domed summit of Tangle Ridge (3000 m) is due north. Later in the descent, you obtain a view of Mt. Alberta (3619 m), tucked in behind Mt. Woolley. Mt. Alberta is the fifth highest mountain in the Canadian Rockies and one of the most difficult to climb. This is the only maintained hiking trail from which it is visible.

You reach the sources of Tangle Creek in a large willow

Disappearing Ice and Disappearing Water

Looking south from Wilcox Pass, eight glaciers are visible: Boundary and "Little A" on Mt. Athabasca; "A-A" between Mts. Athabasca and Andromeda; two unnamed cascading glaciers on Mt. Andromeda; Athabasca; "Little Dome" and Dome. Between 1870 and 1971, Athabasca Glacier receded 1.6 km and decreased 57 percent in area, and 32 percent in volume. Recession continues today at the rate of 1 to 3 m per year.

The glacially streamlined form of Mount Wilcox (2884 m) borders the west side of the pass. Concealed from view on the east side of the pass is a large lake beneath Nigel Peak.

The lake has no surface outlet, indicating the presence of underground or karst drainage in the limestone bedrock. A large spring along Nigel Creek, 5 km south, is thought to be the outlet of this lake. If the park surveyors had known that waters from Wilcox Pass drain south, the area probably would have been included in Banff National Park, not Jasper.

Explorer Mary Schäffer named Tangle Falls in 1907, after an exasperating descent along the creek from Wilcox Pass. Bighorn sheep are often seen near the falls.

"*There remained a high grassy pass to the right, and here after reaching an elevation of 8000 feet, we were encouraged by seeing a long valley running north-west, which we knew must be some part of the Athabasca River. Thus the most critical part of our expedition, the discovery of a pass between the Saskatchewan and Athabasca, was safely accomplished.*"

—Walter Wilcox,
Camping in the Rockies, 1896

meadow. After re-entering the forest and crossing the creek to its south bank, the trail comes to an opening on a rise. In the view west beyond the ice-bound summits of Stutfield Peak (3450 m), is the shoulder of North Twin (3684 m), third highest mountain in the Rockies. In the clearing below this rise is an old campsite, with teepee poles still stacked against the trees. In the following clearing are the ruins of a cabin, possibly constructed by Jimmy Simpson or Bill Peyto in the early 1900s, to serve them on their winter trap lines.

The trail soon emerges from forest at the top of an open, grassy slope, 120 m above the Icefields Parkway. Bighorn sheep frequent this area. Descend south to the grade of the Wonder Road, forerunner of the Icefields Parkway. Follow this grade north to Tangle Creek and trail's end. Untracked bush is known to outfitters as "shin tangle." Tangle Creek and Falls were named in 1907 by explorer Mary Schäffer, following a difficult descent along the creek from Wilcox Pass. From Tangle Falls it is 9.8 km south along the Icefields Parkway to the original trailhead.

Fryatt Creek collects in this pool at the mouth of the Upper Fryatt Valley. In the background is Mt. Xerxes.

27. Fryatt Valley

Route

3-4 days, 23.2 km

Route	Elevation (m)	Distance (km)
Trailhead	1215	0
Athabasca River	1215	7.2
Athabasca Valley viewpoint	1240	8.6
Lower Fryatt CG	1280	11.6
Fryatt Creek bridge	1605	15.9
Brussels CG	1660	17.2
Fryatt Lake	1715	18.7
Headwall CG	1780	21.1
Sydney Vallance Hut	2000	22.0
Upper Fryatt Valley	2035	23.2

Topographic maps: 83 C/12, 83 C/5

Trailhead

Follow the Icefields Parkway (Highway 93) to the junction with Highway 93A at Athabasca Falls, 31.8 km south of Jasper, 70.9 km north of Columbia Icefield Information Centre. Turn west and follow Highway 93A, 1.1 km to the Fryatt Valley-Geraldine Lakes road. This gravel road may be gated, however it should not be locked unless the area is closed. Follow this road 2.1 km south to the signed trailhead for Fryatt Valley. Because this area is frequented by both black and grizzly bears, do not leave *any* food in your vehicle.

After a long approach during which the scenic interest builds gradually, the Fryatt Valley hike culminates in a wonderland of lakelets, pools, meadows, glaciers, disappearing rivers and savage peaks – all that is classic about the Canadian Rockies packed into a valley less than 3 km long.

Both black and grizzly bears frequent this trail. On our first venture to the Fryatt trailhead we saw an enormous grizzly just 40 m from the parking area. The trail is shared with mountain bikers as far as the first campground.

Geraldine Fireroad to Lower Fryatt Campground

The hike begins with an easy fireroad walk along the west bank of the Athabasca River, through a fire-succession forest of lodgepole pine. The resin-sealed cones of the lodgepole generally require the heat of a forest fire to open. The fire that helped create most of these trees took place in 1889, when much of the Athabasca Valley burned.

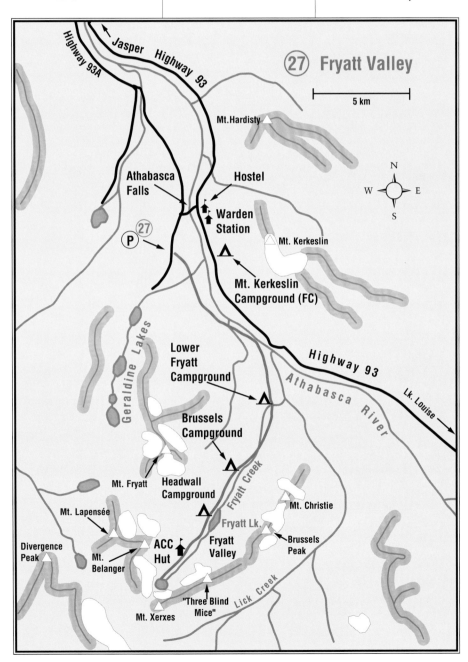

27 Fryatt Valley

Highway 93A

Jasper Highway 93

5 km

Mt. Hardisty

Athabasca Falls

Hostel

Warden Station

P 27

Mt. Kerkeslin

Mt. Kerkeslin Campground (FC)

Geraldine Lakes

Lower Fryatt Campground

Highway 93

Athabasca River

Lk. Louise

Brussels Campground

Fryatt Creek

Mt. Fryatt

Headwall Campground

Mt. Christie

Mt. Lapensée

Fryatt Lk.

Brussels Peak

Divergence Peak

Mt. Belanger

ACC Hut

Fryatt Valley

Lick Creek

"Three Blind Mice"

Mt. Xerxes

Goat tracks

East of the trail are a number of sloughs, formerly kettle lakes, created by melting blocks of ice at the end of the Wisconsin Glaciation. The lakes have filled with sediments that now support aquatic vegetation. They offer good habitat for moose.

At km 2.0 the trail crosses the braided outlet stream from the Geraldine Lakes. This stream is prone to flash-flooding. Over millennia, a large alluvial fan has been built from shales brought down from the mountainsides. Trail crews have difficulty maintaining the bridge over this lively stream. The adjacent trail often becomes a watercourse. You may have to rock-hop the stream and pick your way for a short distance either side. Trembling aspen and balsam poplar trees grow here.

The pleasant stroll through the forest continues. At km 7.2, the trail draws alongside the Athabasca River, with the Icefields Parkway just 150 m away on the opposite bank. The sediment-choked waters of the Athabasca are a formidable barrier to travel.

In the 1800s, the voyageurs of the fur trade called their route across Athabasca Pass "la grande traverse" [the great crossing]—in reference to the difficult ford of this river. From this vantage, you can imagine the harrowing prospect of having to cross this torrent on foot or in a makeshift raft.

At km 8.0 the trail veers away from the river and climbs over a knoll covered in a doghair forest of lodgepole pine. The trail emerges from the forest above the confluence of Lick Creek and the Athabasca River, atop a bank of glacial till. Till banks in this part of the Athabasca Valley are rich in sulphur-bearing minerals. Deer, elk and mountain goats congregate here to lick at the sediments and obtain a natural dietary supplement. The minerals are especially important to mountain goats during late spring, when they shed their winter coats. You may see goat wool clinging to shrubs and tree bark, as well as goat tracks and pellet-like droppings, common on the trail nearby.

The tremendous breadth of the Athabasca Valley fills the view south. It is hard to imagine that this valley was filled with glacial ice a kilometre thick during the Ice Age. Although the eastern slope of the valley is now home to the Icefields Parkway, the western slope, travelled by this trail, is still unspoiled. Look for golden eagles overhead. The inspiring, graceful flight of this raptor perfectly characterizes the wilderness nature of this valley.

Lower Fryatt campground is at km 11.6. This pleasant stopping place is on an alluvial fan beside the considerable torrent of Fryatt Creek. It

From Icefield to Ocean

From its sources on the northern edge of Columbia Icefield, the Athabasca River flows 1230 km to Lake Athabasca in northeastern Alberta. Its waters eventually reach the Arctic Ocean via the Mackenzie River system. Athabasca is Cree for "place where there are reeds," referring to the delta at the river's mouth. The name was one of the first to be used by Europeans in the Rockies, possibly as early as 1790. The 168 km section of the Athabasca River within Jasper National Park was designated a Canadian Heritage River in 1989. The Province of Alberta refuses to participate in the Heritage Rivers Program, so the designation stops at the park boundary.

is likely to be chilly here at night, since cold air will drain down along Fryatt Creek from the valley above.

Lower Fryatt Campground to Upper Fryatt Valley

Cross the creek on a good bridge, and prepare yourself for the climb ahead. The forest becomes more subalpine in character as you ascend the shady slope toward the mouth of the Fryatt Valley. The entrance to the valley is guarded by a quartzite spire to the north. The layers of rock on this outlying peak of Mt. Fryatt are thrust upwards toward the northeast, and are part of the western arm of an anticline. The Athabasca Valley has been eroded downwards

Fryatt Valley is in the centre of this view from Goats and Glaciers viewpoint on the Icefields Parkway.

through this massive, arch-shaped fold. There are many streams to hop at the valley mouth. Two of these are silty. They drain a glacially fed lake on the north slope of Mt. Christie.

Fryatt Valley is a textbook example of a hanging valley. During the Wisconsin Glacia-

tion, glaciers in tributary valleys did not erode as deeply as the ancestral Athabasca Glacier eroded the Athabasca Valley. As a result, when the glacial ice receded, the tributary valleys were left hanging above the floor of the Athabasca Valley. If you look at the topographic map, you

Bear Alley

Buffaloberry is a common shrub in the undergrowth in the Athabasca Valley, and a principal reason why bears frequent the Fryatt Valley trail. The shrub's glossy, dark green leaves are pale and fuzzy underneath, with rust-coloured dots. The red and amber berries are the staple food of bears in late July and August, when they comprise up to 95 percent of a typical black bear's diet. An adult grizzly may eat 200,000 of these berries a day. How does a bear eat something as small as a buffaloberry? Not one at a time. A bear threshes

the branches of the shrub through its jaws, getting a mouth full of berries and leaves. To us, the buffaloberry is sweet, but has a repulsive aftertaste.

If the berry crop is on, you should make lots of noise while hiking this trail. Bears will often be preoccupied with feed-

ing, and may not hear you approach. If a bear perceives you as a threat to its food source, understandably it might become aggressive. Scats containing red berries, tracks in muddy areas, and damage to the shrubs will warn you that a bear is about.

Grizzly bear tracks

will see this graphically depicted. The contours on the southwestern slope of the Athabasca Valley, either side of Fryatt Creek, describe a uniform cliff, more than 15 km in length. Through this cliff, Fryatt Creek and the streams draining numerous cirques to the north and south, plunge toward the Athabasca Valley.

Boats, Bolts and Pitons

The names of the mountains that flank the Fryatt Valley have interesting histories. Mt. Christie (3103 m) was named by James Hector in 1859, for William Christie, who was then in charge of Fort Edmonton. Christie lent assistance to Hector during the winter of 1858-59. Mt. Fryatt (3361 m) was named by the Interprovincial Boundary Commission in 1920 for Charles Fryatt, captain of *The Brussels*, a Belgian merchant vessel that ran interference in the English Channel during World War I. Fryatt was captured by the Germans and executed. The striking turreted form of Brussels Peak (3161 m) honours Fryatt's ship. This summit is one of the more challenging climbs in the Rockies, and was one of the last major peaks near a highway to be climbed. The controversial first ascent took place in 1948, and was aided by the placing of pitons and bolts. Many mountaineers of the day considered such tactics to be "cheating." Today, bolts, pitons and other aids are widely used in rock climbing.

The grade eases, and the trail soon crosses to the northwest side of Fryatt Creek on an imaginatively installed log bridge. From here you obtain your first tantalizing views of the Upper Fryatt Valley. Although the surrounding mountainsides rise steeply, the valley floor here feels quite open after travel through the confined forest below. The trail is rocky and vague in places as it follows the northwest bank of Fryatt Creek. Rock-hop and follow cairns.

Brussels campground is recommended to those who will be day-hiking to the Upper Fryatt Valley. Although Headwall campground is closer to the upper valley, it is a poor camping place, and is best avoided.

The alluvial fan beyond Brussels campground has been created by debris flows and meltwater surges from the tributary valley to the north. The fan almost completely fills the valley floor and has forced Fryatt Creek to the south. The constriction creates a natural dam that impounds the waters of Fryatt Lake. You obtain your first view of this charming body of water as the trail climbs over the fan. The waterfall that drains the upper valley graces the headwall beyond. The glaciated summits are the "Three Blind Mice" (2720 m) to the south (left), and Mt. Xerxes (ZURK-seas) (2970 m). Brussels Peak appears formidable from here. On the base of its southwest ridge is a series of pinnacles that resembles a miniature Stonehenge.

Rock-hop streams on the alluvial fan and descend to Fryatt Lake. Follow a rough track along the northwest shore to Headwall campground. Headwall is a graphic example of where not to place a campground in the Rockies. It is among cow parsnip at the base of a large avalanche slope, a possible haven for grizzly bears. Tent sites are virtually right on the trail. The campground is shaded in the evening and early morning and it lacks a food cache.

Beyond the campground, you climb steeply to the base of the 200 m high headwall that separates the upper and lower valleys. This headwall is one of the most unpleasant sections of "trail" in the Rockies. Outrageously steep, and poorly defined in places, the trail is more a scramble than a hike. Thankfully, this struggle is over in less than a kilometre. From the top of the climb, there are magnificent views northeast over Fryatt Valley. However, the greatest scenic rewards of this hike are yet to come, in the Upper Fryatt Valley to the southwest.

Upper Fryatt Valley

From the top of the headwall in the Upper Fryatt Valley, the raw beauty of the Rockies is revealed with splendor and grace. Fryatt Creek collects in a delightful pool above the headwall. Fringed with meadow and subalpine forest, this pool creates an idyllic foreground for the exquisite

The Upper Fryatt Valley is renowned for its karst features. Here, Fryatt Creek flows into an underground channel.

"*On the Athabasca side, glaciers occupy the heads of the gorges.... With the many lakes it is an attractive corner of the range and in future should become a worthwhile objective for mountain travelers.*"

—Mountaineer Howard Palmer, *Appalachia*, 1926

arrangement of glaciated mountains that ring the Upper Fryatt Valley.

The Alpine Club of Canada's Sydney Vallance Hut, built in 1970, is located nearby. Follow the trail southwest from the hut to the first tributary stream. Keep straight ahead, hop the stream and cross a wet meadow to cliffs where cairns mark the trail.

The limestone bedrock of the upper valley exhibits remarkable karst features. The first example was the pool above the headwall. It drains underground into the waterfall. Now you will see where Fryatt Creek disappears into, and emerges from various underground channels. The final act in the scenic drama of the Fryatt Valley is revealed when the trail winds through a boulder garden, then descends to the shore of an unnamed lake at the foot of extensive moraines below Mt. Xerxes. This is the epitome of cliff, tarn, meadow and glacier that characterizes the Canadian Rockies for so many hikers.

Mt. Olympus (2940 m) is the mountain immediately north of Mt. Xerxes. Olympus was the dwelling place of the gods in Greek mythology. Xerxes was a Persian king from 486-465 BC. Mt. Belanger (bell-ON-zjay) (3120 m) is farther north, with a niche glacier on its southeast slopes. The mountain was named for André Belanger, a fur trader who crossed Athabasca Pass in 1814, and subsequently drowned in the Athabasca River just east of the Rockies. To the south of the lake is an impressive terminal moraine, created during the Little Ice Age.

The Upper Fryatt Valley offers tremendous opportunities for wandering and exploration. If you choose to travel off-trail, please spread out to avoid repetitive trampling of the fragile upper subalpine vegetation. Do not venture onto glacial ice unless you are experienced and properly equipped for glacier travel.

The Ramparts rise in a fortress-like wall above Amethyst Lakes in this view from Surprise Point.

28. Tonquin Valley

Route

3-5 days, 43.7 km loop

Route	Elevation (m)	Distance (km)
Tonquin Valley trailhead	1738	0
Astoria CG	1692	6.8
Chrome Lake jct	1695	8.2
Switchback CG	2100	13.8
Amethyst Lakes jct	1979	16.8
Clitheroe CG	2073	16.9
Surprise Point CG	1982	*19.1
Amethyst Lakes CG	1982	20.2
Moat Lake jct	1982	22.7
Maccarib CG	1997	23.6
Maccarib Pass	2210	31.1
Portal Creek CG	1982	36.0
Portal Creek trailhead	1480	43.7

* Surprise Point campground (CG) is a sidetrip from the loop, and will add 4.4 km to the loop distance.

Topographic maps: 83 D/9, 83 D/16

Trailhead

Follow the Icefields Parkway (Highway 93), 6.7 km south from Jasper to Highway 93A. Turn right and follow Highway 93A south for 5.2 km. Turn right onto the Mt. Edith Cavell Road, and follow this 12.5 km to the Tonquin Valley trailhead parking lot, opposite the youth hostel. Large recreational vehicles and trailers are not allowed on the Mt. Edith Cavell Road. Use the trailer drop-off. A shuttle service is available from Jasper (fee charged). There is a hostel adjacent to the trailhead.

The Tonquin Valley is the backpacking mecca of Jasper National Park. The unbroken precipice of The Ramparts towering above Amethyst Lakes, is a trademark backcountry view, renowned throughout the world.

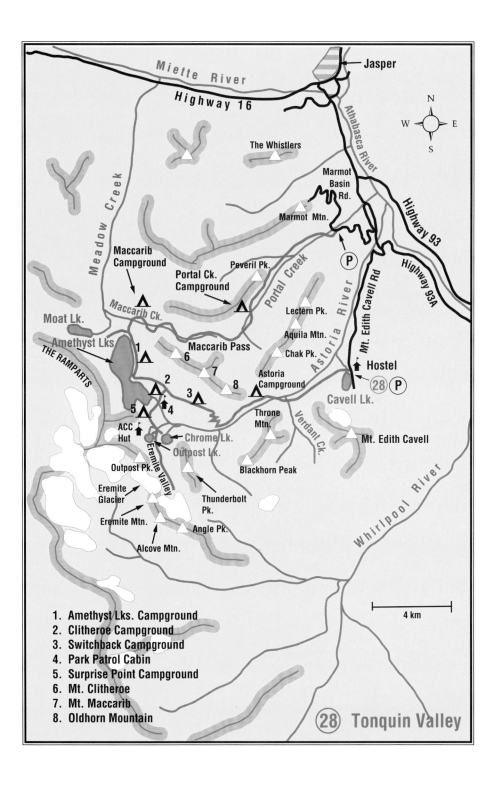

1. Amethyst Lks. Campground
2. Clitheroe Campground
3. Switchback Campground
4. Park Patrol Cabin
5. Surprise Point Campground
6. Mt. Clitheroe
7. Mt. Maccarib
8. Oldhorn Mountain

28 Tonquin Valley

However, despite the scenic attraction, some will find the Tonquin overrun with hikers, horses and mosquitoes. There is no question: solitude is hard to find. In 1993, the maximum number of hikers allowed on the trail at any time was 75. The quota was often filled. There are two horse outfitter's camps on the shores of Amethyst Lake. These may bring two dozen more people into the area daily (along with horseflies). Day-rides also take place in both the Astoria and Portal valleys, where strings of 15 to 20 horses and riders may be encountered.

The Tonquin Valley receives twice as much precipitation as Jasper townsite. The wet meadows near the lakes swarm with mosquitos as thick as anywhere in the Rockies. Although a great deal of money has been spent rebuilding portions of trail to sustain the impact of horses, there remain sections that make for poor hiking during spring runoff and summer rains. Yes, the Tonquin Valley is an extremely beautiful place. However, if you want your experience to be blissful rather than baneful, avoid this outing during early season and spells of poor weather.

Mt. Edith Cavell Road to Clitheroe Campground

The trail is initially road-width and descends to the outlet of Cavell Lake. From the bridge you have an inspiring view south to Mt. Edith Cavell (3363 m), the highest mountain in this area. The mountain was named by surveyor A.O. Wheeler to commemorate British nurse Edith Cavell. Remaining in Brussels after it fell to the Germans in World War 1, she was executed in 1915 for allegedly assisting the escape of prisoners of war.

Keep right at the junction across the bridge. The next 4.7 km are a novelty for the beginning of a hike. The trail de-scends gradually over this distance, crossing Verdant Creek en route. The mature forest at trailside consists of Engelmann spruce and whitebark pine, with an understory dominated by the buffaloberry. Its red and amber berries are a favourite food of black and grizzly bears. You may see tracks and scats of bears in the mud along the trail. Throne Mountain (3120 m) is the prominent peak to the west. The mountain resembles a massive armchair. A deep glacial cirque has been eroded between the two ridges, which create the mountain's "arm rests."

Cross the Astoria River on a bridge and follow the north bank 1.8 km to Astoria campground. The fruits of crowberry, grouseberry, bearberry and bunchberry (dwarf dogwood) colour the undergrowth nearby in late summer. Because of excessive use of the Tonquin loop by horse parties, you should treat water from all sources on this hike before consumption. Be sure to take your water upstream from the trail, to minimize the chance of contamination by horse dung and urine.

Keep straight ahead at the Chrome Lake junction. The approach to Chrome Lake from here is on a poor trail and is not recommended. It is better to day-hike to Chrome Lake from the campgrounds near Amethyst Lakes. Just beyond the junction is a corral used as a lunch stop by the horse day-rides. Please close the horse gate behind you.

The trail is poor and wet

The Tonquin: A Blast From the Past

Fort Astoria was an outpost established by fur-trading magnate John Jacob Astor, near the mouth of the Columbia River in 1811. *The Tonquin* was an ocean-going fur trade vessel belonging to Astor. How did these names come inland to the Rockies? The connection is tenuous. The Athabasca Pass fur-trade route lay 30 km south of the Tonquin Valley, and was used by some of Astor's employees in 1813. The names were applied by the Interprovincial Boundary Survey in 1916.

Astor subsequently sold *The Tonquin* to the Hudson's Bay Company. While it was anchored in Clayoquot (KLAH-kwit) Sound off the west coast of Vancouver Island, Natives boarded the ship and killed most of the crew. Some of the survivors then blew-up the ship, killing all who remained on board.

beneath the quartzite rock-slide on Oldhorn Mountain. On the west side of this slide, the trail switchbacks upward to gain entry to the Tonquin Valley. By the early 1980s, the trail here had been tremendously damaged by horses and extensive rehabilitation was necessary. Heavy machinery was flown in, and sections of trail were crowned and ditched to improve drainage. Soil blanket was installed beneath the tread surface to prevent deep mud holes from developing. Much of the tread surface is gravel, transported here by helicopter. Although the expensive finished product looks out of place in the subalpine meadows, it has significantly reduced the muck and mire underfoot.

The trail levels out near the Switchback campground junction. From this vicinity you obtain your first, tantalizing view of The Ramparts and Amethyst Lakes. Continuing northwest, the trail makes a treeline traverse through delightful meadowland on the slopes beneath Oldhorn Mountain (2988 m). The views continue to improve, and now they include Chrome Lake to the south, and Moat Lake to the northwest. After a short descent, the trail reaches the Clitheroe junction.

You have three options for camping nearby. The Amethyst Lake campground is 3.3 km to the north (right); Surprise Point is 2.2 km to the southwest (left); and Clitheroe campground is 100 m west (left) of the junction. Clitheroe is an Old English name, with Germanic origins and various translations: "hill by the water"; "song thrush hill"; and "hill of loose stones."

A Mountain Fortress

The Ramparts are a lofty precipice of Gog quartzite, 900 m high in places, that extends in an arc for 14 km along the continental divide. Seven of The Ramparts' named summits exceed 3050 m. Many names along The Ramparts were given by the Interprovincial Boundary Survey between 1916 and 1925, and they were inspired by the fortress-like appearance of the mountain wall: Parapet, Dungeon, Redoubt, Drawbridge, Bastion, Turret and Barbican. Moat Lake, at the foot of the northern Ramparts, completes the motif.

Clitheroe Campground Junction to Surprise Point

If you would like to day-hike in the Eremite Valley, you should camp at Surprise Point. The trail to and from this campground will add 4.4 km to the length of the Tonquin loop. The trail to Surprise Point passes directly through Clitheroe campground, and it soon deteriorates into a horse-churned quagmire. The character of the trail improves slightly as it angles south into a large meadow that contains the Amethyst Lakes patrol cabin. In front of the cabin, turn west (right) into forest, and follow signs for Surprise Point.

The trail emerges from the forest into an extensive wet meadow on the east shore of Lower Amethyst Lake. Look for fish and waterfowl in the larger stream channels. Follow metal markers across a cotton grass bog to the bridged outlet of the lower lake. This vantage offers one of the finest prospects of The Ramparts. Surprise Point campground is 400 m beyond, set on a rocky knoll and surrounded by wetland.

The campground provides a panoramic view of the Tonquin and upper Astoria valleys. From here, Mt. Edith Cavell is almost unrecognizable – a rocky chisel scraping the sky. Unfortunately, the campground is often teeming with bugs. The only appealing

Chrome Lake-Outpost Lake-Eremite Valley

20.8 km return from Surprise Point campground

For those who don't mind rough trails, these three destinations can be combined into an energetic and rewarding day-hike from either Surprise Point or Clitheroe campground. This outing requires a challenging ford of Eremite Creek, that should not be attempted by the inexperienced.

Chrome Lake

Head south on a rooted, rocky and muddy trail, that descends 2.1 km to a junction northwest of Chrome Lake. A 200 m sidetrip to the east (left) takes you to the swampy shore of the lake, where bog orchids and spotted frogs may be seen. The upper Eremite Valley, your ultimate destination on this day-hike, is to the south. Backtrack to the junction, and head west on the Outpost Lake trail for 400 m to another junction. Straight ahead (south) is the Eremite Valley.

Outpost Lake

Turn west (right) if you would like to make the 2.4 km return sidetrip to secluded Outpost Lake. The Outpost Lake trail crosses Penstock Creek and climbs steeply onto a knoll of rockslide débris and the forested lakeshore. The Alpine Club of Canada's Wates-Gibson Hut is nearby. The building is named for Cyril Wates and Rex Gibson, two mountaineers who were active in this area from the 1920s to the 1940s. The present hut is the third structure in this vicinity, and it dates to 1967. The foundation and chimney of its predecessor, constructed in 1947, can be seen along the east shore of the lake.

Outpost Lake contains the only non-silty drinking water you will find on this hike. There are many mountaineer's paths in this area. One leads to a sedge meadow south of Surprise Peak. The meadow is frequented by northern bog lemmings. This rodent is one of the most uncommon mammals in Jasper National Park and prefers damp habitats in the upper subalpine. Return via the main trail to the Outpost Lake junction.

Eremite Valley

The Eremite Valley trail follows Penstock Creek south. Mt. Bennington (3265 m) is the prominent peak to the west, named for Bennington, Vermont, birthplace of fur-trader and explorer Simon Fraser. Meltwater from glaciers on the north side of the peak is a principal source of the 1368 km Fraser River.

The origin of Penstock Creek's unusual name is soon revealed. Just north of its junction with Eremite Creek, Penstock Creek flows underground through a bedrock tunnel – a natural penstock. Cross the creek easily on the natural bridge that results.

The ford of Eremite Creek is the crux of this hike. On hot days, the glacial flow is swift, murky and extremely cold. (Remember, the ford will probably be more difficult on your return, when the water level will have risen.) After this moderate to difficult ford, do not follow the well-beaten trail east toward Chrome Lake. Pick up a faint trail heading south. It is on the west side of the bedrock ridge that separates Eremite Creek from Chrome Lake.

After a kilometre of hiking through willows, the trail ascends slightly into a flower-filled

continued on next page

water source is Lower Amethyst Lake, more than 200 m distant. (Bring a water billy.) Surprise Point (2378 m), southwest of the campground, was named because a party from the Interprovincial Boundary Survey was surprised at how long it took them to reach its lowly summit in 1916.

The sedges in the wet meadows, bordering Amethyst Lakes and in the terrain surrounding Astoria River and Maccarib Creek, are important summer food for mountain caribou. The herd that frequents this area contains 30 to 35 animals. Caribou are cold-adapted animals. During the summer they escape the heat by congregating on perennial snow patches in nearby side valleys. Although frequently seen in the Tonquin Valley, caribou are shy and usually flee humans.

Eremite Valley continued

The Eremite Valley is the most rewarding sidetrip on the Tonquin Loop. The rough trail ends at a series of moraines created during the Little Ice Age and provides views of rugged, glaciated quartzite peaks.

glade, and descends again to the creek. This area has been the site of five Alpine Club of Canada mountaineering camps since 1941 The campfire circle, firewood piles and tent poles of the last camp may still be seen. Camping and fires are no longer allowed. Beyond, the trail climbs steeply into upper sub-alpine forest. Eremite Glacier occupies a deep cirque to the west. Fine waterfalls cascade over the ice-worn cliffs beneath it. Where the trail drops into a small draw, take the east (left) branch, and resume the climb over rockslide debris and through a shintangle of krummholz fir.

Upper Eremite Valley

The upper valley is packed with spectacular scenery. A chaos of moraines marks the maximum extent of various glaciers during the Little Ice Age. Arrowhead Lake is dammed by the curving east lateral moraine of Eremite Glacier. The lake is not a picturesque glacial tarn, but a murky, shallow flat where meltwater loaded with sediment collects.

About 4.5 km south of the Outpost Lake junction, the Eremite trail disappears in a meadow bisected by meltwater streams. Boulder-hop the streams and scramble onto the moraines to the south for a marvellous view of the peaks, glaciers and tarns at the head of the valley. An "eremite" is a religious recluse or hermit. The name was applied to the 2910 m mountain west of the valley in 1916, by surveyor M.P. Bridgland. Bridgland considered it "a solitary peak."

Clitheroe Junction to Maccarib Creek Campground

The Tonquin loop continues north from the Clitheroe junction on a rocky trail that descends toward the peninsula that separates the two Amethyst Lakes. The buildings in view are part of a horse outfitter's camp. Across the lake, six glaciers are visible on The Ramparts. Four of these glaciers created horseshoe-shaped terminal moraines during the Little Ice Age.

After it gains the east shore of Upper Amethyst Lake, the trail swings north alongside a marsh to the Amethyst Lake campground.

If you choose to camp here, be aware that outfitters graze their horses nightly along the east and north shores of Upper Amethyst Lake. The tinkle of horse bells

Moat Lk., 3.5 km

The Moat Lake junction is 2.5 km north of Amethyst Lake campground. Although the sidetrip to the lake is scenic, the developed trail has been severely damaged by horse traffic. The final 1.5 km involves a poorly defined track across a boulder meadow covered in willows. However, the rewards are a close-up view of the northern Ramparts, and there is a pleasing prospect of Mt. Clitheroe and Majestic Hill if you return in the light of late afternoon.

Goodair's Final Resting Place

The grave of park warden Percy Goodair is just north of Maccarib campground. Goodair was district warden in the Tonquin Valley in the 1920s, and worked from a cabin located here. On September 12, 1929, he met his end outside the cabin door. When his body was recovered, it was evident it had been mauled and scavenged by a grizzly bear. It is unknown whether the bear killed him, or if he died of natural causes.

Mountaineer James Monroe Thorington characterized Goodair in 1925: "A quiet, pleasant man, he had had the usual interesting career of those whom one runs across in the far places. Studying medicine in London, he enlisted and went to Africa during the Boer War, remaining afterward in the South African diamond fields, wandering as a prospector to strange corners of the earth, and at last finding a life in the Canadian wilderness that pleased and held him. We could quite understand it, and not without a touch of envy."

A mountain west of The Ramparts commemorates Goodair. Another mountain northeast of Lake Louise was named for him in 1986, when six national park wardens who have died in the line of duty were commemorated in the Warden Range.

keeps many a tired hiker awake. The practice of permitting horse grazing in caribou habitat has long been a point of contention between environmental groups and Jasper National Park.

A braided trail leads north from the campground. This area is underlain by bouldery glacial till, which makes for a rough trail. The view of the northwestern arc of The Ramparts from this area was featured in A.Y. Jackson's 1924 painting, "The Ramparts." Jackson was a member of The Group of Seven artists, who specialized in Canadian landscapes. The highest peak in The Ramparts is Mt. Geikie (GEEK-ee) (3270 m). The mountain is entirely in BC, and was named for Scottish geologist, Sir Archibald Geikie.

The Tonquin loop climbs away from the northeast shore of Upper Amethyst Lake through open spruce forest, and then descends to Maccarib (mah-KAH-rib) Creek. Cross the bridge and turn east (right) at the Meadow Creek junction. The sidetrail to Maccarib Creek campground is 50 m farther.

Maccarib campground is shared by hikers and non-

"Maccarib" is a native word that means "caribou." Caribou are rare in Banff and Jasper national parks. The photograph shows Maccarib Pass, one of the best places to see caribou.

commercial horse parties. Situated on a bench above the north bank of Maccarib Creek, it offers exceptional views west to The Ramparts and east to Maccarib Pass. Appropriately, *Maccarib* is Quinnipiac for "caribou." This animal is often seen between the campground and Maccarib Pass.

Tragedy at Portal Creek

In 1992, grizzly bear warnings had been posted for the Tonquin loop for much of the summer. A sow with two cubs, and two individual bears had been frequently observed. However, no bear-human incidents had taken place. On September 15, a couple was surprised by an aggressive grizzly bear as they set up camp at Portal Creek campground. The female hiker attempted to escape by climbing a tree. The bear pursued her and reached into the tree. The male hiker approached in order to draw the bear away. The bear attacked the male and eventually killed him – to date the only recorded bear mauling fatality since Jasper National Park was established. The female hiker escaped with the assistance of another camper, who then ran to the trailhead for help. Park wardens flew to the site three hours after the attack. The bear charged them from the willows and was shot and killed immediately.

Heavy snowfalls had blanketed the Jasper area three times in the previous two weeks. Although surprise is thought to have been the major factor prompting the bear's attack, it is possible the bear was under stress because its regular food sources had been killed by frost and buried under snow.

Maccarib Campground to Marmot Basin Road

The trail to Maccarib Pass ascends gradually through wet upper subalpine meadows, crossing Maccarib Creek and its tributaries numerous times on bridges. Most of the trail has been rehabilitated. Gravel cap has been laid over soil blanket and the edges have been reinforced with timber, creating a finished product called "turnpiking." This costly undertaking was necessary to repair the damage caused by horses. Mt. Clitheroe (2747 m) forms the southern slope of the valley. It features a sizeable rock glacier comprised of quartzite boulders.

Ragwort and common fireweed grow at trailside on the final climb to Maccarib Pass. The tundra of the pass stretch-

Caribou track

es for almost 2 km over the divide between Maccarib and Portal creeks. Low-lying areas feature frost hummocks. These earth mounds are created by churning during repeated freezing and thawing of damp soil. The hummocks are vegetated with western anemone, woolly everlasting, and mountain heather. Snow willow, arctic willow, white mountain avens and moss campion grow in the hollows between them. White-tailed ptarmigan and Columbian ground squirrels may be seen on the pass. Mt. Edith Cavell is visible again to the southwest, over Astoria Pass.

From Maccarib Pass, the trail switchbacks down to Portal Creek through rolling subalpine meadows. The mountains surrounding Portal Creek are composed mostly of reddish Gog quartzite. In 1916, surveyor M.P. Bridgland named two mountains along the creek for golden eagles seen in the vicinity – Chak Peak (2798 m) and Aquila Mountain (2880 m). *Chak* is Stoney for eagle; *aquila* is the Latin word. The slopes of Chak Peak contain a large rock glacier. Farther down the valley is Lectern Peak (2774 m), named for the rostrum of rock at its summit. Directly down the valley, you can see the grey limestone peaks of the Colin Range, northeast of Jasper.

Cross the south fork of Portal Creek to a corral that is used by horse outfitters as a lunch stop. A kilometre far-

ther, the trail levels out along the north bank at Portal Creek campground. Beyond the campground, the trail ascends onto a rocky sideslope and contours across the flank of Peveril Peak before descending steeply through lodgepole pine forest to cross the north fork of Portal Creek.

The remaining 3.7 km of trail continues the steady descent, and passes beside two outcrops of glacial till. Numerous game trails indicate that these outcrops are probably used by goats and deer as mineral licks. From the second outcrop, you have a fine view west along Portal Creek to Peveril Peak (2686 m). This mountain's unusual name was in the title of a novel written by Sir Walter Scott. The last interesting feature on the Tonquin loop is a mass of downed trees to the south of the trail. The weathered trees are apparently ancient avalanche débris from the opposite side of the valley. This slope has since revegetated with mature forest, indicating the avalanche probably took place at least 200 years ago.

Cross the bridge to the south bank of Portal Creek. The Tonquin loop ends a few hundred metres later at a parking lot on the Marmot Basin Road. Turn east (right) to descend this road, 6.5 km to its junction with Highway 93 A. At this junction, turn north (left) for Jasper, or south (right) for the Mt. Edith Cavell Road junction. You should

prearrange transportation for the conclusion of this hike. Otherwise, avoid arriving at the Marmot Basin road late in the day, unless the prospect of a long walk on the road is agreeable.

"*One realizes instinctively in the valley of the Tonquin that the carving of its great rock spires is still in the formative stage. The work is still going on; the mountains are but roughly hewn out, with an impressionistic technique as fantastic as it is fanciful.*"

—James Monroe Thorington, *The Glittering Mountains of Canada*, 1925

The Cavell Meadows trail ascends from barren moraine to rolling alpine meadows and features views of Angel Glacier (above) and the north face of Mt. Edith Cavell.

29. Cavell Meadows

Route

Day-hike, 8.0 km loop

Route	Elevation (m)	Distance (km)
Trailhead	1753	0
Path of the Glacier jct	1799	0.6
Cavell Meadows summit	2043	3.8
Path of the Glacier jct	1840	7.0
Trailhead	1753	8.0

Topographic map: 83 D/9
Best lighting: morning

Trailhead

Follow the Icefields Parkway (Highway 93), 6.7 km south from Jasper to Highway 93A. Turn right and follow Highway 93A south for 5.2 km. Turn right onto the Mt. Edith Cavell Road, and follow this 14.5 km to the Mt. Edith Cavell parking lot. The Path of the Glacier/Cavell Meadows trailhead is on the south side of the parking lot. Large recreational vehicles and trailers are not allowed the Mt. Edith Cavell Road. Use the trailer drop-off at the beginning of the road.

O n the rolling alpland of Cavell Meadows, Angel Glacier and the precipitous north face of Mt. Edith Cavell (3363 m) provide the backdrop for a stunning mid-summer display of wildflowers. This outing describes a loop hike beginning on the Cavell Meadows trail, and returning via The Path of the Glacier, an interpretive trail that explores the forefield of Cavell and Angel glaciers. The forefield was covered by glacial ice as recently as 1920.

Trailhead to Cavell Meadows

From the parking lot, the trail climbs over a terminal moraine and works its way south through the quartzite rubble of the glacier forefield. At the junction in 600 m, turn east (left). The Cavell Meadows trail climbs steeply over a lateral moraine. This landform, and the

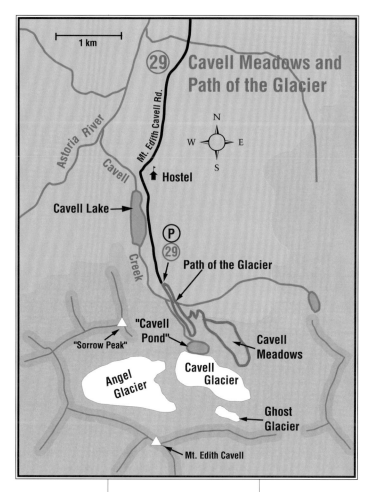

1 km

(29) **Cavell Meadows and Path of the Glacier**

Mt. Edith Cavell Rd.

Astoria River

Cavell

N
W — E
S

↑ **Hostel**

Cavell Lake →

Ⓟ (29)

Creek

Path of the Glacier

△ "Cavell Pond"

"Sorrow Peak"

Cavell Meadows

Angel Glacier

Cavell Glacier

Ghost Glacier ←

△ **Mt. Edith Cavell**

---

terminal moraine crossed earlier, were created by Cavell Glacier when it extended farther down the valley. The coarse quartz sand underfoot has been eroded from the quartzite boulders. Least chipmunk, golden-mantled ground squirrel and pika live in the nooks and crannies of this moraine.

At the top of the moraine, there is an abrupt transition to subalpine forest. This is the trimline of Cavell Glacier. A century and a half ago, the ice of the glacier was thick

enough to reach this far up the valley, and obliterate the mature forest. Some trees near trimline show evidence of roots and trunks damaged by the moving glacial ice.

There are tremendous views of Angel Glacier and Cavell Pond from the lateral moraine. Angel Glacier formerly merged with Cavell Glacier. However, glacial recession caused it to break contact in the 1940s. After a few decades where it maintained a state of equilibrium, it is once again retreating quickly up the

mountain wall. Soon, it will be an angel no more. The lichen trimline of Angel Glacier is clearly visible to the north of the hanging body of ice. The lighter coloured rock was scoured of lichens during the Cavell Advance.

Today, "angel" seems a most appropriate name for the wing-shaped glacier. However, initially the name was not prompted by the glacier's appearance. Mt. Edith Cavell was named for an English nurse who worked behind the lines with the Belgian Red Cross in

Angel Glacier on Mt. Edith Cavell

World War I. She was executed for allegedly assisting the escape of captive troops. It was popular to refer to nurse Edith Cavell as "the angel of mercy," and this is how the name first became associated with the glacier.

After paralleling the moraine crest for a few hundred metres, the trail resumes its climb toward the meadows. The forest here is an ancient one, dominated by Engelmann spruce and subalpine fir. In the winter of 1990-91, a snow avalanche from the north face of Mt. Edith Cavell created a wind blast strong enough to topple some of these trees. One tree cut from the debris by chainsaw shows 232 concentric rings, each recording a year's growth.

Two and half kilometres from the trailhead, the forest becomes a patchwork of tree islands, separated by glades of subalpine meadow. Although the elevation here (1860 m) is low for treeline, the chilling effects of glacial ice, the north-facing slope, and the winter-long shade of Mt. Edith Cavell, combine to preclude the growth of dense forest above this point. Soon the trail emerges from the forest completely. Keep right at the junctions, and follow the trail through a carpet of wildflowers to a cairned knoll. Mountain heather, fleabane, Indian paintbrush, Sitka valerian, western anemone, arnica, everlasting and white mountain avens are just a few of the many wildflowers that grow here.

The upper meadows are part of the alpine ecoregion, and are occasionally visited by mountain caribou and grizzly bear. Some hollows here may hold snow until mid-August. The trickle of snowmelt on warm days provides a water source for moisture loving plants such as leather-leaved saxifrage, northern laurel, white globeflower and red-stemmed saxifrage. The reddish tinge in snowbanks is watermelon snow, caused by an alga with a red eye-spot. Some of the steep slopes above the meadows contain rock glaciers – accumulations of rock that contain just enough ice to allow the whole mass to creep downhill.

Cavell Meadows to The Path of the Glacier

From the high point, the trail loops back through the upper meadows to rejoin the approach trail at treeline. Please keep to the beaten path.

At the Path of the Glacier junction, turn south (left). The trail descends to Cavell Pond in the cirque at the base of Mt. Edith Cavell. The hollow containing this lake was uncovered by the retreating ice in 1963. Icebergs or "growlers" calve from the glacier toe and are often afloat in the water. The surface of the glacier contains several talus (TAY-luss) cones, piles of rocky avalanche debris, transported from the base of Mt. Edith Cavell's north face by the moving ice. Please be aware that there is ice avalanche danger from angel Glacier here.

The trail returns to the parking lot along the principal meltwater stream from the glacier. This section has been washed out in recent years. The rocky soils and cold environment make it difficult for vegetation to become established here. Willows, sedges,

wildflowers and a few stunted spruce trees are all that have taken hold. The contrast between the barren forefield and the lush adjacent forest is striking. Barring another glacial advance, it will be centuries before the forefield supports mature subalpine forest again.

"From the foot of the glacier to the top of the peak there is not a single speck of vegetation, not a blade of living green; but almost at one's feet, within a space formed by the glacier's escaping streams, lies a tiny emerald island, a veritable little oasis, like a patch of lawn left in the ruins of a battlefield ... this little meadow is a perfect garden of wild flowers."

—Mabel Williams,
Jasper, 1949

The Little Ice Age: Cool Detective Work

The most recent advance of Cavell Glacier took place during the Little Ice Age, which lasted from AD 1200 to the mid 1800s. Glaciologists have gained much of their understanding of recent glaciation in the Rockies from studies carried out here. They often refer to the Little Ice Age as the Cavell Advance.

Glaciologists use vegetation near glaciers to assign dates to glacial events. Core samples can be taken from mature trees near trimline. By counting the tree rings in the core, the approximate age of the tree can be determined. If the tree is 300 years old, glacial ice has not

covered its location for at least 300 years. This process is called dendrochronology. If a number of mature trees exist close to a glacier, the date and extent of the most recent maximum advance of the ice can be plotted using this information. Trees growing on moraines formed during the Cavell Advance, or those known to have been damaged by glacial ice are particularly useful in this process.

The presence of rock lichens provides an accurate means for dating the melting back of the ice front here. It has been found that the rock lichen known as map lichen (*Rhizocarpon geo-*

graphicum), grows at a rate of 42 mm per century in its first 110 years, and 11.4 mm per century for the subsequent 140 years. These lichens have been growing on boulders in the forefield since the ice withdrew. By measuring the diameter of the lichens, glaciologists can determine how long it has been since the area was covered by ice.

What have glaciologists learned about Cavell Glacier? Between 1888 and 1975, the glacier receded 988 m. The maximum of the Cavell Advance took place in 1705. This was the greatest advance of the Cavell Glacier during the previous 10,000 years.

Explorer Mary Schäffer named the Opal Hills for the colourful reddish rock and green tundra. The hills provide a striking contrast to the surrounding grey limestone peaks of the Queen Elizabeth Ranges.

30. Opal Hills

Route

Day-hike, 8.2 km loop

Route	Elevation (m)	Distance (km)
Trailhead	1700	0
Schäffer Viewpoint jct	1695	0.2
Opal Hills jct	1960	1.6
Summit of meadows	2160	3.2
Opal Hills jct	1960	6.6
Trailhead	1700	8.2

Topographic maps: 83 C/12, 83 C/13
Best lighting: anytime

Trailhead

Follow Highway 16, 3.7 km east from Jasper to the Maligne Lake Road. Turn east (right). Follow the Maligne Lake Road 44 km to parking lots on the east side of the lake. The trailhead is at the northeast corner of the uppermost parking lot.

The Opal Hills are a delightful island of green set amidst the craggy limestone mountains of the Maligne Valley. This steep loop-hike features interesting geology and with a little extra effort, an exceptional view of Maligne (muh-LEEN) Lake.

Maligne Lake to Opal Meadows

From the trailhead, descend through lodgepole pine forest into a clearing known as the "hummock and hollow meadow." Keep left at the junction 200 m from the parking lot. The Opal Hills are visible directly east. Within a few hundred metres of leaving the meadow, you begin a steep climb to the Opal Hills on a poorly conceived and heavily eroded trail. Persevere, the view is worth the effort.

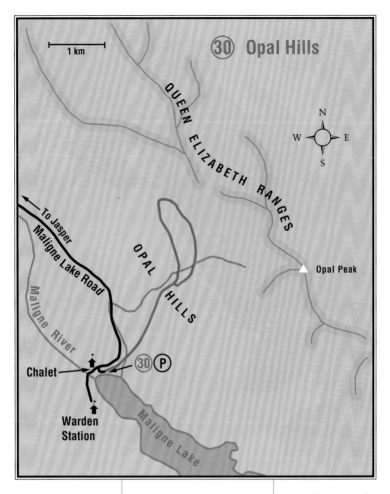

The loop junction is at km 1.6. If you take the right-hand branch, the remainder of the climb is at times withering (a 25 degree slope in places), however the return half of the loop is less steep, consequently safer and easier on your knees.

Immediately above the junction, the fire-succession pine forest gives way to a mature forest of Engelmann spruce and subalpine fir. The trail parallels a shale ravine during the final climb to the meadows that surround Opal Hills. Looking west from the meadows, there is a fine view of the Maligne Valley. The steeply tilted limestones of the front range peaks lie to the east; the older quartzite peaks of the Maligne Range are to the west. The Opal Hills, visible directly north, are hummocks of landslide material from Opal Peak (2789 m). Opals are not found here. Mary Schäffer named the hills for the reddish rock and the green tundra striped with snow.

Opal Meadows

From the first junction in the meadows, a faint track climbs south onto a knoll. By contouring farther south, you are rewarded with a panoramic view of Maligne Lake, more than 400 m below. The lake was known to the Stoneys as "Chaba Imne" (Beaver Lake). Its rumored existence lured explorers in the early 1900s. Maligne Lake is indeed worthy of legend. It is by far the largest of Jasper's 778 lakes and ponds, and it is also the largest natural lake in the

Maligne Lake

Rockies: 22 km long and 96 m deep, with an area of 2066 ha. It is fed by meltwaters from the 25 km² Brazeau (brah-ZOE) Icefield, and other glaciers.

Maligne is French for "wicked." The name was applied to the Maligne River in 1846 by Father Jean de Smet, a Jesuit missionary. His party had trouble fording the mouth of the Maligne where it joins the Athabasca River, 40 km north of Maligne Lake.

The loop trail branches east (left) from the viewpoint junction, and soon branches again – north (left) into the meadows, after crossing the shale ravine. With its abundance of upper subalpine and alpine wildflowers and krummholz tree islands, the shallow vale between the Opal Hills and Opal Peak is a delight. One of the more colour-

Hummocks, Hollows, Rockslides and Moose

In the Rockies, "hummock and hollow" landscapes, like the meadow near the trailhead, usually resulted from the melting of detached blocks of rubble-covered glacial ice at the end of the Wisconsin Glaciation. However, the mounds in this meadow are the remains of frost-shattered boulders.

Elsewhere near the north end of Maligne Lake, the many hummocks and hollows were created by the second largest measured rockslide in the Rockies. This tremendous jumble of rock has an estimated volume of 498 million cubic metres. Mounds of the rockslide debris have become the "hummocks". Depressions in the débris have filled with water, creating lakes and ponds.

The damp, low-lying areas surrounding many lakes and ponds are frost hollows where cold air collects, precluding the growth of mature trees. The wet shrub thickets are excellent habitat for one of the few remaining concentrations of moose in the Rockies. Lack of fire-generated new growth and highway and railway deaths are responsible for the decline in the moose population.

Moose track

ful and uncommon flowers found here is alpine louse-wort. The pinkish and purple blooms of this miniature beauty are scattered across the slopes nearby in late July and early August. The willows on the east side of the meadow provide browse for elk and mule deer.

At the north end of the meadow, the trail curves west and then south, re-entering the forest to commence the sideslope descent to the loop junction. Use caution on the steep grade to the parking lot, particularly if the trail is wet.

"*In the spring of 1908 a small party of six ... unnoticed by a solitary soul, slipped quietly away from civilisation and were lost, so far as the world was concerned, in a sea of mountains to the north. Our quest was a mythical lake spoken of by the Stoney Indians ...*"

—Mary Schäffer,
The 1911 Expedition to
Maligne Lake

Mary Schäffer: Mountain Woman

Mary Schäffer was a Quaker from Philadelphia who made her first visit to the Rockies in 1889. She took to the backwoods life with passion and ease, and endeared herself to Stoney Natives, who called her Yahe-Weha –"mountain woman."

Using a crude map drawn by Stoney chieftain Sampson Beaver, a party organized by Schäffer reached Maligne Lake from the south in 1908, after failing to find it on another foray the previous year. They built a raft, *The Chaba*, and spent three days mapping and exploring the lake, and naming many features. Schäffer was a gifted observer of nature, and a talented artist and photographer. The accounts of her journeys, published in magazines and journals, made her a celebrity. Her 1911 book, *Old Indian Trails of the Canadian*

Rockies, has been republished as *A Hunter of Peace*, and still makes enchanting reading.

ABOUT THE AUTHOR

PATRICIA BOSWORTH was born in San Francisco, California. She attended the Convent of the Sacred Heart and graduated from Sarah Lawrence College with a B.A. degree in English. She is married to novelist Mel Arrighi. Ms. Bosworth was an actress for ten years and appeared on Broadway, on television and in films. She is a member of the Actors Studio. In 1966, while still an actress, Ms. Bosworth began writing articles on the theater and movies for *New York* magazine. After winning a Doubleday Fellowship in writing at Columbia, Ms. Bosworth left acting and became a writer/editor. She has since been articles editor of *Woman's Day*, senior editor of *McCalls*, managing editor of *Harper's Bazaar*. She contributes articles and book reviews regularly to *The New York Times, Esquire* and *Town & Country*.

The Skyline Trail traverses the crest of the Maligne Range from Maligne Lake to Maligne Canyon. In this view, Mt. Tekarra rises above subalpine meadows near the northern end of the trail.

31. Skyline Trail

Route

2-4 days, 44.1 km

Route	Elevation (m)	Distance (km)
Trailhead, Maligne Lake	1680	0
Evelyn Creek CG	1810	4.8
Little Shovel CG	2155	8.3
Little Shovel Pass	2240	10.3
Snowbowl CG	2080	12.2
Big Shovel Pass	2325	17.5
Watchtower jct	2300	17.9
Curator CG jct	2240	19.5
The Notch	2510	22.1
Tekarra CG	2060	30.9
Signal CG jct	2020	35.7
Maligne Lake Road	1160	44.1

Topographic maps: 83 C/12, 83 C/13, 83 D/16

Trailhead

To take advantage of the higher starting elevation, most parties hike the Skyline Trail from south to north. Follow Highway 16, 3.7 km east from Jasper to the Maligne Lake Road. Turn east (right). Follow the Maligne Lake Road 45 km to the parking lot on the west side of the lake. The Skyline trailhead is the most northerly of the two trailheads, west of the parking lot. A shuttle service is available from Jasper (fee charged).

For almost two-thirds of its length, the Skyline Trail travels at or above treeline. Rambling through expansive meadows, crossing high passes and traversing ridgecrests of the Maligne (muh-LEEN) Range, it provides panoramic views of the Athabasca and Maligne valleys, and surrounding moun-

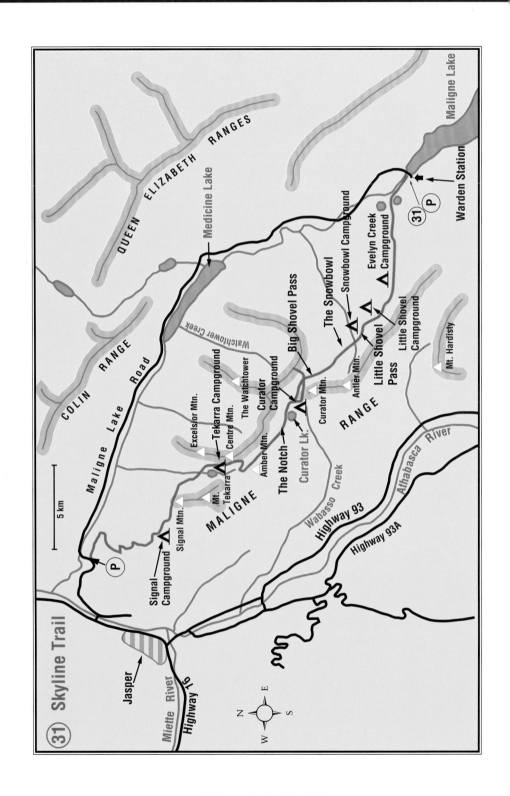

tain ranges. The Skyline is one of the most heavily used back-country trails in Jasper – more than 2000 hikers registered in 1992.

Given its high average elevation, in most years you should not hike the Skyline Trail until after mid-July, when most of the snow will have melted. It is also best avoided during poor weather, for if it's stormy in Jasper, it will be miserable on the exposed ridges of the Skyline. Although it is possible to complete the trail in two days, most hikers spend more time exploring this superb landscape. The summits of the Maligne Range offer many possibilities for ridge walking and straightforward mountaineering.

Maligne Lake to Little Shovel Pass

From the trailhead, a broad path climbs through an open coniferous forest dominated by lodgepole pine. The undergrowth features buffaloberry, feathermosses, twinflower, common fireweed, rocky mountain goldenrod and grouseberry – a member of the heath family. The sweet, red fruit of grouseberry is favoured by ruffed grouse. You may see this bird here.

The trail winds through hummocky terrain, débris from the Maligne Lake rock-slide. The steeply tilted front range mountains on the east side of the valley were under-cut by glacial ice during the Wisconsin Glaciation. After the ice receded, one of the mountainsides collapsed, creating the second largest measured rockslide in the Rockies (estimated volume: 498 million cubic metres). The slide travelled across the valley floor, damming the Maligne River and enlarging Maligne Lake.

At km 2.2 and km 2.4, short sidetrails branch respectively southwest (left) to Lorraine Lake and north (right) to Mona Lake. These lakes occupy hollows in the débris of the Maligne Lake slide. Mona Harrigin Matheson was Jasper's first licensed female trail guide. Lorraine Magstad's parents worked at the Maligne Lake chalet in the late 1920s.

At km 4.8 the trail crosses Evelyn Creek to the first campground. "Evelyn" was one of two persons: the wife of the first resident Superintendent of Jasper National Park in 1913; or the Dutchess of Devonshire, who visited Jasper in 1920.

The trail climbs steeply away from the campground. Although the elevation here is subalpine, lodgepole pine is still the dominant tree. Engelmann spruce and subalpine fir are typically more common in the subalpine, however the combination of dry soils and southerly exposure here creates the perfect niche for lodgepole pines. Many of the pines are twisted and stunted, products of the colder climate at this higher elevation. Two more members of the heath family are now common in the undergrowth: crowberry and blueberry.

Beyond Little Shovel campground, the trail swings north onto the alpine tundra that leads to Little Shovel Pass. The blooms of ragwort, yellow paintbrush and mountain fireweed colour the banks of the stream that drains the pass. Mountain fireweed is also known by the folk name, river beauty.

Looking southeast from the crest of Little Shovel Pass, the ragged limestone summits of the Queen Elizabeth Ranges rise above Maligne Lake. Most prominent is Mt. Brazeau (brah-ZOE) (3470 m), highest mountain in the front ranges. The pass is home to a colony of hoary marmots. Marmots usually prefer to live protected beneath boulderfields. In the absence of protective rocks, they will excavate deep burrows on open tundra, such as

The Making of the Skyline

The section of the Skyline Trail south of Big Shovel Pass was first travelled by Mary Schäffer's second expedition to Maligne Lake in 1911. The northern part of the trail was developed in 1937, when outfitter Fred Brewster sought to make a loop outing for his guided trips to Maligne Lake. Patrons journeyed by road from Jasper to Medicine Lake. From there, they were ferried across the lake. They then boarded horse-drawn carts to lodging at Maligne Lake. Return was on horseback along the Skyline Trail to Jasper.

Little Shovel Pass features views south to the Queen Elizabeth Ranges beyond Maligne Lake, and north into the subalpine basin known as The Snowbowl.

the ones visible here. They must burrow deeply to remain out of the grasp of grizzly bears, their principal predator.

Little Shovel Pass to Curator Campground

The steady descent north from Little Shovel Pass leads into an extensive upper subalpine basin known as The Snowbowl. Sedges and willows here are important summer foods for mountain caribou. This uncommon member of the deer family has a dark brown coat with light patches on the neck, belly, rump and legs. Caribou are officially listed as a "vulnerable" species in western Canada. The Maligne Range herd includes only 10 to 15 animals. Although caribou are accustomed to human presence, they remain shy, and will usually flee. Future protection of Jasper's caribou herds may include seasonal closures of hiking trails in

calving areas, to reduce stress on the animals.

Snowbowl campground is a good base for day-hiking toward Antler Mountain (2557 m) at the head of the valley. Beyond the grove of trees that harbours the campground, the trail descends north into meadows, and begins its rambling and often muddy ascent toward Big Shovel Pass. Moisture-loving wildflowers and

sedges thrive here: fleabane, Sitka valerian, western anemone, ragwort, shooting star, white globeflower, mountain marsh marigold, cotton grass and elephant head. The pink petals of elephant head have three lobes, which create the ears, trunk and mouth of the "elephant." Several dozen miniature "elephant heads" are arranged atop the spike of this showy wildflower.

Immediately west of Big Shovel Pass is Curator Mountain (2624 m), named for its position as custodian of the pass. On its eastern slope is an ice apron, a vestige of glaciation. The cornice bears the unmistakable brilliant blue of perennial snow.

On the north side of Big Shovel Pass, the trail is a faint path beaten into the screes and is easily lost when snow-covered. The trail forks. The branch straight ahead descends directly to Curator campground, and can be used to quickly get "off the skyline" and down to camp when the

Venerable Mountains

The Maligne Range is part of the eastern main ranges. Elsewhere in the Rockies, these ranges are usually among the highest and most rugged. The modest elevations and rounded summits of mountains along the Skyline Trail indicate they were completely covered by glacial ice during the Great Glaciation.

The Maligne Range is comprised almost entirely of early-Cambrian Gog quartzite. Green and black map lichens grow

profusely on this rock, making it appear dark from a distance. However, quartzite can be a colourful rock when viewed close-up: buff, pink, purple and white. Fresh exposures often feature reddish/orange stains caused by iron oxides.

The Maligne Range mountains are in marked contrast to the higher sawtooth and overthrust mountains of the front ranges to the east. These are composed principally of drab, grey limestones.

weather is foul. If you're not in a hurry or do not plan to camp at Curator, take the trail to the right. Although the rocky slopes here appear barren, the keen eye will spot the colourful blooms of moss campion, alpine harebell, Lyall's iron plant, and alpine hawksbeard, scattered across the screes.

About 500 m north of Big Shovel Pass, the trail from the Watchtower Valley descends the ridge from the east. Scamper up to the ridge crest for the view over the hanging valley of Watchtower Creek. The striking summit of The Watchtower (2791 m) was first climbed in 1951. The Watch-tower Valley offers an escape route from the Skyline Trail. The initial descent is north. Then the trail switchbacks tightly to the south, and contours around the swampy basin at the head of the valley. It is 13 km to the Maligne Lake Road by this route.

The Skyline Trail descends to the Curator campground junction, 1.6 km north of Big Shovel Pass. Turn south (left) for the campground. This badly eroded sidetrail loses 120 m of elevation in just 800 m. The pleasant campground is set in a grove of trees beneath a picturesque waterfall. Shovel Pass Lodge is in the meadow below the campground. Unfortunately, all water sources nearby are contaminated with horse dung and urine, making it mandatory to treat drinking water here. This is the head-waters of Wabasso Creek, which Mary Schäffer followed to The Skyline in 1911. *Wabasso* is Cree for "rabbit." The trail along the creek offers a 14 km exit from the Skyline Trail to the Icefields Parkway. However, this arduous route is not recommended.

Maligne Lake, The Hard Way

In 1908, outfitter Billy Warren led a party organized by Mary Schäffer to Maligne Lake. They reached the lake from the south, constructed a raft, explored the waters and named many surrounding features. Schäffer's account of the journey was widely circulated and well received, and made her into a celebrity.

In 1911, the Grand Trunk Pacific Railway was constructed through Jasper. With completion of the railway, the Canadian government sought to publicize the newly created Jasper Forest Park in order to capitalize on the opportunity for tourism. Mary Schäffer was invited to return to the lake, to make an accurate map of it. Schäffer, who lamented the coming of the railway and the changes it would bring to the mountains she dearly loved, reluctantly agreed.

Instead of building another raft to use in the survey, materials for a boat were packed on horseback from Jasper to Maligne Lake. Rather than tackle the trackless wilds of the Maligne Valley with such a load, outfitter Jack Otto chose to cross the crest of the Maligne Range. After ascending Wabasso Creek, Otto led the party along the southern part of to-day's Skyline Trail to the north shore of Maligne Lake.

This unlikely journey was undertaken at an even more unlikely time of year, mid-June, when snows were still deep in the high country. Otto sent an advance party to pack a trail over the high passes. Finding the snow more than they could handle, his men fashioned two impromptu shovels from spruce trees, and used them to scoop out a trail across the passes. The shovels, which Schäffer at first mistook for distant sheep (see closing quote) were left on the high point to greet the following party.

Surveyor A.O. Wheeler subsequently proposed the name "Bighorn Pass" for Big Shovel Pass, because sheep abound in the area. However, Schäffer's more colourful name has endured. The original shovels are now in the collection of the Jasper-Yellowhead Historical Society.

Curator Campground to Tekarra Campground

From the Curator campground junction, the Skyline Trail winds north through boulderfields beside Curator Lake and then climbs steadily to The Notch (2510 m). The Notch is the seventh highest point reached by maintained trail in the Rockies, and was certainly an ambitious place to bring ponies! The Notch often sports a cornice of snow on its east side. Give it a wide berth.

The scree summits flanking this lofty pass are mere walk-ups, and offer superb views of the Athabasca Valley. Mt. Edith Cavell (3363 m) is the prominent peak to the southwest. The Ramparts of Tonquin Valley are beyond. Views south include Mts. Christie (3103 m) and Fryatt (3361 m), Brussels Peak (3161 m) and the northern fringe of Columbia Icefield. Directly below, Curator Lake sparkles like a blue gem in a setting of barren stone. On clear days, Mt. Robson (3954 m) towers above the horizon, 90 km to the northwest.

The next 5 km are the apex of the Skyline Trail, as it follows the backbone of the Maligne Range across the summit ridge of Amber Mountain at 2530 m. Even non-mountaineers will be tempted to walk off trail the few hundred metres to Amber's highest, most northerly point (2544 m).

Hikers cross the summit ridge of Amber Mountain at the apex of the Skyline Trail.

To the east, four parallel ranges of sawtooth mountains are stacked like rocky waves against the skyline. Jasper townsite is visible to the north. Amber Mountain was named because of the colour of its weathered screes.

From the ridge north of Amber Mountain, the trail leaves the "skyline" and switchbacks down toward Centre Lake. The rock glacier that feeds this lake is plainly visible on the west slope of Centre Mountain (2700 m). Bighorn sheep, mountain caribou, white-tailed ptarmigan and hoary marmots may be seen here. Mount Tekarra (teh-KAR-rah) (2694 m), with its massive east-facing cliffs of Gog quartzite, dominates the view north. Tekarra was James Hector's Iroquois guide when the Palliser Expedition travelled to Athabasca Pass in 1859. During your descent to Centre Lake, you pass a gigantic limestone boulder – a glacial erratic. It's a good place to find shade on a hot day.

The remaining 2 km to Tekarra campground involve delightful upper subalpine hiking. Mountain fireweed and cotton grass bloom in the adjacent stream course. The campground is located at the creek crossing, 500 m below the outlet of Tekarra Lake. From this convenient base, mountaineers may make ascents of Mount Tekarra, Centre Mountain and Excelsior Mountain.

Tekarra Campground to Maligne Lake Road

From Tekarra campground, the trail ascends to treeline and contours around the north flank of Mount Tekarra. The sawtooth limestone slabs of the Colin Range are prominent across the Maligne Valley. Between 1835 and 1849, Colin Fraser was in charge of Jasper House, a Hudson's Bay Company outpost in the Athabasca Valley. James Hector named a mountain in this range for him in 1859.

The trail continues across the slopes of Signal Mountain, the northern outlier of Mt. Tekarra. Its slopes command remarkable views north along a 30 km length of the Athabasca Valley, and west beyond Jasper into the Miette Valley. The mountains northwest of Jasper are the Victoria Cross Range. Five summits in this range were named for Canadian soldiers, World War I recipients of the Victoria Cross,

Britain's highest award for military valor. Signal Mountain was formerly the site of a fire lookout.

Turn north (right) where the trail joins the Signal Mountain fireroad. The Signal campground junction is in 50 m. The Skyline Trail concludes with an 8.4 km fireroad walk that descends steadily to the Maligne Lake Road. En route there are views of Roche Bonhomme (ROSH-bun-OMM) in the Colin Range. The mountain's French name

means "good fellow rock," and was probably given by the voyageurs of the fur trade in the early 1800s. The strata near the summit bear a striking resemblance to the face of a man, looking skyward. The patch of dead trees below the summit is the remains of a 1985 forest fire.

Rock Glaciers: Rock and Ice

The Excelsior and Centre valleys contain a number of picturesque tarns, whose colourful waters indicate glacial sources. However, you won't see any glacial ice. The meltwater comes from rock glaciers, piles of rockslide débris that insulate permanent ice within. There are 119 rock glaciers in Jasper National Park. A number of these are here. The photograph shows one on Centre Mountain.

*"*A* mile from the summit ... Jack rather excitedly called our attention to two tiny specks on the skyline and, though he remained sweetly non-committal and suggested they might be a horse or two men, we knew he meant "sheep," and sheep they promptly became ... then we came close enough to analyze our two immovable sheep – only to find them a pair of abandoned shovels which had been hewn from a tree and, in case we needed the same, left standing conspicuously in the snow."*

—Mary Schäffer, the 1911 Expedition to Maligne Lake, in *A Hunter of Peace*, 1980

From Sulphur Skyline you are rewarded with a stunning view of Jasper's front ranges. To the north are the striking cliffs of Ashlar Ridge.

32. Sulphur Skyline

Route

Day-hike, 4.0 km

Route	Elevation (m)	Distance (km)
Trailhead	1372	0
Sulphur Skyline jct.	1662	2.2
Sulphur Ridge summit	2060	4.0

Topographic map: 83 F/4

Best lighting: afternoon

Trailhead

Follow Highway 16 east from Jasper, 42.9 km to the Miette (mee-YETT) Hot Springs Road. Turn south (right) and follow this road 19 km to its end at the Miette Hot Springs parking lot. The trailhead is south of the hot springs pool entrance. The park trail signs refer to this outing as "Sulphur Ridge."

Only in the front ranges of Jasper and Banff National Parks can you travel from a montane valley bottom to an alpine mountain summit in as short a distance as on the Sulphur Skyline trail. The stiff climb rewards you with a panoramic view of wildly contorted peaks in a remote Jasper landscape. There is also interesting geology, and the opportunity to see bighorn sheep. The ridgecrest is usually windy so carry warm clothing.

Miette Hot Springs to Sulphur Skyline

The trail begins as a broad paved lane, leading east from the hot pool building. The mixed forest contains species of both the montane and lower subalpine ecoregions: Douglas fir, balsam poplar, trembling aspen, lodgepole pine and white spruce. When the paved surface

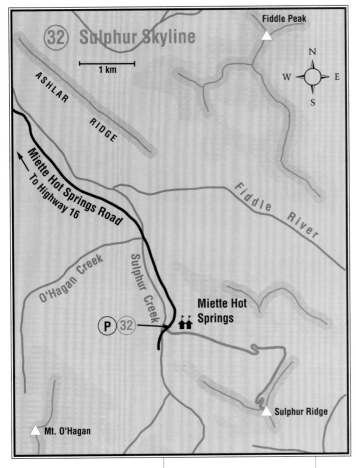

Sulphur Skyline map showing Fiddle Peak, Ashlar Ridge, Miette Hot Springs Road, To Highway 16, O'Hagan Creek, Sulphur Creek, P 32 parking, Miette Hot Springs, Fiddle River, Sulphur Ridge, and Mt. O'Hagan.

quents these slopes.

The trail gains treeline on the east shoulder of Sulphur Ridge, revealing a spectacular view southeast over the Fiddle River valley and the Nikanassin Range. The Nikanassin and the adjoining Miette Range to the north are oriented along the strike of the Rockies, northwest/southeast. The mountains consist of resistant rocks in the upturned edge of a thrust sheet. The valleys on either side have been eroded into the weak shales along the thrust faults, and are known as strike valleys.

The trail levels off briefly at treeline. There is a white quartzite boulder at trailside. If you think it looks out of place among the drab grey of the surrounding limestone – you're right. The boulder is a glacial erratic, transported by glacial ice some 30 km from the main ranges to the west, and deposited here when the

ends at the water supply for the hot springs, continue straight ahead. Keep left at the next unmarked junction. The trail narrows and becomes rough; horses have unearthed many of the rocks underfoot.

After switchbacking across the base of an avalanche slope, the trail contours into a pass that separates Sulphur Ridge from the unnamed peak to the north. At the junction in the pass, turn south (right) and immediately commence a steep climb on a deeply entrenched trail. If you have your head down on this sec-

tion you will miss the rapid transition from lower subalpine to upper subalpine forest. Krummholz spruce and fir trees give evidence of the windiness of this location. A band of bighorn sheep fre-

First Range and First Fiddle

Nikanassin is Cree for "first range." It is the first range of the Rockies in this area when approached from the east. The Fiddle River was called "La Rivière au Violon" (Violon River) by Jesuit missionary Jean de Smet in 1846. There are various origins of the river's name. One claims that the wind makes the sound of a violin when it strikes the ridge of the nearby Fiddle Range. In typical western fashion, de Smet's "violin" was soon corrupted to "fiddle."

ice receded. Erratics provide glaciologists with clues to the places of origin of glaciers in past ice ages.

Sulphur Skyline

The trail leaves the last wind-blasted krummholz and traverses west beneath the summit dome of Sulphur Ridge. It then heads directly upslope – a withering climb on a rocky track to the summit. To the east, foothills and prairie stretch to the horizon. In all other directions is a sea of rugged front range peaks. One of the most prominent mountains is Ashlar Ridge, directly north. "Ashlar" is a form of masonry – thin-dressed stones used to cover brick or rubble. The remarkable 300 m cliff of the upper mountain is resistant Palliser limestone. Utopia Mountain (2560 m) is 3 km to

Moss campion is a pioneering plant of rocky alpine slopes, like those on Sulphur Skyline. A cluster of miniature pink fowers blooms within a mat of evergreen leaves. In the harsh conditions of alpine areas, it may take 20 years for moss campion to bloom. Moss campion helps create and stabilize thin soils, allowing other plants to take root.

The Miette Reef

A legacy of ancient oceans, the mountains in the vicinity of Miette Hot Springs contain a remarkable formation called the Miette Reef. This reef was built by encrusting creatures called stromatoporoids (strome-uh-TOP-or-oids), that lived with coral colonies in warm, shallow seas during the Late Devonian. The Miette Reef amassed to a thickness of 200 m before being entombed in sediments that killed the stromatoporoids and the other reef-building lifeforms. The reef was once again brought to the earth's surface during mountain building; this time, high and dry.

the southwest of Sulphur Ridge. The mountain was named because its summit provided a survey crew with refuge from the flies in the valley bottom.

Less than 10 km east of Sulphur Ridge, outside Jasper National Park, drilling crews are actively tapping petroleum resources in the foothills. If you look east from the summit of Sulphur Ridge, you can see the seismic lines – narrow strips in the forest cut during petroleum exploration. Seismic lines and the roadways constructed to service active wells have disrupted and fragmented much habitat on the eastern slopes of the Rockies.

Sulphur Ridge is an unofficial name for this minor summit, given in recognition of the pungent smell of nearby Miette Hot Springs. The springs are the

hottest (54 ° C) and most aromatic in the Rockies. The "sulphur" smell that emanates is hydrogen sulphide, a gas dissolved in the springwater and released as it reaches the surface. You won't catch a whiff of this gas on the summit. However, on your return to the parking lot, you can follow the boardwalk south past the old hot springs building. Here, at the spring outlets, the "sulphur" aroma is prominent, as is the yellow colour of elemental sulphur. The sulphur is produced as the hydrogen sulphide reacts with oxygen in the atmosphere.

Bighorn Sheep tracks

"Immediately be-hind us, a giant among giants, and immeasurably supreme, rose Robson's Peak. This magnificent mountain is of conical form, glacier clothed and rugged. When we first caught sight of it, a shroud of mist partially enveloped the summit, but this presently rolled away, and we saw its upper portion dimmed by a necklace of light, feathery clouds, beyond which its pointed apex of ice, glittering in the morning sun, shot up far into the blue heaven above ..."

—the first detailed description of Mt. Robson. Milton and Cheadle, *The Northwest Passage by Land*, 1863

Mt. Robson, the "Monarch of the Rockies," reflected in a pond near Berg Lake.

33. Berg Lake

Route

19.6 km to 21.6 km, 2-5 days

Route	Elevation (m)	Distance (km)
Trailhead	862	0
Kinney Lake	985	4.2
Kinney Lake viewpoint	1006	5.2
Kinney Lake CG	985	6.7
Whitehorn CG	1128	10.5
Emperor Falls viewpoint	1493	14.3
Emperor Falls CG	1631	15.0
Marmot CG	1646	17.4
Hargreaves Glacier jct	1650	17.8
Berg Lake CG	1646	19.6
Rearguard CG	1646	20.4
Snowbird Pass jct	1650	20.7
Robson Pass CG	1650	21.6

Topographic map: 83 E/3

Trailhead

Follow Highway 16 to the Visitor Centre at Robson Junction, 84 km west from Jasper or 18 km east from Tête Jaune Cache, BC. Obtain your permit at the Centre. Turn north and follow the paved sideroad 2 km to its end at the Berg Lake trailhead parking lot.

Towering majestically above Berg Lake, the two-kilometre high north flank of Mt. Robson epitomizes the grandeur of the Canadian Rockies. Clad with a magnificent array of glaciers, this monolith of rock, snow and ice is without equal in a range of mountains celebrated for its spectacular scenery.

The Berg Lake Trail, which brings you to the foot of Mt. Robson's awesome northern rampart, is by far the most heavily travelled backpacking route in the Canadian Rockies. In 1992, more than 11,000 people registered for overnight trips and another 50,000 made day-hikes. Strong hikers can reach Berg Lake in one day. However, the presence of well-spaced campgrounds allows the approach to be broken conveniently into two days. Four of the six campgrounds on The Berg Lake Trail (Kinney Lake, Whitehorn, Berg Lake and Robson Pass) have cook shelters with wood stoves. Firewood is provided at great expense. Please help conserve

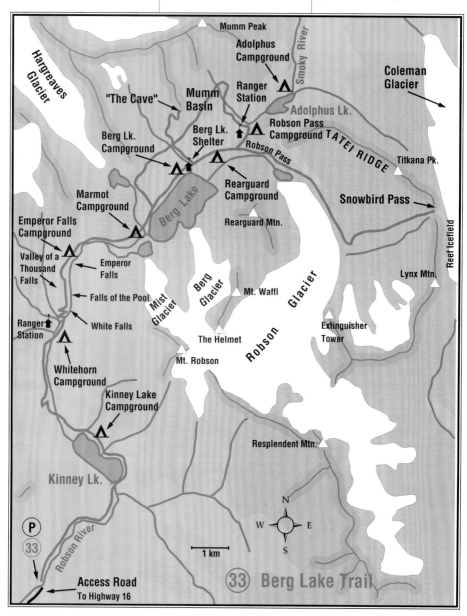

the wood, to reduce maintenance costs and air pollution.

All parties camping on The Berg Lake Trail must obtain a permit at the Visitor Centre on Highway 16. A fee is charged. In 1996, the park instituted a quota system. Call in advance for details: 250-566-4325.

The entire length of the trail is shared with horse traffic, and the first 9 km are shared with mountain bikers. Helicopters land at Robson Pass two days a week, and unfortunately "flightseeing" traffic is common overhead.

Trailhead to Kinney Lake

The broad trail to Kinney Lake is always within sound of the Robson River and showcases diverse vegetation. The low elevation here allows for one of the most moderate climates in the Rockies, and hence the longest growing season (six months). The vegetation features species normally found in BC's Interior Cedar Hemlock Forest zone: western red cedar, western hemlock, western white pine, thimbleberry and devil's club. The trail

The Mountain of the Spiral Road

Although the Robson River Valley at the trailhead is virtually at the lowest elevation of any valley bottom in the central and southern Rockies, the summit of the highest mountain in the entire range is less than 8 km away. Mt. Robson (3954 m) towers more than 3000 m above the starting point of this hike. This staggering vertical relief is hard to grasp. By way of comparison: Mt. Temple rises slightly more than 2000 m from the floor of the Bow Valley at Lake Louise, and Mt. Stephen rises 1900 m above the town of Field.

Mt. Robson is 207 m higher than Mt. Columbia (the second highest in the Rockies) and 528 m higher than Resplendent Mountain, the next highest peak in the immediate area. Why is Mt. Robson so high? The mountain is composed of resistant quartzite, limestone and dolomite rocks. This 3 km thick rock sandwich is one of the more complete, unbroken assemblages of Cambrian rock exposed anywhere on earth. In addition, the sedimentary layers in the mountain are flat-lying, offering additional resistance to erosion. Thus, Mt. Robson has endured the weathering of the ages with more height and bulk than any other mountain in the range.

The strata bend slightly upwards from the centre of the mountain toward the east and west, revealing a broad syncline. This creates the illusion of spiral ramps, angling upwards. Shuswap Natives from the interior of BC knew Mt. Robson as Yuh-hai-has-kun – "mountain of the spiral road." As impressive as it is, Mt. Robson is not the highest mountain in British Columbia. That honour belongs to Mt. Fairweather (4669 m) on the boundary with Alaska.

The quest to find the definitive origin of Mt. Robson's name has been one of the most consuming chores for scholars of Rockies' history. You might think that the monarch mountain of the range was named to honour a politician, official or dignitary. Elsewhere in BC the name "Robson" appears frequently, commemorating John Robson, provincial premier from 1889-1892. However, there is no connection here.

The name "Mt. Robinson" may have been in use for the mountain as early as 1827. Scholars agree that the strongest candidate to lay claim to the name is Colin Robertson, an officer with the North West and Hudson's Bay companies. In 1820, Robertson dispatched a group of Iroquois fur-traders to the area immediately west of Mt. Robson. They may have named the peak for him, and the name was subsequently corrupted through use to Robson.

passes through an old-growth grove of cedars about 2 km from the trailhead. Intensive commercial forestry is quickly wiping out this kind of forest in BC. Even the forestry companies admit old-growth cedars will soon be non-existent outside of parks and other protected areas. At km 3 the trail passes through a mineral lick used by elk, deer, moose and mountain goats.

The outlet of Kinney Lake, sometimes referred to as "the mirror of the mount," is 4.2 km from the trailhead. This tranquil body of water is best appreciated from the viewpoint on its southeast shore, 1 km beyond the outlet bridge. The waters have the remarkable blue and green hues of a glacially fed lake. Avalanche slopes on Cinnamon Peak extend to waterline on the opposite shore. The thickets on these slopes typify the dense bush on the BC side of the continental divide.

Leaving the Kinney Lake

The Reverend Mountaineer

Kinney Lake was named for Reverend George Kinney, who was in the first mountaineering party to attempt Mt. Robson. In 1907, Kinney and A.P. Coleman approached the mountain on horseback from Lake Louise. Poor weather and a shortage of food put end to the exploration before they could set foot on the mountain. Kinney returned in 1908 and again in 1909.

With outfitter Curly Phillips, he nearly reached the summit by a difficult route on the west face in 1909. Given their scant equipment and Phillips' lack of mountaineering experience, it was a bold and remarkable achievement. Later it was tainted because Kinney claimed to have reached the summit, while Phillips admitted the truth of the matter.

viewpoint, the trail climbs over a rise and descends to the lakeshore. The remaining distance to Kinney Lake campground is across an alluvial fan that contains material eroded from the southwest face of Mt. Robson. The delta beyond the campground contains rocky debris that drops from the flow of the Robson River. The seasonal and daily fluctuations of the river create braided streams across the ex-

tensive gravels. The bridges that were installed across some of the braids now stand high and dry, monuments to the temperamental nature of glacial rivers.

Kinney Lake to Emperor Falls

From the north end of the delta, the trail climbs steeply above the west bank of the Robson River into the Valley of

The Alpine Club of Canada-Smithsonian Expedition

Whitehorn Mountain, Mt. Robson's lofty neighbour, was first climbed in 1911 by famed Austrian mountain guide Conrad Kain, during the Alpine Club of Canada-Smithsonian Expedition. Expedition leader and ACC President A.O. Wheeler, was "saving" the ascents of nearby mountains for the glory of a future ACC camp. Kain left camp one afternoon under the pretence of visiting Emperor Falls. When he returned the next morning, it was after having climbed Whitehorn,

solo and in darkness. Wheeler was incensed with Kain's brashness. However, Kain could not tolerate "being among beautiful mountains and not climbing one."

In its outlook, the ACC-Smithsonian expedition was a holdover of the Victorian era. Members shot, trapped and collected almost everything that moved, flew or grew; they carted the samples back to Washington DC for the glory of science. Future mountaineering routes were planned. A.O. Wheeler jealously

considered Mt. Robson to be the sole domain of the ACC. Its first ascent was ultimately accomplished from the 1913 ACC camp in Robson Pass, by two ACC members (one of whom was Canadian), led by Conrad Kain. Despite the fact the 1911 expedition walked heavily on the land, the various reports it generated were instrumental in establishing Mt. Robson Provincial Park, the second in British Columbia – an act of considerable foresight for 1913.

a Thousand Falls. As mountaineer J.M. Thorington observed in 1925: "if not quite a thousand falls come streaming down from the cliffs on either side, the number is at all events most satisfactory and surpassed only by the beauty of their height." There are also three major waterfalls on the Robson River: White Falls, Falls of the Pool, and Emperor Falls.

The trail descends to a suspension bridge crossing of the Robson River. It is safest to cross the bridge one at a time. Whitehorn campground is on the opposite bank. Emergency assistance may be available at the Whitehorn ranger cabin, on the west bank of the river, just north of the bridge. The trail recrosses the Robson River on another suspension bridge 800 m north of the campground. Yellow lady's slipper orchids bloom on the gravels nearby in early July.

To this point the elevation gain has been gentle compared to what lies immediately ahead. In the next 3.7 km, the trail climbs 460 m to the hanging valley that contains Berg Lake. For the 1913 Alpine Club of Canada camp in Robson Pass, outfitter Curly Phillips constructed "The Flying Trestle Bridge," a decked, log structure that made it possible for pack horses to ascend the first cliff. Viewpoints for the three waterfalls on the Robson River provide scenic distraction from the hard work of the climb. Use caution near the unfenced cliff edges.

As you approach Emperor Falls, note the abandoned river gorge immediately east of the trail. The Robson River formerly flowed here. However, downwards erosion allowed the river's course to be captured farther east. In places, the new course of the river is above the present level of the trail. At high water, a trickle of the Robson River spills into the abandoned gorge.

Emperor Falls viewpoint is 150 m east on a sidetrail. The drenching spray is a welcome relief on a hot day, but makes the viewpoint a poor location for photographing the falls. The best vantages for photography are on the main trail.

The trail levels out and draws alongside the Robson River at Emperor Falls campground. The Emperor Ridge of Mt. Robson rises directly opposite. The mountaineering route of Kinney and Phillips lay slightly south of this ridge. Today, the Emperor Ridge is considered one of the harder routes on Mt. Robson and in the Rockies. "Emperor" refers to the fact that Mt. Robson is "monarch of the Rockies."

Emperor Falls to Berg Lake

From Emperor Falls campground, the trail curves east into the upper valley of the Robson River, revealing partial views of the spectacular Mist and Berg glaciers on the north side of Mt. Robson. After contouring above the river on a boulderslope, the trail descends to the river flats. Rock-

Cloud Cap Mountain

From Emperor Falls campground, you can often see how Mt. Robson creates its own weather. Prevailing winds are from the southwest. When the west side of the mountain is clear, the north and east sides may display a banner cloud. Pluming from the summit, this cloud is created where damp air is forced to rise in order to clear the crest. It does not necessarily presage rain or snow.

However, if clouds begin to mass at mid-height on the western side of the mountain, the weather is likely to deteriorate rapidly. Climbers and hikers on the east and north sides may not see this sure sign of approaching storm, and are frequently caught in the foul weather that results.

The tendency for weather to change rapidly on Mt. Robson is one of the principal reasons why its ascent is so difficult. Most of the climbing routes require 3-5 days for a round trip from the highway. In some years, when poor climbing conditions and foul weather persist, Mt. Robson may go unclimbed despite dozens of attempts. Between 1939 and 1953, not a single mountaineering party was known to have reached the summit. When The Overlanders passed Mt. Robson in 1862, their Native guide informed them he had seen the summit only once in his first 29 visits. Not surprisingly, they called it "Cloud Cap Mountain."

hop as necessary. Looking west, Whitehorn Mountain (3395 m) rises majestically above the Valley of a Thousand Falls. As its name suggests, the mountain exhibits a clas-sic horn shape, the product of glacial erosion.

The final kilometre to Berg Lake is routed across a large alluvial fan, created by the creek draining Hargreaves Glacier to the north. From the crest of the fan, Berg Lake comes into view. The trail descends to the northwest shore of the lake at Marmot campground. If you stay here you will escape the crowds at campgrounds farther along

Snowbird Pass, 10.8 km

The glaciers seen from Berg Lake are only a hint of the vast domain of glacial ice concealed on the east slopes of Mt. Robson. More is visible from the Snowbird Pass trail. This outing is strenuous and requires a full day.

Head northeast from Berg

The Snowbird Pass trail parallels Robson Glacier and provides close-up views of this massive river of ice.

Lake campground, past the cotton grass ponds on the Toboggan Creek alluvial fan. Continue through Rearguard campground and onto the glacial flats in the vicinity of Robson Pass. The Snowbird Pass trail branches southeast (right) at km 1.1 just before the pass, and strikes off through the forefield of Robson Glacier. The showy, twisted seedheads of white mountain avens cover the gravels in July and August. Lynx Mountain (3180 m) is directly ahead, between the slopes of Tatei (tat-EH-ee) Ridge (2798 m) on the east (left), and Rearguard Mountain (2720 m) on the west (right). *Tatei* is Stoney for "wind."

The most recent advance of Robson Glacier reached its maxi-mum in 1782. In 1911, A.O. Wheeler marked two large rocks in the forefield, recording the distance from each rock to the toe of Robson Glacier. In 1911, the toe of the glacier was 53 m distant from the western rock. By 1989, it had receded 1249 m, an average of 15.3 m per year.

The rocky knoll east of the trail is a nunatak, a bedrock outcrop that protruded through the glacier during its Little Ice Age advance. This nunatak is remarkable because the terminus of Robson Glacier splayed around it earlier this century, sending meltwater streams east and west from the continental divide. This was one of a few instances in the world where a single alpine valley glacier fed two oceans. (The Chaba Glacier in the Rockies still does this, as does Two Ocean Glacier in Montana.) If you explore off-trail here, you can trace the ancient meltwater courses, and you will see striations – bedrock scratches caused by stone fragments imbedded in the underside of Robson Glacier. The concrete cairns in the vicinity mark the Alberta-British Columbia boundary, and were erected in 1924 by the Interprovincial Boundary Survey.

The toe of Robson Glacier ends in a marginal lake, the source of the Robson River. The western lobe of the glacier toe exhibits massive horizontal crevasses. As the glacier retreats, huge chunks of ice separate along these fissures, and avalanche into the lake. The dark, lengthwise strips of rubble on the glacier's surface are medial moraines, formed by the merging of tributary glaciers "upstream." On the lower mountain-

continued on next page

the trail. However, the exposed gravels of the Hargreaves fan can be a bleak place during poor weather.

Berg Lake

The trail continues along the northwest shore of Berg Lake, passing the Hargreaves Glacier junction. The stunning scenery on the north side of Mt. Robson becomes complete. Berg Lake is the largest lake in the Rockies into which a glacier flows directly. This remarkable image of ice meeting water is the essence of the area's incredible scenic charm. Despite the fact Berg

Snowbird Pass continued

sides flanking the toe, the trimlines of the Little Ice Age advances are evident. There are two trimlines here, indicating advances of different extent. Vegetation below the trimlines was obliterated by the ice.

A rough track angles uphill through moraines east of the marginal lake. Follow cairns where necessary. The graceful horn of Resplendent Mountain (3426 m), one of the most attractive peaks in the Rockies, rises from the head of the glacier to the south. Immediately east of it is Extinguisher Tower, a minor rock summit named for its resemblance to a candle snuffer. Looking northwest, the summits north of Berg Lake rise in parallel, overthrust ramps. The glaciated peak farthest west is Mt. Phillips (3249 m), named for outfitter Curly Phillips. Farthest east is Mumm Peak (2962 m), named for English mountaineer Arnold Mumm, who was in the party that made its first ascent in 1910.

The track climbs steeply through ice-cored moraines above Robson Glacier. In recent years, sections of the cairned route have slumped where the ice-cored moraine beneath has melted. The exposed ice appears black. There is some hazard here, especially if you travel off the beaten track.

Look for glacier tables on lower Robson Glacier. These boulders prevent the melting of ice directly beneath, with the result that they become perched on icy pedestals as the glacier surface melts downward. The lower icefalls on Robson Glacier feature a myriad of free-standing pinnacles of ice, called seracs (sir-RACKS). Seracs form where crevassed glacial ice plunges over irregularities in the bedrock. Slightly east of where Robson Glacier curves to the north, there is a secondary glacier terminus that butts against the lateral moraine. This is a compression lobe of ice – it flows slightly uphill before terminating in seracs that topple onto the moraine.

A steep switchback leads through a cliff to the creek draining Snowbird Meadows. A chaos of cascading ice fills the view west. The icefall at the head of Robson Glacier leads to the rounded summit of The Dome (3090 m). The snow and ice face above is the Kain Face, named for Conrad Kain, who guided the first ascent of Mt. Robson via this route in 1913. At the time, it was the most difficult mountaineering route in North America. Without benefit of the tools and equipment enjoyed by modern mountaineers, Kain chopped more than 600

steps in this icy slope during the ascent. His rope mates, A.H. MacCarthy and W.F. Foster, praised Kain's ability and courage. When the summit was gained, Kain stepped aside and with customary modesty announced: "Gentlemen, that's as far as I can take you." The Kain Face is one of two "regular routes" on Mt. Robson today.

The trail ascends eastward through rolling upper subalpine meadows on the north side of the creek toward Snowbird Pass. These meadows are the hoary marmot capital of the Rockies. Mountain fireweed and yellow mountain saxifrage grow on the gravels in the creek. The trail becomes vague in the upper meadows, and fades into two faint paths. It is easier to approach the pass using the northerly path, which ascends over limestone benches, and follows cairns through the final slopes of scree and boulders.

Snowbird Pass is located on the continental divide and the boundary between Mt. Robson Provincial Park in British Columbia and Jasper National Park in Alberta. It commands a lofty view across the Reef Icefield (25 km^2) and the head of Coleman Glacier to the east. Titkana Peak (2820 m) rises north of Snowbird Pass. *Titkana* is Iroquois for "ptarmigan."

The Snowbird

The name "Snowbird" refers to the white-tailed ptarmigan (TAR-mih-gun), a member of the grouse family common in the high country of the Rockies. Ptarmigan plumage is cryptic; it changes with the seasons. In summer it is a mottled brown, black and white to match the boulderfields; in winter, it is pure white. The tail is always white and the feet are feathered. There is a red spot over the eye. Although ground-dwelling birds, ptarmigan are capable of short bursts of flight in times of danger. These birds are blessed with excellent camouflage. However they are not wary. You often come into the midst of a hen and her clutch of chicks. Alarmed and confused, the birds then provide terrific entertainment, clucking, cooing and running circles around you. Be careful not to step on the chicks.

Glacier still reaches the lake, it is not advancing. It is considerably smaller than when first photographed in 1908. Two lateral moraines flank the terminus and extend into the lake, giving an indication of the glacier's former size.

Berg Lake takes its name from ice bergs or "growlers" that calve from the glacier into the waters. These ice avalanches provide terrific entertainment for campers. A few hours after an avalanche, the prevailing wind usually will have carried the growlers to the lakeshore near Berg Lake campground.

A.P. Coleman named Berg Lake in 1908. However, he called the glacier "Blue Glacier." Subsequently it was called "Tumbling Glacier" – a name already used in Kootenay National Park and hence discarded. Berg Glacier is now the official name.

You should plan on the 2.2 km hike along the shore of Berg Lake taking longer than expected. The incredible north face of Mt. Robson will have you rubbernecking frequently!

Tent sites at Berg Lake campground are on both sides of Toboggan Creek. The Harg-reaves shelter is a day-use facility only. The building was constructed as a guest chalet by the Hargreaves family, owners of Mt. Robson Ranch. It was subsequently donated to BC Parks. The shelter is frequently overpopulated. Store your food in the boxes inside the shelter along the east wall.

If the crowded environs of Berg Lake campground are not to your liking, continue to Rearguard or Robson Pass campgrounds. If you really want to get away from the crowds, Adolphus campground beckons, 4.6 km northeast from Berg Lake in adjacent Jasper National Park. Camping at Adolphus is free, however you will need a park use permit from the Jasper Information Centre.

In recent years, BC Parks has increased the number of day-hiking options from campgrounds near Berg Lake, by clearing one new trail and promoting two others. By far the most rewarding trails are Snowbird Pass and Hargreaves

The rugged Hargreaves Glacier-Mumm Basin trail traverses slopes north of Berg Lake and provides panoramic views of Mt. Robson.

Glacier-Mumm Basin. If you have two days to spend at Berg Lake, include both these outings, for they provide a complete experience of the landscape surrounding Mt. Robson.

Hargreaves Glacier-Mumm Basin loop, 14.8 km

This strenuous outing undulates over diverse terrain on the slopes north of Berg Lake, providing incomparable views of Mt. Robson.

From Berg Lake campground follow the Berg Lake trail southwest for 1.8 km to the Hargreaves Glacier junction. Turn north (right). Ascend a rough, steep track along a dry stream bed, and follow cairns and markers to the east lateral moraine of Hargreaves Glacier. Various routes exist to the crest of the moraine, from where the view opens northwest over the rocky basin containing Hargreaves Glacier and its marginal lake.

Within the last 200 years Hargreaves Glacier filled the basin to the height of this moraine. The glacier faces south and receives a great deal of solar radiation. The rapid retreat of the ice has uncovered a fantastically smooth slab of apricot and grey coloured Tatei limestone and dolomite. Farther south, an upturned lip of this rock, known as a *riegel*, dams the waters of the marginal lake.

The view south from the moraine provides new detail of Mt. Robson. Mist Glacier terminates in a marginal lake, separated from Berg Lake by a horseshoe-shaped terminal moraine. The cliffs between upper Mist Glacier and the Emperor Ridge are known as the Emperor Face. This face was first climbed in 1978. Its ascent has not been

frequently repeated. The ice sheet to the left is the true "north face" of the mountain, first climbed in 1963. The two glaciated peaks immediately northeast of Mt. Robson are The Helmet (3420 m) and Mt. Waffl (2890 m). Newman Waffl died in a 1930 solo attempt on Mt. Robson.

From the Hargreaves moraine, follow the track northeast to treeline. Views ahead include Adolphus Lake in Jasper National Park. The lake was named for Adolphus Moberly, a Métis settler of the Athabasca Valley who guided A.P. Coleman to Mt. Robson in 1908. The lake's clear dark blue colour indicates that its water is non-glacial.

A steep descent through delightful upper subalpine meadows brings you to a crossing of Toboggan Creek and a trail junction 150 m beyond. You can exit this hike to Berg Lake campground by following the track downstream (right), past Toboggan Falls – a slab waterfall that resembles a waterslide. Turn northwest (left) at this junction for a sidetrip to "The Cave," a solution cave high on the shoulder of the next ridge. The track climbs steeply through recently burned forest for approximately 1.5 km to the cave entrance – a horizontal slot in the Eldon limestone.

The cave itself won't be to everyone's liking, however the

panorama of Berg Lake and Mt. Robson from nearby is the scenic climax of this outing. Group of Seven artist Lawren Harris depicted this scene in a work titled "Tumbling Glacier." Looking south, Resplendent Mountain is notched between Mt. Waffl and Rearguard Mountain. If you observe the upper valley of Toboggan Creek carefully, you will see where the creek emerges from underground. The presence of The Cave and this creek outlet indicates karst topography. Bring a flashlight if you'd like to explore The Cave, and beware of ice on the floor.

Return to the junction at Toboggan Creek. The Mumm Basin trail continues east, ascending steeply through whitebark pine forest to treeline. Follow cairns and markers across boulderfields, screes and meadows, on a vague track that climbs into Mumm Basin. Wildflower displays here in mid-summer include clumps of fringed-grass-of-parnassus and the showy seedheads of western anemone.

The trail crosses briefly into Alberta, then descends steeply to Robson Pass by contouring southwest along the brink of a high cliff. After re-entering BC at boundary cairn "4U," look carefully for markers as the trail is easily lost. The steep descent continues on a well-beaten trail to Robson Pass campground. Turn southwest (right) to return to Berg Lake.

Yoho National Park

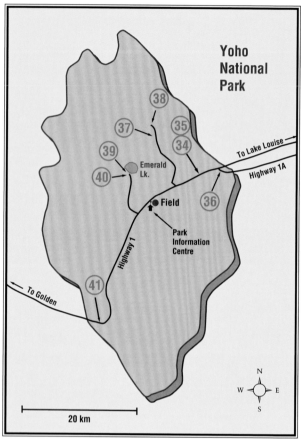

Yoho
National
Park

To Lake Louise

Highway 1A

Emerald
Lk.

Field

Highway 1

Park
Information
Centre

To Golden

20 km

N
W — E
S

Overview map of Yoho National Park showing trailhead locations

The word "Yoho" is a Cree expression of awe and wonder – sentiments affirmed by the many hikers who cherish the park's 350 km of trails. The Classic Hikes in Yoho provide high-level views of the park's spectacular lake-dotted, glaciated landscape. Founded in 1886 as Canada's second national park, Yoho includes 1313 km² on the western slopes of the Rockies in BC.

The village of Field (population 300) is in the centre of the park, 85 km west of Banff, 26 km west of Lake Louise, and 57 km east of Golden on Highway 1. Access is by car and passenger bus. Accommodation and basic supplies are available. The park information centre is on Highway 1 at the Field junction. The park has four frontcountry campgrounds with 286 campsites. There is a hostel at Takakkaw Falls. Yoho is in the same time zone as Banff and Jasper national parks, Alberta.

The site of Paget Lookout was chosen for its unobstructed view of Kicking Horse Valley and much of southern Yoho National Park.

34. Paget Lookout

Route

Day-hike, 3.5 km

Route	Elevation (m)	Distance (km)
Trailhead	1616	0
Paget Lookout jct	1783	1.4
Paget Lookout	2134	3.5

Topographic map: 82 N/8
Best lighting: anytime

Trailhead

Wapta Lake picnic area on the north side of Highway 1, 11 km east of Field, 15 km west of Lake Louise. Eastbound travellers should turn into West Louise Lodge, 500 m east of the trailhead, and approach westbound. The trailhead is adjacent to the picnic shelter.

I n the aftermath of large forest fires in 1936 and 1940, the Dominion Parks Branch surveyed the Rocky Mountain parks to find sites for fire lookout stations. Each site possessed unrestricted views of the major valleys and was in line-of-sight with adjacent stations in the lookout system. Paget (PADGE-ett) Lookout was one of three sites chosen in Yoho National Park, and saw use until the late 1970s. The access trail is still maintained and the lookout building is open as a day-use shelter. From the lookout you obtain a grand overview of southern Yoho National Park.

Trailhead to Paget Lookout

At the unmarked junction, 80 m from the trailhead, make a sharp turn west (left). The next 1.3 km of trail ascends through subalpine forest. In early summer, the undergrowth is coloured with the blooms of the diminutive evergreen violet, and the exquisite calypso orchid. Turn northeast (right) at the junction at km 1.4. The trail crosses and recrosses an avalanche slope beneath Paget Peak. The cliffs to the north contain Cambrian rocks that dip towards the southwest.

Where the trail begins its switchback ascent through the cliffs of Paget Peak, whitebark pine trees become common. The whitebark pine grows in the upper subalpine ecoregion and prefers windswept locations. On younger trees the bark is smooth and silvery-grey; on older trees, it is grey and scaly. The needles are in bunches of five.

The switchbacks provide glimpses of Mt. Niles (2972 m) and Sherbrooke Lake – the third largest lake in Yoho. Sherbrooke Lake is well worth a visit after your descent from Paget Lookout. (See Classic Hike # 35.) Mt. Ogden (2695 m) rises from the western shore of the lake. The mountain was named for Isaac Ogden, a vice-president of the CPR. The Lower Spiral Tunnel is in the west flank of the

mountain.

You often see boreal toads on these switchbacks – one of only 10 species of amphibians in the Canadian Rockies. At the top of the switchbacks the grade eases, and the trail heads northeast to the lookout.

Paget Lookout

Paget Lookout commands a 180° panorama, from Mt. Richardson, the Slate Range, and the Bow Valley in the east; to the lofty peaks surrounding Lake Louise and Lake O'Hara

in the south; and to the Van Horne Range and Kicking Horse Valley in the west. Across the Kicking Horse Valley to the southeast is Narao Peak (nah-RAY-owe) (2974 m). The mountain's name is Stoney for "hit in the stomach," possibly a reference to when James Hector of the Palliser Expedition was kicked by his horse near Wapta Falls in 1858. The forested slopes of Narao Peak show different shades of green, indicating tree stands dominated by different species. Most of the up-

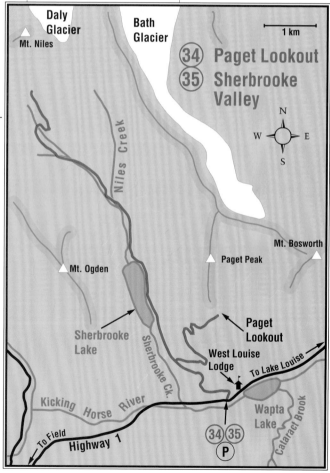

Wapta Lake

per Kicking Horse Valley burned in 1889 in fires caused by railway operations. The lighter green canopy indicates stands of lodgepole pine. The darker, taller canopy indicates more ancient stands dominated by Engelmann spruce and subalpine fir.

In the view from Paget Lookout, you can see how the gradient of the Kicking Horse River, flowing west, is much steeper than that of the Bow River, flowing east from the continental divide. Western river systems have only about 525 km straight line distance to flow between the Rockies and the Pacific Ocean. Eastern river systems flow about 1500 km to Hudson's Bay, or 2200 km to the Arctic Ocean. A steep gradient gives a river much more energy, and enables it to erode a deeper valley. Abrasive sediments in the water also increase a river's erosive power.

The town of Field is 16.3 km west of Kicking Horse Pass as the water flows, at an elevation of 1242 m. At an equal distance east of Kicking Horse Pass on the Bow River, the valley floor elevation is 1533 m.

Mountain goats are often seen at Paget Lookout. Yoho has about 400 mountain goats. Bighorn sheep also share this

Kettles and Sinks

The major east-west passes in the Rockies (Kicking Horse, Vermilion, Yellowhead and Crowsnest) all feature lakes near their summits. These passes were initially scoured by massive ice sheets during the early Pleistocene glaciations, 1.9 million years ago, and have been enlarged by 20 to 30 glaciations since.

Huge blocks of rubble-covered ice detached from retreating ice sheets at the end of the most recent glaciation, the Wisconsin, and came to rest atop mountain passes in the Rockies. As the detached ice blocks melted, the rubble slumped, creating hollows in which water collected. The resulting lakes are known as kettles. Wapta Lake is a kettle, as are Summit Lake and Sink Lake farther east in Kicking Horse Pass. Sink Lake has no visible surface outlet and may drain underground into Wapta Lake. *Wapta* is the Stoney word for "river," and was the original name of the Kicking Horse River.

When Highway 1 was constructed through Yoho in 1956, crews excavating a roadcut near Wapta Lake found permafrost – evidence of remnant glacial ice from the Wisconsin Glaciation.

habitat. For decades, sheep were thought to be absent from Yoho. However, since the early 1990s sheep have been seen at a mineral lick on the lower slopes of Paget Peak, adjacent to Highway 1. They now probably range in this area.

The lower slopes of Paget Peak (2591 m) north of the lookout are bedecked with glacier lilies until early July.

The peak was named for Reverend Dean Paget of Calgary, a founding member of the Alpine Club of Canada, who climbed the peak in 1904. Surveyor J.J. McArthur made the first ascent in 1886.

"We made the ascent of the mountain to the north across Wapta Lake... The view from this mountain presents 5 small lakes, one of which at the time of our exploration was still covered with ice."

—J.J. McArthur, on the first ascent of Paget Peak in 1886, *Report of Department of the Interior,* 1887

Waterbars: Going With the Flow

Hiking trails disturb natural drainage patterns. Waterbars are one of several devices used to prevent water from collecting underfoot. A waterbar is a log imbedded in the trail to divert water from the tread surface to an area off-trail where drainage is better. Waterbars are frequently installed on steep sections of trail that ascend directly upslope, or across a sideslope, like those on the upper part of the Paget Lookout trail. Without waterbars, these sections of trail would erode into channels. Waterbars are ideally located where there is a natural dip on the downhill edge of the trail. In the absence of such a dip, trail crews may bevel the trail where

they install the waterbar to increase its effectiveness. Waterbars are often slippery and pose a genuine tripping hazard to hikers. Step over them, not on them.

"At noon we came upon a fine lake something over a mile in length, whose pale blue waters settled once for all the question as to whether our valley led directly to the glacier."

—Charles Fay,
on the first recorded
visit to Sherbrooke Lake,
Appalachia 1898

Sherbrooke Lake is flanked by avalanche slopes that provide excellent habitat for elk, deer, moose and grizzly. Mt. Ogden is the backdrop in this view from the east shore of the lake.

35. Sherbrooke Valley

Route

Day-hike, 9.8 km.

Route	Elevation (m)	Distance (km)
Trailhead	1616	0
Paget Lookout jct	1783	1.4
Sherbrooke Lake	1814	3.0
Meadow beneath Mt. Niles	2317	9.8

Topographic maps: 82 N/8, 82 N/9

Trailhead

Wapta Lake picnic area on the north side of Highway 1, 11 km east of Field, 15 km west of Lake Louise. There is no sign for eastbound travellers. The trailhead is adjacent to the picnic shelter.

Although the spectacular scenery of Lake O'Hara and the Yoho Valley attracts most of Yoho's hikers, the Sherbrooke Valley has a wilderness quality missing from these other areas. This Classic Hike features one of Yoho's largest backcountry lakes, excellent wildlife viewing opportunities, and classic upper subalpine meadows.

Trailhead to Sherbrooke Lake

At the unmarked junction 80 metres from the trailhead, make a sharp turn to the west (left). From here, the trail climbs moderately to the mouth of Sherbrooke Valley. Keep straight ahead at the junction at km 1.4. The right hand trail leads to Paget Lookout. (See Classic Hike #34.) Strong hikers can link these hikes in an energetic day.

Between the Paget Lookout junction and Sherbrooke Lake, sections of trail have been gravel-capped. Pressure-treated wood decking has been installed to bridge boggy areas. Look for the blooms of orchids here in early summer, including tall white bog orchid and hooded lady's tresses. Mt. Stephen (3199 m) and Cathedral Crags (3073 m) are visible through the trees to the southwest.

At km 3.0 (60 m beyond the first blowdown) a short sidetrail leads west (left) to the shore of Sherbrooke Lake. Early morning visitors often find the lake a tranquil mirror, reflecting the colourful slabs of Mt. Ogden (2695 m) opposite, and the thumb-like form of Mt. Niles (2972 m) at the north

Please see map on page 190

end of the valley. The upthrust sedimentary formations in Mt. Ogden's ridge date to the Cambrian period. In the sequence of formations, the rocks become progressively younger toward the north end of the mountain.

With an area of 35 ha, Sherbrooke is the third largest lake in Yoho. It is 12 m deep and is usually frozen until late June. Glacially formed and fed, its waters change colour from clear, to green, to silty gray as the glacial melt season progresses. Lake trout and rainbow trout are the fish species present. Surveyor J.J. McArthur named the lake in 1887, after the town of Sherbrooke, near his home in the province of Quebec.

The trail follows the east shore. You may see mountain goats high on the cliffs of Paget Peak. Extensive avalanche slopes reach down to west shore. These slopes are good places to look for moose, deer and elk, who browse on green alder, water

birch and willows. The avalanche slopes are also frequented by grizzly bears in their quest for berries, succulent forbs and rodents. Although small in area, the Sherbrooke Valley is habitat for grizzlies, and their tracks and scats are often seen along the trail. Grizzlies dig their dens in mid-autumn, preferring steep north or east slopes in areas of high snowfall, such as upper Sherbrooke Valley. If you are hiking late in the season, be especially mindful of grizzlies. Yoho's first recorded mauling of a human by a grizzly took place just beyond the north end of Sherbrooke Lake in September 1939.

Sherbrooke Lake to Niles Meadows

At the north end of the lake, the trail passes through another blowdown. There are many dead trees in the lake, with root plates still attached. Whereas the downed trees on shore blew over in a windstorm, those in the lake did not. It is likely they were uprooted by avalanches from the slope to the west. Deposited on the frozen lake surface, the trees came to rest on the shallow lake bottom when that winter's ice melted.

Beyond the lake's inlet, the trail ascends beside a small canyon that contains a waterfall, and then emerges into an extensive subalpine wet meadow, dotted with massive boulders. Here Niles Creek, draining the valley to the northeast, converges with up-

Blowdown

Just before Sherbrooke Lake, the trail passes through the first of the valley's blowdown areas. These Engelmann spruce and subalpine fir trees were uprooted during a violent thunderstorm in August 1984. The trail has been cut out of the resulting debris. You may still be able to count the rings on some of the cleared tree trunks. A few of the spruces were roughly 300 years old.

Although it looks like a scene of destruction, this blowdown is one of nature's methods for revitalizing areas of old forest. In the absence of fire, blowdowns create openings in the forest canopy, allowing sunlight to reach the floor. This promotes new growth of shrubs and wildflowers that provide food for deer, elk, moose and bears.

The trail beyond Sherbrooke Lake climbs to alpine meadows beneath Mt. Niles.

per Sherbrooke Creek.

The trail crosses the two channels of Niles Creek and then makes several sharp turns as it works its way through willows to the north edge of the meadow. After a gentle switchback ascent into ancient forest, the grade steepens to crest a rock step alongside a waterfall. Three hundred metres farther, rock-hop the creek to its west bank, or use a fallen tree if present.

The upper reach of Sherbrooke Creek is both avalanche slope and creek bed.

Snow avalanches from the west sweep directly down the creek, and have severed many tree tops at trailside. The prospect of avalanches was not taken into account when a bridge was installed here in 1988. The pressure-treated bridge timbers were crushed by the weight of avalanches the following winter – an expensive trail maintenance lesson. Use what's left of the bridge, or rock-hop to the east side of the creek.

The mountains along the west side of Sherbrooke Valley feature wildly folded and steeply tilted rock formations. Two waterfalls cascade over the cliff at the head of the creek. The trail angles sharply to the southeast (right) and climbs steeply on an open slope, where clumps of false hellebore grow. A hundred metres after cresting this slope, the trail emerges from the trees and swings north into the meadow beneath Mt. Niles. Take note of where the trail leaves the trees. It is easy to miss on return.

A rockslide on the west side of the meadow makes a good place to have lunch. Mt. Niles is the centrepiece in the view north. Its strata show the unmistakable U-shaped fold of a syncline. The mountain was named for William Niles, president of the Appalachian Mountain Club in 1898. Remnant glaciers occupy the cirques on the west side of the valley and to the south are the majestic peaks of the continental divide.

In the Footsteps of Pioneers

The first recorded travellers in this part of the Sherbrooke Valley were mountaineers Charles Fay and party, who without benefit of a trail, used this approach to attempt Mt. Balfour on the Waputik (WAH-poo-tick) Icefield in 1898. Although unsuccessful on Mt. Balfour, Fay's party made the first ascents of Mt. Niles and the unnamed peak immediately south of Mt. Daly.

The trail we now hike originated in 1911, to provide access to the 6th annual Alpine Club of Canada mountaineering camp, which convened at the north edge of the wet meadow. Here and there you will see rotting corduroy bridges that date to the original trail construction.

Odaray Mountain is framed by stands of Lyall's larch on Opabin Plateau.

36. Lake O'Hara Alpine Circuit

Route

Day-hike, 12.4 km loop

Route	Elevation (m)	Distance (km)
Trailhead, lakeshore	2035	0
Wiwaxy Gap jct.	2035	0.3
Wiwaxy Gap	2538	2.2
Lake Oesa jct.	2260	4.2
East Opabin jct.	2287	6.6
Opabin Lake	2287	7.1
All Souls' jct.	2210	8.8
All Souls' Prospect	2500	9.8
Schäffer Lake	2180	11.0
Park patrol cabin	2040	12.4

Lake O'Hara is the most developed and popular hiking destination in Yoho National Park. Within a 5 km radius of the lake, 80 km of hiking trails explore every nook and cranny of an exceptional high country landscape. The Lake O'Hara Alpine Circuit connects sections of seven trails into a rewarding loop, with views of more than a dozen of the area's lakes and ponds, and the

Trailhead

The number of visitors to Lake O'Hara is controlled through a complicated quota system administered by Yoho National Park. Most day-hikers take advantage of bus service along the Lake O'Hara fireroad (fee charged). Reservations are accepted for portions of the bus seating. Call the park well in advance for details (250-343-6433). Foot access is by the Lake O'Hara fireroad (11.2 km) or Cataract Brook trail (12.8 km); however, you will still require a reservation for the Lake O'Hara campground.

To reach the bus staging area and trailheads, follow Highway 1 to the junction with Highway 1A, 12.6 km west of Lake Louise, 13.4 km east of Field. Turn onto Highway 1A, cross the railway tracks and turn west (right) to the Lake O'Hara parking lot. Walk the road or the Cataract Brook trail from the adjacent trailhead. Or meet the park attendant at the shelter inside the fireroad gate if you will be riding the bus. The bus trip takes half an hour. The Alpine Circuit trailhead is adjacent to the park patrol cabin at Lake O'Hara. Follow the path on the south (right) side of the cabin to the interpretive display on the lakeshore trail.

rugged peaks along the continental divide.

Portions of this hike traverse exposed rocky ledges, and about a third of the distance is on rough trails through boulderfields and across scree slopes. In these places, you must pay careful attention to route markers. Avoid this outing during early season, poor weather, electrical storms, and after snowfalls. Opabin Plateau is usually closed until the winter snowpack is melted – July in most years.

Trailhead to Wiwaxy Gap

From the interpretive display, follow the lakeshore trail north for 60 m to the outlet bridge. Cross the bridge, turn east (right) and follow the north shore trail 200 m to the

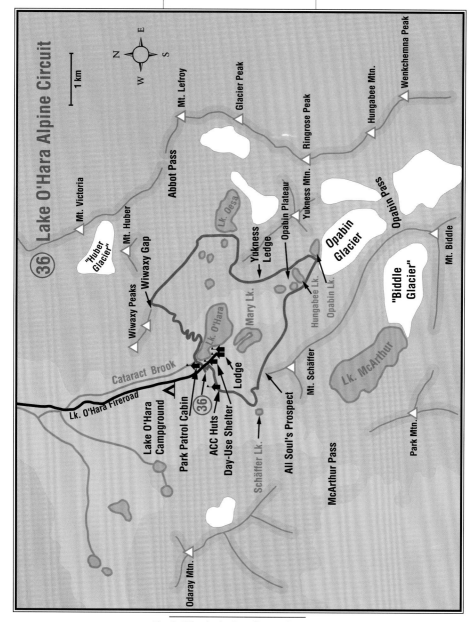

Wiwaxy Gap junction. The "north bay" of Lake O'Hara, adjacent to this section of trail, was closed in 1990 to protect trout spawning and nursery habitat.

Looking west across the lake, Odaray Mountain (3159 m) may be reflected in the still waters of morning. The southern summit of the mountain was first climbed by surveyor J.J. McArthur in 1887. From its slopes, he was probably the first white man to see Lake O'Hara. McArthur told a retired British army colonel, Robert O'Hara, of the lake. O'Hara made at least two visits to the lake in the 1880s and 1890s, and it became known as "O'Hara's Lake."

The climb from the lakeshore to Wiwaxy Gap is the steepest section of trail in Classic Hikes – 503 m of elevation gained in just 1.9 km. The first section switchbacks tightly in a gully that was swept by a debris flow in the summer of 1985. At the top of the gully, you traverse east beneath a 20 m quartzite cliff, and then ascend the cliff on ledges. Wherever the trail becomes faint, the route is indicated with cairns and painted markers: two vertical yellow stripes on a rectangular blue background. Although you may occasionally have to use your hands on the rock for balance, in no place does the route involve technical climbing. If you lose the way or come face to face with an unscalable cliff, backtrack and look for the route markers.

The steep grade resumes. A remarkable Engelmann

Alpine Artists

The Lake O'Hara area has attracted and inspired many artists, among them: J.S. Sargent, W.J. Phillips, Peter and Catherine Whyte, and members of the Group of Seven, including J.E.H. MacDonald. Macdonald in particular was enchanted with Lake O'Hara, and made the first of seven visits in 1924. Several of his works include views of Mt. Biddle, Mt. Owen and Cathedral Mountain from the Lake O'Hara Alpine Circuit.

spruce tree towers over the trail. Two of its roots have grown laterally out of the steep slope, and then upwards to become separate trunks. The diameter of the main trunk is 1.4 m at the base, more than 10 times greater than average for a spruce at treeline. Whitebark pine also grows here.

Your rapid ascent soon provides an overview of Lake O'Hara. The lake has an area of 34.4 ha, and a maximum depth of 42 m. As its vivid colour suggests, the lake is fed by glacial meltwater. If you look southeast into the valley that contains Lake Oesa, you can see that Lake O'Hara is the lowest in a series of five lakes and ponds. Glaciologists call such an arrangement paternoster lakes or a glacial cirque staircase. In past ice ages, glacial ice flowed west and hollowed the basins for each lake at progressively lower elevations. A cascading stream now connects them. As

Lake O'Hara Place Names

Some of the unusual names in the Lake O'Hara area are of Stoney Native origin, and were given by Samuel Allen of Philadelphia. Allen visited the Rockies four times between 1891 and 1895. He learned the names from William Twin, the Stoney most adept at guiding white explorers in the Rockies.

Hungabee (hun-GAH-bee): "chieftain." With an elevation of 3493 m, it is the highest mountain in the area.

Oesa (owe-EE-sah): "ice" (Allen spelled it Oeesa). The lake is often frozen into July.

Opabin (owe-PAY-bin): "rocky." This name appears often throughout the mountains of the US and Canadian West.

Wiwaxy (wih-WAX-ee): "windy." Wiwaxy Gap is indeed a windy place. Allen called the valley to the north "the gorge of the winds."

Yukness (YUCK-ness): "sharpened, as with a knife." The mountain's horn shape was "sharpened" by glacial ice.

Controversy surrounds the mountain called Odaray (OWE-dah-ray), which was apparently named by surveyor J.J. McArthur. Four meanings have been proposed: "many waterfalls," "very brushy," "windfall" or "cone." Since McArthur originally referred to it as "Cone Mountain," the latter was probably the intended meaning.

with most lakes created this way, the deepest part of Lake O'Hara is just beneath the headwall, at what would have been the "upstream" point of the glacier.

Across Lake O'Hara to the southeast, Yukness Mountain (2847 m) scrapes the sky. The glacially sculpted horn of Mt. Biddle (3319 m) looms above Opabin Pass to the south. The north glacier of Mt. Owen (3087 m) is framed to the southwest through McArthur Pass.

The trail traverses across more gullies and continues its steep sidehill ascent. Above treeline, you climb steeply to Wiwaxy Gap, the low point on the ridge that connects the Wiwaxy Peaks (2703 m) to the

west, with Mt. Huber (3368 m) to the east. Daisy and golden fleabanes, Drummond's anemone, spotted saxifrage, alpine arnica, moss campion and white mountain avens are scattered across the screes. Look for the tracks and pellets of mountain goats here too.

For those unaccustomed to high mountain viewpoints, Wiwaxy Gap will seem more like the domain of mountaineers. The view north over Cataract Brook includes Cathedral Mountain (3189 m), and the peaks on the Wapta and Waputik icefields in the northern part of Yoho National Park. Two waterfalls on the cliff to the northeast of Wiwaxy Gap are fed by meltwater from Huber Glacier. Above the

waterfalls, the keen eye can pick out the rocky summit of Mt. Victoria (3464 m). Its western aspect is entirely unlike the familiar view from Lake Louise. True to its name, Wiwaxy Gap is a windy place, and with the sweat you've worked up during the climb, you are not likely to linger.

Wiwaxy Gap to Lake Oesa

Head southeast from Wiwaxy Gap on the trail that aims straight for Lake Oesa. Ignore the paths that lead uphill and downhill, left and right respectively. You can see the trail ahead, scratched across the cliff edge. If this does not look to your liking, or if snow

The Gog Formations

The Lake O'Hara Alpine Circuit is the only Classic Hike that features a single rock formation underfoot for its entire distance. Between lake level and approximately 2750 m, the bedrock is Gog quartzite and siltstone.

Gog quartzite is a metamorphic, quartz-rich sandstone, and one of the hardest and most common rocks in the central Rockies. It is composed of quartz sediments eroded from the Canadian Shield, transported to the southwest by rivers, and deposited in ancient seas during the Early Cambrian period. Deep within the earth's crust, the quartz particles liquefied under intense

Fossilized worm burrowings are common in slabs of Gog siltstone.

heat and pressure. As the rocks were thrust toward the surface during mountain building they were cooled, binding the sandstone together with quartz cement.

Some exposures of Gog quartzite are covered in green

and black map lichens (*Rhizocarpon geographicum*). Where protected from weathering, Gog quartzite is often white, pinkish or purplish; where exposed it can become stained brown and red with iron oxides. The fossilized burrowings of worms and brachiopods are common, as is iron pyrite (fool's gold). Some quartzite boulders contain a conglomerate of fist-sized pebbles and rocks, fused together with quartz. At the Lake Oesa junction, trail builders have imaginatively incorporated colourful ripple rock slabs of Gog siltstone into the walking surface.

lingers, turn back here. Also, beware of snow avalanche danger on this next section if you are hiking before mid-July, or after a snowfall. The 2.2 km to Lake Oesa involves a descending traverse, with fine views to the chain of paternoster lakes. On a calm day, you can hear the cascading water in the cataracts that link the lakes. Across the chasm, Yukness Mountain broods in morning shadow.

Some of the finest views of Lake Oesa are from this section of trail. In a typical year, the lake is still partly frozen in mid-July. The massive mountain wall that backs the lake is part of the continental divide, and extends from Mt. Lefroy (3423 m) on the north, through Glacier Peak (3283 m), to Ringrose Peak (3281 m) on the south. A small drift glacier occupies Lake Oesa's north-

east shore, and a moraine-dammed lake sits above the southeast shore. Lake Oesa is dammed by an upturned, glacier-worn rock slab, known as a *riegel* (RYE-gull).

Lake Oesa to Opabin Plateau: Yukness Ledge

At the first trail junction, turn southwest, downhill to the right. In 150 m you reach the Lake Oesa junction. You want the trail indicated as "Opabin Plateau via Yukness Ledge Alpine Route," which angles southeast from the junction. The trail crosses the rock slabs west of the lake and descends towards the outlet. Follow the large cairns and use caution if the rock is wet or icy. At the third cairn, the trail angles off to the south (right) across a small meadow, and then de-

scends a short cliff to the outlet stream. Rock-hop the stream and follow the cairned route west, climbing across slabs and through boulderfields. Beware of rockfall danger here.

The trail descends a natural staircase with some awkward steps, and then switchbacks on the north end of the terrace that overlooks Lake O'Hara. Pay careful attention to the route markers here. At the next junction, turn sharply south (left). If the weather has turned poor you can exit by going straight ahead at this junction. This will bring you to the Lake Oesa trail at Victoria Lake, where you turn west (left) to descend to Lake O'Hara.

For the next kilometre, the trail traverses Yukness Ledge, offering breathtaking views over Lake O'Hara. Move slowly and carefully near the cliff edge, especially if the rock is wet. You may see a sediment plume issuing from "East Opabin Creek" into Lake O'Hara, where the glacial sediment transported by the creek disperses into the lake. The finest particles, called rock flour, are suspended in the lake water and reflect the blue and green spectrums of light, giving the lake its remarkable colour.

Opabin Glacier comes into view straight ahead, tucked beneath the precipitous flank of Mt. Biddle. Samuel Allen named the mountain for A.J. Biddle, a Philadelphia author and publisher. To the west of the trail is Opabin Plateau, covered with stands of larch

Cairn Building

The rock piles you see marking the route and crowning the highpoints of this hike are called cairns. *Carn* is Gaelic for "pile of rocks". Cairns assist hikers and mountaineers when the way is vague, or during poor weather when visibility is limited.

The cairns in the Lake O'Hara area have evolved over decades. Many are "overkill" for their intended purpose, cluttering the margin of well-defined routes. Some are no more than landscape graffiti – unnecessary and inappropriate. Please do not add to existing cairns or build new ones. When

you move rocks in alpine areas you alter drainage patterns, overturn lichens and disrupt the formation of soils. On the small scale, you may set back the growth of vegetation by centuries.

and dotted with the Opabin Moor Lakes. When you have travelled slightly more than one half of the length above Opabin Plateau, the trail begins a winding and sometimes steep descent through rockslide debris to its junction with the East Opabin Trail at Hungabee Lake.

Opabin Plateau

Turn southeast (left), cross a rock bridge, and ascend the rise to Opabin Lake. Notice the boulders that were inlaid in the walking surface during trail rehabilitation in 1988 and 1989. The thin, clay soils here saturate with water quickly, and create a slippery, poorly drained walking surface. Undisciplined hikers walk off the trail at such times, damaging the surrounding vegetation. The boulders serve as stepping stones, keep feet dry and preserve the adjacent upper subalpine meadows.

Hungabee Mountain, first climbed in 1903, towers to the southeast of Opabin Lake. The broad, northwest face forms part of today's regular mountaineering route from Opabin Pass. Although many mountaineers have this summit on their "wish list," the poor rock on the upper mountain and the frequent presence of snow and ice thwart most attempts to climb it.

The mass of rubble on the south shore of Opabin Lake is a terminal moraine, created during the Little Ice Age advance of Opabin Glacier. The moraine has partly filled the lake. Studies of lake bottom sediments at Opabin Lake and

When you traverse Yukness Ledge, Lake O'Hara is directly below.

Lake O'Hara indicate that the Little Ice Age was the most significant glacial advance here in the last 8500 years. Between 8500 and 3000 years ago, glaciers were absent in this area above the elevation of Opabin Lake. The upper Opabin Valley, now a domain of rock and ice, supported subalpine forest.

Opabin Plateau to All Souls' Prospect

Turn sharply northwest (right) at the junction at Opabin Lake, and follow the West Opabin Circuit. The upper subalpine meadows here are filled with yellow and white mountain heather and frequented by white-tailed ptarmigan. The trail descends rock benches, paralleling West Opabin Creek. You can see where the silty water of Opabin Lake drains beneath a

complex of moraines. The moraines indicate two distinct glacial advances. The lower and larger moraine, covered in lichens, records the maximum advance of the Wisconsin Glaciation, 11,000 years ago. Atop this sits the more colourful rock of the Little Ice Age moraine, approximately 150 years old.

There are fine views ahead of Cathedral Mountain, the Wiwaxy Peaks and the serried flanks of Mt. Huber (3368 m), reflected here and there in the numerous lakes and ponds on Opabin Plateau. Emil Huber was a Swiss alpinist who in 1890 made the first ascent of Mt. Sir Donald, in Glacier National Park, BC.

At all trail junctions on Opabin Plateau, keep to the West Opabin Circuit, which is always either left or straight ahead. After 1.6 km of delightful hiking, the trail begins a steep descent with views of

Mary Lake and Cathedral Mountain directly ahead. The All Souls' Prospect junction is 80 m farther. You may exit the Alpine Circuit at this point by keeping straight ahead to descend to Lake O'Hara. Otherwise, turn west (left), and ascend a man-made rock staircase onto the benches beneath Mt. Schäffer (2692 m). Hoary marmots frequent these benches, and mountain goats are often seen on the cliffs above.

You climb steeply to the west on scree and then traverse northwest on a more reasonable grade. Beware of rockfall danger here. The ascent culminates at All Souls' Prospect. The peculiar name of this viewpoint was given by Dr. George Link, who cleared many trails in the Lake O'Hara area. All Souls' Day is November 2 – a day of prayer for the souls of the faithful departed.

From All Souls' Prospect, you enjoy a tremendous and lofty panorama on a clear day. Due north is the Cataract Brook valley, leading the eye to Mt. Bosworth (2771 m) above Kicking Horse Pass. All the principal peaks of the continental divide in this area are visible, and to the west and southwest respectively, are point-blank views of Odaray Mountain and Mt. Owen. Looking southwest, you can see Neptuak Mountain (3237 m) framed through Opabin Pass. From here, Opabin Plateau appears a desolate place; its meadowlands and larch forest dwarfed to insignificance by a chaos of moraines and rockslides, and

"Picture the colours of morning darting from pyramid to pyramid, then slowly creeping down into the valleys, as sunlight puts a crown upon the summits, while still wrapt in the purple gloom sleep the circling glaciers, the winding stream, and the emerald water of lake Oeesa."

—Samuel Allen
describing the view
from Wiwaxy Gap in 1894

by the sheer precipices that ring the valley.

Descend north from All Souls' Prospect on a rough path beaten into the screes and boulderfields. This is a bone-jarring descent, with one 2 m step that requires downclimbing. The proliferation of trails in the Lake O'Hara area has resulted in many redundant and parallel paths. During this descent, look to the meadows near Schäffer Lake. You can see new gravelled trails, and old trails that have been closed and left to revegetate.

The trail winds through treeline forest and passes the Big Larch junction. Keep straight ahead for 100 m to the Schäffer Lake junction. The lake is a kettle pond fringed with willows. Turn northeast (right) at this junction. As the trail begins its descent to Lake O'Hara, note the gradual transition from larch forest to one dominated by Engelmann spruce and subalpine fir.

The descent brings you to the Alpine Club of Canada's Elizabeth Parker Hut and the erroneously named "Alpine Meadow." The meadow is below treeline and is "subalpine." The buildings date to 1926, and have been operated by the ACC since 1930. Nine other cabins formerly on this site were moved to the lakeshore and are now the outlying cabins of Lake O'Hara Lodge. Keep straight ahead at the junction adjacent to the hut.

The ACC held the first of six mountaineering camps at Lake O'Hara on this meadow in 1909. Between then and 1974, when random camping and group camping were abolished, the meadows suffered severe impact from overuse. East of the hut is a fenced plot on a closed trail. You can see the subtle difference that two decades of natural regeneration has produced in the vegetation – a vivid indication of the harshness of climate at this elevation.

Turn north (left) at the junction 200 m east of the hut. The trail climbs out of the creek bed, swings east and descends to the day-use shelter and patrol cabin on the fireroad. Outbound buses stop here. If you're staying at the campground, turn north (left) and walk 600 m along the road.

> "*An entirely new trail was made this year ... along the upper slopes of ... the Yoho Valley. I suggest that this ... should be completed by connecting the Upper Yoho Valley with the ... trail which goes along the bottom of the valley. If this is done, tourists will be able to make a grand trip ... "*
>
> —Letter from mountaineer
> Edward Whymper to
> Sir Thomas Shaughnessy,
> President of the CPR,
> January 3, 1902

The Iceline contours at the edge of Emerald Glacier and crosses an area covered by glacial ice less than a century ago.

37. Iceline

Route

Day-hike or overnight, 22.0 km loop

Route	Elevation (m)	Distance (km)
Takakkaw Falls parking lot	1509	0
Iceline/Yoho Pass trailhead	1501	0.6
Lower Iceline jct	1646	1.9
Upper Iceline jct	1860	3.4
Celeste Lake jct	2195	6.7
Little Yoho CG	2073	11.8
Laughing Falls jct	1814	15.6
Laughing Falls CG	1608	17.0
Takakkaw Falls parking lot	1509	22.0

Topographic maps: 82 N/7, 82 N/8, 82 N/10
Best Lighting: anytime

Trailhead

Follow Highway 1 to the Yoho Valley Road, 3.7 km east of Field, 22.3 km west of Lake Louise. Go north 14 km to the day-use parking area at Takakkaw Falls. Take the trail from the south end of the parking lot back to the Yoho Valley Road. Cross the road to the Iceline/Yoho Pass trailhead.

I t was 85 years before Edward Whymper's suggestion concerning a high-level hiking route in the Yoho Valley came to fruition.

Constructed in 1987, The Iceline quickly became one of the most popular Classic Hikes. Scratched from glacial rubble, the trail follows a sensational line, contouring the edge of Emerald Glacier for 5 km. Spectacular close-up views of a glacial environment, and panoramic vistas of the Yoho Valley are your rewards for venturing into this harsh domain. The rocky benches traversed by The Iceline are often snowbound until early July.

Trailhead to Iceline

The trail ascends the avalanche slope above the hostel and works its way south. Look back to obtain

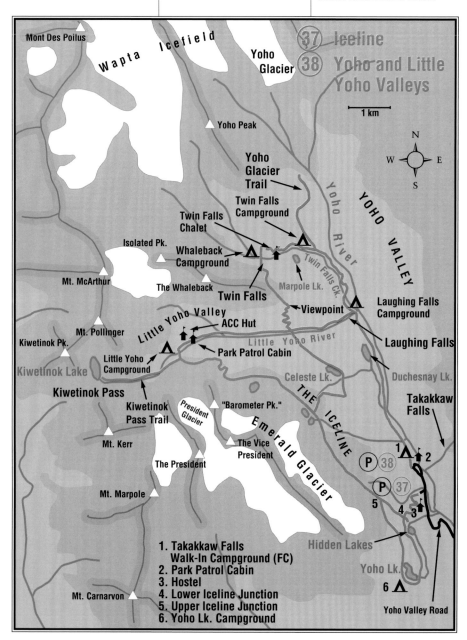

1. Takakkaw Falls
   Walk-In Campground (FC)
2. Park Patrol Cabin
3. Hostel
4. Lower Iceline Junction
5. Upper Iceline Junction
6. Yoho Lk. Campground

fine views of 254 m Takakkaw (TAH-kuh-kah) Falls, one of the four highest in Canada, and Mt. Balfour (3272 m). At the edge of the avalanche slope, the trail enters old-growth forest. Despite the nearby peril of avalanching snow and the wind blasts it generates, some of the Engelmann spruce trees here have attained diameters of 1.2 m at the base. With ages from 300-400 years, these are among the oldest trees in Yoho National Park.

The west slope of the Yoho Valley is terraced, with bedrock strata that dip toward the Yoho River. Just before the trail levels out on the first terrace, the sidetrail to Hidden Lakes branches south. It is only 200 m to these seasonal lakelets. Beyond this junction, the main trail returns to the avalanche slope and ascends steeply along its southern edge. You reach the lower Iceline junction in 100 m. Turn north (right).

For the next 1.5 km, the trail climbs through avalanche forest and dense growths of mountain alder to the upper Iceline junction. You will see bedrock in the trail as you gain elevation. At the junction, turn north (right). Here, you are slightly higher than the brink of Takakkaw Falls across the valley, and you can see the waterfall's source in Daly Glacier. *Takakkaw* is Cree for "it is magnificent!"

Iceline to Little Yoho Valley

To this point, this outing has followed sections of trail that existed before 1987. Just beyond the junction, angle northwest (left) onto the newer trail. The character of The Iceline is immediately evident, as the trail ascends a rock staircase. Construction of The Iceline required imaginative trail building. Boulders and rock slabs were used to create bridges, steps, retaining walls, and drainage culverts. Where the trail crosses bedrock slabs, its margin is defined by rows of rubble cleared from the path. These rocks, and many artistic cairns help guide the way across the bleak, unvegetated forefield of Emerald Glacier. Please refrain from building new cairns.

The Iceline roughly parallels Edward Whymper's route of exploration in 1901, when his party followed the edge of Emerald Glacier from Yoho Pass to the Little Yoho Valley. Whymper, famous for his first ascent of the Matterhorn in 1865, was accompanied by trail guide Tom Wilson, mountaineer James Outram, and four European mountaineering guides. During the trip, party members made first ascents of nine mountains in the Little Yoho, crossed several passes, and named many features.

Emerald Glacier consists of several cirque glaciers tucked under the east flank of The Vice President. During the most recent significant advance, the Little Ice Age, these lobes of ice covered the area now traversed by the trail. Working its way north, the trail climbs and descends a series of lateral moraines. Between the moraines, you cross areas of recently exposed Cathedral limestone bedrock, bisected by meltwater streams. The bedrock displays numerous striations – scratches and grooves etched by stones imbedded in the underside of the moving ice.

The vistas from The Iceline improve with each moraine crossed. Just before the Celeste Lake junction, the trail draws alongside a marginal lake, fed by meltwater from Emerald Glacier. You may have to rock-hop the outlet of

Whiskey Jack Hostel

Whiskey Jack hostel originated in 1922 as a CPR bungalow camp called Yoho Valley Lodge. The open avalanche slope was chosen because it was close to water and offered a view of Takakkaw Falls. However, the builders did not recognize the avalanche hazard. The lodge was damaged by an avalanche in the winter of 1937-38. The surviving buildings were relocated to the south, but not far enough to be out of harm's way. In 1967 another avalanche destroyed the vacant main lodge building. The surviving outbuildings became a hostel in 1969. "Whiskey jack" is a folk name for the gray jay, an inquisitive member of the crow family that is common in the surrounding subalpine forest.

this lake during warm weather, when the glacial runoff is at maximum. The low ridge of debris north of this lake is a push moraine, created by a minor advance of the closest lobe of ice in the 1970s. Directly north, across the Little Yoho Valley, are Mt. McArthur (3015 m) and the rocky prow of Isolated Peak (2845 m). Mt. McArthur was first climbed by surveyor W.S. Drewry in 1891. He named the peak for fellow surveyor, J.J. McArthur.

There is little natural shelter from either poor weather or intense heat on The Iceline. If you are weary, you may choose to exit at the Celeste Lake junction. It is 12.3 km to the hostel via Celeste Lake and Laughing Falls, reducing the outing to 18.4 km total. Continuing on The Iceline, you contour west into the Little Yoho Valley, and reach the apex of the trail on the crest of another moraine. Ahead are the northern aspects of The Vice President (3066 m) and The President (3138 m). These mountains were originally named by members of the 1906 Alpine Club of Canada camp for two officials of the CPR: President, Thomas Shaughnessy; and Vice-President, David McNicoll. After the camp, it was discovered the men's personal names had been previously given to two mountains in Glacier National Park, BC. Thus, their titles were applied to these mountains instead.

Another lobe of Emerald

The forefield of Emerald Glacier

Glacier is nestled on the north flank of The Vice President. Its meltwaters feed a lake that is backed by a lofty, 600 m long lateral moraine. The meltwater stream is building a delta into the lake. Another, smaller moraine-dammed lake lies to the north. As you descend toward treeline, Yoho Glacier, and Mts. Gordon (3203 m) and Balfour are to the northeast. The north ridge of The Vice President is unofficially called "Barometer Peak." It features wildly overturned folds. Purple Arctomys (ARK-toe-miss) shale is common here.

Little Yoho Valley to Whiskey Jack Hostel

The Iceline swings behind the prominent moraine and 500 m later, begins a steady descent through meadow and subalpine forest to the Little Yoho River and campground. The campground is at km 11.1, roughly the halfway point on the hike. The remainder of the distance is on good trail and can be completed fairly quickly if desired. Head east from the campground on the Little Yoho trail for 3.8 km to Laughing Falls junction. Turn south (right) and descend to Laughing Falls and campground in 1.5 km. From there, it is 5.0 km south to the Takakkaw Falls parking lot.

A Glacial Balancing Act

The lobes of Emerald Glacier feature shallow caves. The roofs of the caves frequently collapse and shower the rock benches below with chunks of dense, blue ice. Situated on the shaded lee side of an 800 m high mountain wall, Emerald Glacier receives more nourishment in the form of snowfall and suffers less melting, than many other glaciers in the Rockies. When appraising a glacier's well-being, glaciologists talk of "glacial budget". In years of net loss of snow, a glacier goes into debt and will recede. In years when a net gain of snow takes place, a glacier posts a profit and will advance. In 1993, more than 80 percent of glaciers in the Rockies were in retreat. Although Emerald Glacier has receded significantly during this century, the fact it can avalanche from a cliff in this fashion probably indicates it is presently "holding its own."

Mont des Poilus, Yoho Peak and the western margin of the Wapta Icefield highlight the view north from the apex of the Whaleback Trail.

38. Yoho and Little Yoho Valleys

Route

3-5 days, 29.5 km

Route	Elevation (m)	Distance (km)
Yoho Valley parking lot	1509	0
Takakkaw Falls walk-in CG	1517	0.2
Yoho Valley trailhead	1520	0.4
Pt. Lace/Angel's Staircase	1540	2.3
Duchesnay Lake jct	1616	3.7
Laughing Falls and CG	1600	4.4
Yoho Glacier jct	1616	6.5
Twin Falls CG	1605	6.7
Whaleback jct	1768	8.0
Whaleback Summit	2210	12.5
Little Yoho jct	1905	14.6
Little Yoho CG	2073	17.8
Kiwetinok Pass jct	2073	17.9
Celeste Lake jct	2195	22.7
Upper Iceline jct	1860	26.0
Lower Iceline jct	1646	27.7
Whiskey Jack Hostel	1501	28.8
Yoho Valley parking lot	1509	29.5

Topographic maps: 82 N/7, 82 N/8, 82 N/9, 82 N/10

Trailhead

Follow Highway 1 to the Yoho Valley Road, 3.7 km east of Field, 22.3 km west of Lake Louise. Turn north and follow this road 14 km to Takakkaw Falls. Drive through the large parking lot and park on the right in the Yoho Valley parking lot.

Yoho National Park takes its name from a Cree expression of awe and wonder. The Yoho and Little Yoho valleys contain a concentration of the park's wonders: powerful and picturesque waterfalls, glacier-clad peaks, and pockets of alpine meadow.

The Yoho and Little Yoho valleys are heavily used by both day-hikers and backpackers. Do not expect solitude, except late in the hiking season. The close spacing of campgrounds, the well-developed trails, and the convenient access to treeline and glacial environments makes the area ideal for novice back-packers. Increasing environmental impact in this area may lead to closure of some campgrounds and trails in the future. Please abide by any new regulations.

Takakkaw Falls to Twin Falls Campground

The outing begins along a gravel road to the Takakkaw Falls walk-in campground. The Yoho Valley trail departs north and heads across alluvial flats into forest. This trail originated after the initial expansion of the Mt. Stephen Reserve, as a corduroy carriage road constructed between 1903 and 1909. Corduroy is built by laying sections of whole trees side by side, and covering the bumpy

surface that results with dirt. Sections of old corduroy can still be seen at trailside.

Yoho's interpretive theme of "rockwalls and waterfalls" is exemplified in the Yoho Valley better than any-where else. The massive U-shaped valley trough was carved during the Wisconsin Glaciation. Tributary valleys also filled with ice, but were not as deeply eroded. When the ancestral Yoho Glacier receded, the tributary valleys were left hanging above the main valley floor. Their streams now plunge toward the Yoho River as waterfalls. Takakkaw Falls (TAH-kuh-kah: a Cree expression meaning "it is wonderful"), cascades 254 m, one of the four highest waterfalls in

Canada.

At km 2.3, short sidetrails branch east to the bank of the Yoho River and a view of Angel's Staircase Falls, and southwest to Point Lace Falls. The Yoho Valley trail continues north and climbs Hollingsworth Hill, named for a district warden who used dyna-mite to widen the right-of-way. The Duchesnay Lake junction is at km 3.7. The side-trip to the pleasant lake is less than half the 400 m indicated on the park sign. In most years, the lake is virtually dry by late summer. Moose frequent this area. Back on the main trail, you draw alongside the Yoho River at a small canyon. The tilted, potholed rock exposed in the riverbed is

---

Please see
map on
page 204

Jean Habel: Quest for Hidden Mountain

Laughing Falls was not named because of imaginary voices heard in its cascading waters. The falls brightened up the otherwise glum surroundings during the rain-plagued first exploration of the Yoho Valley in 1897. The expedition was organized by Jean Habel (AHH-bull), a German mathematics professor and mountaineer. Habel was intent on ascending a mountain he had seen from the railway the previous year – a peak he called Hidden Mountain, now named Mont des Poilus.

Habel's party journeyed from Field to Emerald Lake, then over Yoho Pass to the floor of the Yoho Valley at Takakkaw Falls.

This 25 km journey, delayed by the professor's many ramblings, required eight days. Continuing

north in the valley, the party was the first to see Laughing Falls and Twin Falls, and the first to set foot on Yoho Glacier. The expedition was curtailed by a shortage of supplies before any serious attempt could be made to ascend Hidden Mountain. However, Habel's report, published in the journal *Appalachia*, stirred up great interest in the Yoho Valley, and was instrumental in the area being added to the federal park reserve in 1901. In 1986, the previously unnamed mountain on the Wapta Icefield, immediately south of Mt. Baker, was named Mt. Habel in his honour.

Sullivan limestone.

Laughing Falls campground is situated just beyond, on an alluvial fan where Twin Falls Creek and the Little Yoho River join the Yoho River. Since it is so close to the trailhead, this campground is seldom used. For the best views of nearby Laughing Falls, follow beaten paths along the north bank of the Little Yoho River.

Continue north (straight ahead) from the junction just beyond Laughing Falls campground. The trail crosses to the east bank of Twin Falls Creek

and follows cobbled flats alongside the Yoho River. The author once encountered a herd of 23 elk here. The trail then turns sharply south to re-enter the valley of Twin Falls Creek. There are tantalizing views west through the trees to Twin Falls. At the Yoho Glacier junction, the trail to the glacier branches north (right). Turn south (left), and descend to Twin Falls campground in 150 m.

Twin Falls Campground to The Whaleback

Beyond Twin Falls campground, the trail bypasses a small canyon in the creek and climbs toward the Whaleback junction. There is a slab of "ripple rock" in the trail. The rock's undulating surface records the action of wavelets on a prehistoric shoreline. The roar of Twin Falls increases as you approach the Whaleback junction. Here, several of the Engelmann spruce trees are more than 1 m in diameter and 45 m tall.

Yoho Glacier, 2.3 km

If you arrive early at Twin Falls campground, you may want to hike to Yoho Glacier after setting up camp. Backtrack to the Yoho Glacier junction, and head north on a rough trail that rises and falls through an ancient forest of Engelmann spruce and subalpine fir.

At 2.2 km from the junction, the trail makes a short switchback descent and emerges abruptly from the forest on a barren slope overlooking the forefield of Yoho Glacier. The sudden transition from forest to sparsely vegetated terrain marks the trimline of the glacier. In 1844, the toe of the glacier was here. All forest to the north was obliterated beneath the ice. In this harsh climate and on these poor soils, it will take many cen-

Yoho Glacier has receded greatly in the last century. It is now hard to see it from the Yoho Glacier trail. In this view from Yoho Peak, the glacier flows from the slopes of Mt. Rhondda on the Wapta Icefield. Mt. Habel is the rocky summit in the background on the left.

turies for forest to become re-established.

Looking north, you can see Yoho Glacier notched between the cliffs of Mt. Gordon (3203 m) to the east, and the slopes and moraines of Yoho Peak (2760 m) to the west. The glacier has receded almost 3 km in 150 years. Yoho Glacier is one of eight outlet valley glaciers of

the 40 km² Wapta Icefield. Earlier this century, the glacier was the subject of intense scientific study and annual measurement. When glacial retreat made access to the ice difficult for the horses that packed the heavy survey gear, the studies were abandoned.

If you follow a rough track north from the end of maintained trail, you can explore the colourful ice-sculpted and water-worn rock slabs in the forefield of Yoho Glacier. Mountaineers can also follow the cairns to the west lateral moraine of Yoho Glacier. This knife-edge ridge of rubble affords a breathtaking panorama of the glacier, the Wapta Icefield and the Yoho Valley.

Twin Falls Chalet is 80 m south of the Whaleback junction. The Chalet originated in 1908 as a shelter built by the CPR for its mountaineering guides and clients. It was expanded in 1923. It is now owned by Yoho National Park and has been privately operated under lease since 1962. Twin Falls cascades over a 180 m cliff of Cathedral limestone at the mouth of a hanging valley. Paths along Twin Falls Creek provide unobstructed views of the picturesque falls, which are sunlit until mid-morning.

Turn north (right) at the Whaleback junction just north of Twin Falls Chalet. The trail climbs steadily for the next 1.6 km to the mouth of the Waterfall Valley. There are fine views east of Mt. Balfour (3272 m), highest peak in the area, and of the peculiar, castellated summit of Trolltinder Mountain (2917 m). The name means "Gnome's Peak," and was given by Jean Habel because of its resemblance to a peak of the same name in Norway. Glaciers adorning these mountains form part of the

The Yoho is a valley of waterfalls. Twin Falls cascade 180 m over a Cathedral limestone cliff at the mouth of a hanging valley.

32 km² Waputik Icefield. Waputik (WAH-poo-tick) is a Stoney word that means "white goat."

The trail follows the edge of the cliff south to the former site of Whaleback campground. This was not a place for sleepwalkers! Tent sites were less than 10 m from the cliff edge. Fatalities occurred here, from both falls into the creek and over the cliff.

One hiker fell into the whirlpool at the brink of the falls and survived the chill and the inevitable pull of the current for 45 minutes before being rescued. The area is frequented by mountain goats who have become aggressive in recent years. Because of such hazards, and the fact that the underlying bedrock makes construction and maintenance of an out-

Leaving Well Enough Alone

When viewed in context of the relentless force of flowing water and the shattering effects of frost, the limestone column that divides Twin Falls is a temporary feature. Even more so when you consider that unnatural forces have also been at work. In 1924, trail workers used dynamite in an attempt to make the two falls equal in volume. Debris from the blast blocked the southerly channel and had exactly the opposite effect intended. One can well imagine the panic of the workers as they toiled in that perilous place, in their ultimately successful attempt to set matters right!

house difficult, this campground was closed in 1994.

The Whaleback to Little Yoho Valley

A decked I-beam bridge spans Twin Falls Creek just above Whaleback campground. Avalanches from Whaleback Mountain sweep this area, so the bridge is installed and dismantled annually to prevent its destruction. If you are hiking when the bridge is out,

expect a moderate to difficult ford of Twin Falls Creek, best accomplished about 50 m above the bridge site. The water is silty and extremely cold.

To the west is Whaleback Mountain (2633 m), named by mountaineer Edward Whymper. Viewed from the south, the shales of its upper slopes suggest a massive whale breaching the ocean's surface.

The turreted peak at the northwest end of Whaleback Mountain is Isolated Peak (2845 m). It was first climbed in 1901 by a party that includ-

ed Whymper and James Outram.

The next 1.5 km is the scenic highlight of the Yoho Valley. The trail makes a steady ascent south from the creek and winds through treeline into delightful upper subalpine meadows. Prominent in the view north from the apex is the pyramidical form of Mont des Poilus (3161 m) – Habel's "Hidden Mountain." The mountain's present name commemorates French foot soldiers of World War I. Group of Seven artist Lawren Harris

Kiwetinok Pass and Lake, 2.8 km

From the campground, cross the bridge over the Little Yoho River and head west. After climbing beside a small canyon, the trail drops into the forefield of President Glacier. Rock-hop or ford the meltwater stream and follow cairns west across the rubble. Rock-hop or ford (moderate) the

The glaciated flanks of The President dominate the Little Yoho Valley in this view southeast from Kiwetinok Pass.

President. Beyond is Mt. Daly and Daly Glacier.

From Kiwetinok Lake, you can scramble west over boulders to Kiwetinok Pass. Beyond is the Amiskwi River, the largest tributary of the Kicking Horse River. (*Amiskwi* is a native word for "beaver." The river was formerly called Beaver-

Little Yoho River 500 m later to its north bank. A steep climb on a rough track ensues, leading to the rocky basin that contains Kiwetinok Lake.

Kiwetinok is a Stoney word meaning "on the north side." At 2454 m, Kiwetinok has been referred to as the highest lake in Canada. It may well be the highest named lake, but there is at least one unnamed lake in Banff National Park about 50 m higher.

Kiwetinok Lake is often

frozen until early August. The lake is partially fed by meltwater from a small glacier on Kiwetinok Peak (2902 m), hence the remarkable colour of the water. White-tailed ptarmigan will often be seen nearby. Because summer is so brief here, these particular birds never fully develop summer plumage.

Looking east down the Little Yoho Valley, you can see a tremendous overturned fold in "Barometer Peak," the ridge extending north from The Vice

tail.) Kiwetinok Pass was first crossed in 1901 by Edward Whymper's party. They had a miserable time bushwhacking their way back to Field, as has everyone else who has followed since. Whymper named the mountain south of the pass for Robert Kerr of the CPR, the man who had given Whymper free train passage. The mountain north of Kiwetinok Lake was named for Joseph Pollinger, one of Whymper's guides.

depicted this scene in a work entitled "Isolation Peak."

Meltwaters from the glacier in the foreground feed Twin Falls. Mt. Collie (3116 m) and Yoho Peak are to the northeast, separated from Mts. Habel, Rhondda and Gordon by Yoho Glacier. Directly east is Mt. Balfour. To its south are Mts. Daly (3152 m) and Niles (2972 m) at the head of Daly Glacier. Farther south the view includes Mt. Stephen, Cathedral Mountain, Odaray Mountain, and Mts. Victoria, Huber and Hungabee.

A short distance before reaching the south end of Whaleback Mountain, the trail angles sharply right (west). However, continue straight ahead for 80 m to a viewpoint overlooking the Little Yoho Valley. The glaciated mountains directly across the valley are The Vice President (3066m) and The President (3138 m), named for executives of the CPR. The rocky bench beneath The Vice President is the route of The Iceline trail. A cairn on the viewpoint commemorates a skier, killed nearby in a snow avalanche in 1962. Whitebark pine grows in this windswept location.

The trail switchbacks steeply down an avalanche gully to reach the Little Yoho Valley in 2.1 km. Turn west (right) onto the Little Yoho trail, and keep straight ahead at the Celeste Lake junction. The trail climbs gradually through subalpine forest for 3.6 km to Little Yoho campground, passing the Alpine Club of Canada's Stanley Mitchell Hut and a park patrol cabin en route. The campground makes an excellent base for exploration of the upper valley. Although the only "official" sidetrail is to Kiwetinok Pass, mountaineers may make straightforward ascents of many of the surrounding peaks.

Loop Hike Options

The recommended exit from Little Yoho campground is to follow The Iceline, which begins on the south side of the bridge across the Little Yoho River. This 11.1 km route offers spectacular, close-up views of the ice and moraines of Emerald Glacier, and high-level views of Takakkaw Falls and the Yoho Valley. (See Classic Hike #37.)

A great deal of The Iceline's length is on rubble and rock, and if you have knee, ankle or back complaints you may find it rough going with a heavy pack. Alternate exits are: follow the Little Yoho Valley trail east to Laughing Falls, and then to Takakkaw Falls (10.1 km); or follow The Iceline to the Celeste Lake junction, take the connector to the Little Yoho trail, then to Laughing Falls and Takakkaw Falls (16.1 km). Those who want to add another night to this outing can follow The Iceline to the upper Iceline junction (8.3 km), and take the high trail (straight ahead) for 2.4 km to Yoho Lake campground. From Yoho Lake it is 4.7 km to the Yoho Valley parking lot via Whiskey Jack hostel and the Yoho Valley Rd.

"It required no discussion to select a name for this wonderfully beautiful cascade. It named itself; Twin Falls it was called there and then, and so it appears on Habel's map ..."
—Ralph Edwards, guide on the first exploration of the Yoho Valley in 1897, *The Trail to the Charmed Land*, 1950

"After about two hours travel we arrived at a point where the ground seemed to slope downward gently on either side ... About half a mile from this point we emerged from the timber on the shore of a marvellously beautiful little lake, not much larger than a little pond, but of an exquisite ultramarine colour."

—Trail guide Ralph Edwards, on the first crossing of Yoho Pass and discovery of Yoho Lake, 1897, *The Trail to the Charmed Land*, 1950

Yoho Lake reflects Michael Peak, a minor eminence on The Vice President. The peak was named for Professor Arthur Michael who made the first attempt to climb The Vice President in 1900.

39. Wapta Highline

Route

Day-hike or overnight, 21.3 km loop

Route	Elevation (m)	Distance (km)
Trailhead	1302	0
Yoho Pass jct	1310	1.5
Yoho Pass	1838	7.3
Yoho Lake and CG	1814	8.0
Yoho Pass	1838	8.7
Burgess Pass	2195	15.0
Emerald Lake trail	1300	20.2
Emerald Lake parking lot	1302	21.3

Topographic maps: 82 N/7, 82 N/8

Best lighting: anytime

Trailhead

Follow Highway 1 to the Emerald Lake Road, 2.6 km west of Field. Turn north and follow the road 8 km to its end at the Emerald Lake parking lot. The trailhead is at the north end of the parking lot, next to the bridge.

The Wapta Highline completes an energetic high-level circuit around Emerald Lake, Yoho's largest and best known body of water. Few day-trips in *Classic Hikes* gain as much elevation or cover as much distance. Few also highlight such an intriguing assortment of geological, historical and ecological features.

Emerald Lake to Yoho Pass

The first 1.5 km follows the Emerald Lake nature trail. The lush vegetation surrounding the lake is noted for trees uncommon in the Rockies: western red cedar, western hemlock and western yew. At km 1.1, the trail turns east (right) onto an extensive alluvial fan. The Emerald Fan is one of the largest in the Rockies. Many alluvial fans were established between 6000 and 7000 years ago by meltwater surges as the earth's climate warmed rapidly after the Wisconsin Glaciation. The Emerald Fan is slowly filling Emerald Lake. Aerial views indicate 50 percent of the lake's former area is now rubble.

At the second trail junction on the Emerald Fan, branch northeast (left) on the Yoho Pass trail. For the next 2 km, the trail continues across the alluvial fan, offering views north to the impressive peaks that ring Emerald Basin. The centrepiece is a hanging glacier on The President (3138 m).

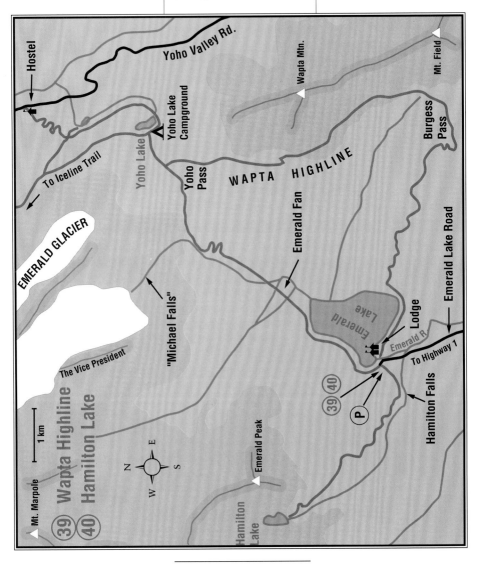

The original road from Field was a log corduroy affair known as the "Tally-Ho Road." It extended across the Emerald Fan, and sections are still visible beside the trail.

From the east edge of the fan, the trail begins its steady ascent to Yoho Pass. The cliffs of The Vice President dominate the view north, exhibiting the Cathedral limestone, Stephen shale, Eldon lime-stone sequence of Cambrian formations. The mountain was named for David McNicoll, a vice-president of the Canadian Pacific Railway. The creek at trailside drains a glacial cirque high above. The Van Horne Range to the southwest, and Mt. Vaux (VOX) (3319 m) to the south, ring the horizon. On calm days, these mountains are reflected in the lake. This scene was painted by Group of Seven artist Lawren Harris in 1924, in a work tilted "Emerald Lake." A similar scene appeared on the Canadian ten-dollar bill, from 1954 to 1971.

The grade eases as the trail traverses an avalanche slope, and then steepens again upon re-entering the forest. Yellow columbine and false hellebore are common at trailside. The entrance to Yoho Pass is

The Emerald Fan: A Tough Place to Call Home

The Emerald Fan is a harsh home for vegetation. Hardy plants such as common juniper, yellow mountain avens, white camas and Indian paintbrush are scattered across the gravels. The evergreen leaves of the mountain avens are lightly coloured on the under-side to reflect the in-tense heat that can ra-diate from the rocks. The showy orchid, yel-low lady's slipper, blooms here from mid-June to mid-July. A few lodgepole pines, gnarled white spruce and white birch comprise the sparse tree cover. Some of the pines have branches on their northeast sides only. They are said to "flag" the prevailing southwest winds. Although the trees look insubstantial, a few of the lodgepole pines are 150 years old – graphic evidence of the inhospitable growing condi-tions caused by poor soil, glacial winds and the fluctuating water table on the fan.

The alluvial fan northeast of Emerald Lake is plainly visible in this moun-taineer's view from the north summit of Mt. Burgess. You can see how the fan is filling the basin occupied by the lake.

You will see various genera-tions of bridges as you cross the Emerald Fan. Glacial melt streams are subject to daily and seasonal fluctuations, and prone to flash floods. The I-beam bridges were installed at great expense over streams that promptly changed their courses, leaving the structures high and dry. The "boardwalk bridges" were designed to be portable, al-lowing trail crews to reposition the bridges as required – a daily ritual during peak run-off in Au-gust. In practice, these heavy bridges are not portable, and they frequently become buried in the débris of flash-floods. At the east edge of the fan is an I-beam bridge that was crushed by a snow avalanche. The forces at work on the Emerald Fan illus-trate that nature's rule prevails, despite human efforts to gain control. Your feet may get wet !

marked by a horse/hiker barrier at a trail junction. The dense, ancient forest on the pass does not allow any distant views. From here you have the option of making a sidetrip across the pass to Yoho Lake (1.4 km return) by continuing straight ahead (east).

Yoho Pass was first crossed in 1897, by the party of Jean Habel. (See box p.208.) Ralph Edwards was guide on the trip. He called Yoho Lake "Marina Lake." In 1906, it was known as "Summit Lake" when the first Alpine Club of Canada camp convened on its shores. The tranquil lake is spring fed and contains eastern brook trout. The cliffs of Wapta Mountain (2778 m) loom to the south. The glacial horn of

The Burgess Shale

The west slope of the ridge connecting Wapta Mountain and Mt. Field is famous throughout the world as the site of the Burgess Shale. "Burgess Shale" is an older name for the Stephen Formation, which comprises the bedrock here. Charles Walcott of the Smithsonian Institution discovered soft-bodied fossils on the slopes above the trail in 1909. During five subsequent summers of collecting, Walcott gathered 80,000 fossil specimens that are now housed at the Smithsonian in Washington DC. Walcott described the specimens with the knowledge of the day, assigning them to categories known from fossil finds elsewhere in the world. It was 60 years before renewed interpretation of the fossils took place, and the significance of this treasure trove of ancient species was realized.

The Burgess Shale contains wonderfully preserved remains of marine animals that lived along the edge of the continental shelf during the Middle Cambrian period, approximately 530 million years ago. The edge of the shelf was marked by a submarine cliff, now called the Cathedral Escarpment. Periodic mud flows from the shallow water platform at the top of the cliff would sweep animals and plants living there into the watery abyss, and bury them on the sea floor along with its resident animals. Since death was sudden and the remains were entombed, scavenging and decay did not take place. As a result, the fossils have been preserved in exquisite detail. Because the animals lacked skeletons, today they appear as flattened chemical imprints in the shale.

The Burgess Shale fossils preserve 140 species. Paleontologists have painstakingly reconstructed the animals' appearances into three-dimensional figures. Some of the fossils represent the earliest known members of many life-form groups (phyla) that exist today. Others are unique in the world and represent species that cannot be classified among contemporary phyla. This suggests that the variety of life at "body-plan" level was greater 530 million years ago than it is today – possibly almost twice as diverse. Standard evolutionary theory dictates an increase in diversity as time passes. The Burgess Shale may indicate that mass extinction events and chance have played a greater role in the evolution of life than was previously realized.

Although you may see researchers working at the Burgess Shale site above the trail, the area is closed to public access without a permit from the park superintendent. Guided tours to the site are available. Inquire at the park information centre at Field. Please remember that collection of rocks and fossils is prohibited in the national parks.

Hallucigenia was perhaps the strangest of the Burgess Shale fauna. The creature was approximately 2 cm in length, and had seven pairs of unjointed legs, and seven tentacles along its spine.

Michael Peak (2696 m), a minor eminence on The Vice President, is to the northwest.

Yoho Pass to Burgess Pass

From the horse/hiker barrier in Yoho Pass, the Wapta Highline turns sharply south. After about 500 m, the trail emerges from the forest beneath the grey Eldon limestone cliffs of Wapta Mountain. This is spectacular hiking with a pronounced feeling of exposure. In places, the cliff overhangs the trail. The Van Horne Range is again visible to the west. To the north, "Michael Falls" drops from the cirque on The Vice President in two lofty cascades. The highest mountain in the area, Mt. Balfour (3272 m), is visible to the northeast. Pikas live in the rocky debris downslope from the trail.

On August 25, 1988, a tremendous rainstorm struck the vicinity of Field. The west-facing slopes of Wapta Mountain caught the full brunt. The rock strata funnelled the runoff into gullies, and surges of water and debris swept the mountainside below, cutting three swaths 4 m deep through the Wapta Highline. The trail contours in and out of these flash-flood courses and works its way onto avalanche terrain on the western slopes of Wapta Mountain. The view west once again includes Emerald Lake, largest of Yoho's 61 lakes and ponds, now almost 900 m below.

The trail continues south to the avalanche gully beneath

The western red cedar is the provincial tree emblem of BC. The damp shaded north slopes of Mt. Burgess contain the largest cedar forest in Yoho Park.

Mt. Field (2635 m). This gully is frequently snowbound until August. Use caution and please keep to the trail if snow patches linger. Look for mountain goats on the slopes above. Across the gully, the trail turns west into Burgess Pass. As you traverse an exposed shale slope on the south side of the pass, there are fine views of Mt. Stephen (3199 m) across the Kicking Horse Valley, Mt. Vaux (VOX) (3319 m) in the distant southwest, and the town of Field.

Burgess Pass to Emerald Lake

The trail to Emerald Lake plunges north from the junction in Burgess Pass. The initial slopes may be snow covered until mid-July. Most of the descent is in dense forest. The imposing north face of Mt. Burgess (2599 m) towers in profile through a break in the trees. The mountain and

pass were named for Alexander Burgess, Canada's Deputy Minister of the Interior in 1886. The last 2 km of this winding and relentless descent passes through the most extensive western red cedar forest in Yoho.

Follow the Emerald Lake trail west from the lakeshore junction. Keep right at subsequent junctions. Watch for moose here late in the day. The trail climbs onto the terminal moraine that dams Emerald Lake and enters the grounds of Emerald Lake Lodge. Originally constructed by the CPR in 1902, the lodge was completely redeveloped in 1986. The main lodge building contains timbers used in the first structure. Complete the loop hike by following the gravel road through the lodge grounds to parking lot.

"I had chosen a high conical mountain which overlooks Emerald Lake on the west side, as a [survey] station, and made the ascent to the foot of the steep broken ridge which leads to its summit; but the rumbling of the slides of the freshly fallen snow, carrying down masses of rocky débris, warned us of the imminent danger, and we abandoned the ascent."

—Surveyor J.J. McArthur describing an incomplete ascent of Mt. Carnarvon above Hamilton Lake. *Report of the Department of the Interior,* 1887

Hamilton Lake is a perfect glacial tarn, nestled in a limestone hollow at the foot of Mt. Carnarvon.

40. Hamilton Lake

Route

Day-hike, 5.3 km

Route	Elevation (m)	Distance (km)
Trailhead	1302	0
Hamilton Falls	1352	0.7
Hamilton Lake	2149	5.3

Topographic map: 82 N/7
Best lighting: mid-morning to mid-afternoon

Trailhead

Follow Highway 1 to the Emerald lake Road, 2.6 km west of Field. Turn north and follow the road 8 km to its end at the Emerald Lake parking lot. The trailhead is at the southwest corner of the parking lot.

On the Hamilton Lake trail you make an unwavering ascent to one of the most picturesque backcountry lakes in Yoho. The outing features rainforest, whitebark pine trees and alpine meadows. A waterfall and a mountain display an ancient geological boundary. If fortunate, you may see moose, hoary marmots, porcupines and golden eagles. Caution: grizzly and black bears may also be present. This steep trail is a good test of fitness. The final approach to the lake is frequently snowbound until early July, and winter ice may linger on the lake's surface equally as long.

Emerald Lake to Hamilton Falls

The trailhead is located in the deep basin that surrounds Emerald Lake. This basin traps storm systems and creates abundant precipitation. Vegetation along the first 700 m contains species typical of the Western Interior Hemlock "rainforest," normally found farther west in BC: western red cedar, western hemlock, western yew, thimbleberry and devil's club. Queen's cup, western meadow rue, foam flower and dwarf dogwood are common wildflowers in the undergrowth. The white flower of queen's cup yields a striking blue-coloured berry in late summer, hence its other folk name: "bluebead." You may see black bear and moose here.

The trail draws alongside

Please see map on page 214

Hamilton Creek and follows it to some large Douglas firs at the shaded base of Hamilton Falls. The damp environment here gives rise to brilliant yellow tree lichens. The features named "Hamilton" honour a prospector who discovered the falls while in quest of more material rewards. Hamilton Creek was formerly the water supply for Emerald Lake Lodge. You may still see artifacts associated with the water intake system and pipeline. The falls are at the mouth of a hanging valley, and are being eroded into Chancellor limestone.

Hamilton Falls to Hamilton Lake

You leave the damp forest as the trail switchbacks to a fenced viewpoint at the upper cascades of Hamilton Falls.

Lighting is best before mid-morning. Here you can see plunge pools and potholes, as well as how the bedrock fault has captured the course of Hamilton Creek. Upstream from the falls is a limestone canyon. Continue up the relatively steep grade. The forest gradually changes from montane lodgepole pine to the combination of subalpine fir and Engelmann spruce typical of subalpine elevations. At km 3.9, you may rest at an opening in the forest that allows a view to Emerald Lake.

Leaving this viewpoint, the trail angles sharply northwest and the grade lessens. White-bark pine indicates that you have reached the upper subalpine ecoregion. One of these pines has six trunks growing from a single base. The bark of many nearby trees has been damaged by porcupines. These rodents strip the outer bark in culinary quest for the sweet, inner cambium layer. A tree girdled of its bark will

An Ancient Boundary

The trailhead is located on the boundary between two geological provinces of the Rockies: the eastern main ranges and the western main ranges. To the northeast are the eastern main ranges. They are typified by the castellated or "layer cake" mountain, whose flanks exhibit resistant cliffs of quartzite, limestone and dolomite, separated by recessive shale ledges. The strata are largely horizontal. To the southwest are the western main

ranges. These older mountains are comprised almost entirely of weak shales and slates, and they have been eroded into more gentle forms that exhibit much folding and faulting. The sediments contained in eastern main range mountains were deposited in relatively shallow seas, whereas those of western main range mountains collected in much deeper water. The trail follows the boundary between the geological provinces all the way to Hamilton Lake.

Hamilton Falls are being eroded into a bedrock fault at the boundary of the eastern and western main ranges.

ant and ancient tree for this elevation. In early July, glacier lilies bloom in profusion on the final approach to Hamilton Lake. The protein-rich bulb is a favourite food of grizzly bears. Two other favourite grizzly snacks, hoary marmots and Columbian ground squirrels, live nearby. Therefore you should use caution here.

Hamilton Lake is at treeline, a tarn dammed by an upturned lip of Chancellor shale. This rock dam precisely marks the boundary between the eastern and western main ranges. The Chancellor Formation is vertically tilted. The eastern main range formations are horizontal. The boundary can be seen bisecting the southeast ridge of Mt. Carnarvon (car-NARR-von) (3340 m), the backdrop to the lake. Beneath the mountain is a massive anticline, an arch-shaped fold in the bedrock. Mountain goats frequent the grassy areas on the mountain's lower slopes.

Although it has been claimed that Hamilton Lake was not "discovered" until 1936, it is in plain view from the south ridge of Mt. Carnarvon, which was first occupied as a survey station in 1887. The mountain was named in 1858 by James Hector for the fourth Earl of Carnarvon, who later was author of the British North America Act. The summit of Mt. Carnarvon was first climbed in 1904. The blocky peak north of Hamilton Lake is known unofficially as "Top Hat." Watch for golden eagles, soaring on thermals overhead.

usually die.

The trail crosses several avalanche slopes, with views southwest to the Van Horne Range. William Cornelius Van Horne oversaw construction of the Canadian Pacific Railway from 1881-1885, and he later served as its president. The peak with two summits is known locally as "Nimrod Peak," after the Stoney guide of the Palliser Expedition. (*Nimrod* means "great hunter.") The higher peak to the north, with the prominent niche glacier, is Mt. King (2892 m), named for a Canadian astronomer and surveyor. The mountain was first climbed in 1892 by J.J. McArthur. The peaks of the Ottertail Range, including glacier-capped Mt. Vaux (VOX) (3319 m), are prominent to the south. To the east (left) of Mt. Vaux are the twin summits of Mt. Goodsir (3562 m, 3525 m), highest mountains in Yoho National Park, and 9th and 12th highest in the Rockies. On the western skyline, 90 km distant, are the granite spires of the Bugaboos in the Purcell Range of the Columbia Mountains.

At a switchback you pass a massive Engelmann spruce, more than a metre thick at the base, and 35 m tall – truly a gi-

Chancellor Peak towers above the Kicking Horse and Beaverfoot Valleys in southwestern Yoho National Park. It presents one of the greatest vertical rises of any mountain at roadside in the Rockies: 2180 m.

41. Mt. Hunter

Route

Day-Hike, 6.6 km

Route	Elevation (m)	Distance (km)
Trailhead	1125	0
Lower lookout jct	1532	3.3
Lower lookout	1532	3.5
Lower lookout jct	1532	3.7
Upper lookout	1966	6.6
Topographic maps: 82 N/2, 82 N/7		

Trailhead

Follow Highway 1, 24.7 km west of Field to the Wapta Falls Road. There is no sign for westbound travellers. Turn south and park in the small parking area adjacent to Highway 1. The trailhead is immediately opposite on the north side of Highway 1. Use caution crossing the highway.

The steep trail to Mt. Hunter's two fire lookouts is usually the first high elevation trail to become snow-free in Yoho.

The early season wildflower displays are exceptional, and you may be fortunate to see elk, deer and moose. Check yourself carefully for wood ticks after hiking this trail in late May or June.

Trailhead to Lower Lookout

From the highway, the trail angles east into a forest of lodgepole pine and white spruce. In mid- to late-June you will be treated to a remarkable display of wildflowers: western wood

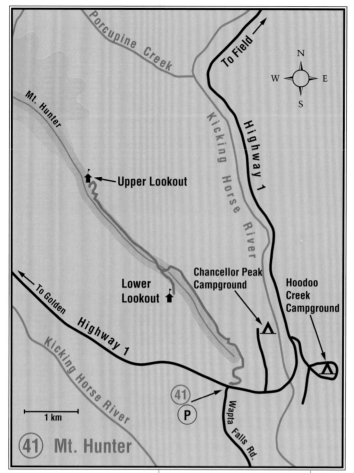

To Field →

← To Golden

Porcupine Creek

Mt. Hunter

Highway 1

Kicking Horse River

Upper Lookout

Lower Lookout

Chancellor Peak Campground

Hoodoo Creek Campground

Highway 1

Kicking Horse River

Wapta Falls Rd.

1 km

(41) P

(41) **Mt. Hunter**

bia Mountains to the west. Vegetation on the lower ridge includes an association of Douglas fir and Rocky Mountain juniper, more typical of the semi-arid, southern Columbia Valley. At about km 1 there is a Douglas fir tree that is 0.9 m diameter. This is a large tree for the Rocky Mountain variety of Douglas fir. (On the west coast of BC, the coastal variety frequently attains diameters of 4 m.) Nearby is a standing dead fir that has been drilled full of holes by woodpeckers – a den tree.

You will see the rain shadow vegetation clearly where the trail draws alongside the cliff edge. Bearberry, shrubby cinquefoil and creeping juniper are common in the undergrowth. For the next 1.5 km the trail parallels the cliff, offering views of the Kicking Horse Valley and the Beaverfoot Range. The Beaverfoot Range is part of the oldest and smallest geological province in the Rockies: the western ranges. Moose and elk are sometimes seen in the sloughs near the highway.

The massive blowdown in this area took place during a windstorm in November 1993. Forestry interests appraised the value of the downed timber at more than $1,000,000

lily, yellow lady's slipper, shooting star, prickly wild rose, yellow columbine, dwarf dogwood, wild strawberry, star-flowered Solomon's seal, Indian paintbrush and blue-eyed grass. Thoughtless hikers often pick the wood lilies and lady's slippers. This illegal practice usually kills the plants, and has led to their disappearance in many areas. Please leave the flowers to play their role in the ecology, and allow others to enjoy them.

After 225 m, the trail climbs to the CPR main line. Carefully cross the tracks and look for the trail sign 10 m to the west. Ascend a rooted trail into the forest to gain the southeast ridge of Mt. Hunter. The author has seen mule deer, great horned owl and grizzly bear here. White birch and aspens at trailside have been used as "rub trees" by elk and deer to remove the velvet from their antlers at the beginning of the autumn rut.

Mt. Hunter is in the montane ecoregion and is also in the rain shadow of the Colum-

Dry sections of the ridge on Mt. Hunter support three varieties of the juniper shrub. Rocky Mountain juniper (photo) is uncommmon elsewhere in Yoho. It is the most tree-like form of juniper and sometimes attains heights of 4 to 5 m. It has flat, scaly leaves that resemble those of western red cedar.

and lobbied for the right to salvage the "wasted wood."

Snags: Den Trees

In the past, foresters regarded standing-dead trees, known as snags, as both a safety hazard and a fire hazard. Now it is known they provide nesting and denning sites, and food for many birds and mammals. With intensive clear-cutting of forests outside protected areas, snags are disappearing at an alarming rate. BC is currently attempting to educate foresters to insure snags are spared for the benefit of dependent bird species. Unfortunately, progress is not a simple matter. With the shelter of adjacent

trees removed in clearcuts, the snags that are spared soon succumb to the wind.

Fortunately, Yoho National Park did not permit the re-

moval and logging of this blowdown. The difference in philosophy underscores the external pressures facing Canada's national parks.

The impressive cliff underfoot is Ottertail limestone. This rock is an anomaly amongst the weak shales and slates of mountains in the western Rockies. Western main range mountains are typically heavily eroded and gentle in appearance. Resistant cliffs of Ottertail limestone are thus conspicuous in this landscape.

A steep climb leads to a junction in a doghair forest of lodgepole pine. Turn south (left) to reach the lower lookout. The tower jack's cabin has been maintained and is open as a day-use shelter. The author once found the paw prints of a grizzly bear on the cabin door and windows. The ladder to the tower is unsafe and should not be used. The huge black panels south of the lookout are part of a microwave communications system.

Across the Kicking Horse Valley, Mt. Vaux (VOX) (3319 m) is the more northerly of the two high mountains. James Hector of the Palliser Expedition named the mountain for William Vaux, a curator at the British Museum. Vaux secured financing so members of the expedition could write and publish their reports. It is likely that Hector named the mountain in gratitude, after his return to England. The more southerly of the two mountains is Chancellor Peak (3280 m), named for the Chancellor of Ontario, who arbitrated a dispute between the CPR and the federal government in 1886. Both mountains were first climbed in 1901.

High Cuisine

In their remote locations, fire lookout tower jacks would be without human contact for several weeks at a time. Their diet was a major concern. The handbook written for lookout keepers continually promoted adequate intake of vitamin C – it recommended canned tomatoes be added to almost every meal. If the delivery of rations was a week late, it didn't mean boredom should prevail at mealtime. Innovative use of other canned items was stressed. One recipe describes canned meatloaf glazed with marmalade. Innovative indeed.

Lower Lookout to Upper Lookout

The trail ascends steadily to the upper lookout through a forest of lodgepole pine and Douglas fir. Some trees at trailside still contain insulators from the telephone system that connected the upper lookout to the warden station at Leanchoil (lee-ANN-coil). Mt. Hunter is set in an angle of the Kicking Horse River. To the northeast, the river has the braided character typical of glacially fed streams. To the northwest, the river's course is more confined, as it plunges into the V-shaped canyon that leads to its junction with the Columbia River at Golden.

The upper lookout was part of the original system of fire lookouts, and was built in 1943. By the 1960s, the facilities were in disrepair, and park managers decided to replace them with a newer structure, lower on the ridge. The tower at the upper lookout was removed in 1992. Although it is a pack rat heaven, the tower jack's cabin still stands.

The view southwest from Mt. Hunter includes areas outside Yoho National Park. Many clearcuts are visible. Commercial forestry is rapidly destroying a great deal of habitat adjacent to the Rocky Mountain parks. Logging roads facilitate access to formerly remote park boundaries. The roads have led to increased hunting, poaching and recreation.

Guides Nimrod and Erasmus

Mt. Hunter (2615 m) was named by James Hector in 1858. Unfortunately Hector did not record for whom he named the peak. Along with several "formal" candidates named Hunter, are two "informal" ones: Hector's Stoney guide Nimrod, whose hunting skills Hector praised; and Peter Erasmus, another of Hector's guides. (Nimrod means "great hunter.") Erasmus made a partial ascent of Mt. Hunter, and shot a goat the following day. Given that Hector's party was desperately low on provisions while in this vicinity, the importance of the "hunters" to the expedition suggests they are the best candidates. Peter Erasmus died in 1931 at the age of 98.

Other rewarding hikes in the vicinity are Leanchoil Hoodoos and Wapta Falls.

"*Peter, I sent up the mountain in the angle of the valley to take bearings, and to see what the mountains were like to the west. He ascended to 3500 feet by the aneroid, but did not get to the highest part of the mountain ...*"
—a partial ascent of Mt. Hunter by Peter Erasmus, guide to the Palliser Expedition, Journal of James Hector, August 29, 1858

Kootenay National Park

Established in 1920 as Canada's tenth national park, Kootenay includes 1406 km² on the western slopes of the Rockies in BC. The park features tremendous geographical and ecological diversity. It is the only national park in Canada in which both cactus and glacier may be found.

Kootenay is not heavily developed, and offers just under 200 km of hiking trails. The four Classic Hikes in the park immerse you in rolling meadows, alpine ridges, wilderness valleys, and glacial barrens that were covered by ice less than a century ago.

The 104 km Kootenay Parkway (Highway 93) bisects the park. This road connects Castle Junction on Highway 1 34 km west of Banff) with Highway 95 at the town of Radium Hot Springs (105 km south of Golden). Access to the park is by car or passenger bus. Park information centres are at the west park gate, and at Vermilion Crossing (41 km west of Castle Junction). Accommodation and basic services are available in the park at Vermilion Crossing and in the vicinity of the Radium Hot Springs pools, where the warden office is also located. More extensive services are available at the town of Radium Hot Springs, locally known

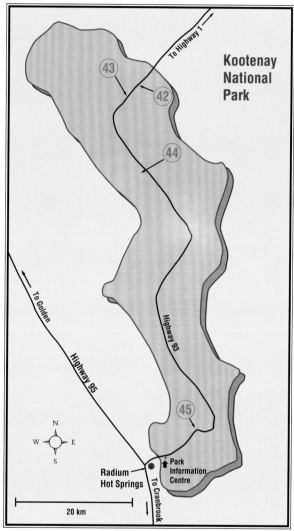

Overview map of Kootenay National Park showing trailhead locations

as Radium, just west of the west park gate. Extensive services are also available at Invermere (14 km south of Radium on Highway 95), and at Banff. Kootenay has three

frontcountry campgrounds with a total of 301 campsites. There are no hostels. The park is in the same time zone as Banff and Jasper national parks, Alberta.

The lobes of Stanley Glacier drape over the cliffs at the head of the Stanley Creek valley. Along with the glacier, the trail features the Vermilion Pass Burn, massive limestone cliffs, and an array of wildflowers. The valley was first explored in 1901 by the party of renowned mountaineer Edward Whymper.

42. Stanley Glacier

Route

Day-hike, 4.2 km

Route	Elevation (m)	Distance (km)
Trailhead	1593	0
Stanley Glacier viewpoint	1921	4.2

Topographic map: 82 N/1
Best lighting: mid-morning to mid-afternoon

Trailhead

South side of the Kootenay Parkway (Highway 93); 13.4 km west of Castle Junction; 91.5 km east of the junction with Highway 95.

The Stanley Glacier trail explores a spectacular hanging valley and offers close-up views of three major processes that have shaped the landscape of the Rockies: fire, avalanches and glaciation.

The valley is renowned for its views of glacial ice in summer and frozen waterfalls in winter. With luck, you may see moose, mountain goats, white-tailed ptarmigan and hoary marmots.

Kootenay Parkway to Stanley Glacier Viewpoint

From the parking lot, the trail descends to the Vermilion River and then switchbacks up into the Vermilion Pass Burn. This lightning-caused fire consumed 2360 ha of subalpine forest in July 1968. Most of the living trees at trailside are lodgepole pines. The resin-sealed cone of the lodgepole requires a temperature of 45°C to crack open, resulting in a mass seeding after the fire. The subsequent dense growth of pines is known as a doghair forest.

The trail climbs steadily through the burn, gaining 220 m of elevation in the first 2.4 km. After it crests a small rise, the trail descends slightly to a footbridge across the creek. The entrances to most hanging valleys in the Rockies are blocked by moraines that were pushed

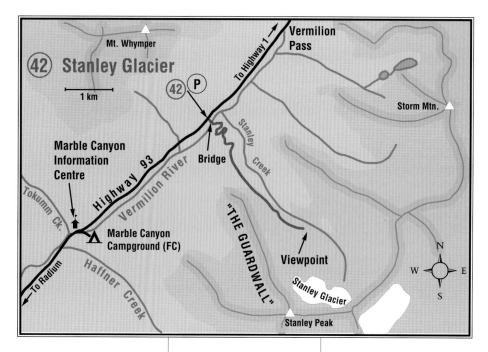

42 Stanley Glacier

Mt. Whymper

Vermilion Pass

To Highway 1

1 km

P 42

Storm Mtn.

Marble Canyon Information Centre

Highway 93

Vermilion River

Stanley Creek

Bridge

Tokumm Ck.

Marble Canyon Campground (FC)

To Radium

Haffner Creek

"THE GUARDWALL"

Viewpoint

Stanley Glacier

Stanley Peak

N W E S

up alongside the larger glaciers in the main valleys. The rise just before the footbridge indicates the moraine at this location.

The next 1.8 km of trail is a hiker's and photographer's delight. With the forest canopy removed by fire, a profusion of sun-loving wildflowers now blooms here. Many are pioneering species that often grow after fires: camas, common fireweed, fleabane, pink wintergreen, arnica, yellow columbine, ragwort, and vibrantly coloured Indian paintbrush. Damp areas feature bog orchids and gentians.

At one point, the trail separates burned and unburned forest. To the west (right) are mature Engelmann spruce; to the east (left) are blackened timbers and stumps. You will not see as many young lodgepole pines as you did near the trailhead. Trees are regenerating slowly in this part of the burn because of the cold air that drains from Stanley Glacier.

The colossal cliff flanking the west side of the valley is known as "The Guardwall." The lower 300 m of cliff is Cathedral limestone and dolomite. It contains a number of solution caves – caverns eroded by naturally acidic rainwater. The upper cliff is

Avalanches and Avalanche Paths

The slopes on the east side of Stanley Glacier Valley feature steep avalanche paths. Near trailside are the sun-bleached remains of trees uprooted by sliding snow and by the winds it generates.

Snow avalanches occur when one or more layers within the snowpack release from other layers, or when the entire snowpack separates from the underlying slope. Avalanches are caused by a complex interplay of temperature, humidity, wind, snow depth, slope aspect and steepness. People and animals travelling on a susceptible slope may trigger an avalanche. Loud noises cannot trigger an avalanche, unless they originate in an explosion that also vibrates the ground.

Although they are destructive, avalanches are also useful – another of Nature's tools for ensuring biodiversity. They remove large vegetation and create open habitat that supports shrubs and wildflowers. These are important foods for moose, elk, bears and deer.

Eldon limestone. In between is a fossil-rich ledge of Stephen shale. These formations date to the middle Cambrian period. The dark streaks on the cliffs are water seeps and rock lichens. In the perpetual shade of winter, the seeps freeze into sheets of ice and become a destination for waterfall ice climbers.

Stanley Glacier Viewpoint

A sign on a rocky knoll marks the end of the maintained trail, and is a good vantage from which to study Stanley Glacier. Several lobes of ice terminate on cliffs. Less than two centuries ago, the glacier flowed over these cliffs onto the valley floor. You may hear the creaking and groaning of the ice as it creeps incessantly forward, and with fortune, witness an ice avalanche. Meltwater cascading over the cliffs is sometimes caught in updrafts, creating waterfalls that disappear in mid-air.

Toward Stanley Glacier the valley is a barren world of boulders and screes, home to mountain goat, hoary marmot, pika and white-tailed ptarmigan. The summit of Stanley Peak (3155 m) is concealed from view. The mountain was originally named "Mt. Ball" by James Hector in 1858. However, that name subsequently came into use for a higher mountain to the southwest. The name Stanley Peak was given by Edward Whymper in 1901, to honour Frederick Stanley, 6th Governor General of Canada. Lord Stanley's name also adorns North American ice hockey's ultimate prize, the Stanley Cup.

Looking north, you can see the U-shape of this hanging valley. Valleys in the Rockies were originally V-shaped, the products of erosion by streams and rivers. As Stanley Glacier advanced, it undercut the surrounding mountainsides. When the glacier receded, the mountainsides collapsed, and the valley floor was widened.

Edward Whymper

The peak framed by the valley walls north from Stanley Glacier viewpoint is Mt. Whymper (2845 m). The mountain was named for Edward Whymper, who was in the first party to climb the Matterhorn, in 1865. Whymper made five trips to the Rockies in the early 1900s. The first three were under arrangement with the CPR. In return for free rail passage and an outfit of mountain guides, Whymper was to pen magazine articles and make suggestions regarding the location and construction of trails and facilities. The railway hoped to capitalize on Whymper's illustrious reputation and make the Rockies into a "new Switzerland."

Whymper had a dour temperament and a legendary capacity for alcohol. He rapidly alienated his mountaineering guides and packers, and accomplished few of his objectives. Perhaps the greatest disappointment for the CPR was that Whymper did not attempt to climb Mt. Assiniboine, "the Canadian Matterhorn," on his first visit. The moguls of the railway soon tired of his scheme. Whymper's most significant mountaineering was completed during the 1901 trip when Mt. Whymper, Stanley Peak and a number of mountains in what is now Yoho National Park were first climbed.

"Mr. Edward Whymper, another veteran of world-wide fame, spent six months in 1901 amongst these summits and returned to England full of enthusiasm and admiration for the immensity of the alpine area, the grandeur of the peaks, and the sublimity of the scenery throughout the entire region ... "

—James Outram, *In the Heart of the Canadian Rockies,* 1905

"On the north were the high mountains of the Desolation Range near Moraine Lake, with Mt. Deltaform towering over all. A small lake lies part way up its heavily wooded flanks, but its upper precipices of ice and rock seemed very difficult of ascent."

—Walter Wilcox, describing the environs of Kaufmann Lake in 1899, *The Rockies of Canada*, 1909

Kaufmann Lake occupies a remote setting in a high valley on the south side of the Wenkchemna Peaks.

43. Kaufmann Lake

Route		
Day-hike or overnight, 15.1 km		
Route	Elevation (m)	Distance (km)
Marble Canyon trailhead	1479	0
Upper falls, Marble Canyon	1494	0.7
Fay Hut jct	1677	10.5
Tokumm Valley CG	1738	11.3
Kaufmann Lake jct	1814	13.6
Kaufmann Lk. and CG	2057	15.1
Topographic maps: 82 N/1, 82 N/8		
Best lighting: afternoon and evening		

Trailhead
Marble Canyon, north side of the Kootenay Parkway (Highway 93); 17.2 km west of Castle Junction; 88 km east of the junction with Highway 95.

Of Kootenay National Park's half dozen large lakes, Kaufmann Lake, set in the wilderness heartland of the northern part of the park, is the most remote and least visited. Caution: This trail ventures into grizzly bear habitat.

Kootenay Parkway to Fay Hut Junction

From the bustling trailhead at Marble Canyon, follow the interpretive trail for 35 m and turn north (right) onto the Tokumm (TOE-kum) Creek trail. *Tokumm* is a Stoney word for the red fox. Curiously, foxes are absent from

Kootenay National Park in the present day.

After 200 m the Tokumm Creek trail merges with an old cart track that formerly led to mining claims in Prospector's Valley. A short sidetrail at km 0.7 leads west (left) to the 39 m upper waterfall in Marble Canyon. Back on the main trail, continue north through an ancient forest of Engelmann spruce and subalpine fir, crossing numerous tributary streams on bridges.

At km 3, the trail narrows and descends to the bank of Tokumm Creek, with views of lush avalanche paths across the valley. Stickseed grows here. This 1 m tall wildflower has numerous powder-blue flowers and looks like a gigantic forget-me-not. By area, almost half of the slopes along Tokumm Creek are avalanche terrain. Many of the avalanche

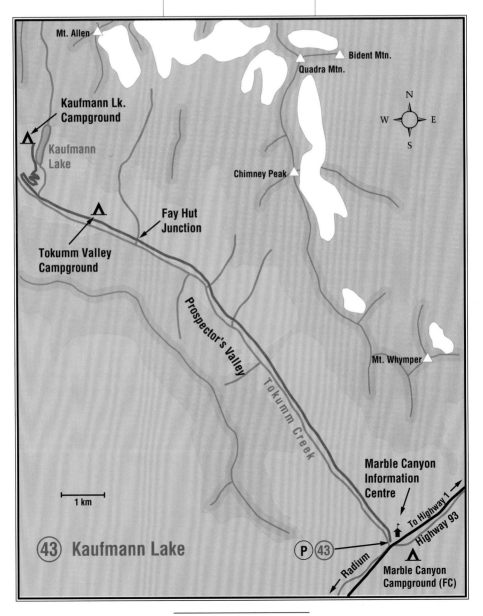

Mt. Allen

Bident Mtn.

Quadra Mtn.

Kaufmann Lk. Campground

N
W — E
S

Kaufmann Lake

Chimney Peak

Fay Hut Junction

Tokumm Valley Campground

Prospector's Valley

Tokumm Creek

Mt. Whymper

1 km

Marble Canyon Information Centre

To Highway 1

Highway 93

(43) Kaufmann Lake

P (43)

Radium

Marble Canyon Campground (FC)

paths extend from ridgetop to valley bottom, and the terrific momentum of avalanches often carries snow and débris across the valley floor and uphill on the opposite slope. These avalanche paths support dense growths of shrubs and forbs and are important habitat for moose and elk, especially in winter.

For the next 7 km the trail is almost always within sight and sound of Tokumm Creek. The trail is rocky and rooted, and you will be constantly adjusting gait. It makes for fatiguing travel. Tokumm Creek has been eroded into a fault that marks the approximate division between the western and eastern main ranges. Most rocks in the western main ranges are drab grey shales and limestones formed from sediments deposited in relatively deep water. Rocks of

the Chancellor group of formations are the most common. The eastern main ranges feature limestones, dolomite and quartzite.

After passing a massive, erratic limestone boulder, and crossing the major meltwater stream from the Wenkchemna Icefield, the trail reaches the Fay Hut junction. Fay Hut is 2.3 km to the east along a steep trail. Built in 1927, it was the first climbing hut erected by the Alpine Club of Canada. The hut was named for Professor Charles Fay, an American mountaineer.

Fay Hut Junction to Kaufmann Lake

Beyond the junction, the views north improve. Prominent is Mt. Oke (2920 m), named by explorer Samuel

Allen for a prospector he met nearby. You might think this is also the origin of the name "Prospector's Valley." However, this name was applied by Walter Wilcox in 1899 when he found an abandoned prospector's camp near the valley mouth. The old prospectors knew what they were doing. Small-scale commercial mining for lead and zinc took place in this valley just north of Marble Canyon between 1914 and 1943.

Given that this valley is prime bear habitat, the Tokumm Valley campground is poorly situated. Tent sites are within 10 m of the trail, and avalanche slopes are nearby. The author once spent a restless night here, listening to things outside the tent go "crash" in the night. North of the campground, Tokumm Creek is often bridged by con-

Icy Headwaters

Most surface water in the Rockies originates in the melting ice of glaciers. At km 8.4, the trail to Kaufmann Lake crosses a frigid, silty, meltwater stream that issues from the Wenkchemna Icefield. This stream also channels cold air into the valley bottom. You will see pink and white mountain heather at an elevation 600 m lower than normal for these plants. Although 6 km distant and 900 m lower than the closest glacier, the banks along this stream bed vividly exhibit the far-reaching effects of glacial ice on the mountain environment.

Pink mountain heather

More than 50 percent of Tokumm Creek valley is avalanche terrain. Deposits of avalanche snow often remain in the valley bottom throughout the summer. This avalanche deposit has bridged Tokumm Creek.

solidated, avalanched snow. Some of these "avalanche plug" deposits contain crevasses, indicating they are perennial features.

The remaining 2 km to the Kaufmann Lake junction is slow going since the trail undulates up and down the gravel creek banks. A 25 m section of trail slumped into the creek in 1992. Soon after you cross the braided outflow of Kaufmann Lake, a sign directs you to the final climb: 243 m of elevation gain in just 1.5 km. This section of trail is old and frustrating – the handiwork of mountaineers and fishing enthusiasts. Initially, the trail works its way south to the outlet stream, rising and falling needlessly. You then mercilessly ascend directly upslope before levelling out in a wet meadow near the lake outlet. Please try to keep to the beat-

en path. You will get your boots wet here.

Your exertions on the final approach are amply rewarded by the view at Kaufmann Lake. The setting features an unfamiliar perspective of familiar mountains. These are the "other sides" of some of the Wenkchemna Peaks, the wall of mountains better known as the backdrop to Moraine Lake. Mts. Allen (3301 m) and Tuzo (3245 m) border the east shore, and Deltaform Mountain (3424 m), the west. The surrounding forest contains scattered Lyall's larch.

Christian and Hans Kaufmann were two Swiss mountaineering guides who worked in Canada between 1900 and 1906. They guided first ascents of a number of mountains in this area, including: Neptuak, Deltaform, Hungabee, Biddle, Tuzo, Allen, Bowlen and Fay.

The lake is named for their father, Peter, who guided briefly in Canada in 1903.

The Kaufmann Lake campground is an ideal getaway for those seeking a night or two of backcountry solitude. The area is frequented by moose, elk, mule deer, and perhaps grizzly bear.

Kaufmann Lake was formerly a popular place for sport fishing. Since fish grow slowly in the cold, nutrient-poor water of high altitude lakes, a century of sport fishing has seriously depleted fish stocks in Kaufmann Lake.

The southwest shore of Floe Lake is dominated by the massive limestone cliffs of The Rockwall. Sunrise here can be one of the most memorable sights in the Rockies.

44. The Rockwall

Route

4-6 days, 55.0 km

Route	Elevation (m)	Distance (km)
Floe Lake trailhead	1338	0
Floe Lake CG	2058	10.5
Numa Pass	2370	13.2
Numa Creek CG	1530	20.0
Numa Creek jct	1530	20.4
Tumbling Pass	2256	25.3
Tumbling Creek CG	1890	27.9
Wolverine Pass jct	2188	31.0
Rockwall Pass	2253	31.7
South fork Helmet Creek	1936	35.3
Limestone Summit	2174	36.3
Helmet Creek CG	1753	39.5
Goodsir Pass jct	1761	40.1
Ochre Creek CG	1494	48.7
The Paint Pots	1464	54.0
Paint Pots parking area	1448	55.0

Topographic map: 82 N/1

Trailhead

West side of the Kootenay Parkway (Highway 93); 32.6 km west of Castle Junction; 72.1 km east of the junction with Highway 95.

The Rockwall is amongst the cream of the Classic Hikes – a remarkable outing that epitomizes the spectacular landscape of the Rockies. Peak, pass and precipice; meadow and stream; glacier and tarn – The Rockwall weaves these quintessential elements into one of the most rewarding backpacking excursions in the range.

The roller-coaster nature of this outing will make demands on your fitness. You cross four passes, involving a total vertical gain of more than 2600 m. The corresponding descents total 2250 m. The good news: excellent trails and

Natural Snowfence

The cliffs of The Rockwall are oriented southeast/north-west along the grain or strike of the Rockies. This is at right angles to the prevailing southwesterly air flow. Moisture-laden air from the Pacific is inter-cepted by the cliff and forced to rise. As the air rises and cools, mois-ture condenses into clouds, and precipitation falls.

In the alpine, more than 75 per-cent of the annual precipitation is snow. The prevail-ing winds scour snow from the southwest slopes of The Rockwall and deposit it into niches and basins on the northeast side. Here it accu-mulates to form and sustain drift glaciers, like the one that feeds Floe Lake. Not only does the cliff help create the glacier, but the perpetual shade it casts sustains the ice.

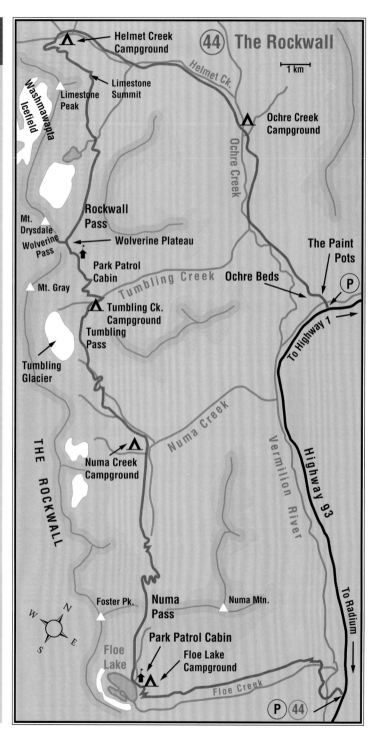

Helmet Creek Campground

(44) The Rockwall

Helmet Ck.

1 km

Washmawapta Icefield

Limestone Summit

Limestone Peak

Ochre Creek Campground

Ochre Creek

Rockwall Pass

Mt. Drysdale

Wolverine Plateau

Wolverine Pass

The Paint Pots

Park Patrol Cabin

Tumbling Creek

Ochre Beds

P

Mt. Gray

Tumbling Ck. Campground

Tumbling Pass

To Highway 1

Tumbling Glacier

Numa Creek

Numa Creek Campground

Vermilion River

THE ROCKWALL

Highway 93

N W E S

Foster Pk.

Numa Pass

Numa Mtn.

Park Patrol Cabin

Floe Lake

Floe Lake Campground

To Radium

Floe Creek

P (44)

five campgrounds allow you to break the hard work into short sections. The passes are usually snowbound until early July. Drinking water is scarce on this hike. Carry an extra water bottle and top up whenever you draw alongside a clear stream.

Kootenay Parkway to Floe Lake

The trail initially descends to cross the Vermilion River at a canyon eroded into Chancellor shale. The river's name refers to the red stains of iron oxides found along its banks upstream. Here, the river is often chalky gray in colour, choked with glacial sediment. The trail follows the riverbank northwest to Floe Creek, which you cross on a suspension bridge. At time of publication, there were three such bridges on The Rockwall. Two were in disrepair. Cross with care, one person at a time.

In the lower valley of Floe Creek, the lush forest includes a few specimens of Douglas fir and devil's club. Massive Engelmann spruce grow in the upper valley. These trees are more than 1 m in diameter and exceed 40 m in height. The dense shrubs and succulent forbs on the many avalanche paths offer excellent food for moose, deer, elk and bears. Bear cautions are common on this trail. Make lots of noise as you travel along Floe Creek.

At km 8.0 the trail reaches the valley headwall and you commence an excruciatingly

Water Worn and Scoured by Snow

Floe Creek occupies a steeply walled, V-shaped valley, typical of the western main ranges. The weak shales and slates of the underlying bedrock erode readily to create the deeply entrenched valley. The valley walls become natural paths for snow avalanches. Avalanche slopes comprise almost half the area along Floe Creek.

steep climb, gaining 400 m in the next 2.5 km. The toil ends a few hundred metres before Floe Lake campground, where there is an abrupt transition to an upper subalpine treeline forest, dominated by Lyall's larch.

Floe Lake

Floe Lake occupies an inspiring setting that contains all the classic features of The Rockwall: meadow, cliff, mountain, glacier and water. The lake is named for the ice floes or "growlers" that calve from the glacier beneath The Rockwall. You will often hear the cracking and booming of the glacier as it advances, and with fortune, you may see an iceberg calve into the lake. Sunrise here is one of the most memorable sights in the Rockies.

The Rockwall trail takes its name from the Ottertail limestone cliff that extends 53 km through western Kootenay and southwestern Yoho national parks. The cliff forms the backdrop to Floe Lake and is 900 m high in places.

Most of the surrounding

Pressure-treated Timbers: Designed and Built to Specifications

Floe Lake campground has been "hardened" to accommodate heavy use: gravel trails, gravel tent pads, and picnic tables built from "pressure-treated wood." The timber used is treated with the preservative copper-chromium-arsenate, and is advertised to be rot-resistant for 30-50 years. The preservative is deadly poison, but supposedly becomes inert once applied. However, err on the side of caution. Keep your food and hands from contacting the wood directly.

In the mid- to late-1980s, pressure-treated wood was used extensively for trail and campground structures in most of the Rocky Mountain parks. This wood is expensive, requires transport by helicopter to most sites, and contributes toxins to the environment. Pressure-treated wood structures are ugly, and look more like the precision work of engineers than the craft of trail builders.

At time of publication, park managers were re-evaluating the use of pressure-treated wood in the backcountry. Hopefully, natural timbers obtained on-site will once again be used for backcountry bridges, boardwalks and tables. Unfortunately, most trail crews are now unfamiliar with the skills required to work with natural materials.

The Rockwall is a remarkable limestone cliff, 900 m high in places. It extends 53 km through western Kootenay and southwestern Yoho. In the southern half of this distance the cliff has only one significant break: Wolverine Pass.

western main range mountains contain weak shales and slates. These mountains are generally described as being more eroded and gentle in appearance than the craggy peaks to the east. The Ottertail limestone of The Rockwall is a remarkable exception. Sediments comprising western main range shales and slates were deposited in deep sea water, largely devoid of marine life.

Originally, Ottertail sediments were deposited in shallow sea water that supported abundant marine life. Incredibly, the skeletal remains of marine creatures created this thick deposit of limestone. The Ottertail limestone imbues the western main ranges with some of the precipitous character of the mountains to the east along the continental divide.

Floe Lake to Numa Creek

From Floe Lake, the trail crosses the campground to the park patrol cabin, and then ascends steeply across a series of benches to Numa Pass. The hard work is on a delightful trail, which winds through upper subalpine larch forest and glades that feature tremendous displays of wildflowers. Given the high elevation and heavy snows here, the blooms of these flowers are at their peak in early August – a few weeks later than average.

The final kilometre to Numa Pass is across shales and alpine tundra. Repeated freezing and thawing churns the soil into mounds called frost hummocks. A few scraggly larch trees in krummholz form have taken root in the hummocks. The black-tipped

sedge, *Carex nigricans*, is common in the hollows, as are mountain heather, woolly everlasting and white mountain avens.

Numa Pass is the high point on The Rockwall trail. Mt. Temple (3543 m) and the "back sides" of the Wenkchemna Peaks are featured in the view north. Foster Peak (3204 m) rises west of the pass. *Numa* is Cree for "thunder." Numa Mountain (2550 m) was originally known as "Roaring Mountain."

The trail traverses west from the pass on a track beaten into the screes, and then descends north to treeline. The drop to Numa campground is one of the most abrupt on any of the Classic Hikes (840 m in 6.8 km). The basin north of Foster Peak contains a cirque glacier whose meltwater cascades over cliffs into the upper reaches of Numa Creek. The cliffs rise above avalanche paths that provide excellent habitat for bears. Travel with caution here. The lush vegetation at the edge of the avalanche paths has a rainforest ambience. Several fallen spruce trees cut from the trail show more than 400 annual rings.

Cross the south fork of Numa Creek on a felled tree bridge – hazardous when wet. The red berries of dwarf dogwood, wild strawberry and dwarf raspberry are common here in late summer. Tent sites at Numa Creek campground are on both sides of the tributary stream. Porcupines frequent this campground. Don't leave your boots or packs unattended!

Numa Creek to Tumbling Creek

At the junction 400 m beyond Numa Creek campground, you can make a quick exit from The Rockwall. The trail straight ahead (northeast) follows Numa Creek 6.4 km to the Kootenay Parkway. Otherwise, turn west (left) to ascend to Tumbling Pass.

Avalanche slopes flank the north fork of Numa Creek. The heavy precipitation in this area supports incredibly lush vegetation. In few places in the Rockies will you see shrubs this tall, such a variety of succulent forbs, and such an abundance of berries. Red elderberry is common. The author's field notes refer to

this section of trail as "a grizzly grocery store." Visibility is often poor, and the sound of the creek will obscure all but your most vocal noise-making efforts.

The well-conceived trail switchbacks steadily upward through the course of a glacially fed tributary stream. The torrent can be considerable on a hot afternoon. Rockhop or ford as required. Much of the rubble at trailside is moraine that was pushed over the cliff edge during the last advance of the glacier concealed above. During the climb you can see Mt. Ball (3311 m) to the east.

After completing the climb, the trail rambles through a kilometre-long boulder meadow – a delightful upper subalpine garden. From the north end of the meadow, you climb steeply over the scree shoulder east of Tumbling Pass. The extra climb detours around a lateral moraine that blocks the true low point of the pass. Ahead is the next instalment of spectacular Rockwall scenery, dominated by the convoluted, rubble-covered mass of Tumbling Glacier.

The trail descends from Tumbling Pass alongside a lateral moraine that marks the trimline of Tumbling Glacier. To the east of the trail is forest, to the west is a barren land of rocks and ice-cored moraine. During the peak of the Little Ice Age, Tumbling Glacier advanced this far east, obliterating the forest.

After you reach the north end of the lateral moraine, an-

gle northeast and descend steeply to Tumbling Creek. You can exit from The Rockwall at this point 10.3 km along Tumbling and Ochre creeks to the Kootenay Parkway. There are campgrounds en route.

The Tumbling Creek campground is 300 m west of the bridge. The water in Tumbling Creek is usually too silty to drink. The creek you cross just east of the campground may be dry lower down, however it should be flowing a few hundred metres to the north. It provides clear drinking water. The next water source is in 7.4 km.

Tumbling Creek to Helmet Creek

If you stay at Tumbling Creek campground, the ascent to Wolverine Plateau is a rude awakening, beginning directly from the tenting area. However, now that you are accustomed to the roller-coaster rigours of The Rockwall, this climb will seem short. The trail makes a sharp turn on a slope overlooking the extensive moraines of Tumbling Glacier. The view northeast includes a surprising landmark – the tower of Castle Mountain in the Bow Valley. The ascent continues through ancient larch forest, leading to the extensive upper subalpine meadows of Wolverine Plateau. The displays of western anemone and Indian paintbrush here are astounding. In 1985, a Lyall's larch with a circumference of 3.86 m was found nearby. This is the

The Rockwall trail climbs and descends repeatedly from forested valleys to upper subalpine passes. The photograph shows Tumbling Glacier and The Rockwall from Wolverine Plateau.

thickest Lyall's larch recorded in BC.

At the first knoll on the plateau, a sidetrail branches northeast to Wolverine patrol cabin. With its idyllic setting, this rustic shelter has epitomized mountain heaven for many a park employee. The Rock-

wall trail contours the western edge of the plateau, on an outcrop of Chancellor shale. The Wolverine Pass junction is 3.1 km from Tumbling Creek campground. Turn west (left) for the short sidetrip to the pass. The Rockwall trail continues straight ahead to Rockwall Pass.

Rockwall Pass is unquestionably the scenic climax of this outing. The 4 km long precipice of Ottertail limestone between Mt. Drysdale and Limestone Peak (2878 m) dominates the view northwest. This monolithic example of natural architecture is rarely duplicated in form or

Wolverine Pass (2207 m), 225 m

It is only half as far to Wolverine Pass as the park trail sign indicates. The short walk takes you to the boundary of Kootenay National Park, and the only significant break in the rampart of The Rockwall. By scrambling a short distance up the scree slopes north of the pass, you are rewarded with a view over Dainard Creek to the Beaverfoot Valley and distant Purcell Mountains. Extensive clearcuts scar the valley, a vivid

reminder of the considerable environmental pressures caused by resource extraction just outside national parks. This loss of habitat affects wildlife populations within protected areas, by eliminating travel routes and concentrating animals where they compete to mutual detriment. In addition, a forestry road leads along Dainard Creek to within 2 km of Wolverine Pass. The easy access granted is at the heart of a chronic poaching

problem in this part of the national park.

The peaks flanking Wolverine Pass are Mt Gray (3000 m) to the south and Mt Drysdale (2932 m) to the north. Charles Drysdale was a geologist, and William Gray his assistant. The two drowned on the Kootenay River while conducting geological fieldwork in 1917. Dainard Creek was named for Manuel Dainard, an outfitter from Golden in the late 1890s.

extent elsewhere in the Canadian Rockies. Another drift glacier lies at the base of the cliff. Its meltwaters drain into a substantial marginal lake. With the alpine meadows of Rockwall Pass as the foreground, the scene is unforgettable.

The surface of the unnamed glacier beneath Mt. Drysdale features alternating dark and light bands called ogives (OWE-jives). These result from different rates of glacial retreat and advance during summer and winter. Black exposures in the extensive moraine system on the near side of the glacier are ice-cored moraines. The melting

of these ice-cored moraines sustains a number of small lakes.

Five couloirs on the north face of Mt. Drysdale funnel snow, ice and rock onto the glacier. The ice is dotted with talus cones – piles of débris that the moving ice has transported away from the mountain wall. The series of lateral moraines adjacent to the trail records at least five distinct advances of glacial ice during the Little Ice Age. It is not often you will see a sequence this well preserved. Usually, the largest of the advances obliterated evidence of the lesser ones. In this case, apparently none of the existing

moraines was overridden during subsequent advances.

The trail descends to cross the outlet of the marginal lake, the headwaters of the south fork of Helmet Creek. Downstream, there is a picturesque waterfall and canyon. The number of game trails in the area indicates mountain goats visit the canyon to lick sulphur-bearing minerals from the shales.

The climb to Limestone Summit is interrupted by a flat meadow. Looking south, you obtain a final, grand close-up view of The Rockwall. Limestone Summit is not a true mountain pass, but a larch-covered spur of Limestone

The Wolverine: A Bad Reputation, A Grim Situation

Wolverine Pass is named for the largest terrestrial member of the weasel family. The adult male wolverine is about 1 m long and half that high at the midpoint of the back, and it weighs 14 to 21 kg. The thick fur is generally dark, with a highlight across the forehead and down each flank. Considerable colour variation occurs. The animal secretes a rank-smelling musk, which gives rise to one of its folk names: "skunk bear," Although the animal is not frequently seen, the wolverine's range includes the upper subalpine zone of areas like Wolverine Plateau.

The wolverine is an opportunis-

tic scavenger, eating carrion, small birds and mammals. The animal has a fierce reputation, hence its other folk name: "devil-beast." It has been reported that a wolverine will protect a kill from an approaching grizzly bear. The animal's formidable appearance no doubt has contributed to its reputation. The wolverine has beady eyes and sharp teeth, which it will bare at any intruder while making an array of intimidating sounds. You can imagine

the smell of its breath! A face-to-face encounter with a wolverine is not-soon forgotten.The

wolverine is officially classified as "vulnerable" in western Canada – at risk because of low or declining numbers. The animal requires vast terrain – 2000 km^2 is typical for an adult male. Wolverine fur is desired for parka hood trimmings because it resists ice build-up. Habitat disruption and trapping outside national parks are the two major pressures facing this animal. Its survival in the Rocky Mountain parks hinges on protection of its life and habitat on adjoining provincial lands.

Wolverine tracks

Peak. The steady descent north from Limestone Summit brings you to the alluvial flats at Helmet Creek campground. En route there are fine views of Helmet Falls.

With a total drop estimated at 352 m, Helmet Falls is one of the four highest waterfalls in Canada. Surveyors argue about whether all the cascades, or just the highest, should be included in a waterfall's height. Although Della Falls on Vancouver Island is unquestionably the highest in Canada, Helmet, Hunlen and Takakkaw falls each have proponents that claim them to be "second highest."

The South Tower of Mt. Goodsir (3562 m), northwest of Helmet Falls, is the highest mountain in the Rockies between Mt. Assiniboine and Columbia Icefield. Although you might think this huge thrust of rock is another resistant outcrop of Ottertail limestone, it is the opposite – crumbly shales and slates of the McKay (muck-EYE) group of formations. Just why one of the weakest rocks in the Rockies comprises one of the highest mountains, yet awaits an explanation.

James Hector named Mt. Goodsir in 1858 for John Goodsir, an anatomy professor in Edinburgh. The South Tower was first climbed in 1903, and the North Tower in 1909. The popular climbing routes are on the southwest slopes of the mountains, however both north faces have been climbed.

The headwall that flanks Helmet Falls is a good place to look for mountain goats. This animal is the symbol of Kootenay National Park, which is home to 200 goats. Another 400 goats live in neighbouring Yoho. To the north of Helmet Falls, an underground stream discharges from the cliff in a small waterfall.

Helmet Creek to the Kootenay Parkway

The Rockwall concludes by following Helmet Creek east to its confluence with Ochre Creek, and then southeast along Ochre Creek to the Paint Pots and the Kootenay Parkway. It's a pleasant hike involving a gradual descent through lush subalpine forest. Red and white baneberry and the lily, twisted stalk, are common in the undergrowth, along with the wildflowers dwarf dogwood and queen's cup.

From the suspension bridge crossing on Helmet Creek, there is a distant view west to The Rockwall, featuring Helmet Mountain and part of the Washmawapta Icefield. An icefield is a substantial body of ice that sends tributary glaciers into more than one valley. The Washmawapta is the southernmost feature in the Rockies to which the term "icefield" is officially applied. *Washmawapta* is Stoney for "ice river."

Downstream from the bridge, the trail skirts a shale canyon at the mouth of Helmet Creek and climbs through forest before descending to Ochre Creek. Many of the sub-

The Ice River Alkaline Complex: Protected and Exploited

North of Helmet Falls, Sharp Mtn. (3049 m) contains an outcrop of the Ice River Alkaline Complex. The complex is the largest assemblage of igneous (once molten) rock known in the Canadian Rockies. This molten blob of magma intruded into older sedimentary formations approximately 245 million years ago. Many rare minerals occur. In total, the complex covers 19 km². The portion within Yoho and Kootenay national parks is a Special Preservation Area. Access and collecting are prohibited.

There have been various attempts to extract the iron-rich mineral, magnetite, from this complex. All have failed because of the remoteness of the location. In 1991, a mine was proposed for upper Moose Creek, west of The Rockwall, and just 300 m from the boundaries of Yoho and Kootenay national parks. The developers hope to take advantage of a forestry road scheduled for construction along Moose Creek. The road itself, the logging it will bring, and the mine will severely disrupt habitat crucial to grizzly bears, elk and mountain goats, and destroy an opportunity to establish a "buffer zone" along the national park boundaries in this area.

alpine fir trees in this vicinity have been stricken with a needle-cast disease that has defoliated them. As you descend to Ochre Creek, notice the V-shape of the Helmet and Ochre valleys.

Cross Ochre Creek to a pleasant campground. The trail crew has provided an imaginative set of lumberjack lawn furniture. At the junction just beyond the campground, turn south (right), and follow signs at the subsequent junctions for "Highway 93." At the far side of the Ochre Beds, the Rockwall Trail crosses the Vermilion River on a well-built suspension bridge and ends at the Kootenay Parkway (Highway 93), 12.9 km north of the Floe Lake trailhead.

"From the snow-covered top the view was superb. One could see most of the great peaks of the Rockies and Selkirks, range after range fading away into the blue distance."
—Katie Gardiner describing the view from The Rockwall summit of Foster Peak, on its first ascent, July 8, 1933, *Canadian Alpine Journal,* 1934

The Red Earth

The last points of interest on The Rockwall are the Paint Pots and Ochre Beds. "Ochre" is clay stained yellow and red with iron oxides. This "red earth" was a valuable trading commodity for Kutenai Natives from the Columbia Valley in the 1700s. The Kutenais collected the ochre, shaped it into cakes and baked it in fire. The resulting compound was mixed with fish grease or animal fat to create a body paint used in rituals. The Kutenais would stop at the Ochre Beds to gather ochre on their way to Kootenay Plains on the North Saskatchewan River. Their travel route, "The Kutenai

The Ochre Beds are deposits of clay that have been stained red and yellow by iron-rich water. The water percolates to the surface nearby at the outlets of three cold mineral springs, the Paint Pots. This ochre was an important trading and ritual commodity for Kutenai Natives.

Trail," took them north over Goodsir or Ottertail passes, through what is now Yoho National Park, and across Amiskwi and Howse passes.

The iron-rich water that stains the clay percolates from three cold mineral springs – the Paint Pots. The ochre has

stained rocks downstream in the Vermilion River – the origin of its name. Please do not disturb or remove the ochre.

Kootenay or Kootenai was the name applied to the Natives by tribes east of the Rockies. It means "people from beyond the hills." Anthropologists now use the spelling Kutenai. The Kutenais referred to themselves as Ksanka, which means "Standing Arrow." For more information on the Paint Pots and Ochre Beds, see *Walks and Easy Hikes in the Canadian Rockies.*

The Kindersley loop features a variety of wildflowers in early season. Between Kindersley Pass and Kindersley Summit, the trail traverses steep avalanche slopes that are frequented by bighorn sheep.

45. Kindersley Pass and Summit

Route

Day-hike, 10.1 km; or 17.4 km loop

Route	Elevation (m)	Distance (km)
Kindersley trailhead	1335	0
Lookout Point Ridge	1936	6.0
Kindersley Pass	2210	8.4
Kindersley Summit	2393	10.1
Sinclair Creek trailhead	1433	16.1
Kindersley trailhead	1335	17.4

Topographic maps: 82 J/12, 82 K/9

Best lighting: anytime

Trailhead

Kootenay Parkway (Highway 93), 10.5 km east of the junction with Highway 95, 94.2 km west of Castle Junction. The small parking area is on the south side of the highway. This is a dangerous turnoff for westbound travellers. The trailhead is on the north side. Use caution crossing the highway.

The Kindersley Pass and Summit trail travels from dense valley bottom forest to barren alpine ridge crest, and showcases diverse vegetation. The wildflower displays of early summer are superb. Although it gains 875 m in 8.4 km, the trail to Kindersley Pass is one of the best constructed in the Rockies, and the grade is seldom steep. Kindersley Pass and Summit are usually snowbound until late June.

Kootenay Parkway to Kindersley Pass

From the Kootenay Parkway, the trail initially ascends through a damp forest dominated by Douglas fir. This tree is the climax species of forests in the montane ecoregion of the southern Rockies. Its fire-resistant bark enables it to

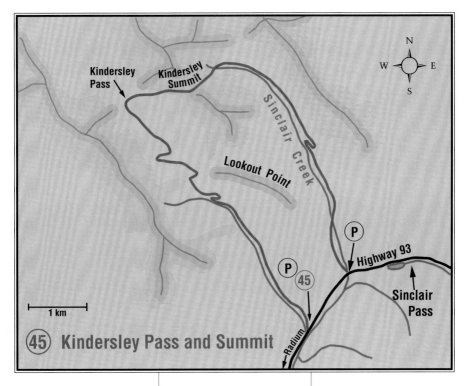

45 Kindersley Pass and Summit

withstand the periodic hot ground fires that remove competing vegetation. Western Canada violet, white geranium, western meadow rue, yellow columbine, baneberry, birchleaf spirea, and prickly wild rose are common wildflowers and shrubs in the undergrowth. Where the trail climbs away from the creek onto drier soils, lodgepole pine and massive white spruce grow, with Oregon grape in the undergrowth. This hollylike shrub has yellow flowers that produce blue berries. In autumn, the thick, waxy leaves turn purple and red.

At km 2.8, the trail draws opposite an avalanche path. The lush vegetation here includes cow parsnip and other succulents that are favourite foods of black and grizzly bears. The shrubs offer browse for elk and mule deer. In fact, this unnamed valley is excellent habitat for many mammals. An abundance of prey species (mice, voles, squirrels, deer and snowshoe hares) sustains predators such as American marten, coyote, cougar, lynx and wolf. The ancient trees offer good habitat for flickers and woodpeckers.

The trail returns briefly to the valley bottom. Then the switchbacking resumes. During the next 5 km, you may see the blooms of more than 30 species of wildflowers if you are hiking early in the season. Two of these flowers have bulbs that are favourite foods

The Ice-Free Corner of the Rockies

From a steep sideslope at km 4.0, you can clearly see the V-shape of this unnamed valley. Many valleys in the southwestern part of Kootenay National Park are V-shaped. This indicates they have been eroded principally by water, not by glacial ice. If the bedrock here was resistant limestone or dolomite, the flowing water would have created a slot canyon. Since the bedrock consists of weak shales and slates, the V-shape has resulted. The western ranges between Golden and Invermere do not contain any glaciers today.

Wolf tracks

of grizzly bears: glacier lily and western spring beauty.

At km 6.0, the trail crests the forested west ridge of Lookout Point, and contours into an avalanche basin that contains Lyall's larch trees. Look for the tracks and scats of wolves here. The stream at trailside now drains east into upper Sinclair Creek. More switchbacks through avalanche terrain lead to the final approach to Kindersley Pass: a confined, snowmelt stream course, adorned with western anemone. The consolidated avalanche snow here frequently endures the summer.

Kindersley Pass to Kindersley Summit

Kindersley Pass is on the national park boundary, and offers only limited views north into the Brisco Range. Cutblocks scar upper Kindersley Creek – a reminder of the pressures just outside national parks. Follow a steep track northeast along the park boundary to an errant sign indicating "Kindersley Pass," perhaps erected here because the view is better than on the true pass below. The trail angles sharply southeast (right), and begins a treeline traverse across avalanche gullies to Kindersley Summit. Krummholz tree islands of Engelmann spruce and subalpine fir dot the mountain-

side. Taller spruce grow out of the twisted mats of firs.

Bighorn sheep frequent these slopes in summer.

Kindersley Summit is the high point on this hike. Used in this sense, the word "summit" means the highest point reached by trail in a valley. Properly speaking, Kindersley Summit should be called "Sinclair Summit," as it is at the head of the Sinclair Valley, not the Kindersley Valley.

Kindersley Summit to Kootenay Parkway

The most straightforward exit from Kindersley Summit is to retrace your route to the trailhead. For the more adventurous, trail markers lead east from Kindersley Summit into the avalanche basin at the head of Sinclair Creek. Follow a steep, sketchy path for 1 km, after which the trail becomes better defined in the vicinity of the creek, which you hop to

The steeply walled valleys of the western ranges feature many avalanche paths. These openings in the forest are important habitat for many species of wildlife.

its east bank. From here on it is easy travelling on a steep trail that descends through the lush vegetation of this V-shaped valley. You cross to the west side of the creek 1.7 km before the trail's end at the Kootenay Parkway. The original trailhead is 1.3 km southwest (right) along the Koote-

nay Parkway. Use caution with regard to traffic. Sinclair Creek was named for James Sinclair, who in 1841 led a group of 120 settlers from Manitoba through the Rockies via Sinclair Pass to the Oregon country.

"The characteristics of the range vary largely in its long-drawn sweep from sunny south to icy north; the structure and scenery change from time to time as one passes from one section to another along its mighty length."
—Mountaineer James Outram,
In the Heart of the Canadian Rockies, 1905

An Eagle's View

Mountaineers may readily ascend the two unnamed peaks southeast (2515 m) and northwest (2683 m) of Kindersley Summit. Both offer detailed views of a tremendous length of the continental divide. Mt. Joffre (3449 m) looms in the distant southeast and Mt. Goodsir (3562 m) dominates the skyline in the northeast (distant centre of above photograph). Directly east is an unfamiliar view of a well-known mountain: Mt. Assiniboine (3618 m), highest point in the southern Rockies, and sixth highest in the range. The Purcell Range of the Columbia Mountains forms the skyline to the west. Look for golden eagles on the thermals overhead.

From the northerly summit, the view also includes the Co-

lumbia Valley and the complete length of the western ranges, from northeast of Golden to south of Invermere. The western ranges (photograph) were the first to be thrust above sea level in the Rockies, more than 120 million years ago. Their weak shales and slates exhibit extensive folding and faulting.

Waterton Lakes National Park

Established in 1895 as Canada's fourth national park, Waterton Lakes includes 525 km² in the extreme southwestern corner of Alberta. The park's theme is "where the mountains meet the prairie." From many viewpoints along the park's 225 km of trails, the remarkable effect of the front ranges rising from the plains is the scenic focal point.

Waterton Lakes National Park is 264 km south of Calgary via highways 22 and 6; and 130 km southwest of Lethbridge via Highway 5. There is passenger bus service to Pincher Creek and Fort Macleod, from where a shuttle service provides access to the park. Otherwise, access is by car.

The town of Waterton Park offers supplies, services and accommodation. The nearby towns of Cardston and Pincher Creek also cater to travellers. The park has three frontcountry campgrounds with 391 sites. Backcountry campgrounds each have a quota and campers require a wilderness pass. You can obtain passes in person at the park information centre, 24 hours in advance of your trip. The park information centre and warden office are just north of Waterton Park townsite, on Highway 5. There are no hostels in the park.

Overview map of Waterton Lakes National Park showing trailhead locations

Bertha Lake occupies a fiord-like hanging valley. The lush green vegetation and red argillite of the surrounding slopes contrast with the dark water of the lake.

46. Bertha Lake

Route

Day-hike or overnight, 5.8 – 7.5 km

Route	Elevation (m)	Distance (km)
Trailhead	1295	0
Upper Waterton Lk viewpoint	1410	1.4
Lakeshore jct	1400	1.5
Lower Bertha Falls	1475	2.9
Bertha Lake viewpoint	1495	5.4
Bertha Lake CG	1755	5.7
Bertha Lake shelter	1755	5.8
Pond west of Bertha Lake	1760	7.5

Best lighting: early morning at the east shore, afternoon at the west shore

Trailhead

In Waterton Park townsite on Evergreen Avenue, 500 m south of Cameron Falls.

The Bertha Lake trail climbs steeply to Waterton's most accessible backcountry lake, a charming fiord-like body of water surrounded by lush forest. The hike is renowned for its diverse vegetation. The campground and shelter at the lake are frequently crowded. Therefore, this outing is recommended as a day-hike only. The trail is shared with horses.

Townsite to Lower Bertha Falls

From the townsite, the trail climbs gradually through a mixed montane forest towards Bertha Creek. Fleabane, false hellebore, white geranium, bear grass, harebell, yarrow, paintbrush, fireweed and pearly everlasting line the trail. Trembling aspen, mountain ash, poplar, white birch, Douglas maple and lodgepole pine are the common trees. Many of the pines are stand-ing-dead. A mountain pine beetle infestation between 1976 and 1983 killed 50 per-cent of the lodgepole pines in the park, and as many as 75 percent of the trees in some stands.

Other trees in this forest have been toppled by severe winds. Beetle infestations and blowdowns open the forest canopy and allow new growth. The sunlit areas that result support shrubs and wildflow-ers, and are important feeding areas for many large mam-mals. One of the common shrubs here is buffaloberry, whose red and amber berries are a staple food of black bears.

At km 1.4, a short path

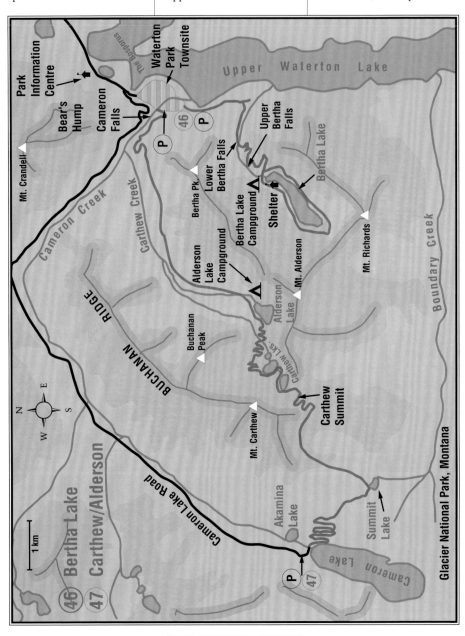

Vegetation near Lower Bertha Falls is typical of forests in BC's interior rather than those of southern Alberta.

leads straight ahead to a viewpoint that overlooks Upper Waterton Lake. In September 1998, a forest fire consumed much of the forest on the east shore. Across the lake to the southeast is Mt. Cleveland (3190 m), highest mountain in Glacier National Park. It was named in gratitude by conservationist George Bird Grinnell in 1898 for Grover Cleveland, US president. Cleveland had established the Lewis and Clark Forest Reserve the year before. The Reserve included the area that became Glacier National Park in 1910.

Limber pine grows at this viewpoint. Like the whitebark pine, this tree has needles in bunches of five and prefers windy locations. However, it is generally a tree of the montane forest, whereas the whitebark pine grows in upper subalpine forest. Showy

brown-eyed Susans also grow here.

South of the viewpoint across Bertha Bay is a fire succession forest of lodgepole pine. In August 1935, a forest fire raged between Boundary Creek and Bertha Creek along the west shore of Upper Waterton Lake. The conflagration threatened the townsite of Waterton Park. It was extinguished by the efforts of 533 firefighters, aided considerably by wet weather and a change of wind. The young pine forest is a legacy of this burn.

Backtrack to the main trail and descend to the west. Keep straight ahead at the junction in 40 m. The trail contours around a limestone bluff of the Altyn Formation, whose layers plunge towards the southwest. This is the *dip* of the underlying rock forma-

tions in Waterton. Whether you look at a small cliff or a mountainside, you will see this orientation consistently exposed. Wild bergamont, Jacob's ladder, creeping beardtongue, stonecrop, yellow false dandelion and bearberry grow on the dry, gritty soils at the base of the bluff.

As you approach Bertha Creek the vegetation quickly changes to species characteristic of damp subalpine forests. Waterton has the most diverse vegetation of any Rocky Mountain park. It is home to 870 vascular plant species – 55 percent of the total found in Alberta. Of these, 113 are rare in Alberta, and 34 are unknown in the province outside the park. A prominent storm track along the 49th parallel brings significant moisture into the southern part of the park, creating normally found in BC. Western yew and devil's club once grew along lower Bertha Creek but have not been seen for many years.

Lower Bertha Falls cascades over another outcrop of the Altyn Formation. At the base of the falls, the water is eroding into the seam between two upturned edges of rock. This creates a natural gutter that captures the flow and channels the water away to the southeast, along a right-angle turn in the stream course. When bedrock dictates the flow of a stream in this fashion, it is called *structural control*. Downstream are a series of step-like cascades, each caused by an upturned edge of rock in the creek bed.

Lower Bertha Falls to Bertha Lake

Cross the bridge at the falls and begin a relentless switchback ascent on the lower slopes of Mt. Richards. This is excellent bear habitat; make lots of noise. After about 2 km, there are views through the trees of the 75 m Upper Bertha Falls cascading over a cliff of Altyn limestone. The trail angles away from the falls. From openings in the trees there are fine views east to Upper Waterton Lake and Vimy Peak (2379 m). The trail makes one final switchback along the base of a cliff before descending to the mouth of the hanging valley that contains Bertha

Lake. The campground is 110 m beyond the outlet stream bridge, and the shelter is an additional 100 m around the north shore of the outlet bay.

With an area of 30.2 ha and a depth of 50.3 m, Bertha Lake is the second largest and second deepest of Waterton's backcountry lakes. The lake is dammed by upturned rock strata, and it occupies a hollow eroded in the shattered shales of the Greyson Formation (formerly called the Appekunny Formation). The lake is backed by a tremendous cliff of Siyeh limestone and dolomite, 500 m high. This cliff extends from Mount Alderson (2692 m) on the northwest, to Mt. Richards (2416 m) on the south. Bertha Peak (2440 m) stands to the

Bear Grass

The showy white bloom of bear grass is the floral emblem of Waterton Lakes National Park – the only national park in Canada in which it is found. Growing from a stem that is 50 to 120 cm tall, the bear grass flower graces meadows throughout Waterton from mid-June to mid-July. Some bear grass plants exhibit a peculiar crook in the upper stem. It is thought these bends occur when the flower head matures during wet periods. The stalk is bent by the weight of the extra moisture. Individual bear grass plants bloom sporadically, averaging one to three times in every ten years. It is especially important not to pick this attractive flower.

The bear grass flower is eaten by sheep, deer and elk.

Mountain goats eat the mature leaves, and bears eat the younger leaves in spring. Natives reportedly wove the leaves into baskets and items of cloth-ing. Although the leaves appear grass-like, the plant is a member of the lily family. Bear grass does not occur north of Crowsnest Pass.

north of the outlet. A waterfall tumbles down its south slopes.

It is thought that the name "Bertha" was originally applied to the lake we know today as Alderson Lake. Bertha Ekelund was an early Waterton resident, reportedly jailed for passing counterfeit money. This made her into a folk hero. She was also a sometime companion of Joe Cosley. A true mountain man, Cosley was at various times a prospector, trapper, and Glacier park ranger and guide, between 1890 and 1930. He probably knew the landscape of Waterton/Glacier better than anyone else alive in his day. Cosley named many features for himself, his friends, and in the case of Bertha and other lakes, for his female companions. An earlier name for this lake was "Spirit Lake."

Circuit of Bertha Lake

To fully appreciate Bertha Lake and its valley, allow time to make a circuit of the lake. However, use caution. The upper valley is excellent bear habitat. You may also see a cougar or wolverine here. Just north of the shelter, a prominent trail branches west (right). Follow this along the north shore of the lake, alternating between meadows and stands of ancient subalpine forest. In early to mid-July there are tremendous displays of bear grass here.

The trail crosses two red bluffs of Grinnell argillite that dip towards the lake. They fea-

ture a colourful assortment of wildfowers: mariposa lily, stonecrop, umbrella plant, creeping beardtongue, meadowsweet, and spotted saxifrage. Together with shrubby cinquefoil and juniper, they give the illusion of montane meadow at a subalpine elevation. Between the two bluffs the trail follows the lakeshore with a gravelly beach of red argillite underfoot. In wetter areas, you may see red monkey flowers.

Rock-hop the principal inlet stream. Just beyond is an abandoned campsite and the remnants of an old shelter. Camping is not permitted here. The trail climbs over a bluff, crosses two more inlet streams, and descends to a small pond beyond the western shore of the lake. An abandoned stream course tells of days-gone-by when this pond fed directly into Bertha Lake. The stupendous cliffs above are home to mountain goats.

The return trail follows the south shore and cuts through several argillite gullies. From the open scree slope near the lake's east end, you obtain fine views of the lake, which is only 50 m wide at this spot. The scree slope is a fan of rubble that extends into the lake, and creates the constriction. The circuit concludes at the stand of dead trees near the lake's outlet. Climb up to the approach trail and descend to Waterton Park townsite.

"Colour in the rocks, colour in the flowers, colour in the skies! Colour indeed seems to be the principal attribute of Waterton Lakes National Park; even its history is marked by that quality."

—Donald Buchanan, *Canadian Geographic Journal,* February 1933

Separated by natural dams of glacier-worn rock and ringed with red argillite, the Carthew Lakes occupy a series of glacial hollows on the north side of Carthew Summit.

47. Carthew-Alderson Trail

Route

Day-hike or overnight, 19.9 km

Route	Elevation (m)	Distance (km)
Trailhead	1661	0
Summit Lake jct	1931	4.3
Carthew Summit	2311	7.9
Upper Carthew Lake	2195	9.3
Lower Carthew Lake	2159	9.9
Alderson Lake jct	1811	13.1
Cameron Falls, Waterton Park townsite	1295	19.9

Best lighting: anytime

Trailhead

Follow the Akamina Parkway for 16 km from Waterton Park townsite to the parking lot at Cameron Lake. The trailhead is across the footbridge at the outlet of Cameron Lake. Daily shuttle service (fee charged) is available to Cameron Lake. Inquire at the Tamarack Mall in Waterton Park townsite.

The Carthew-Alderson trail traces a spectacular route from Cameron Lake to Waterton Park townsite.

It immerses you in ancient forests, takes you across an alpine ridge crest, and visits five delightful backcountry lakes. The vistas span everything from mountain top to prairie. The trail is usually passable by mid-June, however the north slopes of Carthew Summit can be snowbound into July. Avoid this outing during poor weather and when thunderstorms are forecast. The trail is shared with horses.

Trailhead to Summit Lake

The Carthew-Alderson trail begins at the outlet of Cameron Lake in the heart of a dense subalpine forest. Engelmann spruce, subalpine fir, false hellebore, cow parsnip, foam flower, water birch, bear grass, arnica, queen's cup, thimbleberry, feathermosses, grouseberry and ferns grow at trailside. In a few places, you may see red monkey flowers, whose attractive blooms are frequented by hummingbirds. As you climb towards Summit Lake you pass some of the oldest trees in the park, aged 250-300 years. As elsewhere in Waterton, there are many standing-dead trees. Tree lichens, notably *Bryoria* species and wolf lichen, cling to their branches.

The trail to Summit Lake was constructed in 1910, and it illustrates how trailbuilders can tackle a very steep slope, yet create a walking surface that is seldom steep. Long switchbacks across this 50-degree sideslope result in a gentle, well-graded ascent. Through breaks in the trees you enjoy views of Cameron Lake, Akamina Lake and Akamina Pass. *Akamina* (ah-kah-MEE-nuh) is a Kutenai

Please see map on page 248

native word that means "high bench land."

At km 3.7 the trail levels out and traverses through treeline forest towards the Summit Lake junction. Open meadows here are filled almost entirely with bear grass. The meadows are frost hollows that stunt the growth; hence most plants do not support stalks and blooms. There are some fine examples of ripple rock at trailside.

At km 4.3 you reach the Summit Lake junction. Summit Lake is nearby; a shallow kettle pond, often teeming with bugs. You may see mule deer here, licking at the mineral-rich mud. Mt. Custer and Chapman Peak (2867 m) are reflected in the lake on calm days. Robert Chapman was a superintendent of Glacier National Park in 1912.

Glaciologists believe that Summit Lake once drained northwest into the Akamina Valley. However, glacial overdeepening of the Cameron Lake basin altered

drainage patterns. Today, Summit Lake drains south into Boundary Creek in the US.

Summit Lake to Carthew Summit

At the Summit Lake junction, turn northeast (left). After a gradual climb of about 500 m, the trail traverses beneath a rock bluff decorated with bear grass, creeping beardtongue, fleabane, and white draba. The surrounding forest contains Lyall's larch trees. In the basin south of the trail is a tributary of Boundary Creek. The surrounding slopes support a ghostly forest of ancient standing-dead trees.

The trail breaks through treeline and contours across a steep avalanche-swept slope, climbing gradually towards Carthew Summit. From the open scree slopes there are pleasing views southwest over lush, wet meadows. This foreground contrasts with the forbidding north face of Chapman Peak beyond. Picturesque Lake Wurdeman lies at the base of the peak, fed by meltwater from an apron of glacial ice. Lake Wurdeman is a textbook example of a cirque lake. The lake's name commemorates yet another topographer with the 1861 US Boundary Survey – J.V. Wurdeman. The lake was known to Peigan (pay-GAN) Natives as "Bird Rattle Lake," after one of their warriors.

The red rock underfoot is argillite (ARE-jill-ite) of the Kintla Formation, and is 1.3 to 1.5 billion years old. Argillite is

Cameron Lake

Early morning is one of the best times to appreciate Cameron Lake. The lake is 39 m deep and has an area of 172 ha. It occupies a hollow excavated by glacial ice and is dammed by a glacial moraine. The lake was named for Donald Cameron, who led the British party that surveyed the international boundary in 1874. The summit of Mt. Custer (2708 m) at the south end of the lake lies entirely within Glacier National Park, Montana. The mountain was not named for the famous general, but for Henry Custer, a topographer with the US Boundary Survey who worked in this area in 1860 or 1861. The avalanche paths at the south end of the lake are frequented by grizzly bears.

created from muddy sediments that were deposited on a river delta. This mudstone is red because its sediments contain oxidized iron. The sediments were exposed to the air after deposition, and the iron "rusted." Kintla argillite is thinly layered and easily eroded. It comprises the many colourful scree ridges in the western part of Waterton Lakes National Park.

The final climb to Carthew Summit is on a series of long switchbacks. Scorpionweed, sky pilot, yellow draba and alpine forget-me-not dot the red screes. Please follow the orange-painted markers and keep to the beaten path. Summit Lake, Cameron Lake and Lake Nooney are now visible to the west and south.

Carthew Summit

The scenic climax of this hike bursts into view to the northeast as you crest Carthew Summit. Framed between the ridges of Mt. Carthew (2630 m) and Mt. Alderson (2692 m), the Carthew Lakes lead the eye through a rugged hanging valley to the distant prairie. By their arrangement, the Carthew Lakes are known to glaciologists as a glacial cirque staircase, or paternoster lakes. This Latin expression means "beads on a rosary." The lakes occupy basins eroded by glacial ice as it flowed down the valley. Each basin is at a progressively lower elevation. Although significant glaciers are now absent from Waterton, their legacy in creating this exceptional landscape is

Mule Deer

The mule deer is the more numerous of the two species of deer in the Canadian Rockies, and is abundant in Waterton. To distinguish the mule deer from the white-tailed deer, look first at the tail. The mule deer's tail is narrow and white with a black tip. The white-tailed deer's tail is broad, and is the colour of the coat above, and white underneath. The antlers of mule deer bucks are equally branched, whereas those of white-tailed bucks branch upwards from a forward-reaching beam. The coats of both species are reddish brown in summer, changing to grey in winter. The rumps are white.

Deer graze on grasses and wildflowers in summer. In autumn and winter they browse on leaves and buds. In late winter, mule deer may resort to strip-

ping tree bark to get at the sugary cambium layer beneath. The mountain lion is one of the principal predators of deer. The abundance of mule deer is one reason why mountain lions are common in Waterton.

Waterton's mule deer are not shy. Accustomed to humans and to handouts, many have lost their wildness. However, please remember that these animals can inflict serious injury by kicking with their front hooves. Do not approach a doe with fawns, or any deer during the autumn rut. If a deer approaches you, scare it away by shouting and waving your arms.

evident.

The screes that flank Carthew Summit feature roseroot, Sandberg's wild parsley, and sky pilot. The pygmy (dwarf) poppy also grows here. This yellow-flowered plant is rare in Canada. Most of the places that it has been found are in Waterton. Lt. William Carthew was a Canadian land surveyor who worked with the Interprovincial Boundary Survey that delineated the Alberta-BC boundary between 1913 and 1925. As part of his duties, he climbed Mt. Carthew in 1914.

Many hikers ramble south a short distance from Carthew Summit and scamper onto the bluff that affords views south over Boundary Creek. Avoid this high point if poor weather is approaching.

Carthew Summit to Alderson Lake

The descent from Carthew Summit to Upper Carthew Lake may be complicated by perennial snow patches on the trail. At first, the trail angles slightly northeast. Then it switchbacks down to the southeast to skirt the largest of the snow patches above the west shore of Upper Carthew Lake. Please keep to the beaten path, and for your safety, stay off large snow patches.

The trail follows the north shore of Upper Carthew Lake to an ancient krummholz forest at the lake's outlet. The rock dam that separates the upper and lower lakes is known as a *riegel* (RYE-gull). Compressive forces during mountain building, thrust

rock layers upwards to the northeast. The resistant leading edges of some thrusts have endured as the natural dams that impound many of Waterton's backcountry lakes.

You switchback down alongside pretty cascades between the upper and lower lakes. Rock-hop the outlet stream to its south side. As you descend to the west shore of Lower Carthew Lake, you will probably encounter more snow. The trail makes a hairpin turn to the north (left) and follows the west and north shores of the lake. Rock-hop the inlet stream. When the lake level is high, you may have to traverse some rocks just above the water. Two bodies of water comprise Lower Carthew Lake. The largest is 7.3 ha in area and 11 m deep. It is separated from the much smaller Carthew Pond by a dam of rockslide débris.

The trail climbs the crest of the cliff that separates the lower lakes from Alderson Lake. Wildflowers that prefer dry habitats cling to the thin soils here: stonecrop, rocky mountain goldenrod, spotted saxifrage and scorpionweed. After this short climb, the trail angles north and then east, descending steeply into the basin between Mt. Carthew and Buchanan Peak (2409 m). The cliff is limestone of the Siyeh Formation. It contains an intrusion of igneous rock called the Purcell Sill. You may see eroded fragments of this dark, crystalline lava-like rock on the trail.

The outflow from the Carthew Lakes cascades in a

Lightning!

Waterton experiences more electrical storms than other areas described in *Classic Hikes*. You should avoid the park's passes and high ridges when thunderstorms approach. Hikers and mountaineers time their outings to insure they are off high ridges and on their way down from summits by 1 p.m., after which time thunderstorms are more common. However, any time you see a thunderstorm approaching or hear a buzzing sound emanating from metallic objects or your hair, it is time to head down quickly.

What do you do if you are caught in a high place during a

thunderstorm? First, descend at least 100 m vertically from a summit or ridge crest. Then, avoid open meadows, lakes, glaciers and snow patches. Do not seek shelter under isolated rock pinnacles or trees. Crouch at the base of a cliff, or in a depression that does not have tall trees or large boulders nearby. Keep a metre away from the cliff or depression walls, since these channel the current of a local strike. The metallic objects you carry will not attract a lightning strike. However, they may cause burns if there is a strike within 30 m. Remove these items from your pack and pockets.

Tlhe Carthew-Alderson trail descends steeply from Carthew Lakes to Alderson Lake.

fine waterfall to your right. Rock-hop its stream. The adjacent meadows are decorated with colourful wildflowers. Continue the steep descent through a ragged krummholz forest and across scree slopes, with views of Alderson Lake ahead.

It is often said that there are no glaciers in Waterton in the present day. However, if you look carefully at the west shore of Alderson Lake, you will see a series of remnant glaciers that have pushed up terminal moraines. These moraines were probably formed during the Little Ice Age, which ended in the mid-1800s. Glaciers in other localities in the Rockies advanced as much as 3 km during the Little Ice Age, and they often extended beyond the cirques that housed them. Evidence shows that no glaciers in Waterton have advanced beyond their cirque basins in the last 10,000 years. The remnant glacial ice at Alderson Lake is sustained by snow avalanches from the 600 m high cliffs above. These cliffs are a good place to look for mountain goats.

The trail turns northeast above the north shore of Alderson Lake. The slopes below the trail are festooned with bear grass. You might expect that Carthew Creek, flowing through the meadows to the north of the trail, would empty into Alderson Lake. Alderson Lake has been impounded by a moraine, and the trail travels along the crest. This moraine diverts

Late-Lying Snow

The novelty of encountering snow patches in July and August lures many unwary hikers into trouble in places like the basin above Upper Carthew Lake. Because these snow patches have been through many freeze and thaw cycles since the previous winter, they contain a significant amount of ice. This ice sometimes appears snow-like, especially near the edges, where footing can be treacherous.

If you fall on the granular snow and ice, your skin may be cut badly. In addition, you may begin to slide downslope, out of control towards boulderfields. If nothing worse happens you will likely be soaked and cold afterwards. Unless you have an ice axe in hand, are competent at using it for self-arrest, and you are dressed appropriately, stay off late-lying snow! The reddish tinge in these snow patches is called watermelon snow and is caused by an alga with a red eye spot.

Carthew Creek away from the lakeshore.

With a maximum depth of 60 m, Alderson Lake is the deepest of Waterton's backcountry lakes. It has an area of 10.2 ha. The lake was probably the original "Bertha Lake." Its name was changed in 1915 to honour Lt. General E.A.H. Alderson, who commanded Canadian Forces in France during World War I.

At km 13.1 you reach the Alderson Lake junction. You have the option of staying overnight at the campground on the lakeshore. However, most people do not want to haul heavy packs over Carthew Summit to camp here, when Waterton Park townsite is only a few hours' hike away. The campground is 250 m east (right) of the junction. The campground shows excessive wear and tear from overuse and horse traffic, and it can be very buggy in midsummer.

Alderson Lake to Waterton Park Townsite

A few hundred metres beyond the campground junction is an alternate route to the campground. Keep left. The lush upper subalpine forest along Alderson Creek is similar to the one at the trailhead near Cameron Lake, except most of the trees are not as old. The trail crosses numerous avalanche paths that are excellent bear habitat. Make lots of noise here since visibility is limited. If you look up the valley from open slopes,

"This is what I have seen in my dreams, this is the country for me."
—Kootenai Brown, 1865

you can see the waterfall on the headwall below the Carthew Lakes. Rock-hop tributary streams as required.

The descent of this valley may seem interminable if you expended all your energy earlier in the day. However, it is hardly a "boring walk in the woods." The subtle transition in the forest is of great interest. As you lose elevation, notice the change from species of the damp subalpine forest to Douglas fir and lodgepole pine – dry montane forest species. About halfway along the valley, just to the north of the trail, is an incredibly large Engelmann spruce tree, 1.4 m in diameter at its base.

At long last, the trail switchbacks down and you can see Waterton Park townsite through open forest. The trail parallels a fence at the brink of Cameron Creek canyon. In the creek bed you can see structures built for flood control and the former water supply for the townsite. The temperamental creek has exhibited a 1000-fold increase in volume of flow between November and the following July. In June 1964, runoff from Cameron Creek and other tributaries raised the level of Upper Waterton Lake 2.8 m

above its previous record high, inundating Waterton Park townsite. The most recent serious flood was in 1995. Sediments deposited by Cameron Creek have built the alluvial fan on which the townsite is situated.

At an unmarked junction, turn sharply north (left), and descend into a poplar grove at trail's end – Cameron Falls. The 10 m high falls are being eroded into an outcrop of 1.5 billion-year-old Waterton limestone, the oldest rock formation visible in the Canadian Rockies.

Crypt Lake is concealed in a hanging valley atop a 175 m limestone cliff. The photograph was taken from the lake's south shore in Glacier National Park, Montana.

48. Crypt Lake

Route

Day-hike or overnight, 8.6 km

Route	Elevation (m)	Distance (km)
Crypt Landing	1279	0
Lower Hell Roaring Falls jct	1350	0.4
Upper Hell Roaring Falls jct	1500	3.0
Burnt Rock Falls	1600	5.6
Crypt Lake CG	1900	7.9
Crypt Lake Tunnel	1925	8.1
Crypt Lake	1945	8.7

Best lighting: late afternoon

Trailhead

Book round-trip passage on the shuttle boat from the marina at Emerald Bay in Waterton Park townsite (fee charged). There are two departures each morning, and two pick-ups each afternoon – check the times at the marina. The fifteen minute boat trip delivers you to the trailhead at Crypt Landing on the east shore of Upper Waterton Lake.

The Crypt Lake hike is unique in the Rockies. You begin by crossing Upper Waterton Lake by boat. Then you follow a steep trail from montane shoreline to timberline through a valley of picturesque waterfalls. The diversity of the approach culminates with a 25 m crawl through a limestone tunnel and an airy traverse on an imposing cliff. As if all this isn't exotic enough, you can follow a rough track around Crypt Lake and cross the international border into the US.

This hike cannot be done early in the season. The headwall below Crypt Lake must be free of snow. Also, do not undertake this outing if you fear heights or enclosed places. This is not a hike for those seeking solitude. In peak season, two shuttle boats may deposit more than 100 hikers at the trailhead within a few minutes. The trail passes through prime bear habitat. The valley of Hell Roaring Creek can be torrid in mid-summer, so carry lots of water. The trail is shared with horses as far as the campground.

Crypt Landing to Crypt Lake Camground

From Crypt Landing, head south and begin the switchback ascent toward the drainage of Hell Roaring Creek. The forest near the trailhead is extremely damp and diverse, with a mixture of montane and subalpine tree species: Douglas fir, white spruce, white birch, Douglas maple and subalpine fir. Note the large Douglas firs, with bark cloaked in tree lichens. You would not normally expect this damp a forest at low elevation in Waterton. However, the bay of Crypt Landing is sheltered from the ever-present winds that would otherwise dry the soils and foliage. Thimbleberry, false Solomon's seal, fairy bells, arnica, and western meadow rue dominate the undergrowth.

At km 0.4 you reach the lower Hell Roaring Falls junction. This sidetrip is best left until your return, when the falls and canyon may be sunlit. At approximately km 1.5, the main trail switchbacks across an open west-facing slope, surrounded by a more typical low-elevation Waterton forest – one dominated by

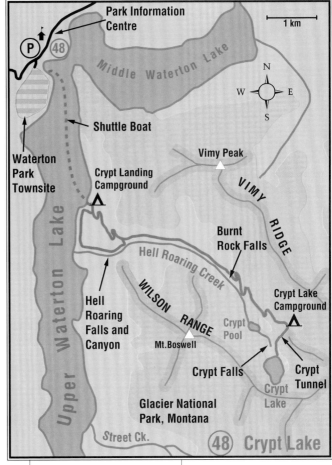

lodgepole pine with sun-loving flowers in the undergrowth. This slope provides open views of Upper Waterton Lake and the valley of Bertha Creek. Please do not shortcut the switchbacks.

The trail traverses southeast into the drainage of Hell Roaring Creek and contours above the creek through open pine forest. Buffaloberry is common here, and this southfacing slope is frequented by both black and grizzly bears. Use caution. "Hell Roaring" is a most appropriate name for

the turbulent creek. It is thought the name was connected with a mining claim in this area in the late 1800s. Keep straight ahead at the upper Hell Roaring Falls junction. The grade eases and the trail contours in and out of drainage gullies. Rock-hop as necessary. Across Hell Roaring Creek are Twin Falls, cascading from a hanging valley on the north slope of Mt. Boswell.

The trail swings southeast, following Hell Roaring Creek to its sources. You cross some avalanche slopes and pass through another pocket of damp subalpine forest. The shales underfoot have been washed down in flash floods from the mountainside to the east, creating an alluvial fan that has spread through the forest. When you reach the stream that has created the fan, you get your first view of Burnt Rock Falls.

Now the hard work begins. In the next 3 km the trail climbs approximately 300 m and is often rocky. As you switchback away from the creek, you get several close views of Burnt Rock Falls. The red or "burnt" rock at the base of the falls is iron-rich Grinnell argillite. Above it is older pale Altyn limestone. Why is older rock above younger rock? The two formations are

separated by the Mt. Crandell Thrust Fault. During mountain building, the bedrock underlying this area fractured, and the Altyn Formation slid upwards and northeastwards over younger layers along the fault. Note the massive hollow eroded into the weak Grinnell Formation at the base of the falls. The Altyn Formation resists the flow of water and endures as the brink of the waterfall.

As you draw equal with Burnt Rock Falls, use care as you rock-hop the tributary stream that crosses the trail on a bare rock slab. Now Crypt Falls comes into view, tumbling 175 m down the Crypt Lake headwall. Beneath the falls is a shallow lake known as Crypt Pool. The remainder of

the steep climb to Crypt Lake campground is across avalanche gullies. At trailside are bear grass and krummholz balsam poplar trees, an unusual form for this species.

At time of publication, Crypt Lake campground was in poor repair and scheduled for re-design. All of the backcountry campgrounds in Waterton Lakes National Park can be reached in less than a day from the closest trailhead. Some, like this one, can be reached in a few hours. Thus, many who use these campgrounds are not familiar with backcountry travel and the techniques and necessity of no-trace travel and camping. After decades of such use, the campgrounds are unappealing.

The Waterton Lakes – Big Water

With a maximum depth of 157 m, Upper Waterton Lake is the deepest lake in the Canadian Rockies. It is 11.1 km long, has an area of 941 ha, and is by far the largest of Waterton's 80 lakes and ponds. It holds approximately 645 million cubic metres of water. The southern reach of the lake extends 4 km into Glacier National Park, Montana.

There are 17 native species of fish in Waterton Lakes National Park and eight introduced species. Fish were important to Natives in Waterton. A Native fishing camp was located on the west shore of The Bosporous between Upper and Middle Waterton Lakes. Evidence indicates that it, and other camps nearby, were in use for 8000 years. The

largest fish on record in the park was a 23.2 kg lake trout caught in Upper Waterton Lake in July 1920. Reports from the early 1900s describe individuals taking 500 fish from Upper Waterton Lake in a day. Principally as a result of overfishing, fish are not as numerous today.

Blackfeet Natives knew the Waterton Lakes by several names, one of which meant "big water." Thomas Blakiston of the Palliser Expedition named the lakes in 1858, to commemorate Charles Waterton, an eccentric British naturalist who roamed South America and the Caribbean between 1812 and 1829. Charles Waterton is best known for introducing curare (cure-RAH-ree) to western medicine and for establishing the

world's first bird sanctuary at his home in England. It housed more than 800 species. He never visited the lakes. Blakiston, only 25 at the time he saw the lakes, was a budding naturalist, and evidently thought highly of Charles Waterton.

In the late 19th century the lakes were known locally as the "Kootenai Lakes," after the Kutenai Natives. Kootenai Brown, Waterton's most famous resident, settled on the shore of Lower Waterton Lake in 1878. Kootenai Brown promoted the establishment of a national park at Waterton. He became the first warden when the reserve was established in 1895, and later he became its superintendent.

Looking north from the top of the Crypt Lake headwall to Crypt Pool and the valley of Hell Roaring Creek. In the distance is Vimy Peak.

Crypt Lake Campground to Crypt Lake

Rock-hop or ford (straightforward) the creek immediately south of the campground, and follow the trail that angles southwest through the boulderfield. You may hear the shrill whistle of hoary marmots here, and with luck see these large rodents, the self-appointed guardians of the Crypt Tunnel.

Near the eastern portal of the tunnel is a sign that warns you to stay on the trail – as if you have much choice here! The Crypt Tunnel is a natural, waterworn fissure that extends 25 m laterally through the limestone of the Crypt Lake headwall. The tunnel has

Windy Waterton

More often than not, it is windy on Upper Waterton Lake. The average daily wind speed at Waterton Park townsite is 32.5 km per hour, and gusts of 180 km per hour have been recorded in winter. At such times, spray from the lake collects on the windows of the Prince of Wales Hotel 150 m away and 40 m above the lakeshore. Many of the windy days in winter and spring are caused by chinooks (shih-NOOKS). A chinook occurs when a Pacific storm system sheds its moisture on the western slopes of the Rockies. The air is forced high to clear the crest of the range. As the dry air sweeps down the eastern slopes and its pressure increases, the temperature rises 1.5°C for each decrease in elevation of 100 m.

Chinook is a Native word that means "snow eater." In nearby Pincher Creek, the warm winds once raised the temperature 21°C in four minutes. Chinooks keep the mountain front snow-free for much of the winter, creating ideal winter habitat for elk, deer, sheep and goats, who require accessible grasses and browse. The winds also prevent the formation of ice on the Waterton Lakes in some years.

Sinks and Solutions

Crypt Lake is impounded by a series of glaciated bluffs, called *riegels*. Limestone in the area is readily eroded by naturally acidic rainwater in a process called *solution*. The rock at trailside just before the lake contains *rillenkarren*, miniature grooves eroded into its surface. Over time, cracks in the surface of limestone bedrock are deepened by rain and meltwater into fissures. The fissures connect into systems that create underground drainage channels called *karst*. Crypt Lake has no surface outlet, and drains through a karst system. It is known as a *sink lake*.

Access to the eastern entrance of the Crypt Tunnel is by a metal ladder. Beyond the tunnel, the trail traverses an exposed cliff.

been slightly enlarged to ease passage. Gain the eastern portal by climbing a 2 m high metal ladder. The tunnel narrows and angles down toward the west. Then, at its narrowest point, you will be obliged to crawl on your hands and knees. Two cautions: watch for ice on the tunnel floor, and do not enter the tunnel wearing a bulky pack – particularly one with an external frame. If your pack gets caught, take it off and push it ahead of you. Exit the western portal over an awkward 1.3 m rock step.

The section just beyond the western portal of the Crypt Tunnel gives this hike its notorious reputation. For 50 m, you traverse and ascend an exposed cliff, which may intimidate those afraid of heights. A steel cable has been installed here. Use it as a handrail. Another caution: take care not to bump your pack against the cable or its anchor posts, especially during descent. This could throw you off balance.

The airy traverse beyond the tunnel delivers you to the crest of the Crypt Lake headwall. North along Hell Roaring Creek are Vimy Ridge and Vimy Peak (2379 m), named for the ridge in France taken by Canadian forces in World War I. The forest on the headwall is distinctly upper subalpine, and tufts of pink mountain heather grace the clearings.

The final section of trail traverses beneath a low limestone bluff. At an unmarked junction, you may follow a sidetrail west to the underground outflow of the lake and the brink of Crypt Falls. Use caution. The main trail angles south from the junction, ascending an old watercourse that may have been Crypt Lake's outlet before the karst system developed. Descend gradually to the north shore of Crypt Lake.

Crypt Lake

Crypt Lake has an area of 13.5 ha and a maximum depth of 44 m. It occupies a cirque eroded into shales of the Greyson Formation, (formerly called the Appekunny Formation).

The word "crypt" is derived from the Greek *kryptos,* which means "hidden." With its difficult approach, the lake is indeed hidden in its high cirque. The outlet stream is also hidden within the bedrock. The lake is ringed by cliffs and summits of the Wilson Range, including Mount Boswell (2439 m) on the west. W.G. Boswell was a veterinary surgeon with the British Boundary Commission of 1872-1876. The name was officially applied in 1917. Before that time, the mountain had been called Street Mountain, after Jack Street, a Mountie who died in an avalanche on its slopes. The cliffs of Mount Boswell are a good place to look for mountain goats.

A rough track leads around Crypt Lake, although during times of high runoff some of the route will be underwater. At its most southerly point, this track takes you into Glacier National Park in the US. A portion of the circuit crosses the rubble-covered surface of a remnant glacier at the water's edge. It should be crossed with great care.

The southeast shore of the lake contains an ancient alluvial fan, now partially vegetated. Atop this, is a fan of more recent origin that contains material eroded and transported by water and avalanches from a gully in the cliffs above. The east shore of the lake is bordered by a subalpine meadowland through which cascades a pretty stream

The "undefended border" at the south end of Crypt Lake typifies the spirit of the Water-

ton/Glacier International Peace Park. Established in 1932 as a gesture of friendship between Canada and the United States, the two existing national parks were combined into the world's first peace park. Today, the two parks work together on resource conservation issues. It is particularly fortunate that this spirit of cooperation was forged so early, for protection of Waterton/Glacier is vital to the integrity of the greater Crown of the Continent Ecosystem.

On a pleasant day, and after the exertions of the approach, you will be tempted to wile away the hours at Crypt Lake. However, be sure to leave yourself enough time to catch your return boat from Crypt Landing – 2.5 to 3 hours is recommended.

Hell Roaring Falls

On the way back to the trailhead you may visit Hell Roaring Falls and Canyon. From the upper junction approximately 3 km from Crypt Landing, take the left-hand trail. This descends steeply to the canyon and falls, which have been eroded through colourful vertically tilted rock. Bears are frequently seen in this vicinity.

As it angles away from the canyon, the trail offers a view over the alluvial fan at the mouth of Hell Roaring Creek. The trail then contours above the lakeshore through lodgepole pine and Douglas fir for 1 km, before joining the Crypt Lake trail, 400 m from the trailhead. This sidetrail will add about 500 m to the overall length of the outing.

Mt. Blakiston rises above the Lineham Lakes in the view north from Lineham Ridge Summit, the apex of the Tamarack Trail.

49. Tamarack Trail

Route

3 days, 36.1 km

Route	Elevation (m)	Distance (km)
Trailhead	1600	0
Lower Rowe Lake jct	1940	3.9
Rowe Meadow	2010	5.2
Upper Rowe Lakes jct	2015	5.5
Lineham Ridge Summit	2560	8.5
South fork of Blakiston Ck	1870	13.6
Lone Lake Summit	2250	15.7
Lone Lake and CG	1990	17.7
South Kootenay Pass jct	1940	21.5
Blakiston Creek jct	1935	21.6
Twin Lake Summit	2150	23.5
Upper Twin Lake and CG	1970	24.7
Sage Pass jct	1970	24.9
Snowshoe CG	1740	27.9
Red Rock Canyon	1495	36.1

Trailhead

Follow the Akamina Parkway for 10.5 km from Waterton Park townsite to the Rowe-Tamarack trailhead.

Although not as strenuous an outing as The Rockwall Trail in Kootenay National Park, the Tamarack Trail is cut from the same undulating cloth. This energetic excursion parallels the eastern slope of the continental divide, traverses the heads of three valleys, and crosses a mountain ridgecrest that provides a panoramic vista of the southern Rockies. It travels through excellent habitat for mountain goats, bighorn sheep, mule deer, cougar and grizzly bears. The two campgrounds are located at back-country lakes, and sidetrails lead to other lakes. The Tamarack Trail is shared with horses. Lineham Ridge, the apex of the trail, is the fourth highest point crossed by maintained trail in the Rockies. Do not un-

dertake this hike until the snow cover melts: mid-July in most years.

The park closed the Rowe Meadow campground in 1993, necessitating a difficult 17.7 km day at the beginning of this outing. Upper Rowe

Lakes is described here as a sidetrip from the Tamarack Trail. However, closure of Rowe Meadow campground makes this impractical since there is now no safe place to cache your packs. Since the Upper Rowe Lakes are one of

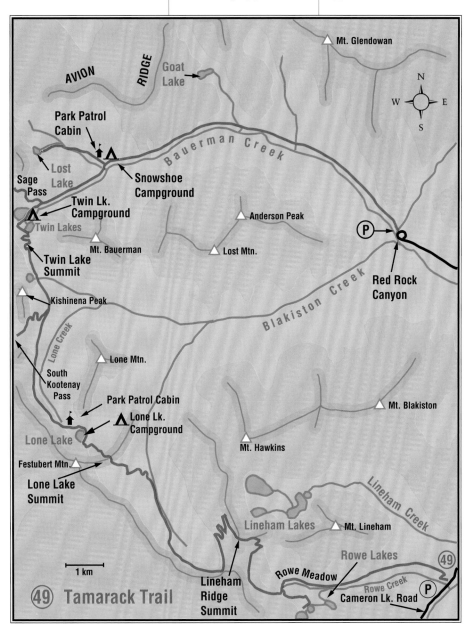

Mt. Glendowan

AVION RIDGE

Goat Lake

N
W E
S

Park Patrol Cabin

Bauerman Creek

Lost Lake
Sage Pass

Snowshoe Campground

Twin Lk. Campground

Twin Lakes

Anderson Peak

Mt. Bauerman

Lost Mtn.

Twin Lake Summit

Kishinena Peak

Blakiston Creek

P

Red Rock Canyon

Lone Creek

Lone Mtn.

South Kootenay Pass

Park Patrol Cabin

Lone Lk. Campground

Mt. Blakiston

Lone Lake

Festubert Mtn.

Mt. Hawkins

Lone Lake Summit

Lineham Lakes

Mt. Lineham

Lineham Creek

Rowe Lakes

49

1 km

49 Tamarack Trail

Lineham Ridge Summit

Rowe Meadow

Rowe Creek

Cameron Lk. Road

P

Cougar tracks

the scenic highlights of Waterton, you may want to visit them as a separate day-hike from the Akamina Parkway.

Trailhead to Upper Rowe Lake Junction

The trail begins on the alluvial fan that Rowe Creek has built at its confluence with Cameron Creek. The broad path leads uphill into a doghair pine forest. At the prominent corner at 0.3 km, you can see where Rowe Creek is eroding into red mudstone – argillite of the Grinnell Formation. The trail climbs away from the creek onto a dry open slope, where the wildflowers stonecrop, yarrow, umbrella plant, yellow beardtongue, low larkspur and pearly everlasting grow. You then pass through an older subalpine forest. In the undergrowth are bear grass, thimbleberry, cow parsnip, queen's cup, and the delicate mariposa lily.

At approximately km 2.4, the trail emerges from forest onto avalanche slopes beneath the cliffs of Mt. Lineham. These slopes provide excellent food sources for bears and Waterton's numerous mule deer. Views back down the valley include Buchanan Ridge (2400 m) and Mt. Crandell (2378 m).

At km 3.9, the sidetrail to Lower Rowe Lake branches south (left). It is 300 m to the lake's outlet. Walled by the east ridge of Mt. Rowe, and dammed by a rockslide, the lake beckons as a rest stop.

The inlet stream is a waterfall that drains the Upper Rowe Lakes, situated in the hanging valley above. The talus slopes to the west are frequented by hoary marmots and pika. A cougar was seen here in 1993.

Beyond this junction, the trail re-enters forest and crosses Rowe Creek several times en route to Rowe Meadow at km 5.2. The meadow is surrounded by the amphitheatre-like cliffs that connect Mt. Rowe to the south with outliers of Mt. Lineham to the north. The meadow is home to a boisterous colony of Columbian ground squirrels and swarms of horse flies. The campground was closed in order to rehabilitate the meadow and because of frequent interactions between bears and campers. Do not camp here unless the facility is reopened. The trail leads southwest across Rowe Meadow to a bridge over Rowe Creek. The Upper Rowe Lakes junction is 20 m south of the bridge.

Upper Rowe Lakes Junction to Lone Lake

Rowe Meadow marks the end of easy hiking for the next day and a half on the Tamarack Trail. There are no water sources in the next 8 km. Insure your water bottles are full. Turn west (right) at the Upper Rowe Lakes junction, and begin a tortuously steep climb for 500 m onto a bench beneath the cliffs of the continental divide. The cliffs contain the two elements of the Siyeh Formation. The lower, more weathered part of the cliff is siltstone and sandstone. The upper, more blocky part is limestone and dolomite. Geologists in the US have subdivided the Siyeh accordingly, calling the lower part the Empire Formation, and the upper part the Helena Formation. The Purcell Lava Sill, an injection of igneous rock, occurs in the Helena Formation as a thin, dark green or black layer. The Siyeh Formation is the backbone of the continental divide in Waterton, and it flanks the Tamarack Trail between here and Twin Lakes. The formation takes its name from *saiyi,* a Blackfoot Native word that means "mad" or "rabid."

The grade moderates and the trail undulates needlessly through some depressions. Blazed as a horse route, the Tamarack Trail makes many such superfluous climbs and descents in the next 20 km. The hard work created for hikers would be unnoticed by someone on horseback, although probably not by the horse! There are fine examples of ripple rock at trailside. The pockets of avalanche meadow contain glacier lilies and western anemone. From treeline, the trail begins a sweeping rise towards the west ridge of Mount Lineham, on a path beaten into red screes of the

Kintla Formation. Use caution if you must cross late-lying snow patches. Scan the slopes above for bighorn sheep.

As you gain elevation, views open to the south, including Mt. Custer (2708 m) and Chapman Peak (2867 m) south of Cameron Lake; and Mt. Cleveland (3190 m), the highest mountain in Glacier National Park. Soon, the three Rowe Lakes are visible, along with the spectacular peaks in western Glacier. Treeline is high on the northern slopes of Rowe basin, and the trail skirts a krummholz forest that features lifeless, silvery spars of wind-blasted, sun-bleached whitebark pine. Centuries old, these skeleton trees serve an important purpose. They anchor the screes, stabilizing thin soils and allowing other vegetation to take root.

Follow the painted orange markers as the trail switchbacks westward to Lineham Ridge Summit – the apex of the Tamarack Trail in both elevation and views. A remarkable 360° panorama takes in most of Waterton and Glacier national parks, BC's Akamina-Kishinena Recreation Area, and the Rockies north to Crowsnest Pass. The Lineham Lakes lie nestled in the basin directly northeast. The lakes are known individually as: Water Cudgel, Hourglass, Ptarmigan, Channel and Larch. John Lineham was an Alberta businessman of the 1880s with interests in oil, lumber and ranching. Mt. Blakiston (2920 m), highest in Waterton, rises northeast of Lineham Basin.

After traversing north for 1 km, the trail switchbacks to the south and begins a mercilessly steep descent on scree into the south fork valley of Blakiston Creek. Follow the orange trail markers. The pale mauve blooms of sky pilot dot the slopes. The grade moderates when you reach the larch forest in the valley bottom. The trail then curves northwest and parallels the continental divide, heading north towards Lone Lake Summit.

Upper Rowe Lakes (2168 m), 1.2 km

Keep straight ahead at the junction on the south side of Rowe Meadow. The trail switchbacks on an open slope and then ascends eastward into a treeline forest of Lyall's larch. After rounding the spur on the northern flank of the valley that harbors the Upper Rowe Lakes, the trail descends to the southwest and delivers you to the shore of the upper lake. Its east shore features a thick krummholz forest that includes Lyall's larch. Krummholz means "crooked wood" in German. Another translation sometimes given is "elfin timber." These

Upper Rowe Lake

gnarled and ragged trees do suggest a fairy-tale forest.

As with most of Waterton's backcountry lakes, the two Upper Rowe Lakes are situated in a cirque at the head of a hanging valley, and they occupy hollows scooped from the bedrock by a glacier. Although glacial ice is no longer present, perennial snow drifts cling to shady recesses along the south shores of the lakes. The lakes are separated by a natural dam of resistant rock and are connected by waterfalls. The outflow of the smaller lake cascades more than 150 m to Lower Rowe Lake. The abundance of larch trees and bear grass, and the opportunity to see bighorn sheep and mountain goats add to the charm of this destination.

For the most part, it is pleasant hiking through upper subalpine woods, with a few chronic muddy spots. You will appreciate the shade of the cliff on a hot day, and the fact your toes are no longer being jammed into the front of your boots! Springs issue from the cliffs and may offer water. Soak your hat here if you need help to cool off.

The next climb is the most trying of this long first day, especially if you have expended your reserves crossing Lineham Ridge Summit. The trail climbs 380 m in 2.1 km. This hard work would be more tolerable if the trail didn't ramble and undulate so much during its interminable climb, adding many needless metres of elevation. Your first steady descent is *not* to Lone Lake campground. There is still much uphill to come. Rock-hop streams as required. A section of trail is routed directly along a rocky, seasonal stream course. It will be a torrent during heavy rains.

From Lone Lake Summit on the east ridge of Festubert Mountain (2520 m), the near-by campground at Lone Lake beckons. The mountain commemorates a village in France where Canadian troops fought

Bighorn Sheep

Rowe Basin is one of the best places to see bighorn sheep in the backcountry of the Rockies. A sheep's coat is tawny brown with a white rump patch and a dark brown tail. The bighorn ram stands approximately a metre tall at the shoulder. And when mature it has a set of thick brown horns that spiral forward. These horns are never shed. Together with the skull, they can account for 13 percent of the animal's 125 kg weight. It is possible to determine the approximate age of a ram by counting the annuli, or rings, on one of its horns. Each annulus contains a dark and light band, together representing one year of growth. The female sheep (ewe) grows horns too. These are less spectacular and curve backwards.

The rams flock together in high places during summer and early autumn. The dominant ram must constantly defend his place. Usually, this is done without battle in what is called the "present" (pree-ZENT) – when two rams turn their heads sideways, to allow each to inspect the horns of the other. As the autumn rut approaches and the issue of who will breed with a harem of ewes becomes more crucial, diplomacy wanes. The rams duel, charging head-long at each other and meeting with a mighty crash. Thick armour bones beneath the horns usually prevent serious injury. However, duels to the death take place.

Grasses are the most important foods for bighorn sheep. The animal cannot tolerate snow depths of more than 0.3 metres. Deep snow limits its travel and access to food. Hence, wind-scoured slopes in the front ranges offer the best winter habitat for bighorns. A 1986 estimate for Waterton yielded 129 sheep, down from a previous high of 315 in 1982. The die-off was caused by parasites and hard winters. Grizzly bears, wolves and cougars are the animal's principal predators. They often achieve success by forcing sheep to run over a cliff. Poaching along the western boundary of Waterton also takes a toll on these animals.

Bighorn sheep are generally accustomed to humans and will often allow us to approach closely. This puts both humans and sheep in peril. With their horns and sharp hooves, sheep are capable of inflicting serious injury. Accustomed to nutrition-poor handouts from people, sheep may not be able to endure a hard winter. If a sheep approaches you, scare it away.

in World War I. The view northeast features the whaleback scree peaks of northern Waterton.

You will probably cross a snow patch as you leave Lone Lake Summit. The descent north switchbacks through a remarkable Lyall's larch forest. It is not often you see this tree species in such a uniformly aged and widely spaced stand. Lyall's larch grows at high elevation on rocky soils, and consequently is seldom consumed by fire. Several of the trees here are more than a metre in diameter at their bases, indicating ages of 300 years or more.

The descent ends at an avalanche path that contains a conical mound of landslide debris. As you gain the southeast shore of Lone Lake, pause to admire the view northeast over the U-shaped valley of Blakiston Creek. Rock-hop the outlet of the lake, and follow the trail along the cliff edge,

north to the campground.

Lone Lake is 13 m deep and has an area of 2.5 ha. Glaciologists speculate that it once drained entirely north into Lone Creek. A moraine subsequently blocked the drainage, forcing most of the outflow to spill northeast over the cliff into the upper reaches of Blakiston Creek. As with all Waterton's backcountry campgrounds, the one at Lone Lake has suffered greatly from abuse and overuse. Please do your part to minimize impacts. And don't forget your insect repellent. This is one of the buggiest spots in the Rockies. A park patrol cabin is on the lake's northeast shore.

Lone Lake to Twin Lake

After the rigors of the first day, your second day on the Tamarack Trail brings two options, both of which are much less energetic. You can hike to

Twin Lake campground in 7 km, or Snowshoe campground in 10.2 km. Short sidetrails to South Kootenay Pass and Sage Pass can be added to your itinerary.

The trail north from Lone Lake alternates between delightful upper subalpine meadows and ancient forest as it descends gradually to the Blakiston Creek junction. This is excellent habitat for grizzly bears. You cross two wet meadows from which you can study the cliffs of the Siyeh Formation, immediately west.

Fifty metres north of the South Kootenay Pass junction is the Blakiston Creek junction. You may exit the Tamarack Trail at this point, by turning east (right), and following this trail 10.1 km to Red Rock Canyon. Otherwise, keep straight ahead.

Hop the outlet stream of the pond in Blue Grouse Basin. From appearances, the pond formerly occupied a much larger area. Now it is gradually being filled with vegetation. The blue grouse is one of six grouse species in the Rockies, and prefers upper subalpine habitats like this one, where it feeds on berries and insects. The cliffs of Kishinena Peak (2450 m) are to the west. The mountain's name is probably a Kutenai word that means "balsam fir" or "white fir."

After the tiring climbs on day one, you will hardly notice the modest ascent to Twin Lake Summit. From the crest of the climb, you get glimpses through the larch forest of the Twin Lakes to the north. After

Tamaracks or Larches?

The name "tamarack" is commonly applied throughout North America to three species of coniferous trees that shed their needles annually: tamarack, Lyall's larch and western larch. The tamarack is the most common of these three trees in Canada and is found in every province and territory. However, it is not widespread in the Rockies, occurring only in low-elevation wetlands on the eastern slopes north of the North Saskatchewan River. The western larch is found principally in southeastern British Columbia, with a few stands in southwestern Alberta.

The deciduous conifers along the Tamarack Trail are not tamaracks, they are Lyall's larches. This tree species often forms treeline forests, but does not occur north of Clearwater Pass in Banff National Park. The tree was catalogued by Eugene Bourgeau, and named for David Lyall, a naturalist and surgeon with the British Boundary Commission of 1872-1876.

South Kootenay Pass (2160 m), 1.7 km

The South Kootenay Pass trail was part of a historic route used by Kutenai Natives and the first white explorers in this region. Known as the Buffalo Trail, this route connected Kutenai territory west of the continental divide with seasonal hunting and fishing grounds on the prairies. The Kutenai had been displaced to the western side of the divide by hostile Stoneys and tribes of the Blackfoot Confederacy in the early 1700s. South Kootenay Pass maintained the Kutenais' access to bison, the animal on which their culture was based. They used the trail until bison were eliminated from the wild in the 1880s.

The Kutenai traded with the Salish, Nez Percé and Flathead peoples west of the continental divide, from whom they obtained obsidian for making arrowheads and tools. This material has been found at some of the more than 200 Native archeological sites in Waterton. The Buffalo Trail followed Blakiston Creek to Lower Waterton Lake. Fifty-six of the park's archeological sites are in the Blakiston Valley. The ruts made by travois – sleds that were pulled by dogs, and later horses – are found on the Blakiston Creek alluvial fan. Evidence of five Native camps, along with scattered artifacts and rock cairns has been found on South Kootenay Pass.

Two fur-trade scouts may have crossed the pass in the early 1800s. The first undisputed crossing of the pass by Europeans was from west to east in 1858, by a group led by Thomas

Cliffs of the Siyeh Formation parallel much of the Tamarack Trail and form both the continental divide and the western boundary of Waterton Lakes National Park. You can see the two elements of the Siyeh Formation clearly in this photograph: the greenish Empire Formation below, and the grey Helena Formation above.

Blakiston, an officer of the Palliser Expedition. Blakiston applied the name Pass Creek to the stream now known as Blakiston Creek. It is not likely that today's trail to the pass follows the precise route of The Buffalo Trail. In places you can see where a much older, windfallen trail cuts across, taking a steeper grade to the pass. Ancient trees in the area carry blazes

that mark the original route.

For all its history, South Kootenay Pass is not particularly scenic. The sparsely forested saddle offers limited views west into the logged Akamina-Kishinena Recreation Area, and east over Lone and Blakiston creeks. You will be obliged to carry your packs on this sidetrip, since there is no safe place to cache them.

Lost Lake (1875 m), 1.9 km

Head north from Snowshoe campground. At the junction in 0.9 km turn northwest (left). The trail ascends gradually through a damp forest to the lush shore of jade-coloured Lost Lake. Cow parsnip and bear grass grow in abundance along the trail and at the lake. The lake is backed by steep avalanche slopes that are excellent bear habitat. Travel accordingly.

Lost Lake was stocked with fish in the past, but avalanche deposits in the lake have killed them. These events underscore the fact that some lakes in the Rockies are naturally barren, and they highlight the inappropriateness of introducing fish species where they don't belong. The ecology of most lakes in the Rockies has been altered by stocking to promote sport angling. It is only recently that national parks policy has been revised to suspend this practice.

a steep descent, the trail contours across a scree slope at the head of the cirque that contains Lower Twin Lake. The campground at Upper Twin Lake is 200 m straight ahead from the next junction. The 300 m sidetrail to the east (right) leads to the lower lake.

Given the pleasing scenery in this area, the campground at Upper Twin Lake is a disappointment. It is set amid seeps and is out of view of the lake. However, it does make a good base for exploring Sage Pass.

Twin Lake to Red Rock Canyon

Hop the outlet stream of Upper Twin Lake. The trail turns east and begins a steady descent along upper Bauerman Creek, named for H.B. Bauerman, a geologist with the British Boundary Commission. After about 1.5 km the trail draws alongside the creek. The meadow here contains many wildflowers and shrubs typical of the montane ecoregion – a strip of prairie in the heart of a subalpine valley.

You cross Bauerman Creek

The Crown of the Continent

The phrase "Crown of the Continent" was first coined by George Bird Grinnell. Grinnell was a conservationist and the strongest proponent of the establishment of Glacier National Park in the US, which was achieved in 1910. He later founded the Audubon Society.

Grinnell envisioned a series of protected areas that would preserve the backbone of the southern Rockies. Today, environmentalists still push for recognition and protection of the

Crown of the Continent Ecosystem – extending from central Montana to Crowsnest Pass. In the face of the habitat disruption and fragmentation that has accompanied ranching, logging, mining and petroleum drilling, protection of this ecosystem has become as crucial as it is elusive. It is now recognized that if wide-ranging carnivores and unique natural processes are to survive in the southern Rockies and elsewhere, existing national parks must be connected with other reserves; to offer more than small pockets of protected habitat. So far, the political will to protect the Crown is lacking, and the diminishment of its integrity continues.

Sage Pass (2131 m), 1.4 km

Head north from Upper Twin Lake campground and hop the outlet stream of Upper Twin Lake. The trail turns east. In 100 m, the Sage Pass trail branches north (left) and climbs steadily to the treed pass. Sagebrush is a shrub of the montane ecoregion and is common just across the pass, in southeastern BC.

to the Snowshoe campground and patrol cabin 3.2 km after leaving Upper Twin Lake. From here it is an easy 8.2 km walk along the undulating fireroad to Red Rock Canyon. The fireroad is shared with mountain bikers. You pass the sidetrail to Goat Lake en route. The steep hike to the lake is not recommended to those with heavy packs unless you plan to spend the night there.

Some of the rocks along the fireroad feature star-shaped crystals of feldspar. Isolated large crystals in a fine-grained igneous rock are called phenocrysts. As you approach Red Rock Canyon, note the change in the character of the forest. Balsam poplar becomes common, and the rustle of its leaves on the ever-present wind heralds your arrival at trail's end.

Red Rock Canyon is 23 m deep and is being eroded into red and green argillite of the Grinnell Formation. The red rock contains the mineral hematite. The circuit of the canyon is only 700 m, and is highly recommended.

"*Far away in northwestern Montana, hidden from view by clustering mountain-peaks, lies an unnamed corner – the Crown of the Continent. The water from the crusted snowdrift which caps the peak of a lofty mountain there trickles into tiny rills, which hurry along north, south, east and west, and growing into three rivers, at last pour their contents into three seas. From this mountain-peak the Pacific and the Arctic Oceans and the Gulf of Mexico each receive its tribute.*"

—G.B. Grinnell,
The Crown of the Continent,
Century Magazine,
September. 1901

The Other Side of the Divide

If you ascend to Sage Pass, you may be shocked at the view northwest over the upper reaches of Sage Creek. Logging roads and clearcuts scar the landscape. How can this be – so close to a national park?

The landscape west of Waterton is in BC, and the desires of the forest industry dictate most of the land-use in that province. Despite the negative effects on adjacent protected parks and reserves, and the ease of access that new logging roads offer to formerly remote areas, BC's Ministry of Forests routinely allows clearcuts in the headwaters of remote drainages like Sage Creek. North of Waterton, the same holds true on Alberta's forestry lands.

We should be thankful that the Rocky Mountain national parks were established with such foresight. We must now each do our part to limit use, and eliminate waste, of wood and paper products; thereby slowing the consumption of remaining boreal forests. See Issues and Contacts in the Reference section.

General Information

Hiking boots are your most important backpacking equipment. Things to consider when choosing boots are: use, durability, cost, and any chronic foot, ankle or knee complaints you may have.

Leather Boots

If you intend to backpack frequently, and care to treat your feet with the respect they deserve, leather boots with a Vibram sole are the best choice. You can also purchase orthotic inserts to correct for chronic problems in the lower leg and back. Although expensive, orthotics decrease the chance of incurring tendonitis and other injuries resulting from the pounding your feet, ankles and knees take while carrying a pack on the trail. The orthotic technician may also recommend specific exercises and stretches to help correct problems with gait and foot strike. Invest 5 to 10 minutes at the trailhead doing these exercises before each hike.

Take your hiking socks and orthotics with you when you try on the boots in the store. There should be enough room at the rear of the boot for you to slip your index finger between the boot cuff and your achilles tendon. Insure your toes do not feel crowded, especially while walking down a flight of stairs or a ramp. Bring a loaded backpack with you to see how the boots feel when you are carrying weight. Spend a half hour in the pair of boots that feel the best, to be sure you (and your feet) like them. It is a good idea to break the boots in – around the house, or on short walks – before using them for an extended trip.

Lightweight Boots

Lightweight hiking boots are those with canvas or synthetic uppers. They have captured a large share of the footwear market. As a result it is now often difficult to find a good pair of sturdy leather boots. Lightweight boots are well suited to day-hikes on well-maintained trails. They have three advantages: they cost less than good leather boots; they cause less damage to trails; and they require less energy. (Every kilogram carried on your feet is equivalent to six carried on your back.) However, for backpacking, lightweight boots have drawbacks:

- They are less durable than leather boots and cannot be resoled.
- They are not waterproof. You are thus more likely to step off the trail to avoid wet spots or snow patches, causing more damage off-trail than heavier boots cause on-trail.
- They cannot be effectively edged into the surface when descending steep or slippery trails, scree or snow slopes.
- They do not offer much ankle or arch support, especially to those with chronic foot problems.
- They are not as warm as leather boots, wet or dry.

Boot Care

Treat leather boots to enhance their ability to repel water. There are a number of synthetic and natural compounds available. Apply these to clean and dry boots only, three or four times a season. Remember, even properly treated boots will eventually soak through, given enough exposure to moisture. To help dry a pair of waterlogged boots, stuff them with newspaper; changing the newspaper as it becomes wet. Do not attempt to dry boots with direct heat or in an oven. A pair of soggy boots will often dry out on their own during a sunny day on the trail. Leather boots can be cleaned with a stiff brush and warm water. If you can afford two pairs of boots, use them on alternate days or trips. This will allow each pair to dry out between use, and will prolong the life of the stitching. Do not glue or seal the stitching, since this prevents the boot from breathing.

If you plan to store your boots for a long period of time, the leather will be less likely to dry out if they are treated first. When stored, insure the boots maintain their proper shape. Check them before storing to see if they require resoling, new laces, or stitching in the uppers. Plan these repairs during the off-season.

Socks

Wool or wool blend socks are the warmest and most durable choice for outer socks. Calf-length socks are suitable most of the time. Carry two pairs and wear them on alternate days, or exchange them as they become wet. Thin polypropylene or nylon inner socks help reduce the chance of developing blisters, and also help wick moisture away from your feet into the outer sock. A knee-length pair of socks will make camp life more comfortable early and late in the season.

Gaiters

You should always carry a pair of gaiters. They should cover the lower leg from the boot laces to just below the knee. To prevent the gaiters from riding too high at the heel, they should have a tie, strap or cable which passes under the sole of the boot.

Gaiters are useful on rainy and snowy days, and on muddy trails. They also keep débris out of your boots when descending scree and snow slopes, and they help keep feet and legs warm on cold, windy days. You can tie wet gaiters to the outside of your pack to dry as you hike.

Advice for the Blister Prone

A blister is a localized inflammation of the skin, caused by friction. Blisters contain plasma leaked from the affected tissue and can be painful. They may also become infected.

With some backpackers, they are a chronic condition. The cause of blisters is almost always poorly fitted boots, or boots that fail to provide enough arch support.

No amount of socks stuffed into boots which are too large will entirely cure a blister condition. If you have a pair of boots which do not fit properly, and wish to enjoy pain-free hiking, all you can do is purchase another pair that do fit.

With a correctly sized pair of boots on your feet, there is a simple technique to reduce the likelihood of blisters: wear a thin inner sock, and a thicker outer sock. Much of the friction that could create blisters now takes place between the inner and outer socks. Also, try wearing the inner socks inside out. This places smoother material against your skin. If your boots are too tight across the toes, skip the front lacing lugs to reduce tightness in that area.

Apply a blister dressing, such as Moleskin, immediately when you detect a "hot spot" on your feet. Prompt action may help prevent many kilometres of misery. Do not "burst" blisters while out on the trail, since infection may result.

Tips for Foot Comfort

There are two strategies to consider when fording streams. If you leave your boots on when the water is deeper than your boot tops, you will avoid the possibility of cutting your feet on the rocks.

You will also be more sure-footed when your feet are numbed by the cold water. However, if you take your boots off when fording streams, you will avoid walking in wet boots – wet boots or wet socks can cause blisters. The best solution for fording streams, if you can afford the extra weight, is to carry a light pair of sneakers, thongs or "river shoes".

It is often not possible to see bottom in glacial meltwater, and your feet can be cut badly on sharp rocks. Use a bandana or handkerchief to dry your feet after you get them wet. Also, a wet pair of feet will quickly make you cold at camp.

Do not go barefoot at camp in porcupine country!

At the end of a long, hot day on the trail, soak your feet in a stream or lake. The cold water will help alleviate swelling, and despite the initial shock, your feet will be refreshed.

Packs

Backpacks, like backpackers, come in all shapes and sizes. If you will be hiking a variety of trails, you will probably require two models: a day pack and an overnight pack. Packs made from coated ripstop nylon are lightweight and relatively waterproof. Those made from Cordura (packcloth) are more durable. Some packs use both fabrics to create a waterproof body and a durable base. A waterproof pack cover can be purchased, made, or improvised from a large plastic bag. Whatever packs you select, insure they have durable zippers and buckles that you can operate while wearing mitts or gloves.

Overnight Packs

For overnight trips, most people require a pack in the 60-80 litre range. Although it is true that a larger pack tempts you to take more gear than is required, a smaller pack with odds and ends strapped all over the exterior is the makings of backcountry disaster. You might lose gear or have it soaked in the rain, and you will have to unpack and repack every time you want to get inside the main compartment. This kind of pack will also sap your energy since the centre of gravity will shift away from your back, throwing you off-stride.

Overnight packs should have: an internal or external frame, an adjustable shoulder yoke, compression straps, one or two easily accessible outer compartments, and adequate padding. Some models of overnight packs come in tall, regular and small sizes. Insure you are choosing the correct size. Have the pack fitted to your torso by a knowledgeable salesperson before you leave the store. With the pack fully loaded, the hip belt should take most of the weight.

If your pack does not have zipper pulls when purchased, add short loops of 3 mm cord or bootlace to create your own. Zipper pulls make access to your pack easier while you are wearing gloves or mitts, and also lengthen the life of the zippers.

What do you do with your pack when camped in the backcountry? Some people choose to hang their packs with their food at night. In theory, this is the safest thing to do, since it minimizes the chance that scents on your pack will attract a bear to your tent. However, if it rains your pack will be soaked. Worse, squirrels and jays may damage it. A pack left on the ground or low in a tree may be eaten by porcupines. Many campers tuck their empty packs under the tent fly, outside the

tent. That way, they will probably be awakened by any animal that attempts to eat the pack during the night.

Day Packs

Day packs need not be fancy. A pack volume of 30 to 35 litres is adequate. Excessive padding and multiple compartments are not required. A zippered hood compartment and a single storage compartment are all you need. For the day-hiking options on overnight trips, carry a small nylon teardrop pack (15-20 litre capacity), or condense your main pack using the compression straps.

Tents

Buying a tent has become a baffling experience in recent years. More than with any other item of camping equipment, tent talk has become ridiculously technical. Keep the following in mind when you go tent shopping, and don't let the sales jargon intimidate you.

- Choose a tent that will accommodate your party comfortably (one-person, two-person, four-person).
- Choose a tent that is light enough to carry without complaint, and one with components that can be shared among party members to distribute weight.
- Choose a tent that has a large fly.
- Choose a free-standing tent. They are easier to set up, and they can be dried quickly by hanging them from a tree on a windy day. More important: some of the tent pads at campgrounds on popular trails have been "hardened" in recent years, and are almost impossible to peg.
- Choose a light-coloured tent. They are more cheerful when it is pouring outside, and you are stuck inside. They dry more quickly and it is easier to read inside them. It is also easier to spot mosquitoes and bugs inside.
- Choose a tent you can afford.

No backpacking tent is entirely waterproof, so don't spend a fortune on one that claims to be. The tent fly is what will keep you dry. Seal all tent seams (especially those on the fly) before each season. Nylons and tent materials decay and shrink in sunlight, so do not leave your tent pitched when you won't be using it. Most tent fabrics are highly flammable. Do not cook, smoke or use a candle in a tent. Follow all the manufacturer's care recommendations. You may want to carry a small sponge to soak up drips inside your tent, and an aluminum sleeve to slip over the break in a snapped tent pole.

Some backpackers may be accustomed to sleeping on the ground in a bivouac sac. In drier, warmer climates this is a viable option. However, it is not recommended in the Rockies.

Sleeping Bags

Even in mid-summer, nights in the Rockies are usually cool. Frost and snow are possible on any night at any location. Most backpackers opt for a three-season synthetic bag, or a summer down-filled bag. Early and late in the hiking season, you may be more comfortable in a winter bag. Carry your sleeping bag inside your backpack. Most people line the inside or outside of the sleeping bag stuff sack with a large plastic bag, for extra protection against rain and sweat.

Whatever sleeping bag you choose, an insulated sleeping mat is essential. The most comfortable and most expensive mats are inflatable. Less expensive and less effective are closed-cell foams. Your sleeping mat should be carried in a stuff sack to keep it dry and to protect it from scuffing and punctures.

Drinking Water and Giardiasis

For many visitors, one of the most attractive things about the Canadian Rockies is the abundance of fresh water. Backpackers often reach the headwaters of mountain rivers, or meltwater streams close to their glacial sources. This is some of the purest water on earth. Is it safe to drink?

Unfortunately, although the water in many streams is still safe, some water is not. The parasite *Giardia lamblia* is now present throughout the Canadian Rockies. *Giardia* (zjee-ARE-dee-ah) is a protozoan parasite transmitted in feces. The complaint it produces, giardiasis, is commonly called "beaver fever," because the *Giardia* cyst can be carried by beavers. *Giardia* can also be carried by most mammals, including dogs and humans. Wherever *Giardia*-contaminated fecal matter enters a watercourse, the cyst may be present. Once a stream becomes contaminated, any mammals using the stream may spread the contamination.

Giardia produces general weakness and gastro-intestinal upset. Diarrhea, abdominal cramps, foul-smelling gas and feces, and lack of appetite are symptoms. Lower abdominal pain while walking downhill is a classic indicator. The symptoms occur 10 to 14 days after ingestion of the cysts, so if you get sick on your first backcountry trip of the season, blame your cooking, not the water! *Giardia* is diagnosed through a stool sample, and controlled by the drug Flagyl. Undiagnosed, *Giardia* symptoms may become a chronic and unpleasant condition.

Obviously, responsible attitudes toward human waste in the backcountry will help reduce the spread of *Giardia*. (See Backcountry Cleanliness.) Since dogs are carriers of Giardia, and may also track the feces of other animals into watercourses, it is a good idea not to take dogs into the backcountry. (At time of publication, most parks did not allow dogs in the backcountry overnight.)

Chlorine, iodine and halizone do not kill *Giardia* cysts. You must bring water to a hard boil to kill the cysts. At sea level, three minutes of boiling is recommended, with an additional minute for each 600 m of elevation gained. So boiling times to kill *Giardia* at campgrounds on the Classic Hikes will range from five to seven minutes. Portable water filters with pores 0.4 microns or smaller will remove the cysts. These filters are available in a variety of configurations and price ranges. Most are lightweight and are suitable for extended trips.

Dehydration

How much water should you drink each day? Dehydration affects the body's ability to digest food, to stay warm in cold weather, and to stay cool in hot weather. It also contributes to altitude sickness. Symptoms may occur at elevations as low as 2450 m.

The amount you should drink varies with temperature, wind, humidity, activity and your metabolism. The best gauge of adequate rehydration is to check the frequency of urination, and the volume and colour of your urine. You should urinate at least three times in a 24 hour period. If your urine is clear, you are drinking enough fluids. If your urine is not clear, drink at least a litre of water. Any time you feel thirsty, you probably lack at least a litre. Avoid beverages that contain alcohol or caffeine, since they contribute to dehydration. For every cup of coffee you drink, you eliminate 1.3 cups of fluid by urine.

Use durable one-litre water bottles for carrying drinking water. Plastic, such as those manufactured by Nalgene, or anodized aluminum, such as those made by Sigg, are the best choices. In survival situations, if you have a cigarette lighter, a piece of candle to start a fire, and a metal water bottle, you will almost always be able to make a hot drink.

Water sources are not always close to backcountry campgrounds. Carry a "water billy" to cut down on the number of trips you must make to get water. The refillable liners from four-litre wine or juice boxes work well as water billies. They compress when empty and weigh little. Depending on your taste, it can be fun draining the liner of its original contents. You will be reusing an otherwise discarded product, and reducing the number of unnecessary trails that develop in the backcountry.

Stoves and Fuel Bottles

A camp stove is a backcountry necessity in the Rockies, because fires are generally not allowed in high-use areas. Even if allowed, cooking with a wood fire can be time-consuming – a fact you will not appreciate during inclement weather, when a quick, hot cup of tea or soup might save the day.

Water boils at a lower temperature at high altitude: 1°C less for each 300 m above sea level. The boiling point at campgrounds on the Classic Hikes will range from 92°C to 97.5°C. Use the windscreen provided with your stove to cook efficiently and minimize time.

Take care not to scorch or burn picnic tables at campgrounds. Place your stove on bare ground, on a flat rock, or on top of a metal firebox.

Backpacking stoves manufactured by MSR and Coleman are the most popular. These stoves are lightweight, dependable, stable and have built-in pressure pumps that allow for easy priming. This compensates for pressure losses due to cold weather and altitude. The stoves burn white gas (naptha, Coleman fuel) – a fuel that is readily available at townsites and most service stations.

Carry a repair kit for your stove. Test and clean your stove before each trip, and learn how to troubleshoot. The 22 ounce (US) MSR bottle is usually sufficient to cook breakfasts, dinners and hot drinks for two people during a three day and two night outing. You will use more fuel if you boil your drinking water.

Carry extra fuel in aluminum bottles, such as those manufactured by Sigg and MSR. A combination of one-litre and half-litre bottle sizes will allow you to most efficiently use the space in your pack. Recycle the original fuel containers. White gas tends to be expensive locally. If you see it at a good price, stock up.

Fuel cartridges are usually available locally for butane stoves. However, these stoves do not perform well in cold weather or at high altitude. Kerosene is not generally available.

Matches

Carry two cigarette lighters as well as waterproof, strike-anywhere matches. Keep the lighters in different places. A wet lighter can always be dried in a pocket. Wet matches may take days to dry, and usually disintegrate. Waterproof your matches by dipping them in melted wax.

Pots and Utensils

Stainless steel cooking pots are more durable than aluminum pots. Insure your set includes a pot holder. Two cooking pots should be carried for a party of two to three people. Use one for boiling water, and the other for cooking food. This simplifies clean-ups, and prevents the unforgettable experience of drinking tea that tastes like spaghetti sauce. Carry your stove and pots in stuff sacks, and hang them with your food at night. To prevent squirrels and birds from eating your trail mix and cereals (their favourites), store these foods inside your cooking pots.

Each person should carry a pocket knife, a plastic bowl, a spoon, and an insulated travel mug for hot drinks. Most beverages taste better if made directly in the mug, rather than in an aluminum or stainless steel pot. The drinks stay warmer too.

Food

Backcountry cuisine has evolved considerably from the freeze-dried fixation of the late 1970s. Backpackers now rely less on prepackaged meals, freeze-dried or otherwise. Prepackaged meals tend to be expensive, and portions are not always sufficient. Many backpackers buy bulk grains and pastas, and create their own dried sauces, either from recipes or by combining commercially available mixes and soups. Bulk foods avoid excessive packaging. Reclosable plastic bags can be used to carry meal-sized portions. Write instructions in ink, directly on the bag. With care, the bags can be washed and reused many times.

The foods you choose to eat in the backcountry will obviously be governed by your tastes, your pocket book, the amount of weight you are willing to carry, and the length of time the foods will keep. Another important consideration: choose foods that do not attract bears.

Do Take:
Dried grains and cereals, granola mixes
Instant soups and sauces
Bread (pita is an excellent choice)
Pasta
Cheese
Dried fruit
Nuts and seeds
Seasonings
Teas
Instant hot or cold beverage mixes
Powdered milk
Sweets and candies
Dessert mixes

Do Not Take:
Fresh, dried or canned fish or seafood
Fresh, dried or canned meat
Peppermint tea
(These foods may attract wildlife, particularly bears.)

Also, do not take anything that is strongly scented into the backcountry: toothpaste, deodorant, perfume or cologne, shampoo, hair spray or gel, or scented soap.

Insure your diet includes fresh vegetables and fruits. These can easily be taken on overnight trips, and will keep for the first two or three days of longer outings. A daily vitamin/mineral supplement is a good idea to help compensate for a lack of fresh foods, especially if you are backpacking for an entire summer. Salt tablets are hard on your digestive system. Add extra salt to your food instead, to help maintain your electrolyte balance.

Many people find they eat more than normal while hiking, and require trail snacks. Mixtures of nuts, raisins, seeds and candies are a standby. Save money by buying these items in bulk, and create your own mixtures. You lose much time when travelling in groups if stops must be made as each group member becomes hungry. Trail snacks should always be at hand, allowing the growlies to be quickly staved off until an agreed upon mealtime. If you feel yourself becoming lethargic or cranky, eat! Low blood sugar is often the culprit, and snacking will usually improve your energy and outlook. Handy snacks will also allow you to keep moving if foul weather makes stopping at the predetermined lunch spot disagreeable. They may become survival food in an emergency, especially if you become separated from the person carrying dinner!

Bulk foods are available in Banff, Golden, Canmore and Jasper. If you have a vehicle, keep your food in a mouse-proof metal box. With planning and proper storage, you can spend weeks backpacking without a resupply trip to town.

Always pack a few extra soups and hot drink mixes. These can be used for a hot lunch during inclement weather, or as emergency rations if your trip takes one night longer than planned.

Backcountry Cleanliness

What do you need to carry to stay respectably clean and comfortable in the backcountry? Toothbrush, dental floss, brush or comb, toilet paper, baking soda (in a plastic film canister), any essential medications, and nylon rope to use as a clothesline. If you wear contact lenses, make a small travel kit with your required solutions, and don't forget your eyeglasses and a hard glasses case.

It is unnecessary to fuss excessively over personal cleanliness and hygiene in the backcountry. Soap, deodorant, toothpaste, gel, cologne and perfume are potential pollutants, and contain scents that may attract bears. You are wise to leave these cosmetics at home. Besides, your pack will be lighter. You can brush your teeth with warm water. Once a day, add some baking soda to the toothbrush.

After a sweaty day on the trail, you are probably not going to be as clean as you would like to be. On hot days, rinse your head, underarms, legs and feet in creeks or lakes. If you are brave, go for a dip. If body odour is a problem, it can be completely controlled by natural "deodorant stones" available at health food stores. These weigh but a few grams. They work for foot odour too.

Dirty T-shirts, underwear and socks can be rinsed without soap in creeks and hung on a clothesline while at camp, or on your pack while on the trail. They won't be squeaky clean, but they will be tolerable for another day. String a cord inside your tent and hang damp clothes on it at night. At night, the clothesline can be put to use as a food storage rope in areas where a food storage system is not provided.

Do not wash your pots and dishes in lakes or streams. Choose an area on well-drained ground, away from watercourses and tent sites, and bring the water to this location. Use warm water and a plastic scouring pad. If food is burned onto your pots, use a small amount of baking soda or sand as an abrasive. Scatter the waste water over a wide area, or use it to douse campfire coals. If the waste water contains many food particles, you may strain it first through a porous cloth. Pack out the strainings or burn them.

Even in hot weather, this simple cleansing will keep dishes suitably clean throughout a five day trip – assuming your food does not include excessive fats, fish oils and the like. When you get back to civilization, by all means wash your pots, dishes and utensils in hot, soapy water to avoid having a backcountry science project growing in your pack next time you hit the trail.

If possible, always rinse your hands in a stream or creek after eating lunch or snacks. This will help prevent the spread of food odours over your pack and clothing.

Answering Nature's Call

At campgrounds and trailheads, please use the outhouses provided. The facilities you will encounter on trails range from fibreglass structures resembling sentry pillboxes, to rustic cedar biffies, to open pits and don't fall backwards! Toilet paper is not provided, except in the core areas of Mt. Robson and Mt. Assiniboine provincial parks.

If an outhouse is unusable because of negligence or damage, or nature calls while you are on the trail, the following guidelines apply. Urinate well off trail, away from tenting areas and at least 50 metres from all watercourses. Avoid urinating directly on vegetation, since uric acid burns foliage. Human urine contains about 3 percent sodium on average. Mule deer, bighorn sheep, porcupines and marmots are attracted by the salt, and eat urine-soaked turf. If you urinate near your tent, you may find one of these animals chomping on your front lawn soon after.

When you defecate, dig a small "cat hole," maximum 10 cm deep, in the dark, biologically active layer of the soil, at least 100 metres away from any watercourse. Cover your feces, including toilet paper, with the excavations. Alternately, you may pack your used toilet paper to the next outhouse, or toss it in a burning campfire. Use unscented, undyed, unpatterned toilet paper.

Clothing

Versatile backcountry clothing incorporates a series of layers that can be donned or shed quickly as required. Avoid cotton, denim and leather, as they soak easily and become clammy. Choose wool, pile, fleece, polypropylene and other synthetic fabrics.

In the Rockies you will need extra layers of clothing to combat the chill of stormy weather and high altitude. Always carry a set of long underwear – tops and bottoms – and liner gloves and a pair of heavier outer gloves or wool mitts. Fingerless wool gloves are useful. A pair of knee-length socks and a down vest make camp life comfortable early and late in the season. Also bring a warm winter-style hat, such as a toque with ear flaps, or a balaclava.

Rains in the Rockies are often extremely cold. Although your backpack helps keep you warm and dry, you should invest in a full suit of good raingear, with adjustable cuffs, and a snug hood. Full or partial zippers on the legs assist ventilation. Choose a rain jacket size larger than normal to allow warm clothing to be worn underneath, and to compensate for the fact that a full backpack will make your jacket bunch at the shoulders. Ponchos are not effective in the Rockies. The wind blows them and they tear easily on shrubs and trees. Remember, no fabric is completely waterproof. The purchase of expensive "miracle fabrics" may not be money well spent. A good coated nylon rainsuit will usually suffice. It can double as a windsuit when required.

What about the sunny days? Shorts, T-shirts, and a sun hat should be part of your layered system. The effect of solar radiation is more intense at high elevations. Skin burns more rapidly. Carry an effective sunscreen (SPF 30), and apply it liberally. Zinc ointment is the best for fair-skinned people. Apply it to noses, lips, cheek bones and ear lobes. Light-coloured fabrics will keep you cooler, and tend to dry more quickly when soaked through with sweat. Sunglasses that block most UV radiation should always be in your pack. A large cotton handkerchief or bandana can be used in a number of ways: scarf, head cover, towel, sling and pressure dressing.

Campground Etiquette

On all but a few of the Classic Hikes, backcountry camping is permitted at designated campgrounds only. Please do not camp elsewhere. The standards for designated backcountry campgrounds differ widely among the various parks. In Banff, all sites are equipped with outhouses, a food storage system, and rustic picnic tables. In Jasper, only the most heavily used campgrounds have these facilities. The tent pads and trails in popular campgrounds in Yoho and Kootenay have been "hardened" with gravel. And picnic tables have been built from pressure-treated wood. Four of the campgrounds along the Berg Lake Trail at Mt. Robson have cooking shelters and wood stoves.

If fires are allowed it will say so on your park use permit. As a general rule, if a metal firebox is not provided, campfires are not allowed. (See Campfires.)

In designated campgrounds, camp on an established site. Do not dig drainage trenches around your tent. Share picnic tables, campfires and food storage cables with other parties if the campground is crowded. Observe quiet hours between 10 p.m. and 7 a.m., and please, do not take tape decks, cellular phones or radios into the backcountry. Groups larger than six persons are discouraged, and those of 10 or more require permission of the park superintendent. Respect the right of others to solitude.

At night or when you will be away from camp, hang your food on the storage cables, where provided. Be sure to clip the cables to the eye hooks after use. Unattached cables are a hazard to elk, moose and deer. If an antler snags in a cable late in the autumn, the animal may die a slow death from starvation.

The sun's first rays often function as a natural alarm clock. If you plan an early start, choose a tent site that will not be shaded in the morning. If there is frost, rain or snow overnight, a sunny tent site will also aid greatly in drying out before you repack.

Random Camping

For many people, random camping is the essence of backcountry travel. The ability to select a campsite without constraint is linked to a sense of freedom. Random camping demands that we show tremendous responsibility and care toward the environment. Historically, this responsibility has been lacking. The backcountry of the Rockies is dotted with many old camps, where the local impact has been damaging.

To help curtail the proliferation of damaged sites, the Rocky Mountain parks have been zoned to regulate conflicting activities and uses. Opportunities for different backcountry experiences are thus scattered throughout these parks in a manner that insures they do not detract from each other, or further damage the environment. The zoning also helps protect wildlife and natural features. Rather than being tempted to break the rules, consult a park information centre to discover which areas of the parks suit your desired backcountry experience.

Only a few of the Classic Hikes contain areas where random camping is permitted: #20 in the Dolomite Creek drainage; #22, in the Howse River and Glacier River drainages (no fires); and the section of #7 between the Banff boundary and the Mt. Assiniboine core area.

A park use permit is required for random camping (except Mt. Assiniboine). The campsite must be at least 5 km from the nearest trailhead and 50 m from both the closest trail and water source. Either choose a site that hasn't been used before – one that has no vegetation or durable vegetation cover; or choose a site that is already heavily impacted. In this case, confine your movements to areas that are already trampled, to avoid enlarging the disturbed area. Do not camp on game trails. If more than one tent is pitched, keep the tents well apart. Tent sites must be moved every three days. Maximum group size is 10.

You will need to carry a 30 m piece of nylon rope and a carabiner to hang your food at night. String food, pots and stove so they are suspended at least 5 m off the ground, halfway between two trees at least 5 m apart. In many cases this is much more easily said than done! Do not be tempted to store your food in a less than satisfactory manner. Sling the rope over dead branches if possible, to avoid damaging tree bark.

Campfires

The campfire is an irresistible aspect of trail life; one in which we all indulge from time to time. Campfires are not allowed in many backcountry areas. However, where they are permitted, ask yourself: do I need a fire? Campfires consume wood and oxygen, and release tremendous amounts of carbon into the atmosphere. There is irony in travelling lightly during the day, only to burn half a cord of wood around the campfire each night.

Treat campfires as a luxury, not as a necessity. Even where campfires are permitted, do not go into the backcountry expecting to cook over them. Cooking over a campfire is time consuming, undependable and wastes firewood. Use a lightweight camping stove for cooking. For emergency or wet weather situations where a fire is absolutely necessary for warmth or safety, carry a small piece of candle to use as firestarter.

Light fires only in the metal fireboxes provided. If random camping in a pristine area, build a fire ring from carefully gathered rocks, and dismantle the ring afterwards. Or, build your fire in a river bed on a gravel bar below high water line. When random camping in a heavily impacted area, use an established fire ring. In all cases, keep your fire on mineral soil, not in the organic layer. Do not burn wood more than 8 cm in diameter. Campsites littered with half-burned logs are an ugly sight and set a bad example for future campers.

Be aware of fire bans posted during times of extreme forest fire hazard. Remember that nationwide, improperly tended or unextinguished campfires are the leading cause of forest fires. (Cigarette smoking is the second leading cause.)

Most fire pits in the backcountry are tarnished with garbage left behind by inconsiderate backpackers. Do burn the following: tea bags, coffee grounds, paper, and paperboard. Don't burn: tin cans, other metals, aluminum foil and bags, multi-laminate soup or sauce packages, Tetra-paks, and twist ties. Make the effort to pack out all items and recycle those that you can.

To extinguish your fire, pour water on the coals and mix the slurry thoroughly with a stick. Douse the coals again.

Lastly, share your campfire with fellow campers. Sharing campfires reduces air pollution and the impact caused by wood gathering, and it adds to your experience of the backcountry.

Firewood

Where fires are allowed, be responsible in gathering firewood. Use only deadfall that is already in small pieces. Do not gather driftwood from stream beds, or break branches, living or dead, off living or downed trees. Do not drag dead wood out of the duff layer, thereby disturbing feathermosses and lichens, and promoting erosion. Keep the wood in its natural lengths until ready to burn. That way, unused wood can be scattered and will appear natural.

Your Vehicle

Vehicle break-ins and thefts at trailheads are increasing. What do you do with your wallet, money and vehicle keys while out on a hike? Do not leave them in your vehicle. Carry valuables in a zippered compartment or small wallet, preferably in the hood of your pack. Each person in your group should carry a vehicle key. All valuables left in your vehicle should be in the trunk, or in a locked compartment in the box of a pick-up truck. Leave nothing on the dash to indicate how long you will be away from your vehicle.

Bugs

Although bugs in the Rockies are nowhere near as numerous as in the far north or the lake country of the Canadian Shield, you will undoubtedly become acquainted with black flies, horse flies, deer flies, no-see-ums and the 28 species of mosquitoes that call these mountains home. Biting bugs are attracted by body warmth and by exhaled carbon dioxide. From the bugs' points of view, some people are more attractive than others. However, almost everyone finds the need to apply a repellent at some time during the summer.

Biting bugs generally become noticeable in late June or early July, and are gone by late August. Cool weather kills them off. Warm, damp weather helps them proliferate. Campsites near lakes are usually bug heaven, and the bane of backpackers in mid-summer. Some of the buggiest backcountry campgrounds are: Luellen Lake, Baker Lake, Amethyst Lake, Lone Lake, Surprise Point and Lake Magog.

Insect Repellents

In recent years, many backpackers have been using bug repellents made from natural substances. Most of these are comprised principally of oil of citronella. Although they need to be applied more often, natural repellents are easier on the human body. The manufacturing process is easier on the environment too.

Chemical repellents containing at least 75 percent DEET by volume are effective against most bugs. Unfortunately, DEET dissolves plastics and removes paints from metal surfaces. It will foul your film, camera, tent fly, and synthetic fabrics. Who knows what DEET is doing to your skin and the membranes in your mouth, nose and eyes, where it invariably ends up. It tastes awful too. Chemical repellents also contain small amounts of alcohol. Alcohol destroys skin tissue in bites and cuts, and may result in scarring. DEET-covered hands dipped into backcountry watercourses introduce chemical pollution.

Whatever repellent you choose, avoid aerosol sprays. Purchase repellents in lotion form, or in pump-spray bottles. Carry the repellent in a reclosable bag, in case the container should leak.

If you have severe reactions to the bites of mosquitoes, you may want to carry an oral antihistamine to help alleviate the swelling. Cool compresses using stream or lake water will provide temporary relief from itching. Many people experience strong reactions to the first bites of the season, but suffer less as the body builds its seasonal immunity.

Wood Ticks

Whereas the bites of flying bugs are usually nothing but a painful nuisance, the bite of the Rocky Mountain wood tick is potentially a more serious matter. Ticks resemble tiny flattened spiders, and are related to them. Ticks are usually encountered in the montane ecoregion from early April until mid-June. Areas frequented by bighorn sheep, elk and deer are havens for these parasites.

Ticks climb up grasses and low shrubs and await their prey: mammals that pass by. Once lodged in the fur or clothing of a potential victim, the tick seeks out fleshy areas to inflict its bite and draw its meal of blood. The mouth parts penetrate the skin and the tick's body balloons with the fluid of its host. You will often see the flanks of elk and deer covered in swollen ticks.

The dangers to humans from tick bites are: Rocky Mountain spotted fever – the complications can be fatal; and tick paralysis – a reaction to tick-induced toxins that can impair functions of the central nervous system. A tick must usually be imbedded for at least 24 hours before the symptoms appear. Lyme disease is carried by deer ticks and has not yet been reported in the Rockies. However, it will eventually appear here.

What can you do to protect yourself? Avoid grassy meadows during May and June. After any outing in tick terrain, search your clothing, skin and hair thoroughly. Have a friend check your scalp, neck and back, and the places where the elastic straps of underwear press against your skin. A tick will usually roam the skin of a potential host for several hours before biting. Ideally, you are trying to find it before it bites you.

If you find a tick, grasp its hind quarters with a pair of tweezers and pull gently. If the tick comes away easily, its mouth parts are probably not attached. If there is slight resistance, the tick has bitten. Increase the force of your pull, however try not to break off the mouth parts, which if left imbedded, can still cause problems. Once the tick is removed, wash the bite with soap and water.

If you only get the body of the tick, go after the imbedded mouth parts with a sterile needle, or see a physician as soon as possible. If after removing a tick, you detect a red circle around the bite, or swelling persists, see a physician promptly. Do not attempt to squash a removed tick – burn it with a match.

Stream Crossings

You will encounter three varieties of unbridged stream crossings on the Classic Hikes: rock-hops, where the soles of your boots may get wet; boulder-hops, where the uppers of your boots may get wet; and fords, where your boots would be totally submerged. Good balance, and the ability to plan the sequence of rocks and boulders to be used, are all you need for rock-hops and boulder-hops. Take extra care during cold weather, in case the tops of the rocks are icy. Also, beware of the slick surfaces of wet boulders covered with algae, glacial silt or moss.

Fords

Fords add to the wilderness nature of remote outings, and are a serious undertaking. Most rivers and streams in the Rockies are glacially fed. The water is extremely cold and often silty. Water levels fluctuate daily, with glacial melt at a maximum in the evening and a minimum in early morning. Water levels also fluctuate seasonally. Peak runoff from snowmelt is in late May and early June. Peak runoff from glacial melt is in early August.

Any experienced backpacker will tell you that fords are the most difficult and dangerous aspect of trail travel in the Rockies. A missed step at even a "straightforward" ford can lead to soaked or damaged equipment, or hypothermia – the makings of a backcountry disaster.

The fords you will encounter on the Classic Hikes are rated as follows:

Straightforward: ankle to knee deep, good footing

Moderate: calf to knee deep, boulders and uneven footing

Difficult: knee to thigh deep, boulders and uneven footing, wide crossing

Many people carry a pair of old running shoes or "river shoes" on trails that involve fords. The extra weight is well worth the comfort and decreased chance of a foot injury while fording a stream. Wearing running shoes may render a moderate ford as straightforward.

Develop a routine for fords. Stow your camera inside your pack and strap your boots onto the outside so they cannot be lost if you fall into the stream. Unbuckle waist and chest straps. Insure your pack will not slip out of position and throw you off balance. Wear shorts and make sure your socks, sweater and long pants will remain dry inside your pack.

Fords are best accomplished by facing upstream and sidestepping. Take a diagonal line, upstream to the opposite bank. Use a stout stick to aid balance. However, do not lean entirely on it. Keep your weight over your feet, and move one foot at a time. Move as quickly as you can. Your feet will soon begin to ache or go numb, and if you move slowly, the pain and difficulty of the remainder of the crossing will increase.

From the bank, most fords look easier than they are once you are in the water. If a ford appears truly formidable, do not attempt it. On straightforward and moderate fords, one person should cross at a time. Those on the bank should have their packs off, and be prepared to enter the stream to help a person in trouble.

On difficult fords, choose the widest possible location, which is generally where the stream will be shallowest. The places where horses cross are not necessarily the best places for hikers. However, game trails may indicate good crossing places. Cross as a group. Groups of two or three should brace arms over each others' shoulders and cross in a line, facing upstream. The strongest or tallest people should be on the outside. Groups of four or five can form a circle, with the strongest person facing downstream.

Water is most turbulent adjacent to submerged boulders. Water directly downstream from a large boulder can be calm. Be careful when stepping out on the far bank, especially if it is on the outside of a curve in the stream. This is often where the current is deepest and

fastest. Dry your feet thoroughly before putting on your socks and boots.

A stream crossing for a group of two to five persons may require 15-25 minutes. Insure at least one person in the party makes noise at regular intervals, in order to alert any bears nearby to your presence. If you find a stream uncrossable late in the day, you may choose to camp (where permitted) and attempt the crossing early next morning, when the water level usually will have dropped.

Additional Day-Hikes

Some of the overnight Classic Hikes include destinations that can be day-hiked from the trailhead. For information on these outings, refer to the hike number in parentheses. The day-hikes marked with an asterisk depart from the trailhead at the *end* of the hike described in the text.

Arnica Lake (#8)*
Boulder Pass (#18)
Floe Lake (#44)
Healy Pass (#8)
Hidden Lake (#18)
Kinney Lake (#33)
Laughing Falls (#38)
Lineham Ridge (#49)
Little Shovel Pass (#31)
Maccarib Pass (#28)
Nigel Pass (#25)
Rowe Lakes (#49)
Signal Mountain (#31)*
Sunshine Meadows (#7)
The Whaleback (#38)
Twin Falls (#38)
Twin Lakes (#8)*
Yoho Glacier (#38)

First Aid

Your first aid kit should include: blister dressings, adhesive dressings, closure strips, adhesive tape, sterile gauze, pain killer, tensor bandage, triangular bandage, tweezers, latex gloves, pencil and paper. Splints can be improvised from branches or tent poles, or from a rectangular piece of stiff cardboard. Carry required medications and inform your hiking partners of your allergies and conditions. People with chronic conditions should wear a

Medic-Alert bracelet or necklace.

A detailed description of first aid is beyond the scope of this book. What do you do if someone is injured? In a nutshell: If the injury is minor, patch up the wounds and carry on. If the injury is grave:

- Do not move the person unless the local environment is life-threatening.
- Insure the person is breathing adequately. Assist with rescue breathing if required.
- Control all deadly bleeding, preferably with sterile dressings.
- Immobilize fractures.
- Treat the person for shock. Most patients should be kept supine (on their back), unless this compromises their breathing. Keep the person warm and comfortable. Be reassuring. For medical complaints or difficult breathing, allow the person to choose the position of greatest comfort.
- Give no food or drink unless rescue is more than a day away.
- At least one person should stay with the injured.
- If the party is large enough, one or two persons should seek help, taking a written description of the injury and patient's location with them.

Repair Kit

Makeshift equipment repairs are sometimes necessary in the backcountry. Carry: needle and thread, a length of duct tape, a length of fibreglass tape, 3 mm cord, light gauge wire, adhesive nylon patches, and a spare bootlace. A short metal sleeve can be used to bind a broken tent pole. Flagging tape may prove useful for marking a route in an emergency.

Hypothermia

Hypothermia is the lowering of the body's core temperature, and is one of the principal risks you confront in the backcountry. Its onset is insidious and the development of symptoms progressive. Untreated, it can lead to death. The three factors that set the stage for hypothermia are: cool or cold air, wind, and precipitation. Any one of these can make you hypothermic. It is possible to become hypothermic simply from a chilly breeze on an otherwise sunny day.

The initial symptom of hypothermia is shivering, an intense muscular activity intended to produce heat. Extremities then become cold as blood is shunted towards the body's vital organs. Pulse and respiration rates increase. If the victim makes no attempt to seek shelter or put on warm and dry clothing, the shivering will change to muscular rigidity. He or she will stumble while walking. Fine motor skills will be lost. Speech will become slurred and thinking will become slow. Pulse and respiration rates will decrease and weaken. If the condition is allowed to progress, the victim will become unconscious, and without expert medical intervention, will probably die. This progression of symptoms can take place over a period of days or in a matter of hours.

Your ability to resist the onset of hypothermia is determined by age, body size, fitness, diet and effectiveness of clothing. Protect yourself and your companions by eating and drinking adequately, and carrying and using appropriate clothing. Turn back if conditions are foul. Remember that 55 percent of the body's heat is lost through the top of the head. So wear a warm hat when it's chilly! Watch your companions carefully for the onset of symptoms. Insist they wear more clothing if you think they are at risk. Conversely, take their advice if they offer the same to you.

Flashlight

Twilight is long-lasting during summer in the Rockies, and a flashlight is seldom required. However, you should have one available for emergencies and for hiking early and late in the season. A penlight or headlamp is recommended. Use rechargeable batteries.

Photography

There are two approaches to backcountry photography: snapshot and single lens reflex (SLR). The snapshot photographer should choose a model with a fast (< f 2.8) lens, a focal length of 35 mm, and a built-in flash. Carry a mini-tripod for low-light and self-portrait shots. A film speed of 100 ISO is suitable for most applications.

The SLR photographer requires more and

heavier equipment. The author carries a 35 mm camera body and three lenses: 24 mm, 28-80 mm zoom, and 70-210 mm zoom. The lenses are equipped with 1B filters. The camera body is fitted with the 28-80 mm lens, and carried over the shoulder in a tele-zoom camera bag. The 24 mm lens and a spare roll of film are also carried in the camera bag. A sturdy tripod, cable release, and additional film complete the equipment, which weighs 4 kg total.

If photographing wildlife is your passion, you may want to add a 300 mm lens. Polarizing and graduated filters can be used to good effect in the harsh lighting conditions you will often encounter. Insure there is space in your backpack to put everything away during heavy rains. Carry durable plastic bags to help keep your equipment dry.

The author shoots Kodachrome 64 and 200 reversal films. Fujichrome films are also popular. These films and 35 mm print films are available locally, although they tend to be more expensive than if purchased in major centres.

Wild Animal Count

The following summarizes the wildlife observations we made in 1992 and 1993 on the trails during fieldwork for this book. We did not keep records of songbirds and common rodents.

bighorn sheep	55
boreal toad	1
caribou	2
common loon	3
duck	10
falcon	1
golden eagle	7
grizzly bear	1
grouse	20
hawk	14
hoary marmot	59
moose	3
mountain goat	69
mouse	8
mule deer	35
northern bog lemming	3
osprey	2
owl	7
pika	20
porcupine	14
snowshoe hare	4
spotted frog	1
vole	17
white-tailed deer	3
white-tailed ptarmigan	21

Metric-Imperial Conversions

Metric	Imperial
1 millimetre (mm)	0.0394 inches
1 centimetre (cm)	0.394 inches
1 metre (m)	3.28 feet
1 kilometre (km)	0.62 miles
1 hectare (ha)	2.47 acres
1 sq. kilometre (km^2)	0.386 square miles
1 kilogram (kg)	2.205 pounds
1 tonne (t)	0.9842 UK tons
	(1.102 US tons)
1 litre (L)	0.22 UK gallons
	0.264 US gallons
1° Celsius (C)	1.8° F

The freezing point is 0°C (32°F).
One hectare is 100 m by 100 m.

Imperial	Metric
1 inch	2.54 centimetres(cm)
1 foot	0.305 metres (m)
1 mile	1.61 kilometres (km)
1 acre	0.405 hectares (ha)
1 square mile	2.59 sq. kilometres (km^2)
1 pound	0.4536 kilogram (kg)
1 UK ton	1.016 tonnes (t)
1 US ton	0.9072 tonnes (t)
1 UK gallon	4.55 litres (L)
1 US gallon	3.78 litres (L)
1° Fahrenheit	0.55° C

The freezing point is 32°F (0°C).

A quick formula for converting distances and heights from metric to their approximate Imperial equivalent is to multiply the metric distance by 3 and add 10 percent of the product. For example: 30 m x 3 = 90, plus 9 = 99. Therefore, 30 m equals approximately 99 feet.

Bears

Bears are synonymous with the Canadian Rockies. They are the stuff of fear and fascination, and it seems every visitor wants to see one. In truth, there are far fewer bears than most people realize. Perhaps 150-200 grizzlies range through the parks visited by Classic Hikes. Even fewer black bears occupy the same area.

You are more likely to see a bear while you are driving along the Icefields Parkway or Maligne Lake Road, than you are in the backcountry of the Canadian Rockies. In 11 years of backcountry travel in the Rockies, and a total distance hiked of roughly 11,000 km, the author has met eight grizzly bears and six black bears on the trail.

Most backcountry bears will not tolerate human presence. With its keener senses, a bear will usually detect you and leave an area before you become aware of it. As a result, in the backcountry, you may often be near a bear but oblivious to it, far more often than you realize.

Bears are both a possible peril to humans, and a dwindling promise for the perpetuation of wilderness. Wildlife biologists refer to grizzly bears as an "indicator species." Where the grizzly survives, wilderness survives. Remove the grizzly and the uncertain outcome of encounter, and the raw edge will be gone from the beauty of the Rockies.

In profile, the prominent shoulder hump and dished face are the key features that distinguish the grizzly bear from the black bear.

Problem Bears and Problem People

The number of hikers in the Rockies has remained fairly constant during the last decade, while the populations of black and grizzly bears have declined. However, principally as a result of human presence in bear habitat, bear-human encounters still take place. To understand why, we must take note of certain aspects of bear behavior, and the pressures affecting bears in the Rockies.

Both black and grizzly bears spend almost every waking moment in quest for food to tide them through their five to seven month winter hibernation. At the peak of their feeding, in August, an adult grizzly may feed for 18 hours per day, and consume 36 kg of food, representing 40,000 calories. Bears work hard to get most of this food. However, they are also opportunists, and will gladly take a kill left unattended by wolves or coyotes, garbage generated by humans, or improperly stored camping food.

A fed bear is a dead bear. A bear conditioned to food acquired from humans quickly loses its innate fear of people. The bear protects the garbage, picnic cooler or backcountry food cache just as if it were other "kill." "Aggression" is observed in the bear's reaction to approaching humans. If the bear has cubs in its care, they receive inappropriate lessons in encounters with humans, making the solution to the situation more complex.

Running Out of Chances

For the bear habituated to human food in the Rocky Mountain parks, the outcome is usually "three strikes and you're out." Park managers will often give a bear two chances, relocating it and its cubs to remote terrain where possible. The relocations may take a bear onto provincial lands where it may be legally hunted. If not shot by a hunter, an habituated bear often returns to the place where the pickings are easiest. When time comes for the third relocation, a bear known to be conditioned to human food is usually destroyed. In BC's provincial parks, the management outlook with regard to "problem bears" is not as forgiving. In 1992, two black bears in Mt. Robson Provincial Park were destroyed on their "first offence," despite the fact they had been lured into trouble by improperly stored camping food. The hikers responsible were not identified or penalized.

Black Bear

Grizzly Bear

In 1992, eight black bears (perhaps 13 percent of the park's population) died or were destroyed in Banff. Four other black bears were relocated from the park and did not return, and could also be considered as "deaths" in the context of the protected population. In 1993, as of early September, 12 black bears had died on the highways and railway in Jasper National Park. These kinds of population drains may already have triggered an "extinction vortex," where the black bears' slow reproductive rate cannot keep pace with deaths, both natural and unnatural.

Grizzlies in some areas have fared little better. Of 12 grizzlies radio-collared in Yoho and Kootenay parks between 1988 and 1990, 11 were dead by June 1992. These were bears that enjoyed the "protection" of national parks over a sizeable part of their range. Two of these bears were legally hunted outside the parks.

Clearly, the pressures confronting protected bear populations are becoming inescapable. The key pressures are:

1. Habitat loss and disruption on lands adjoining the parks.
2. Habitat alienation within the parks due to the overwhelming human presence associated with townsites, transportation corridors, and recreation – including hiking.
3. Mortality along transportation corridors within the parks.
4. Legal hunting along park boundaries.
5. Poaching and the lucrative foreign trade in bear parts.
6. Bears lured into interactions with humans by improperly stored food or garbage.

Mom's Point of View

The female grizzly or sow breeds an average of every three to five years. So the offspring enjoy a lengthy apprenticeship with their mother: two summers, sometimes three. This training is required for the young to become familiar with the incredibly diverse and seasonally varied sources of food that comprise bear diet.

Breeding commences at age five to seven years. The litter in the Rockies is usually a single cub. This represents the lowest reproduction rate among large North American mammals. Mortality rate for cubs is 10 to 40 percent in the first 18 months.

These are not the kind of statistics that will sustain the species if unnatural threats are also present. The mother bear will vigorously protect her young in order to insure their continuation. Hence, coming between a grizzly sow and her cubs is the ultimate backcountry blunder, and should be avoided at all costs. If nothing worse happens, the hiker who commits this transgression will have a front row seat for the heart-stopping experience of a bluff charge from 200 or more kilograms of Nature's greatest fury.

The bluff charge is not "aggression." It is a

natural, programmed reaction on the part of the mother bear. The bluff charge has been compared to the agitated response of a guard dog when you approach it, or its domain, too closely. If the sow is with two-year old cubs, she may send them after you as well, as a training exercise. In 1992, a Banff warden (luckily on horseback) was charged by a sow and her *four*, 2-year-old offspring!

Possible Causes for a Bear Attack

- You are between a sow and her cubs, or have presented a perceived threat to the cubs.
- You have encroached on a buried kill, or are passing through an area that offers a secure food source – a lush berry patch, a

Travelling Smartly and Avoiding Bears

Nothing will guarantee that you will not encounter a bear. Analyses of some bear-human encounters reveals no fault on the part of the people, other than simply being in the wrong place at the wrong time. However, by heeding the following list of do's and don'ts, you will certainly minimize the chances of raising the ire of a backcountry bear.

Do:

- Become familiar with how to identify the black and grizzly bear. Read the pamphlet: *You Are in Bear Country.*
- Inquire at a park information centre regarding recent bear activity for your proposed outing. Make note of the posted bear cautions and the species.
- Travel with a partner or two, and stay close together.
- Make noise while hiking. A bear bell is not sufficient on its own. Shouting is the best technique. Don't be self-conscious, this is self-defence. Choose a sound that requires little effort and does not make your voice hoarse. You will be making this often.
- Shout more loudly and more often when travelling alongside streams, through tall shrubs, and across avalanche slopes.
- As an alternative to shouting, rattle pots or tin cans. A bear is almost certain to run from a creature crazy enough to hike down a trail rattling a rock in a tin pot.
- Continue to make noise at intervals during rest stops and while fording streams.
- Observe avalanche slopes and berry patches keenly before you cross them. Be cautious on trails lined with buffaloberry bushes in fruit.
- Pay attention to bear sign on the trail. Look for

tracks and scrapes in muddy areas. Note the direction of travel. Are they the tracks of a mother and its young? Learn to recognize bear scat (droppings) and diggings. Make more noise if the sign is fresh.
- Leave the area immediately if you discover an animal carcass.
- If you see a bear, give it a wide berth. Verify whether it is a sow with cubs.
- Be especially observant on trails marked with a bear caution sign.
- Cook 50 m downwind of your tentsite. Eat all you cook.
- At night or when away from camp, hang all food, snacks, pots, stove and strongly scented non-food items from the food storage cables provided, or by rigging your own food storage system.
- Pack out all your garbage.
- Report any bear sighting or encounter to a park information centre or park warden, for the safety of those who follow.

Do not:

- Enter an area that is closed due to bear activity.
- Cook or eat in or near your tent.
- Store food or pack in your tent, or at your campsite.
- Leave your pack unattended.
- Stop or camp in areas where there is fresh bear sign.
- Dispose of food, food wastes or fish viscera in tenting areas.
- Take fresh meat, fish or seafood into the backcountry.

field of glacier lilies, a marmot colony, etc.

- You surprise a bear on the trail, in close quarters.
- A heavy snowfall in late summer or early autumn has driven bears to lower elevations where there is less food, and they are more intolerant of human presence.

What to Do If You Encounter a Bear

First, remember that bears are unpredictable. Second, in many encounters, the bear will be as startled and surprised at seeing you, as you are at seeing it. A bear you meet on a trail probably wants an escape route, and also wants to know you mean it no harm. Most encounters usually last but a few seconds, and are governed by the instinctive reactions of both bear and human. You will do what seems right, and the bear likewise. If you keep some of the following in mind, experts believe there is less chance you will provoke a non-aggressive bear to attack.

Bears frequently use trails. Muddy sections of trail are the best places to detect bear tracks. Scrapes, scats, diggings and flipped-over rocks are also clues to bear presence. If the bear sign appears fresh, you should assume that there is a bear nearby. The tracks in the photograph were made by a grizzly.

- Do not run. Running provokes a natural predator-prey response. A close quarters situation may be one in which the bear is not interested in you at all, but simply wants to continue along the trail in the direction it was going. Yield the trail. Back away slowly.
- Avoid direct eye contact. Among bears, staring in the eye is considered a challenge or threat.
- Talk quietly to the bear.

- Given that you and the bear are now observing each other, how do you know if the bear might charge? If it clacks its teeth together, slaps the ground with its paws, sweeps its head from side to side while eyeing you, or grunts loudly, the bear is agitated and may be considering a charge. However, if it stands broadside and lowers its head to one of its front paws, the bear is probably indicating non-aggressive behaviour.
- If the bear approaches slowly and you are below treeline, turn your head slowly to choose a tree to climb. Back toward the tree. To escape a grizzly, you must climb 5-10 m. Climb quickly. Bears have hauled people out of the lower branches of trees by grabbing their legs. If the bear climbs toward you, climb as high as you can. Kneel or squat on the uppermost sturdy branch. Do not leave your legs dangling. Climbing a tree is not a sure escape from an approaching black bear. It can climb higher than a grizzly (up to 30 m). However, in a black bear encounter, climbing a tree is recommended over "playing dead."
- If it is obvious you must climb a tree, drop your pack only if the pack will prevent you from climbing. A dropped pack may keep the bear nearby for hours, possibly days, while it gorges on the contents.
- In situations where a bear charges, remember: the initial charge is *usually* a bluff. The bear will usually stop several metres short of contact. (This would be the time to use a bear spray – see below.) In this situation, if

Grizzly bear tracks

Black bear tracks

you present no threat to the bear, it may leave. However, groups of six or more people should shout at a bear in this situation, to scare it off. At time of publication, there was no documented instance of a bear attacking a group of six or more people.

- If a grizzly makes contact, do not fight back. Play dead. Curl up in a ball, pack on your back, knees tucked under, hands clasped over the back of your neck. Stick your elbows out for stability. The bear may try to roll you over. You may have to stay in this position for hours. Unresisted attacks by grizzlies are often a matter of one forthright swat and it's over with. The victim often lives, although the injuries may be grave.

- If, on approach, a black bear lowers its head to the ground and sweeps it from side to side while eyeing you, it may be about to attack. The bear may also circle to try and get behind you, in order to knock you over. If a black bear makes contact, fight back. In the rare instance of deliberate attack by a black bear, the bear may be intent on killing for food. Fight for your life. Use a stick, rocks, pocket knife, anything.

- Above treeline, encounters are usually with grizzlies. Try to get a fix on cubs or carrion in the area, and stay clear of them. Back away slowly and yield the trail to the bear. The bear may call off the pursuit once convinced you are intent on leaving the area. If in a group, remain together. If the bear continues to approach directly, you must choose between two admittedly poor options: playing dead, or running for your life. However, remember: you cannot outrun a bear. Run only if a lake or cliffs are nearby. They may provide escape routes.

- After any encounter, abandon your planned route if it will keep you near the bear. Do not camp in the area.

Bear Deterrents

In recent years, some hikers have begun carrying devices that might deter an attacking bear. "Bear bangers" are self-launching fireworks that explode with a loud bang, generally sufficient enough to scare away a bear. That is: if you don't launch the banger so that it explodes behind the bear, scaring it toward you; and if the banger doesn't strike a tree after launching, in which case it doesn't explode.

Bear sprays are aerosols that contain an irritant – usually cayenne pepper. The fog of the spray is intended to temporarily blind an attacking bear, allowing you to escape. A bear spray is used in close quarters, 4 to 6 m. It is possible that an attacking bear's momentum will still carry it onto you, and there is the danger of the spray affecting you also if you spray it into the wind. Because they have been used in criminal activities, bear sprays have been classified as restricted weapons. Purse-sized pepper sprays are now illegal. In the frontcountry, you can be charged under the Criminal Code for carrying a bear spray, if you are not on your way to or from a trailhead.

If you choose to carry bear bangers or bear spray, remember: they offer some hope as a last chance, but in no way replace the care, common sense and sound judgement that is required to travel in bear country.

Bear Facts and Fiction

Bears are revered by Native peoples as mythic animals, to whom they ascribe many powers and influences. In a manner that reflects our muddled interaction with Nature, non-Native North Americans have attributed a vast lore of false behaviour to bears. Some of the more common misconceptions, which might adversely influence your behaviour in bear country, are listed below.

1. Bears have poor eyesight.

Although the sense of smell is more important and developed in bears, both black and grizzly bears possess excellent eyesight.

Grizzly bears may excavate entire meadows in quest of marmots, ground squirrels and the roots of glacier lilies and hedysarum. You can tell if a digging is fresh by examining the vegetation on flipped-over sod. If still green, the digging is probably recent.

2. Bears cannot run downhill, because their front legs are shorter.

Bears can run wherever they please, at speeds up to 61 km/hour.

3. If you wear the colour red, you will provoke a bear to attack.

There is no documentation that colour of clothing influences the outcome of an encounter.

4. Grizzly bears cannot climb trees.

Grizzlies are not inclined to climb trees, but can climb 5-10 metres if they desire. Standing erect, a large grizzly can reach 4 metres into a tree.

5. If a grizzly stands on its rear legs, it is going to attack.

Grizzlies stand on their rear legs to get a better view of the unknown, and to smell the wind. However, rising and falling repeatedly into the two-legged stance indicates extreme agitation.

6. Bears are marauding hunters and carnivores.

Bears are omnivorous – they eat anything. In the Rockies, 90 percent of the grizzly's diet is vegetable matter, as is 75 percent of the black bear's diet. Individual bears may become good hunters, but as a rule in the Rockies, live animals are not often taken.

7. "Grizzly" describes the species' ferocious temperament.

"Grizzly" refers to the grizzled fur of white-tipped guard hairs.

8. Colour and size are the best clues to differentiate between black and grizzly bears.

Both black and grizzly bears vary in colour from black to brown to cinnamon to blond. The adult grizzly is substantially larger than the adult black bear (males weigh 50 to 90 percent more), and has a dished face and prominent shoulder hump. The muzzle of the black bear is straight in profile, and there is frequently a white chest patch. Black bears in Waterton exhibit more colour phases than those in the more northerly parks.

9. *Black bears are more common than grizzly bears.*

In Canada, yes (290,000 black bears, to 22,000 grizzlies). In the Rockies, no. Grizzlies outnumber black bears 2:1 in Banff and Jasper national parks.

Something You Can Do For the Bears

Although bears are protected in the Rocky Mountain parks, (except in areas of Mt. Assiniboine open to seasonal hunting), mounting pressures are creating a grim situation for these animals. With their low reproductive rates, and their need for large areas of undisturbed habitat, grizzly bear populations may soon reach a critical level where mortality outstrips natality – an "extinction vortex." Some researchers estimate the grizzly bear will be locally extinct (extirpated) in the Rockies within a century at best, and perhaps as soon as 30 years.

The Rocky Mountain parks simply aren't large enough to stave off the mounting threats to bears. It has been estimated that the combined area of these parks is at least 50 percent too small to sustain a viable grizzly bear population. The provincial agencies that administer adjoining lands must adopt supportive management policies to help protect bears, thereby increasing the amount of safe habitat available.

For the grizzly bear, this is particularly true in British Columbia, which has a population of 6000 to 10,000 grizzlies. Between 8 percent and 25 percent of this estimated population dies each year, with legal hunting being the leading cause of death. Typically, more grizzlies are legally hunted in BC each year than exist in the Lower 48 US states. Illegal and "accidental" hunting kills also take a significant toll. World Wildlife Fund Canada has recommended a 3 percent maximum "harvest rate" for grizzlies in any jurisdiction. This target is easily being exceeded in BC.

The Committee on the Status of Endangered Wildlife in Canada first classified the grizzly bear as vulnerable in 1991. This means the species is: "particularly at risk because of low or declining numbers." The BC government does not recognize that the Rocky Mountain segment of the province's grizzly population is small, under pressure, and separated from the main coastal population. In reality, the grizzlies are "endangered." For example, 33 grizzly hunting tags were issued in the three wildlife management units adjoining Yoho, Kootenay, Banff and Mt. Assiniboine parks in 1992. Eleven bears were legally killed as a result – an extraordinarily high success rate. There are two open hunting seasons on black bears in the same wildlife management units, together lasting 4.5 months each year. It is estimated that 29 black bears were legally killed in 1992. Fourteen other black bears were recorded killed as "nuisance" bears. You might think that with these success rates, the quota would be dropped. This was not the case. Thirty-three hunting tags for grizzlies were issued again in 1993.

Bear hunting, and the attendant threat of poaching, must be stopped in the Canadian Rockies. The current spate of road construction associated with forestry, and mineral and gas exploration must also cease. For every 2 km of road constructed in bear habitat, the 2 km strip plus an additional 200 m^2 of habitat are rendered unusable to bears. Ten percent of the forestry land base in BC is roads. Many existing logging roads should be closed, and bridges removed, to prevent access to remote park boundaries. Decisions on these matters are the responsibilities of several ministries in Alberta and British Columbia.

In a promising move, British Columbia and Alberta have banned trade in bear parts. Legislation and enforcement is required to curtail this driving force behind poaching. If you would like to help the bears, write to provincial public servants and make requests for forward-thinking bear management policies. Express your support for seasonal protective closures within national parks to park managers.

Issues and Contacts

At time of publication, the following issues directly affected the Rocky Mountain parks. For each issue, a contact is provided, along with the number of the hike where the issue is described in the text.

Mountain Caribou (25, 28, 31)
> The Honourable Premier of Alberta
> Legislature Buildings
> Edmonton, AB T5K 2B6

Forestry and Petroleum Exploration on Adjoining Lands, Alberta (32, 49)
> The Honourable Minster of Forests
> The Honourable Minister
> of the Environment
> Legislature Buildings
> Edmonton, AB T5K 2B6

Forestry on Adjoining Lands, British Columbia (41, 44, 45, 49)
> The Honourable Minster of Forests
> Parliament Buildings
> Victoria, BC V8V 1X4

Helicopter Use, Mt. Robson Provincial Park (33)
> Zone Manager
> Box 579
> Valemount, BC V0E 2Z0
Copy to: The Honourable Minister of Environment, Lands and Parks, Parliament Buildings, Victoria, BC V8V 1X4

Helicopter Use, Mt. Assiniboine Provincial Park (7)
> District Manager
> Box 118
> Wasa, BC V0B 2S0
Copy to: The Honourable Minister of Lands and Parks, Parliament Buildings, Victoria, B.C. V8V 1X4.

Helicopter and fixed-wing overflights, "flightseeing" (7, 33)
> The Honourable Minister of Transport, MP
> House of Commons
> Ottawa, ON KIA 0A6
> (no postage required if mailed in Canada)

Horse traffic, Jasper National Park (25, 28, 31)
> The Superintendent
> Box 10
> Jasper, AB T0E 1E0

Horse traffic, Banff National Park (5, 6, 13, 15, 18, 19, 20, 23)
> The Superintendent
> Box 900
> Banff, AB T0L 0C0

National Parks

For inquiries, comments and concerns regarding a particular national park write to:

Banff National Park
> The Superintendent
> Box 900
> Banff, AB T0L 0C0, 403-762-1500

Jasper National Park
> The Superintendent
> Box 10
> Jasper, AB T0E 1E0, 403-852-6161

Yoho National Park
> The Superintendent
> Box 99
> Field, BC V0A 1G0, 250-343-6324

Kootenay National Park
> The Superintendent
> Box 220
> Radium Hot Springs, BC V0A 2KO,
> 250-347-9615

Waterton Lakes National Park
> The Superintendent
> Waterton Park, AB T0K 2M0, 403-859-2224

Public Input Mailing List
If you wish to be informed about long-range planning for the five Rocky Mountain national parks write to:
> Public Consultation Co-ordinator
> Parks Canada
> Box 2989, Station M
> Calgary, AB T2P 2M9

Provincial Parks

For inquiries, comments and concerns regarding a particular provincial park, write to:

Mt. Robson Provincial Park
> Zone Manager
> Box 579
> Valemount, BC V0E 2Z0, 250-566-4325

Mt. Assiniboine Provincial Park
> Zone Manager
> Box 118
> Wasa, BC V0B 2S0, 250-422-3212

Selected Environmental Organizations

Your membership in the following organizations will increase the power of preservation efforts in western Canada. These organizations appreciate copies of correspondence sent to park superintendents and ministries. It helps them gauge public response to issues.

World Wildlife Fund, Canada
90 Eglington Ave E
Toronto, ON M4P 2Z7
(Focus: habitat loss, endangered species, establishment of protected areas)

Canadian Parks and Wilderness Society
Suite 1150
160 Bloor St E
Toronto, ON M4W 1B9
(Has local chapters in Calgary, Edmonton and Vancouver. Focus: national park planning and management, establishment of new parks, and protected areas, development issues)

Alberta Wilderness Association
P.O. Box 6398, Station D
Calgary, AB T2P 2E1
(Focus: protection of existing parks, creation of new parks, habitat loss, provincial legislation affecting the environment)

Western Canada Wilderness Committee
20 Water St
Vancouver, BC V6B 1A4
or
9526 Jasper Ave, #6
Edmonton, AB T5H 3V3
(Focus: forestry, water quality, mining, and habitat loss)

Bow Valley Naturalists
Box 1693
Banff, AB T0L 0C0
(Focus: issues affecting Banff townsite, Banff National Park and the Bow Valley)

Jasper Environmental Association
Box 2198
Jasper, AB T0E 1E0
(Focus: issues affecting Jasper townsite, Jasper National Park and the Athabasca Valley)

Recommended Reading

General Reference
Gadd, Ben. *Handbook of the Canadian Rockies.* Jasper: Corax Press, 1986. If it's not in this Handbook, it's not in the Rockies.

Hart, J. *Walking Softly in the Wilderness: the Sierra Club Guide to Backpacking,* San Francisco: Sierra Club Books, 1984.

Kals, W.S. *Land Navigation Handbook.* San Francisco: Sierra Club Books, 1983. How to use a map and compass.

National Outdoor Leadership School, *Leave No Trace.* Lander, (US): 1992. A useful, inexpensive booklet that describes no-trace travel and camping techniques.

Pole, Graeme. *Canadian Rockies Super-Guide.* Banff: Altitude Publishing, 1991. A frontcountry guide that features highlights of human history, geology and ecology.

Pole, Graeme. *Walks and Easy Hikes in the Canadian Rockies.* Banff: Altitude Publishing, 1992. A companion guide to *Classic Hikes,* packed with frontcountry outings.

Hampton, B. and D. Cole. *Soft Paths: How To Enjoy Wilderness Without Harming It.* Harrisburg: Stackpole, 1988. The "bible" on responsible backcountry travel.

Birding
Griggs, Jack. *All the Birds of North America.* New York: Harper Collins, 1997

Holroyd, G.L. and Howard Coneybare. *Birds of the Rockies.* Edmonton: Lone Pine Publishing, 1990

Scotter, G.W., Ulrich, T.J. and E.T. Jones. *Birds of the Canadian Rockies.* Saskatoon: Western Producer Prairie Books, 1990. Excellent photography.

Van Tighem, Kevin, and Andrew LeMessurier. *Birding Jasper National Park.* Jasper: Parks and People, 1989.

Wildlife
Burt, W.H. and R.P. Grossenheider. *Mammals.* Boston: Houghton Mifflin, 3rd edition, 1980. The standard Peterson reference for North America.

Murie, O.J. *Animal Tracks*. Boston: Hougthon Mifflin, 1974. An excellent field guide with a wealth of information on animal behaviour.

Schmidt, D. and E. Schmidt. *Alberta Wildlife Viewing Guide*. Edmonton: Lone Pine Publishing, 1990.

Ulrich, T.J. *Mammals of the Northern Rockies*. Missoula: Mountain Press, ca. 1988.

Van Tighem, Kevin. *Wild Animals of Western Canada*. Banff: Altitude Publishing, 1992.

Geology

Ford, Derek and Dalton Muir. *Castleguard*. Ottawa: Minister of the Environment, 1985. A clear and lavishly illustrated description of natural processes at Castleguard Cave and Meadows, but relevant to the alpine region throughout the Rockies.

Sandford, R.W. *The Columbia Icefield*. Banff: Altitude Publishing, 1993.

Vegetation

Anonymous. *Trees and Forests of Jasper National Park*. Jasper: Parks and People, 1986.

Bush, C. Dana. *Wildflowers of the Rockies*. Edmonton: Lone Pine, 1990. Colour illustrations.

Hosie, R.C. *The Native Trees of Canada*. Toronto: Fitzhenry and Whiteside, 1979. The standard reference.

Kershaw, Linda J. MacKinnon, A. and J. Pojar. *Plants of the Rocky Mountains*. Edmonton: Lone Pine, 1998.

Kujit, J. *A Flora of Waterton Lakes National Park*. Edmonton: University of Alberta Press, 1982. Most of the species that occur in the Rockies are found in Waterton. An excellent reference for both novice and expert. Illustrations. Now out of print.

MacKinnon, A., Pojar, J. and R. Coupé. *Plants of Northern British Columbia*. Edmonton: Lone Pine, 1993. Flowers, grasses, trees, shrubs, mosses and lichens in the Central Rockies; particularly those of the subalpine and alpine regions.

Moss, E.H. and J.G Packer. *The Flora of Alberta*. Toronto: The University of Toronto Press, 1983. The standard technical reference. No illustrations.

Porsild, A.E. and D.T. Lid. *Rocky Mountain Wild Flowers*. Ottawa: National Museum of Natural Sciences, 1979. Colour illustrations.

Scotter, G.W. and H. Flygare. *Wildflowers of the Canadian Rockies*. Toronto: McClelland and Stewart, 1992. Good colour photographs.

Stanton, C. and N. Lopoukine. *The Trees and Forests of Waterton Lakes National Park*. Forestry Service and Environment Canada, undated. A free brochure available at Waterton Lakes National Park Information centre.

Zwinger, A. H. and B.E. Willard. *Land Above the Trees: A Guide to American Alpine Tundra*. Tucson: University of Arizona Press, 1989. An excellent guide to ecology above timberline.

Human History

Boles, G., Laurilla, R., and W. Putnam. *Place Names of the Canadian Alps*. Revelstoke: Footprint, 1990.

Hart, E.J. *Diamond Hitch*. Banff: Summerthought, 1979. Stories of trail life and an illustrated history of the guides and outfitters who opened up the Rockies.

Holterman, Jack. *Place Names of Glacier/Waterton National Parks*. Glacier Natural History Association, 1985.

Marty, Sid. *A Grand and Fabulous Notion*. Toronto: NC Press, 1984. The founding of Banff National Park and Canada's national park system.

Pole, Graeme. *The Canadian Rockies: A History in Photographs*. Banff: Altitude Publishing, 1991. Human history from 1884 to the 1950s, illustrated with 130 photographs.

Sandford, R.W. *The Candian Alps*, Banff: Altitude Publishing, 1990. A history of early mountaineering in western Canada.

Schäffer, Mary T.S. *A Hunter of Peace*. Banff: The Whyte Foundation, 1980. On the trail to Maligne Lake with Mary Schäffer.

Food and Cooking

Axcell, Claudia, Cooke, Diana and Vikki Kinmont. *Simple Foods for the Pack*. San Francisco: Sierra Club Books, 1986. Wholesome variations on standard backcountry fare.

Geological Table for the Central Rockies

Age*	Formation Name	Rock Types	Maximum Thickness
80-60	Brazeau	sandstone and shale	4000 m
93-80	Alberta Group	shale and sandstone	750 m
124-93	Blairmore Group	shale, sandstone, lava	2000 m
144-97.5	Cadomin	conglomerate	20 m
169-07.5	Nikanassin	siltstone	600 m
169-97.5	Kootenay Group	siltstone and sandstone	1000 m
208-144	Fernie	shale, siltstone, sandstone	600 m
245-208	Spray River Group	shale, siltstone, sandstone	740 m
320-245	Ishbel Group	dolomite	150 m
320-245	Spray LakesGroup	slate and dolomite	300 m
360-320	Rundle Group	limestone and dolomite	900 m
360-320	Banff	dolomite and shale	820 m
363-358	Exshaw	shale	10 m
366-363	Palliser	limestone and dolomite	620 m
367-366	Sassenach	dolomite	200 m
375-367	Fairholme Group	limestone and dolomite	250 m
458-421	Beaverfoot	dolomite and limestone	540 m
478-438	Mt. Wilson	quartzite	170 m
478-458	Owen Creek	dolomite, shale, sandstone	190 m
488-458	Skoki	dolomite	230 m
505-478	Tipperary	quartzite	300 m
505-478	Outram	limestone and shale	440 m
505-500	Survey Peak	shale	400 m
523-505	Lynx	limestone and dolomite	1060 m
523-505	Mistaya	limestone	160 m
523-505	Bison Creek	limestone and shale	210 m
523-505	Lyell/Ottertail	limestone and dolomite	600 m
523-505	Sullivan	shale, limestone, siltstone	200 m
505-458	Glenogle	shale	700 m
523-458	McKay Group	shale	1600 m
540-505	Chancellor Group	shale and limestone	3000 m
540-523	Waterfowl	dolomite and limestone	200 m
540-523	Arctomys	shale and siltstone	340 m
540-523	Pika	limestone and dolomite	275 m
540-523	Eldon	limestone and dolomite	430 m
540-523	Stephen	shale	150 m
540-523	Cathedral	limestone and dolomite	350 m
540-523	Mt. Whyte	shale, limestone, siltstone, sandstone	200 m
570-540	Gog Group	quartzite and siltstone	4000 m
730-570	Miette Group	sandstone, shale, slate, gritstone	9000 m

*Millions of Years

Geological Table for Waterton

Age*	Formation Name	Rock Types	Maximum Thickness
1500-1350	Missoula Group	argillite, sandstone, limestone (includes Kintla Formation)	2500 m
1500-1350	Siyeh	limestone, dolomite, Purcell lava	1000 m
1500-1350	Grinnell/Spokane	argillite	335 m
1500-1350	Greyson/Appekunny	argillite	820 m
1500-1350	Altyn	limestone, argillite, dolomite	425 m
1500-1350	Waterton	limestone and dolomite	135 m
*Millions of Years			

Glaciation in the Canadian Rockies

Name of Glacial Event	Began	Ended
Little Ice Age (Cavell Advance)	AD 1200	AD 1850
Crowfoot	11,000 BP*	9000 BP*
Late Wisconsin	20,000 BP	11,000 BP
Early Wisconsin (two advances)	75,000 BP	64,000 BP
Great Glaciation (Illinoian Advance)	240,000 BP	128,000 BP
Early Pleistocene	1.87 million years BP	
	"BP" means "before the present."	

Geological Time Periods

Time Period*	Name
1.07 – present	Quaternary
65 – 1.87	Tertiary
140 – 65	Cretaceous
210 – 140	Jurassic
250 – 210	Triassic
290 – 250	Permian
360 – 290	Carboniferous
410 – 360	Devonian
440 – 410	Silurian
500 – 440	Ordovician
570 – 500	Cambrian
900 – 570	Hadrynian
1700 – 900	Helikian
*Millions of Years BP	

Equipment Checklist

Day-hike

- ❏ bandana
- ❏ binoculars (if desired)
- ❏ boots
- ❏ camera/lenses/film/spare battery (if desired)
- ❏ compass
- ❏ extra sweater
- ❏ first aid/repair kit
- ❏ food
- ❏ gaiters
- ❏ gloves or mitts
- ❏ guidebooks (if desired)
- ❏ insect repellent
- ❏ long underwear
- ❏ paper and pencil
- ❏ pocket knife
- ❏ rainsuit
- ❏ shorts
- ❏ space blanket
- ❏ sun hat
- ❏ sunscreen and lip balm
- ❏ T-shirt
- ❏ toilet paper
- ❏ topographic maps
- ❏ trail snacks
- ❏ UV sunglasses
- ❏ water bottle
- ❏ winter hat

Overnight Hike

- ❏ bandana
- ❏ binoculars (if desired)
- ❏ boots
- ❏ bowl/mug/spoon
- ❏ camera/lenses/film/spare battery (if desired)
- ❏ compass
- ❏ day pack for day-hiking options
- ❏ extra sweater
- ❏ first aid/repair kit
- ❏ food and storage bag
- ❏ fuel
- ❏ gaiters
- ❏ gloves or mitts and winter hat
- ❏ guidebooks (if desired)
- ❏ headlamp/flashlight
- ❏ insect repellent
- ❏ lighters (2) and waterproof matches
- ❏ long underwear
- ❏ paper and pencil
- ❏ piece of candle
- ❏ plastic bags
- ❏ pocket knife
- ❏ pots/potholder/scouring pad
- ❏ rainsuit
- ❏ rope (30 m) and carabiner for hanging food
- ❏ running shoes for fording streams
- ❏ shorts
- ❏ sleeping bag
- ❏ sleeping mat
- ❏ socks
- ❏ stove
- ❏ stuff sacks for /stove/pots
- ❏ sun hat
- ❏ sunscreen and lip balm
- ❏ T-shirt
- ❏ tent/poles/fly/pegs
- ❏ toilet kit and toilet paper
- ❏ topographic maps
- ❏ trail snacks
- ❏ underwear
- ❏ UV sunglasses
- ❏ water bottle

Index

About the Author

Graeme Pole has lived and worked in the Rockies since 1983. During this time he has cultivated a multi-faceted knowledge of these mountains. Among his jobs, he spent three summers on trail crew in Yoho National Park. His three previous books are: *Canadian Rockies, Walks and Easy Hikes in the Canadian Rockies* (both are Altitude SuperGuides) and *The Canadian Rockies: A History in Photographs*. When not working on books, enjoying the outdoors and taking photographs, Graeme serves with the British Columbia Ambulance Service as an Emergency Medical Assistant and Unit Chief at Field.

With royalties from the sales of this and other books, Graeme supports the reforestation work of *Trees for the Future*.

Photographs

All colour photographs are by Marnie Pole and Graeme Pole: Mountain Vision.

Historical photographs are courtesy of the Whyte Museum of the Canadian Rockies, Banff, Alberta. The historical photos on page 173 are courtesy of the Jasper-Yellowhead Historical Society.

Graeme Pole

Graeme Pole and Marnie Pole

Graeme Pole is the best-selling author of five non-fiction books that describe the human history and natural history of the Canadian Rockies. Three of his books have been finalists in the Banff Mountain Book Festival. *Classic Hikes in the Canadian Rockies* won the Mountain Exposition category in 1994. He has been a runner-up for the Andy Russell Nature Writers' Award, a finalist in the Crown of the Continent Nature Writing Award, a recipient of a Northwest Outdoor Writers' Association "Excellence in Craft Award," and a recipient of the Teddi Brown Award for Nature Writing. His first novel, *Healy Park*, was published in 1998.